UNIVERSITY OF
WOLVERHAMPTON

Theory, Culture & Society

Theory, Culture & Society caters for the resurgence of interest in culture within contemporary social science and the humanities. Building on the heritage of classical social theory, the book series examines ways in which this tradition has been reshaped by a new generation of theorists. It will also publish theoretically informed analyses of everyday life, popular culture, and new intellectual movements.

Also in this series

Reproduction in Education, Society and Culture
Revised edition
Pierre Bourdieu and Jean-Claude Passeron

The Tourist Gaze
Leisure and Travel in Contemporary Societies
John Urry

Theories of Modernity and Postmodernity
edited by Bryan S. Turner

Global Culture
Nationalism, Globalization and Modernity
edited by Mike Featherstone

The Body
Social Process and Cultural Theory
*edited by Mike Featherstone, Mike Hepworth
and Bryan S. Turner*

Consumer Culture and Postmodernism
Mike Featherstone

Talcott Parsons
Theorist of Modernity
edited by Roland Robertson and Bryan S. Turner

Religion and Social Theory

Second edition

Bryan S. Turner

SAGE Publications
London • Newbury Park • New Delhi

First edition 1983
Second edition 1991

The first edition was published by Heinemann Educational
Books, London, and Humanities Press, New Jersey. We are
grateful to Gower Publishing Group for permission to prepare
this new edition.

SAGE Publications Ltd
6 Bonhill Street
London EC2A 4PU

SAGE Publications Inc
2455 Teller Road
Newbury Park, California 91320

SAGE Publications India Pvt Ltd
32, M–Block Market
Greater Kailash – I
New Delhi 110 048

Published in association with *Theory, Culture & Society*,
Department of Administrative and Social Studies,
Teesside Polytechnic

British Library Cataloguing in Publication Data

Turner, Bryan S.
  Religion and social theory — 2nd ed.
  I. Title
  306.6

  ISBN 0-8039-8568-1
  ISBN 0-8039-8569-X pbk

Library of Congress catalog card number 91-53015

Typeset by AKM Associates (UK) Ltd, Southall, London
Printed in Great Britain by J. W. Arrowsmith Ltd, Bristol

For Adelaide and Nicolas

Contents

Acknowledgements

This study of religion is also a contribution to the development of a sociology of the body. In the evolution of this intellectual project, Mike Featherstone, Arthur Frank and George Stauth have been especially helpful and supportive. My interest in the sociology of religion was originally stimulated and later supported by Roland Robertson. The editorial group around *Theory, Culture & Society* provided the general intellectual environment that made all of this possible. I am particularly grateful to Stephen Barr whose editorial advice has been invaluable.

Bryan S. Turner
Wivenhoe 1991

Introduction to the Second Edition

The constitution of social theory

Two issues have been central to the development of sociological theory since the classical foundations of the discipline in the 1890s. First there is the matter of social order, which is often posed as a question: how is society possible? The problem of social order, which is also referred to as the Hobbesian problem of order, concerns the social foundations of social stability and social cohesion; it involves an analysis of the complex relationships between consensus and constraint in social life. Characteristically, sociologists have posited the existence of a common moral order or system of values which binds people together into a community as an explanation of social integration. These normative systems, rituals and communal practices are treated as the central fabric of social relations; they are thus an essential feature of all communal activity. In sociology, religion has been universally regarded as a central component of this integrative value system (Parsons, 1991). Religion is a social cement, binding individuals and social groups into a communal order.

This is not to say that sociology has some conservative foundation. The problem of social order necessarily involves a sociological enquiry into the essential processes and circumstances which disrupt and challenge the contingent and fragile order of social life. A sociology of social order inevitably implies the study of social conflict, dissent and change. Religion often binds people into alternative and competing social groups or collectivities; inter-religious violence is a common feature of modern social life.

Secondly, sociology examines the social meaning of collective life, the significance of social action and the forms of knowledge and understanding, which are a necessary feature of all social relations. In part this question about social meaning is an attempt to differentiate between the notions of 'action' and 'behaviour'. In sociology it is argued that the essential feature of human action is that it is in principle meaningful to the participants: it is not simply an unreflexive form of behaviour responding to external circumstances or stimuli. Social action involves knowledge and reflexivity on the part of social actors, a process in which the social agent constantly reflects upon the nature of action and its meaningful quality. The assertion that human social action is meaningful is also therefore a definition of what it is to be human. The behaviour of animals is contrasted with human action on the grounds that animal behaviour is not reflexive. Animals have no consciousness, and hence no conception of history or time. For Nietzsche, it was this sense of the passing of time which was part of the tragedy of human beings.

Human action then is purposeful, involving reflection upon the conditions of action; it involves the choice of alternative means for achieving alternative ends. In this sense, human action and interaction are open-ended, contingent events, the outcomes of which can never be fully predicted or known. This uncertainty in human life is at least one sociological source of religious phenomena, because religious practices can be conceptualized as means for structuring human relationships. Religion constructs, in the words of Peter Berger (1969), 'a sacred canopy' which by providing stable meanings organises and structures reality. Religion, as it were, deals with social complexity (Luhmann, 1984).

These two problems (the problem of social order and the meaningful nature of human interaction) are obviously very closely interrelated. Social action presupposes some stable set of assumptions or norms by which social action can be guided. Social order, that is, some stability of norms and values, is necessary for social action and interaction to occur. Social action is characterised by its reflexivity, and hence by the 'knowledgeability' of the social actor (Giddens, 1979). As a consequence, the existence of social order is something about which social actors must constantly reflect and ponder. All social actions require an inter-pretation of situations, understanding of the intentions of other social actors, and predictions about future consequences of action. Sociology can thus be defined as an interpretive science of meaningful social action and interaction (Weber, 1949, 1968).

Disruptions of and threats to social order question the meaningful character of social action. In traditional societies, natural disasters, or at least crises which are seen to be 'natural', such as earthquakes, droughts and pestilence represented major dislocations of social life, which were not easily repaired. These 'natural disorders' had to be reconciled with human interpretations of the divine order. Within a naturalistic fallacy, the disorders of nature were a mirror of the disorders of society. Social disorder in the form of warfare, inter-social violence and human cruelty is equally a challenge to the idea of normality and continuity. The uncertainty of social action, the problem of risk, and the unpredictable nature of future conditions force human beings into a collective response to the shapeless and contingent nature of 'reality'. The problem of risk, uncertainty and meaning is thus a threat to our 'ontological security', that is, to our emotive sense of our own continuity and selfhood (Giddens, 1990, p. 92). Religion is an aspect of the 'repair work' that we do on reality in order to counter the risks of disorder.

Because sociology reflects upon the two issues of meaning and order, religion and sociology stand in an intimate relationship to each other. Religion may be defined as a system of symbols and values which, through their emotional impact, not only bind people together into a sacred community, but induce a normative and altruistic commitment to collective ends. Religion produces community as the consequence of collective ritualistic practices and a common sharing of belief. Religion creates powerful symbols of social life and human existence which generate a powerful experience of social membership. In Emile Durkheim's terminology, religion is an essential feature of collective life as such; religion is collective social thought (Durkheim, 1957). In this specific sense, any social group may be regarded also as a religious group, because the sense of community can be regarded as an experience which transcends individual or private existence.

However, religion is intimately connected with both the problem of social order and the meaningful nature of social relations. By approaching religion from the point of view of order, sociology may appear to neglect the individual and individual experiences of the sacred. Some definitions of religion appear to give more prominence to the idea of the individual experience of Otherness (Wach, 1971, p. 13). Religion is simply this experience of the Holy. From a sociological perspective, however, there is no substantial difference between the social nature of religious activity and the personal character of religious experience. In Durkheim's sociology of religion, it is collective ritual practice which produces profound experiences of transcendence and Otherness.

I have argued that sociology is an interpretive science which attempts to explain social order and understand the nature of social action. Order and meaning are also central to the nature of religious life. Given the importance of these issues, it is not surprising to discover that the 'founding fathers of sociology' in very different ways and with different sets of assumptions were forced to address these two issues, and to consider these problems of the constitution of society by reference to religious phenomena, and the relationship between the individual and the social. Durkheim and Weber may be taken as the classical illustration of this contention, although other leading figures in sociology were also involved in the development of the sociology of religion — such as Georg Simmel (1906).

Durkheim's sociology was an attempt to create a scientific study of moral facts, and therefore he remained primarily concerned with the moral order of society. In *The Elementary Forms of the Religious Life*, Durkheim (1961) provided a general sociological account of the sacred order of society which is produced by common beliefs, collective social rituals and shared religious experiences. For Durkheim, the essential nature of religion was that it addressed the division between the sacred and the profane, and generated a common consciousness which was the foundation of sentiments of social belonging. Thus, for Durkheim religion was a system of symbols and ritual practices concerning the sacred which created a moral community and, in the collective experiences of the social group, individuals experienced what he referred to as the social effervescence of religious practice. This affective consequence of religious practices tied the individual to the social group in a bond which was emotional in character. In this respect, Durkheim's social theory of morals, knowledge and religion was a sociological critique of the individualism and rationalism of Kant's philosophy (Meštrović, 1990). Durkheim rejected the idea that a sense of rational obligation was the foundation of moral life; instead he insisted on the social origins of the feeling of obligation, just as he insisted on the social foundations of our experience of Otherness. Rudolf Otto's notion in *The Idea of the Holy* (1929) that the religious experience is characterised as the *mysterium tremendum et fascinosum* was for Durkheim always a social experience.

In the case of Weber, the analysis of religion was at the core of his sociological research. Unfortunately, sociologists have too frequently concentrated almost exclusively on the two famous essays which were published as *The Protestant Ethic and the Spirit of Capitalism*. Because so much emphasis is placed on the Protestant Ethic thesis (Turner, 1974), Weber has been somewhat exclusively treated as a historical sociologist whose main concern was to chart the religious foundations of modern industrial capitalism. In fact, we have to see Weber's *Sociology of Religion* within a much broader framework, namely as the study of the salvational drives of the various world religions (Tenbruck, 1980). Weber was concerned to understand sociologically the general social consequences of various systems of soteriology in the shaping of social values, institutions and personality. Weber's sociology of religion is thus a study of how religious ethics produce various types of personality and in this sense Weber's sociology might be described as a 'characterology' (Hennis, 1988). 'Personality' in this context meant the conscious development of a life plan, or a rational order of existence. Weber's general sociology involves the comparative study of the life orders which are produced by systems of ethical belief and how these life orders interact with the personalities associated with the various ethical systems. The development of the Calvinistic personality was an essential feature of the origins of modern society.

It has become somewhat commonplace to treat Durkheim and Weber within different frameworks, and this division may be in part consequence of Talcott Parsons's interpretation of their position within the development of sociology (Parsons, 1981). For Parsons, Weber's major question was how religious world-views provided a revolutionary critique of the world, and how these radical religious responses to social order produced revolutionary transformations of society. Religion is an essential component of the radical utopian mentality which challenges the stable order of routine existence. Thus, Parsons saw Weber as providing a historical sociology of religion which was to some extent a refutation of Marx. By contrast, Parsons treated Durkheim as a sociologist who made a major contribution to the analytical understanding of the foundations of social order. In Parsons's interpretation, Durkheim's analysis of the impact of religious values on the emergence of the concept of community was primarily a contribution to the sociology of social order. However, we do not need to posit an opposition between Weber and Durkheim in terms of their sociological analysis of religion.

Recent interpretations of Durkheim have, for example, pointed to Durkheim's dependence on the philosophy of morals which had been developed by Schopenhauer. As I have already argued, within this perspective, Durkheim's analysis of moral systems was in fact a reply to Kant, since Durkheim rejected Kant's individualism and rationalism, adopting instead Schopenhauer's emphasis on emotion, feeling and compassion as foundations of moral action. Moral obligation had to rest on foundations other than individual motive and social sanction. Durkheim's sociology of morals was an attempt to provide a sociological analysis of the moral problems of contemporary society. For Durkheim, modern societies have been shaken to their roots by industrialisation and by the rise of utilitarian individualism. We can see that one of the central questions of Durkheim's sociology was: how is a meaningful moral order possible in a secular and differentiated society?

We also now realise more fully that Weber's sociology was profoundly shaped by the philosophy of Nietzsche, who had also questioned the rationalistic assumptions of Kantian idealism (Stauth and Turner, 1988). Since Nietzsche was the principal follower of Schopenhauer, we can now identify certain convergences between Durkheim and Weber over questions of religion and morals, but we can also see that historically the sociological questions of order and meaning have always been interrelated in various complex ways. Order and meaning as analytical issues are closely interwoven, and as a consequence there is no justification for establishing a sharp division between Weberian historical sociology and Durkheim's analysis of the elementary forms of the sacred.

The problem of theodicy

While I have argued that religion is a system of symbols and practices which produce social commitment through emotional experience, religion also produces an intellectual account of the world. Religion offers a perspective on social existence which requires a rational reflection on social reality. In its highly elaborate and articulate form, this religious knowledge becomes a theology which, through the work of religious experts and specialists, evolves into a complex cosmology of human beings and their place in the world. Under the impact of rational elaboration, it becomes a theodicy. These cosmologies are thus general explanations of the nature of reality, the place of human beings in that reality and God's working of salvation in history (Lapointe, 1989).

In general terms, the core of this religious knowledge is organised around the central problem of theodicy, which in its literal meaning is a vindication of God's providence in view of the inevitable presence of evil in the world. In terms of Christian theology, the central problem of theodicy is to explain how an omnipotent God can both be loving and compassionate, and allow evil to exist. Furthermore, how can human beings be held responsible for their actions if God is an omnipotent Author? These fundamental problems in Christian thought were eventually elaborated by philosophers such as Gottfried Leibniz as a religious response to rational scepticism about God in relation to the universe.

However, in sociology, and especially in the work of Weber, theodicy came to refer to any general ideology which provides a religious explanation of injustice and human suffering. Weber developed the concept to provide a comparative understanding of religious responses to social stratification and inequality.

When I first wrote this book, I gave a special emphasis to the problem of human embodiment in relation to theodicy, because I wanted to argue that a social theodicy is an inevitable consequence of the universalistic feature of human embodiment. Although relativism has become one of the dominant themes of modern philosophy and sociology, there are grounds for believing that we can discover a common phenomenology of the human body which provides universalistic problems and solutions. The fact of human embodiment also forces human beings to address or to cope with problems such as pain, reproduction and death. The body and theodicy are intimately connected, because the central features of theodicy are a number of distinctive intellectual responses to the problem of human pain, the nature of sexuality and the moral problems of death. While all religions have a theodicy in response to questions of human reproduction, the nature of the human body is problematic in the Abrahamic religions. Sexuality and embodiment appear to have been especially problematic concerns in Christianity, which developed the concept of the body as flesh. While Adam was created in the image of God, Christianity elaborated a strong theory of evil as a consequence of Man's fall from grace. Since this fall from grace was deeply associated with the problematic nature of human sexuality, Christianity institutionalised a strongly ascetic response to the problem of the body. In theology, 'the world', that is, the profane regions of life, was defined essentially by the nature of the human body and by the destructive forces of human sexuality.

Thus in the theodicy of the Abrahamic religions, the body came to be associated with the broader problem of truth, subjectivity and salvation. It was only by subordinating and regulating the body through ascetic practices such as diet that the soul could achieve full knowledge of itself and thereby gain salvation. The regulation of the body via painful exercises produces the truth of the self. Thus, in Christianity 'the truth, obligations of the faith and the self are linked together. This link permits a purification of the soul impossible without self-knowledge' (Foucault, 1988, p. 40). However, this problem of sexuality was not an un-differentiated or general problem, but came to define the specific relationships between men and women and their characteristic sexualities.

In this book I argue that the Abrahamic religions were specifically patriarchal in their theology and practice, and that the masculine character of the Divine cannot be ignored or forgotten. The masculine character of God and Christ in New Testament Christianity created a social system of patriarchal power in which women were assigned to and inscribed in inferior and subordinate positions, because it was the sexual nature of Eve and her transgression which played such an important part in the Christian mythology of the exclusion of Adam and Eve from the Garden of Eden. Although in Christianity the theology of the priesthood and sacrament continued to enforce and reproduce this foundational patriarchy, the Roman Catholic Church came to embrace Mariology; through the figure of the Virgin Mary a channel was found for a fuller expression of female spirituality, albeit within a dominant patriarchal framework (Warner, 1976).

In this approach to the sociology of religion, the elementary forms of the religious life are concerned with the problems of order and meaning as these two issues have been shaped by the contingency of human embodiment. However, we have to understand these elementary forms from a historical perspective, since the creation myths of the major world religions have been transformed by historical change and by interaction with each other. Sociologists have not simply been concerned to understand the general contribution of religion to the social fabric; they have addressed a number of more specific questions such as the contribution of the Abrahamic religions to the formation of western capitalism, that is, what is the relationship between religion and the processes of modernisation?

From modernity to postmodernity

Weber's sociology of religion continues to be important because in the Protestant Ethic thesis he provided a striking picture of modernisation in terms of the process of rationalisation. He argued that the long-term consequence of Calvinistic asceticism and rationalism was a secular reality (or an iron cage) in which there is a plurality of values in competition with each other. As a consequence, the very meaning of social order is threatened. In other words, Weber provided a compelling picture of the process of secularisation, whereby religious values lose their social force, and world-views become increasingly pluralistic and fragmented. The world we live in is a world of competing polytheistic values where there are no common agreements such that these competitive struggles could be authoritatively resolved. The ultimate consequence of this process is that, alongside the dominance of instrumental rationalism and experimental science, religious values become attenuated and symbols are emptied of their content.

Weber's version of the transition from *Gemeinschaft* to *Gesellschaft* can be seen as an argument which is to some extent parallel to Durkheim's analysis of the contrast between mechanical and organic solidarity. In *The Division of Labor in Society*, Durkheim (1964) drew a distinction between premodern societies, which are based upon mechanical solidarity, and contemporary societies, in which, as a result of social differentiation, the nature of social order changes to organic solidarity. In the mechanical solidarity of so-called primitive societies, social consensus is based upon a common set of beliefs, a shared ritualistic system and a dominant symbolic code, which in general terms constitute the *conscience collective*. With the social division of labour and the growing complexity of social life, this collective consciousness begins to break down as social beliefs are no longer generally held and society comes to rest on the reciprocal relations between social actors in a complex division of labour. However, in modern society, the speed of social change, the emphasis on egoistic individualism and the absence of civic morals have produced an extensive anomie in society. Durkheim believed therefore that some form of collective consciousness or civil religion would be necessary in modern societies, possibly based upon some form of nationalism (Durkheim, 1957).

In the first edition of *Religion and Social Theory* I adopted a fairly strong version of the secularisation thesis, arguing that indeed religious symbols had lost their force and there was no longer a common religious framework dominating social life. I rejected the 'golden age' theory of religion in order to suggest that feudal society, for example, was not necessarily based upon a common culture, but was culturally divided between various estates, each of which had a rather separate system of belief and symbolisation. For various reasons, I would now take a rather different position on this problem and in this section I want to outline briefly how I would conceptualise the problem of secularisation and modernisation in relation to the contemporary debate about post-modernity.

Locating these issues within a historical framework, I believe that we should regard the Protestant Reformation as not only one source of modernisation, but also its defence against magic, superstition, witch-craft or mysticism. Calvinistic Protestantism was crucial in the development of modern forms of individuality, rationalism and asceticism; it generated and preserved many of the essential features of what we mean by the notion of modernity. Talcott Parsons therefore made an important point when he argued that modernisation in America was not only compatible with American Protestantism but had been generated by it so that secular modernism was to some extent the logical outcome of the long historic development of Protestant rationalism (Parsons, 1963).

If we regard Protestantism as the cultural seedbed of modernity, then we have to regard the Counter-Reformation and baroque culture in the seventeenth century as an anti-modernist movement. The Counter-Reformation sought to bring about major institutional changes within the Roman Catholic Church which would counteract the individualistic and rational challenge of Protestantism. However, we should also view the Counter-Reformation within the broader changes in social and political life which were associated with absolutism and the baroque.

For Perry Anderson (1974), absolutism was a response to the challenge presented by Protestant bourgeois social movements, on the one hand, and to the collapse of military–feudal institutions with urbanisation, on the other. The crisis of the seventeenth century, especially in societies such as France and Spain, was partly the outcome of certain fiscal problems following the transformation of the world economy but it was also connected with deep urban problems related to population growth and social unrest. But these social changes also influenced societies such as Germany (Vierhaus, 1988). The rise of an absolutist state represents the attempt on the part of a threatened feudal nobility to recreate the old order and to re-establish the authority of the moral system by developing a mass culture of emotionality, which through the stimulation of emotions would ideologically reassert the authority of the old order over various social classes emerging in the new urban economy. One aspect of these social changes was the rise of the theodicy of Leibniz (that we live in the best of all possible worlds) as an ideological justification of political absolutism. The Sun King was the living embodiment of baroque virtue in which the King's body was a description of the state (Marin, 1988). The cultural core of the baroque included Shakespeare's explanation of the oedipal complex in *Hamlet*;

Monteverdi's music, which can be regarded as an alchemy of sound; the façades of churches such as Santa Maria della Pace in Rome; an emphasis of the persuasive force of religious images, as in the work of Francisco Zurbaran; and finally the eroticisation of divinity in such works as Bernini's adoration sculptures, especially the Ecstasy of Saint Teresa (Argan, 1989). Against the plain white interiors of northern Protestant churches therefore the baroque culture of the south developed an elaborate interior of colour, emotion and sound which was to capture the masses through the stimulation of emotional affect.

Within this perspective, the recent critique of modernity by post-modern theorists may be regarded as a contemporary manifestation of a much longer set of oppositional movements against the rationalising tendency of the modern project. If modernity can be regarded, from a Weberian perspective, as a process of rationalisation and secularisation within the context of an urban industrial civilisation, then we can trace a number of oppositional social movements which have been critical of the dominance of modernity. These oppositional movements will include not only the Counter-Reformation and baroque culture, but the romantic movement, the various elements of the conservative critique of modernity and, in contemporary societies, feminism and various components within the green movement. These social movements are clearly not identical and they are also not necessarily related to each other. However, they have in various ways challenged the uni-dimensional notion of rationality in modernity, the emphasis on reason rather than emotions, the concept of a grand narrative, and a teleological view of history. This picture of the relationship between modernity and postmodernity appears to me to be historically more satisfactory than alternative positions which suggest that postmodernism has its specific origins in, for example, post-war developments in communication technology or in the development of new middle classes in a consumerist culture. The secular version of modernity which we find within Protestantism has, therefore, found its alternative in a variety of social movements which have questioned the authority of rational and individualistic views of reality.

If this position has any validity then the conceptualisation of secularisation becomes much more complex. First, in the contemporary world the major threat to Calvinistic or Protestant forms of religiosity may no longer appear in the guise of rationalism as in the nineteenth century but in the challenge of postmodernity and consumerism. The challenge of rationality, as described, for example, by Mrs Humphrey Ward in *Robert Elsmere* in 1888, no longer appears as the most significant opposing force against the type of religion represented by western Protestantism. The postmodernisation of society has produced a profound critique, at least at the level of intellectual exchange, of the idea of grand narratives, concepts of unity, a unified notion of rationality and the authoritative dominance of western forms of reasoning. These changes in intellectual culture are in my view potentially far more profoundly damaging to the intellectual core of the Protestant version of modernisation. In so far as Christianity is the grand narrative, the postmodernist technique of deconstruction and the critique of textuality is a direct analytical challenge to the biblical authority of the Christian tradition, especially the Protestant version of that tradition. At the same time, the hedonistic life-styles of consumerism provide an equally profound challenge to religious asceticism and capitalist modernism. According to the arguments of Daniel Bell, Fredric Jameson, Scott Lash, Michael Featherstone and others, if postmodernism is associated with the consumerist life-style of the new middle classes of advanced capitalism then these life-styles become globally significant through the extension of the world economic system and the globalisation of culture (Featherstone, 1988). Consumerist hedonism and postmodernist relativism challenge Christianity at both the intellectual and experiential levels by providing alternative sources of value, life-style and perspective.

We also need to take account of the various ways in which the feminist critique of patriarchal religions and the postmodern critique of rationalism interact to provide yet another source of alternative values to traditional Christian systems. The primary assumptions of the Abrahamic faiths have been patriarchal since they are based upon notions of the Fatherhood of God, divine Sonship and a patriarchal priesthood. Therefore, the feminist critique of the patriarchal discourse of the Abrahamic religions provides a powerful alternative. In so far as we treat western rationalism as a patriarchal form of thought, postmodernism and feminism are equally hostile to the grand narratives of patriarchal Christianity and the instrumentalist rationalism of western capitalist systems.

The point of this argument is not to claim that the baroque was postmodern, but rather to identify a series of contrasts in western history which either prefigured or imitated some of the contrasts of the contemporary opposition between modernity and postmodernity. I have identified Protestant rationalism, especially in the Calvinistic form developed in the liberal bourgeois environment of northern Europe, with modernist tendencies, and therefore I have tried to argue that the Counter-Reformation and baroque culture represented an alternative set of values, practices and institutions which, to some extent, mirrored the modern development of postmodernity. I also want to argue that instrumental rationalism, because it is based upon what Weber regarded as an ethic of world mastery, tends to be patriarchal in its format and its assumptions. The development of Mariology inside the

Roman Catholic Church represented in principle an alternative to the patriarchal figure of God and gave expression to feminist principles; in particular Mary contrasted with the vengeful God of the Old Testament. I am not suggesting, of course, that Mary is a postmodern figure. On the contrary, Roman Catholicism continued to embrace the patriarchal assumptions of the Old Testament, and the whole structure of the Church from the Pope downwards was obviously an institution which was dominated by men and largely expressed male values. Furthermore, some feminists would want to argue that various values, namely celebration of family life, familiarity and intimacy, reproduced a patriarchal division between the head and the heart. In addition, the patriarchal defence of absolute kingship derived from conservative patterns of thought in Europe, while Protestantism tended to be associated with secular kingship and the liberal values of an emerging capitalist order. Nevertheless, it is interesting to consider the notion that, within a modernising Europe, there were always counter-tendencies which emphasised different values, practices and institutions (Buci-Glucksmann, 1984, 1986). My argument therefore is that the contemporary distinction between modernity and postmodernity was prefigured by various social and cultural movements in Europe which can be traced back to the opposition between the Reformation and the Counter-Reformation.

This set of oppositional movements complicates the conventional debate about secularisation by suggesting that modern forms of fundamentalism, far from being necessarily conservative in their content, are actually a defence of the old pattern of modernity in its Calvinistic and Protestant form. While Protestantism may be held in part responsible for unleashing the modern pattern of rational secularism, the Protestant version of religion is also a defence of the modernising project.

The utopian mentality

Believing that the modern world on a global scale is going through a process of secularisation would be somewhat odd, given the central place of religion in many forms of political change in the world order. The rise of fundamentalist Islam is the most obvious example, and its involvement in the modern politics of Iran, Iraq and Pakistan is clear. The struggle for power inside Afghanistan would be yet a further example. However, this is not simply a question of Islamic fundamentalism, since religion has been deeply involved in the political struggles of Northern Ireland, and in the late 1980s religious protest in Poland, Rumania and East Germany were important aspects of the eventual 'gentle revolution' of eastern European communism. One could multiply these examples almost indefinitely.

There is, of course, a long tradition of analysis in the sociology of religion in which religion has been seen to be fundamental to the emergence of utopian thought as a challenge to existing ideology and social practice. Karl Mannheim's *Ideology and Utopia* (1991), which was written originally in 1929, is the leading example. The nature and importance of utopias are topics which have continued to exercise sociological theory (Levitas, 1990). Within a context of secularisation, however, it is not clear whether powerful utopian discourses can emerge which have the capacity to motivate modern social movements.

Why does religion continue to play an important part in social movements and political change? The most obvious answer is that religious ideas and religious mythology provide major vehicles for the expression of social political protest, especially against secular regimes. Thus, Islamic fundamentalism has been important in mobilising urban and peasant opposition to western secularism and consumerism. In this type of explanation, religion functions as a substitute or as a companion to nationalism. For example, what it is to be Polish, or what it is to be Irish is inextricably bound up with a religious identity. In a similar fashion it is difficult to separate the identity of secular Israel from the identity of a profoundly Jewish experience.

Although this explanation is attractive, I put a slightly different interpretation on the continuity of religious mythology in political movements. Sociologists have argued that postmodernism empties existing symbolism by irony, relativism, playfulness, simulation and fragmentation. The volume and velocity of social signs in the modern world, according to postmodern theory, eventually denude symbolism of its real meaning and significance. While mainstream Christianity has been subject to these processes, producing a liquidation of its pristine meanings, some areas of religious symbolism have survived (especially fundamentalism) and these symbolic systems, even in the modern world, may still provide the sort of utopian motivation which is necessary for massive social change. The imagery of the Old and New Testaments continues to provide a vocabulary of protest against injustice which, in both radical Catholicism and radical Protestantism, creates a utopian mentality, which is the basis for a radical critique of existing societies. However, if we examine these developments within a global perspective, we can argue that northern Europe and North America are areas of weak religious mobilisation, because it is within these geographical regions that the processes of modern pluralism and relativism have been most significant. This heartland of the project of modernity now finds itself surrounded by a global Islam which is at the forefront of anti-western protest. Although Islamic fundamentalism has been almost universally anti-western and anti-secularist, my argument is that Islamic radicalism is not anti-modernist. On the

contrary, it embraces precisely those values which have been characteristic of national Calvinistic Protestant modernity, namely asceticism,
anti-magical beliefs and rational practices. The anti-consumerist ethic
of many fundamentalist movements, but especially within Islam, is thus
not necessarily anti-modern, but is almost certainly anti-western in
orientation.

Conclusion: the struggle for the body

The German philosopher Helmuth Plessner has made a valuable
distinction between the 'animate-organismal body' and the 'objectual-
instrumental body' by reflecting on the contrast which is possible in
German between *Leib* and *Körper* (Honneth and Joas, 1988, p. 72).
While *Körper* is related to the hull of a ship, *Leib* is connected with
womb and personality. *Körper* is corpse; *Leib* is an emotive, lived body.

These approaches to the 'lived body' in social theory, for example, in
Gehlen (1988), depend eventually on the social philosophy of Nietzsche
(Deleuze, 1983), who claimed that human beings are a 'not yet
determined animal' (*noch nicht festgestelltes Tier*). The human animal is
'world-open', not fixed by instincts, and thus a species which is not
environmentally fixed. Humans are flexible with respect to their mode
of orientation to their habitus. This environmental openness requires
discipline, constraint and training. These ideas have now become
relatively familiar in philosophical discussions about the body (Leder,
1990), but they have yet to make a significant impact in general on
sociological theory.

These philosophical ideas about the body were, however, the
background to the notion that religion is a sacred canopy which provides
a structure or security for the anomic soul. In the work of Berger (1969)
and Luckmann (1967), the sociology of religion came to develop an
important philosophical anthropology in which religion is a necessary
feature of the socially constructed environment which protects these
'not-yet-finished animals' from the threat of death and chaos. In
mainstream sociology, however, the origins of these ideas in the
philosophical anthropology of the nineteenth century and the *Lebensphilosophie* of the twentieth century remained somewhat obscured from
view. The legacy of Gehlen and Plessner has often been highly
conservative in its emphasis on the necessity of social order as a
protection or canopy against disturbance and disorder. In developing
that line of argument in the sociology of religion, the revolutionary role
of the utopian mentality in world history — a theme which is central to
Weber's comparative sociology of theodicy — is denied or minimised.

When I first wrote this book I was primarily influenced by Nietzsche
and Foucault rather than by Gehlen and Plessner. It was not until I
came to write *The Body and Society* (Turner, 1984) that the work of

philosophical anthropology became more dominant in the way in which I presented the sociological question of sensual practice. Hence the book was directed at problems raised by Foucault in his analysis of knowledge/power and soul/body. Both theoretical approaches (in *Lebensphilosophie* and Foucaultian philosophy) appear to be analytically important, although not mutually compatible, in any sociological attempt to understand religion in relation to the body as practice and as discourse.

References

Anderson, P. (1974), *Lineages of the Absolutist State*, London.

Argan, G. C. (1989), *The Baroque Age*, New York.

Berger, P. L. (1969), *The Social Reality of Religion*, London.

Buci-Glucksmann, C. (1984), *La raison baroque*, Paris.

Buci-Glucksmann, C. (1986), *La folie du voir: de l'esthétique baroque*, Paris.

Deleuze, G. (1983), *Nietzsche and Philosophy*, London.

Durkheim, E. (1957), *Professional Ethics and Civic Morals*, London.

Durkheim, E. (1961), *The Elementary Forms of the Religious Life*, New York.

Durkheim, E. (1964), *The Division of Labor in Society*, New York.

Featherstone, M. (ed.) (1988), *Postmodernism*, London.

Foucault, M. (1988), 'Technologies of the self', in L. H. Martin, H. Gutman and P. H. Hutton (eds.), *Technologies of the Self: A Seminar with Michel Foucault*, London, pp. 16–49.

Gehlen, A. (1988), *Man, his Nature and Place in the World*, New York.

Giddens, A. (1979), *Central Problems in Social Theory*, London.

Giddens, A. (1990), *The Consequences of Modernity*, Cambridge.

Hennis, W. (1988), *Max Weber, Essays in Reconstruction*, London.

Honneth, A. and Joas, H. (1988), *Social Action and Human Nature*, Cambridge.

Lapointe, R. (1989), *Socio-anthropologie du religieux: le cercle enchanté de la croyance*, Geneva and Paris.

Leder, D. (1990), *The Absent Body*, Chicago and London.

Levitas, R. (1990), *The Concept of Utopia*, New York.

Luckmann, T. (1967), *The Invisible Religion: The Problem of Religion in Modern Society*, New York and London.

Luhmann, N. (1984), *Religious Dogmatics and the Evolution of Societies*, New York and Toronto.

Mannheim, K. (1991), *Ideology and Utopia*, London.

Marin, L. (1988), *Portrait of the King*, London.

Meštrović, S. G. (1990), *The Coming Fin de Siècle: An Application of Durkheim's Sociology to Modernity and Postmodernity*, London.

Otto, R. (1929), *The Idea of the Holy*, London.

Parsons, T. (1963), 'Christianity and modern industrial society', in E. A. Tiryakian (ed.), *Sociological Theory, Values and Social Cultural Change*, New York, pp. 33–70.

Parsons, T. (1981), 'Revisiting the classics throughout a long career', in Buford Rhea (ed.), *The Future of the Sociological Classics*, London, pp. 183–94.

Parsons, T. (1991), *The Social System*, London.

Simmel, G. (1906), *Die Religion*, Frankfurt.

Stauth, G. and Turner, B. S. (1988), *Nietzsche's Dance: Resentment, Reciprocity and Resistance in Social Life*, Oxford.

Tenbruck, F. H. (1980), 'The problem of the thematic unity in the works of Max Weber', *British Journal of Sociology*, vol. 31, pp. 316–51.

Turner, B.S. (1974), *Weber and Islam: A Critical Study*, London.

Turner, B. S. (1984), *The Body and Society*, Oxford.

Vierhaus, R. (1988), *Germany in the Age of Absolutism*, Cambridge.

Wach, J. (1971), *Sociology of Religion*, London and Chicago.

Warner, M. (1976), *Alone of All Her Sex: The Myth and the Cult of the Virgin Mary*, New York.

Weber, M. (1949), *The Methodology of the Social Sciences*, edited by E. Shils and H. Finch, Chicago.

Weber, M. (1965), *The Protestant Ethic and the Spirit of Capitalism*, London.

Weber, M. (1966), *The Sociology of Religion*, London.

Weber, M. (1968), *Economy and Society*, 2 vols., Berkeley, Ca. and London.

Introduction to the First Edition

The world we live in is a mistake, a clumsy parody. Mirrors and fatherhood, because they multiply and confirm the parody, are abominations. Revulsion is the cardinal virtue. Two ways (whose choice the Prophet left free) may lead us there: abstinence or the orgy, excess of the flesh or its denial. (Jorge Luis Borges, A Universal History of Infamy, *1973*)

Indeed I wonder whether, before one poses the question of ideology, it wouldn't be more materialist to study first the question of the body and the effects of power on it. (*Michel Foucault,* Power/Knowledge, *1980*)

A materialist interpretation of religion

These two quotations from the Argentine essayist Borges and the French philosopher Foucault encapsulate the essence of religious interpretations of the world and hence the perennial concerns, when properly understood, of the sociology of religion. The central and recurring theme of the stories of Jorge Borges is that the world is a puzzle, our existence is mysterious and any commitment to the notion that reality has a meaning is less than rational. The problem is that, at least for a time, we find ourselves in that world. In this sense, the Borgesian world is fundamentally religious, since religious beliefs and rituals are basic to any human response to the problem of meaning. The question of theodicy, the vindication of divinity in the face of evil, is thus a necessary component of religion (Kolakowski, 1982) and a basic issue in classical sociology of religion, especially in the sociology of Max Weber (1966).

Religious discourses on evil, justice and human freedom are not, however, abstract speculations of a remote, metaphysical nature; they enter into the basic rhythm of mundane life — birth, procreation, ageing and death. Questions about religion cannot, in my view, ever be divorced from questions of the body. The finitude of our corporality is part of the 'mistake' and the reproduction of bodies, confirmation of the parody. Hence, sexuality sooner or later challenges any rational interpretation we may attempt to foist on the labyrinth of reality. As Borges drily notes, religious practices tend to divide around either ascetic control or orgiastic release. The debate over the social roles of Dionysian and Apollinian forces provides a major linking theme from Nietzsche (1967) to Gouldner's study of classical Greece and the origins of sociology (1967).

The study of religion is thus a materialist enterprise, since our corporality is constitutive of our experience of the parody of existence. In religious systems, the body is a vehicle for the transmission of holiness and a major symbol of evil as 'flesh'; it is the means by which the soul is educated and the obstacle to our salvation; our health and our salvation are necessarily conjoined, but our sickness may be either a sign of religious election or a mark of damnation. Tradition has it that Jesus and Muhammad were respectively physically handicapped (Vermes, 1973) and epileptic (Rodinson, 1961).

A materialist interpretation of religion normally implies reductionism. It suggests that religion can be 'explained away' by demonstrating that religion is merely a reflection of more basic social processes or simply the expression of economic interests or a rationalisation of psychological needs. In this study, I argue that the historical and sociological importance of religion as fundamental to human life can only be grasped by an analysis of the relationship between religion, the body, family and property. My notion of 'materialist' starts, therefore, with Foucault's observation that we must pose 'first the question of the body' rather than ideology. By implication, I am critical of the whole trend in the sociology of religion to treat 'the question of meaning' as a theoretical rather than material issue. Sociologists have treated the Borgesian 'parody' as simply cognitive rather than corporeal.

In this study, I follow Weber's introductory statement in *The Sociology of Religion* that the 'elementary forms of behaviour motivated by religious or magical factors are oriented to *this* world' (1966, p. 1). The two features of this world which are crucial for the social functions of religion are the control of property through the family and the organisation of bodies in social space. In theoretical terms, these two features bring together the traditional concerns of Marxism and the more recent perspective of structuralism. A materialist interpretation of religion does not, therefore, regard religious data as mere epiphenomena of more fundamental social processes; on the contrary, it locates religion at the centre of social production and reproduction.

Most textbooks in the sociology of religion are themselves highly ritualistic. The routine rehearsal of traditional themes has the function of integrating a community of scholars around a common set of beliefs. Like the Arunta tribe in Durkheim's classic study of aboriginal religion (1961), sociologists are also bound by *religio*, in the form of sacred texts and professional rituals. The contents page of any major textbook on the sociology of religion over the last fifteen years has a predictable range of topics: the origins of the discipline, the Protestant Ethic thesis, the church—sect typology, secularisation and modern cults (Schneider, 1970; Budd, 1973; Hill, 1973; Towler, 1974; Wilson, 1982). Although some of the major collections of essays in the discipline show a wider range of empirical and analytical interests (Schneider, 1964; Birnbaum and Lenzer, 1969; Robertson, 1969), the sociology of religion has followed a remarkably narrow range of theoretical interests. The central analytical question has been: 'What is religion?' and the difficulty of providing a satisfactory answer to that question has consequently dominated the debate about secularisation in industrial societies (Martin, 1978a). The question is, without doubt, significant in both the philosophy and sociology of religion, but it has had the effect of inducing a certain theoretical sterility and repetitiveness within the discipline. The endless pursuit of that issue has produced an analytical cul-de-sac. It seems appropriate to attempt to raise new questions and topics of a wider theoretical interest and therefore definitions of religion may, at least for the time being, be relegated to an appendix. Although this is heretical, the device has a certain economic utility.

Weaknesses of contemporary sociology of religion

The contemporary state of sociology of religion can be said to exhibit three major weaknesses. First, it has not played a role in or constituted a part of any major theoretical debate in modern sociology. The sociology of religion is a theoretical side-show in relation to, for example, neo-Marxist debates about modes of production and ideology, French structuralist discussions of subjectivity and power, and critical theory's discussion of knowledge, the state and legitimacy. The sociology of religion has tended to regard the crude metaphor of base/superstructure in classical Marxism as the only possible Marxist account of ideology in which religion is simply a reflection of economic relations of production.

Recent developments in neo-Marxism concerning the nature of ideology have been side-stepped so that sociologists of religion have not engaged with the theoretical discussions generated by Louis Althusser (Althusser and Balibar, 1970), Nicos Poulantzas (1973) and Barry Hindess and Paul Q. Hirst (1975). They have ignored the controversy about the role of legitimacy in the modern state which followed from the work of Jürgen Habermas (1976) and Nicos Poulantzas (1978). They have even neglected the contributions to historical analysis by Braudel (1980) and Ladurie (1981). It is difficult to see how the sociology of religion could be taken to be a serious subject in the light of its absence from contemporary debates in sociology. This absence is, in my view, at least partly explained by the fact that sociology of religion has remained deeply embedded in a conventional frame of knowledge and focused on a narrow range of topics.

The second characteristic of much modern sociology of religion is its primary concern with the subjectivity of the social actor, manifested in the analysis of religious beliefs, world-views, definitions of alternative realities, commitments to the sacred cosmos and so forth. There are clearly good credentials for such a position in the interpretative sociology of Max Weber, in Talcott Parsons's critique of rational positivism (1937), in G. H. Mead's social philosophy of action (1934) and generally in the phenomenological tradition of writers like Alfred Schutz (1972).

This concentration on individual subjectivity has, however, a number of limiting consequences within the sociology of religion. It draws attention to the cognitive dimension of religious activity, so that rituals and practices take second place. Attempts to spell out a number of dimensions of religiosity in the work of Charles Glock and Rodney Stark (1965) have left religious beliefs in a central location to theory and research. The preference for hermeneutical and phenomenological perspectives has meant that much sociology of religion remains content with detailed descriptions of the nature and content of religious belief and subjective experience, whereas explanations of the origins, functions and effects of religious practices and institutions are neglected. Dissatisfaction with both the structural-functionalism of an earlier tradition (Davis, 1948) and Marxism has meant that the question 'What is religion, from the subjective perspective of the social actor?' has replaced the question 'What are the social effects of religious phenomena in society?'

This study of religion is, by contrast, mainly concerned with a range of theories which are engaged with the problem of the social consequences of religion for class relationships, family organisation, state legitimacy and the control of individuals and populations. By examining these problems, the book looks backwards to the tradition of Nietzsche, Weber, Engels and Freud, but forwards to the modern contributions of Lévi-Strauss, Foucault, Elias, Sennett and Ladurie. Traditional analyses of religion and secularisation can thus be set in the context of debates about ideology, modes of production, power and knowledge.

Such an approach takes sociology away from the approach of Peter Berger, whose *The Social Reality of Religion* (1969) dominated sociology of religion in the 1970s. By defining religion as a process of constructing symbolic worlds (the sacred canopy), Berger was able to forge an interesting and important alliance between the sociology of religion and the sociology of knowledge. However, Berger took sociology back to Feuerbachian anthropology by claiming that, in essence, man is a religious animal, forced to construct a meaningful world. The approach ignored the Marxist argument that 'the person' is an effect of an ensemble of social relations which, in turn, reflect the complex structure of class positions (Seve, 1975). The *prevalence* of religious beliefs in human groups cannot be equated with the *effectivity* of religious beliefs in the coherence of classes, the operation of the legal system, the distribution of property and the transformation of relations of production.

It is difficult to move from Berger's highly general statements about the subjective reality of sacred worlds and the religious essence of the human enterprise to specific analyses of the role of religion, for example, in class societies. This study of religion largely follows, therefore, a theoretical position developed in *The Dominant Ideology Thesis* (Abercrombie, Hill and Turner, 1980) which criticised sociologists for assuming that the social presence of beliefs was evidence that such beliefs have direct and specific societal consequences. A second argument of that study was that sociologists too frequently examine the articulate and literary beliefs of a dominant class as evidence of the existence of a general, dominant ideology. Sociologists of religion are far too ready to take theological beliefs as their data and recent attempts to analyse 'common religion' do not radically avoid this problem (Towler, 1974).

The third limitation of contemporary sociology of religion is its narrow empirical focus on western forms of religion. In practice, the sociology of religion is very largely the sociology of Christianity. This narrow empirical range was especially characteristic of British sociology in the 1960s and 1970s; *A Sociological Yearbook of Religion in Britain* was illustrative of the competent work done in this genre. This tradition has been supplemented by good ethnographic studies of cults and sects in America (Zaretsky and Leone, 1974) and Britain (Wilson, 1970a), alongside a rich crop of publications on Hare Krishna, Divine Light Mission, the Unified Family and, more exotically, Yaqui spirit-possession (Castaneda, 1968; Silverman, 1975). The trend towards the sociology of cults has now gone so far that mainstream Christianity has to some extent been neglected. The principal exception to this picture is provided by the social history of Catholicism (Bossy, 1975; Delumeau, 1977).

Comparative sociological studies of world religions

Despite the continuing centrality of Max Weber to the sociology of religion, comparative sociological studies of world religions are rarely attempted. Although the sociology of religion has incorporated a number of major theoretical developments in anthropology (Eliade, 1959; Douglas, 1966; Geertz, 1966; V. Turner, 1969), it has not fully measured up to the rich tradition of anthropological and ethnographic studies of other religions (Rasmussen, 1931; Crapanzano, 1973; Gilsenan, 1973; Barnes, 1974; Tambiah, 1976). Comparative sociology of religion is, of course, hazardous, both epistemologically and methodologically. Our understanding of 'other religions' is not achieved naively, as it were, but through the mediation of traditional perspectives or discourses that shape and control the ways in which we encounter and account for other cultures and belief systems. Comparisons of Occidental and Oriental religions, in particular, are formed in terms of an Orientalist discourse.

In this study, my treatment of the problematic of 'other religions' depends heavily on the work of Edward Said, whose *Orientalism* (1978) provides a brilliant account of the discourse by which western culture has appropriated 'Islam'. The peculiarity of the contemporary interest in the epistemological issue of comparisons is that the sociology of religion has been absent from the debate. This is paradoxical, given the fact that understanding other belief systems (Wilson, 1970a) was part of the stock-in-trade of the traditional sociology of religion. Although comparisons, like translations, are philosophically problematic, this study draws heavily on comparative data from Islam, Judaism and Christianity.

Continuities and discontinuities among the Abrahamic religions

In *Orientalism* Edward Said noted that the existence of a discourse generates a series of contrasts (differences) which sets off our familiar reality from alien cultures. Max Weber's sociology of religion is full of such contrasts: rejection of the world in Christianity versus accommodation in Confucianism; the rationality of Calvinism versus the non-rationality of Taoism; opposition to magical practices in Protestantism versus pragmatic acceptance of magical rites in popular Buddhism; the centrality of personal salvation to the Protestant sects versus the quest for land in militaristic Islam. This accounting system of absence/presence provided the conceptual framework within which the question of the origins of capitalism could be successfully posed.

Whereas the discourse of 'other religions' tends to focus on issues of discontinuity and difference, in the case of Judaism, Christianity and Islam there is a strong warrant for emphasising continuity and sameness. The paradox is, of course, that these three dimensions of the 'Abrahamic faith' have traditionally stressed their separate theological identities. The notion of an 'epistemological break' (Althusser and Balibar, 1970) in the structuralist analysis of developments in scientific knowledge could, therefore, be equally applied to shifts and discontinuities in theology and religions. Thus, Christianity by conceptualising Judaism as a pharisaical, ritualistic religion emphasises revelation, prophecy and personal salvation as key components in its 'epistemological rupture' against Jewish traditionalism. The contrast hinges on spirit versus law. In turn, Islam regards its pure monotheism and prophetic scripture as a rupture with Christian trinitarianism or, from an Islamic perspective, polytheism.

Despite the fact that members of the Abrahamic faith emphasise their mutual differences, there are very strong sociological continuities between them. The orthodox core of these religions exhibits a common set of components: a high god, scriptural tradition, prophetic revelation, salvationism. They characteristically spawn popular religious movements which are organised around saints, popular cults, mystical alternatives to puritanical versions of scripturalism and magical practices. The cultural tradition and sociological organisation of Jewish Hasidism, Islamic Sufism and Christian popular mysticism are strikingly similar. Although there may be significant differences between the 'great tradition' of Christianity, Judaism and Islam, their 'little traditions' within the folk community tend to converge (Redfield, 1955 and 1965).

As Gellner (1969b) argues, in Islam there is an oscillation between the puritan asceticism of the town and the hierarchical saintship of the countryside, because the illiteracy of the tribesmen excludes them from the literate, scriptural tradition of the urban mosque. The services provided by saints in Islam and elsewhere are very diverse and not simply confined to that of spiritual mediation. In particular, the popular saints of the Abrahamic religions provide crucial healing services in societies where illness behaviour has important symbolic significance and where modern medical systems are underdeveloped (Beattie and Middleton, 1969). Within these folk traditions, the human body stands in a significant relationship to notions of spiritual and physical well-being. For example, the blessing (charisma) of holy men in the Catholic and Hasidic popular traditions is transmitted by physical contact between lay followers and saints. In popular Islam, the gift (*baraka*) of the saint (*agurram*) is transmitted by blood, urine, spittle and excrement (Westermarck, 1968). Similarly, the confession of sins and purification rites typically involve spitting, washing the body and changing of clothes (Pettazzoni, 1954).

There is, therefore, a convergence within folk religiosity towards an adherence to popular saints who provide medical and symbolic services for the body and towards a cosmology in which the body and its secretions are fundamental to the notion of salvation. There is a convergence of practice, regardless of discontinuities and rupture at the level of formal theological systematisation. The political implications of continuity/discontinuity for global religious conflicts are obviously important, given the role of religion in the definition of citizenship in Israel and in Islamic societies.

Religion, individuals and populations

This study is materialist, therefore, in two senses. To follow a distinction made by Michel Foucault, my aim is to trace the relationships between religion and the body of individuals, and between religion and the body of populations. The term 'religion' is derived from *religio*, the bond of social relations between individuals; the term 'sociology' is derived from *socius*, the bond of companionship that constitutes societies. Following Durkheim (1961), we may define religion as a set of beliefs and practices, relating to the sacred, which create social bonds between individuals. We may define sociology, naively, as the 'science of community' (MacIver, 1917, p. 45). Sociology in general and the sociology of religion in particular are thus concerned with the processes which unite and disunite, bind and unbind social relationships in space and time.

The body of individuals

The theme of this study is that religion has the function of controlling the sexuality of the body in order to secure the regular transmission of property via the family. Because property transmission through primogeniture within the patriarchal family is crucial in securing the economic and political unity of the dominant class, any general theory of the social effects of religion has to concern itself with the question of social class. The importance of religion for subordinate social groups is very different from its importance in the dominant class. Among subordinate groups, I follow the tradition of Engels (1965), Weber (1966) and Mannheim (1960) in arguing that religion can express opposition through millenarianism, sectarianism and chiliasm in the form of resentment (Nietzsche, 1968). Alternatively, religion offers hope, compensation and accommodation. In general, however, I take a critical view of any argument that suggests that religion is a social cement which binds social classes together within a common world-view.

The notion that religion involves the social control of the body and has major consequences for the distribution of wealth and authority can be expressed diagrammatically as:

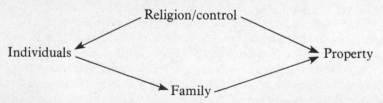

This treatment of religion presupposes that society is organised in terms of family units, laws of inheritance and private property. More precisely, it assumes that wealth is transmitted from one generation to the next through the family and that the family unit is the major source of wealth. In feudalism, religious control of sexuality, especially the sexuality of wives and sons, was crucial to the control of private feudal rights to land; the confessional, penance and other sacraments were important in the social control of women and the production of legitimate offspring (Turner, 1977b). In competitive capitalism, religious control of sexuality was again important in the distribution of property; where the capitalist family was the primary source of future investment for accumulation.

The body of populations

In societies where the state and public ownership are more prominent than private ownership, religion has a different role in relationship to individuals. In late capitalism, where there is a degree of separation of ownership and control (Hill, 1981), the importance of the family for economic accumulation declines and there is less emphasis on the importance of legitimacy and monogamy. There is no longer an economic requirement for sexual restraint among property-owners, since the public corporation rather than the family firm dominates the economy. There is, however, a strong social requirement for the regulation of urban populations in order to achieve public order and to secure taxation.

Traditional religious controls over the body are now transferred to public disciplines which are exercised within the school, factory, prison and other 'total institutions'. Religion may continue within the private space of the body of individuals, but the public space of the body of populations is now subordinated, not to the *conscience collective*, the sacred canopy or the civil religion, but to secular disciplines, economic constraint and political coercion. The public realm is desacralised in western industrial societies. In global political terms, for a variety of contingent reasons, militant Islam and orthodox Judaism assume a significant political role in the context of post-colonial struggles. In western societies, the disappearance of religion from the political arena undermines the legitimacy of the state, which is forced to depend on constraint as the principal basis of stability. This argument takes the form:

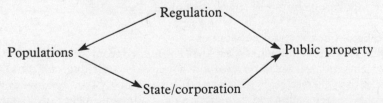

In late capitalism, the state has a major role in the economy, and the private capitalist family is generally replaced by national and international corporations. Although there is considerable inequality in the distribution of private wealth, the nature of the class system changes because managers exercise considerable social and political power through their control over large-scale enterprises (Poulantzas, 1975). Religious pluralism and diversity can now be 'tolerated' because there is, for economic reasons, less emphasis on the sexual control of women. Despite inequalities in the labour-market, women now have greater access to divorce and separation. The moral unity of the dominant class decreases, but at the same time there is the need to control the urban population which developed alongside the maturation of competitive capitalism.

Secularisation and bureaucratisation
The two models of society thus imply a secularisation thesis, namely the declining importance of religion for the unity of the dominant class. However, late capitalism is not the only society in which the state is dominant in civil society or where there is a requirement to control large human populations. This form of argument might also apply to civilisations based on slavery, to societies that Wittfogel (1957) referred to as centralised hydraulic empires, to classical Greece or to the bureaucratic system of the Incas. The variable relationship between coercion and constraint in pre-capitalist societies, such as Egypt and Athens (Carlton, 1977), is particularly important in this respect. Wittfogel's thesis that the origins of the state were located in the problem of bureaucratic control in hydraulic empires has been discredited; the precise contribution of environmental and societal factors in the emergence of pre-capitalist states remains controversial (Moseley and Wallerstein, 1978). Although the regulation of large populations by bureaucratic means precedes capitalism, it is evident that regulatory disciplines tend to intensify with the development of capitalism (Touraine, 1974). The welfare functions of the modern state, which in part serve to incorporate the working class, also require greater regulation and co-ordination of populations (Bell, 1976). Modern capitalist societies are thus characterised by a contradictory relationship between an emphasis on the expressivity of the external body and the regulation of populations by bureaucratic disciplines.

Religion, society and economics
This analysis of religion is sharply differentiated from those approaches which either treat religion as simply a matter of individual subjectivity or satisfy themselves with descriptive accounts of the organisational forms of sects, cults and denominations. Following Weber, this study of religion is primarily concerned with the institutional linkage between religion, society and economics. This concern involves two separate arguments.

First, it rejects the sociological importance of the subjective orientation of social actors in the explication of social regularities. This position follows from theoretical arguments first elaborated in *The Dominant Ideology Thesis* (Abercrombie *et al.*, 1980), in which social actors and social classes were treated as primarily carriers of structural arrangements. In turn, this position depends on the notion that the relations of production in society impose a certain logic on the behaviour of individuals: human agency always operates within the constraints established by the dominant mode of production (Plekhanov, 1940).

Second, it does not follow from this argument that my interpretation of religion entails *vulgar* reductionism. There is never a mechanistic fit between base and superstructure, because, at the level of the social formation, numerous contingent relations between classes, groups and institutions 'deflect' the logic of economic reproduction. The requirements of the dominant mode of production are never entirely satisfied or provided at the level of the social formation. The economy is dominant only in 'the last analysis'; many features of the culture of a society — aesthetics, doctrines concerning Christ's messianic status, theories of scriptural authority, hymnology, ecclesiology and so forth — may have little or no bearing on the operation of economic forms and thus enjoy a relative autonomy from the economic base. Sociologists who wish to devote their academic lives to belletrist analyses of these cultural forms are at liberty to do so, but they do not seriously advance sociology as a systematic science of society.

As a materialist perspective on religion, this text is written against the grain of conventional accounts within the sociology of religion. In order to defend the autonomy and importance of the study of religion within sociology, sociologists of religion have laboured the point that religion is an autonomous cultural phenomenon which cannot be reduced to economic interest or political requirements, that religion significantly influences individual behaviour and that religion is a crucial human interpretation of the existential condition of individuals. The sociology of Max Weber figures large in this interpretation of religion as an independent symbolic activity, because Weber gave special emphasis to religious theodicies and to religion as pre-eminently 'meaningful behaviour'.

This approach to Weber's study of religion tends, however, to minimise Weber's crucial concern for the linkages between religion, economics and politics; in these areas, Weber often wrote in a reductionist fashion in treating the 'ethics' of the world religions as fundamentally shaped by the social location of their carriers. For example, Weber saw the theological content of Islam as determined by the worldly interests of warriors (Turner, 1974a). Furthermore, in

Weber's view, religion as such grew out of specifically this-worldly concerns for health and wealth.

The theological systematisation of theodicy is the product of a stratum of religious intellectuals. Theodicy is not the outcome of purely metaphysical speculations about the 'meaning of life' in general, but is rooted in the immediate issues of our corporeal finitude. A materialist perspective on religion can, therefore, be seen as a play upon the terms *corporalis* and *corporare*. This study is primarily concerned with the corporality of the individual and the corporation of society, with the place of religion in the production of societies and the reproduction of individuals or, in Foucault's terms, with 'the body of individuals and the body of populations':

The discipline of the body and the regulations of the population constituted the two poles around which the organisation of power over life was deployed. (Foucault, 1981, p. 139)

A materialist sociology has to be concerned with the production of wealth and the production of bodies, with the relationship between the social distribution of bodies and commodities, and with the social institutions (the family, religion and the state) which mediate these basic processes of production and reproduction.

A historical-materialist perspective
A materialist perspective on religion does not treat religious beliefs and practices as inconsequential and trivial. On the contrary, it situates religion in our experience of physical and physiological reality. As such, materialism is perfectly in tune with the physicality of the Christian tradition and by extension with the Abrahamic roots of Islam and Judaism. The theological and symbolic core of traditional Christianity is focused on the fatherhood of God, the incarnation of Christ, the suffering on the Cross, the glorious resurrection of the body and the life of the world to come. It is difficult to escape the materialism of the eucharistic feast of Christ's blood and body or the materialistic metaphors of Christ's body and the body of the Church.

This perspective is not, furthermore, merely characteristic of Catholic cosmology, since it is, for example, prominent in Protestant worship and hymnology. The rapture of Charles Wesley's hymns, for example:

> O let me kiss Thy bleeding feet,
> And bathe and wash them with my tears!

is typical of the Methodist response to Christ's physical suffering. This is not to deny that, at various points in the history of Christianity, there has been a profound spiritualisation of religion, breaking the connection between body and spirit, and presenting Christianity as a superior manifestation of the religious quest by virtue of its negation of the equation of sin and sickness, of flesh and evil. The Holy Family thus becomes a denial of the earthly family, or at least a perfected simile (Martin, 1978). But this very process of spiritualisation continues to rely on 'primitive' analogies, metaphors and duplications of matter and spirit, body and soul, the subjectivity of conscience and the objectivity of society:

In the hallway there is a mirror which faithfully duplicates all appearances. Men usually infer from this mirror that the library is not infinite (if it really were, why this illusory duplication?); I prefer to dream that its polished surfaces represent and promise the infinite. (Borges, 1970, p. 78)

A materialist interpretation reduces religion to its elementary forms in the production and duplication of material existence — the corporality of individuals and the corpus of society. Religion thus lies at the crucial interchange between nature and culture in the formation of societies and the creation of human attributes (Hirst and Woolley, 1982). This interchange cannot, however, be understood in general, but only in the context of the material mode of production of individuals and societies. The materialist theory of religion is, by definition, a historical-materialist perspective; it is, as Engels noted in *The Origin of the Family, Private Property and the State*, the study of the production of the means of subsistence and of the production of human beings.

1   Other Religions

The sociology of religion can be said to exist in order to define its subject-matter. Indeed it was in large measure founded by the attempt of Emile Durkheim (1961), in *The Elementary Forms of Religious Life* of 1912, to subdue the multiplicity of religions to the uniformity of religion. The introductory and concluding sections of this sociological classic are allocated to the demolition of existing definitions which treated religion as a mistaken attempt to make sense of the world by reference to such concepts as 'god', 'soul' or 'spirits'. Durkheim proposed that religion can only be understood by concentrating on its social role in uniting the community behind a common set of rituals and beliefs. The defining feature of religion is that it bifurcates the world into the sacred and the profane; the social consequence of such practices towards the sacred realm is the creation and reproduction of a *conscience collective*, a social unity binding members into homogenous units.

Given this celebrated sociological definition, the religions of humanity are so many variations on a theme since they are all constructed on the basis of these 'elementary structures'. Having satisfactorily defined religion as a 'social fact' of human collectivities, the problem of religion appears to disappear from Durkheim's sociological gaze, apart from one rather important difficulty. Durkheim thought that the traditional forms of religious consciousness in European societies were rapidly disintegrating under the impact of secular industrialism; to some extent industrial society was based on a new principle of social integration in which an extensive division of labour created modern bonds of reciprocity and co-operation. During the First World War, however, Durkheim observed the effects of nationalism on the French community and in two wartime articles he implied that nationalism had the same social effects as traditional religions. Was nationalism a religion? One problem with Durkheimian definitions of religion is consequently that their conceptual net is too open; it drags in a diverse catch of social phenomena from baseball to nationalism, from Celtic hogmanay celebrations to royal weddings under the general rubric of 'religion'.

While Durkheim argued for the methodological principle that precise definition of terms must always precede sociological inquiry, Weber (1966) characteristically started *The Sociology of Religion* with the observation that, given the infinite diversity of religious behaviour,

general definitions of religion could only be imposed by fiat. Furthermore, it was not his intention to grasp the 'essence of religion', but only
to lay bare its 'conditions and effects'. Thus:

To define 'religion', to say what it *is,* is not possible at the start of a presentation
such as this. Definition can be attempted, if at all, only at the conclusion of the
study. (Weber, 1966, p. 1)

Weber can be criticised for operating with an implicit definition of
religion which permitted him to discuss magic, Buddhism, Confucianism, Hinduism, Islam, Christianity, taboo, totemism and occultism
under the heading of *Religionssoziologie.* Weber did not finally provide
an explicit, succinct definition of religious phenomena, but it is clear
that his approach to religion was ineluctably historical, rich in empirical
detail and sensitive to the complex significance of 'religion' for different
national and class categories. For example, Weber was, at one level,
concerned to examine the various ways in which the problem of making
sense of the world ('the need for meaning') was worked out in terms of
different theories of salvation and how 'salvational anxiety' has definite
social consequences. These cognitive maps of the human condition
were the result of religious intellectualism and religious professionalism
which had become somewhat detached from the everyday reality of
ordinary people, confronted by the mundane task of mere survival. By
contrast, the historical origins of religion resided in the search to
control the empirical world for entirely secular and instrumental
purposes:

The most elementary forms of behavior motivated by religious or magical
factors are oriented to *this* world. (Weber, 1966, p. 1)

Weber was not, however, concerned with the essential nature of
religion and did not offer a social history of the meaning of 'religion'.
His sociology was, in practice, an analysis of the social effects of religion
on economic and political development as a preface to his central task of
'understanding the characteristic uniqueness of the reality in which we
move' (Weber, 1949, p. 72). In this sense, both Durkheim and Weber
presented reductionist theories of religion. In sociology, the nature of
religious phenomena is to be explained in terms of social consequences,
not in terms of the meaning of religion for human action.

Weber has been criticised as a result of this reductionism and for his
'critical attitude' towards religion by Joachim Wach, who sought to
reconcile sociology and hermeneutics. Weber's sociology is flawed by
its failure to pay sufficient attention to the 'original meaning' of religion
(Wach, 1971, p. 3), whereas hermeneutical sociology would more
adequately conceptualise the objective nature of religious experience.
Following Rudolf Otto's *The Idea of the Holy* (1929), Wach (1971, p.
13) defined religion simply as 'the experience of the Holy'. The point of

the hermeneutic exercise in the sociology of religion is to bring the meaning of situations to the foreground of interpretation and 'to grasp the meanings attached to various situations strictly in terms of the components of the respective people's own mental worlds' (Towler, 1974, p. 2). Within this perspective, the explanation of religious beliefs becomes a matter of correct interpretation, that is, of understanding the meaning of beliefs in their social context (Winch, 1958; Runciman, 1969). Comparative sociology of religion becomes a matter of correct translation, that is, of rendering their meanings in terms of our language (Evans-Pritchard, 1965). The hermeneutic and phenomenological approaches to religion tend, therefore, to commit us to the actor's definition of reality. The way in which an individual describes the world is definitive, at least from the actor's own perspectives. The description which I give to the manner of God's speaking to me has priority over another's sociological explanation of my religious experiences. Within comparative religion, the phenomenological position has been forcefully stated with respect to interpretations of the Prophet Muhammad — 'what Muslims say about Muhammad is absolute and final' (Royster, 1972, p. 68).

There are at least three major difficulties with the hermeneutic or phenomenological approach to religion and religions. In the first, by concentrating on the meaning of social actions, they tend to ignore the way in which the social structure shapes or limits actions and they typically have no conception of the unintended consequences of behaviour (MacIntyre, 1967c). Secondly, this perspective cannot develop any notion of the importance of ideology in social life or of the importance of systematically distorted or erroneous views of the world, or of the role of false beliefs in maintaining political inequality. By treating situational beliefs from the actor's perspective as by definition authoritative, anthropology and sociology run the risk of excessive contextual charity (Gellner, 1970). Finally, hermeneutic sociology must find it difficult to deal with those situations where actors systematically disagree among themselves about the meaning of contexts, or where an actor is involved in self-contradiction as to the significance of his beliefs. In reply to Royster's view that Muslims' views of Muhammad must be definitive, one wants to know what happens when Muslims disagree as to the real nature of Muhammad's human and prophetic status (Turner, 1974a, p. 38).

Religious differences
Semantic debates in the sociology of religion as to the meaning of religion and religions are clearly important, but they can also represent a theoretical labyrinth which, as in a Jorge Borges's story, has the appearance of purposeful endeavour, but in fact has no centre, exit or

direction. One can detect this sense of frustration with epistemological niceties in Friedrich Engels's objections to Ludwig Feuerbach's anthropological defence of religion as a universal human need:

The word religion is derived from *religare* and originally meant a bond. Therefore, every bond between two people is a religion. Such etymological jugglery is the last resort of idealist philosophy . . . sexual love and sexual union is glorified as a 'religion', solely in order that the word religion so dear to idealistic memories may not disappear from the language. (Engels, 1976, pp. 29-30)

The danger with our frustration over 'etymological jugglery' is that it may permit ethnocentric attitudes to go unchallenged when sociologists turn to the problem of other religions. We become unwittingly locked in our own linguistic conventions and we covertly deploy the nature of religion in western Europe as a privileged model of all religious phenomena: our religion provides the yardstick of their religions, the latter appearing as pale reflections or bastard imitations of the former. Marx was certainly aware of this problem, to which he alluded in his history of bourgeois political economy, in discussing a resemblance between political economists and theologians. In his *Poverty of Philosophy*, Marx observed that economists tend to regard the economic institutions of feudalism as artificial, whereas those of capitalism are somehow necessary and natural. Similarly, theologians treat all religions 'qui n'est pas la leur, est une invention des hommes, tandis que leur propre religion est un émanation de Dieu' (Marx, 1847, p. 113). The language of comparison is the language of differences and, although Marx identified the obvious problem of religious comparisons as a contrast between the necessary and the artificial, Marxism was certainly not free from this difficulty. Marx wrote with a cultural arrogance towards other societies which is no longer acceptable in serious journalism, let alone in serious scholarship. In his journalistic commentary on Indian society, Marx commented that the village organisation of the agrarian economy had:

brought about a brutalizing worship of nature, exhibiting its degradation in the fact that man, the sovereign of nature, fell down on his knees in adoration of Hanuman, the monkey, and Sabbala, the cow. (Marx and Engels, 1972, p. 41)

Marx and Engels, despite their pungent criticisms of the effects of British colonial rule, reproduced the language of cultural dominance which traditionally shaped conventional views of other religions. The epistemological problems of relativism in the comparative analysis of other cultures did not come high on the list of Marx's theoretical interests. By contrast, the problem of other cultures has very much dominated the social sciences in the twentieth century. The reason for this epistemological priority is closely tied to the crises of global politics and, in particular, to the location of Islam with respect to the energy requirements of industrial societies.

The way we talk about other people is a central problem of all human interaction and one of the constitutive debates within the social sciences. Although as a matter of fact we do talk about other people and other cultures apparently without too much difficulty, there are major philosophical problems which throw doubt on whether we can *really* understand people who belong to alien groups and foreign cultures. The philosophical issues are ones of translation and relativism. Sociologists and philosophers have come to see the meaning of words as dependent on their usage within a particular language, which in turn depends upon its setting within the way of life of a particular society. The philosophical task of understanding the meaning of an expression in another culture cannot, according to this view of language, be separated from the sociological problem of providing an exposition of the social structure within which that language is embedded (Winch, 1958). Taken as a strong doctrine about the dependence of meaning on social structure, such a philosophical position would render translation, if not impossible, at least uncertain and problematic. Unless there is extensive comparability of social structures, one language cannot be intelligibly translated into another. The paradox is that translation is a routine practice and becoming proficient in another language may be difficult, but not impossible.

The question of translation can be treated as a specific instance of the more general problem of cultural relativism. The problem of relativism is as old as western philosophy itself, since it was Herodotus and Aristotle who confronted the fact that 'Fire burns both in Hellas and in Persia; but men's ideas of right and wrong vary from place to place'. If all beliefs and knowledge are culturally specific, then there are no universal criteria of truth, rationality and goodness by which social practices could be compared or evaluated. There are, however, a number of familiar difficulties with relativism, because, taken to its logical conclusion, it demonstrates that our knowledge of the world is merely ethnocentric, subjective preference. It would mean that no objective valid comparisons between societies could be made, and yet it would be difficult to conceive of knowledge which was not comparative or at least contained comparisons. To know something is, in principle, to be able to speak about it and language necessarily involves contrasts and comparisons between sameness and difference. As with translation, we constantly compare, despite the apparently insoluble philosophical difficulties of doing so.

The questions of translation and relativism inevitably confront the sociologist who attempts a comparative study of two religions, such as Christianity and Islam. In fact, the question of adequate comparisons is so fundamental that it may appear to rule out such an enterprise from inception, since the implication of much sociological analysis of Islam is that it is not a 'religion' at all, but a 'socio-political system'. The trouble with this implication is that it takes Christianity as a privileged model of what is to count as a 'religion' in the first place; perhaps in this respect it is Christianity, not Islam, which is the deviant case. One way into these conceptual puzzles may be to recognise that our contemporary views of other religions, such as Islam, are part of an established tradition of talking about alien cultures. We understand other cultures by slotting them into a pre-existing code or discourse which renders their oddity intelligible. We are, in practice, able to overcome the philosophical difficulties of translation by drawing upon various forms of accounting which highlight differences in characteristics between 'us' and 'them'. The culture from which comparisons are to be made can be treated as possessing a number of essential characteristics — rationality, democracy, industrial progress — in terms of which other cultures are seen to be deficient. A table of positive and negative attributes is thus established by which alien cultures can be read off and summations arrived at. Any comparative study of religions will, therefore, tend to draw upon pre-existing assumptions and scholarly traditions which provide an interpretational matrix of contrasts and comparisons. The principal balance sheet by which Islam has been understood in western culture may be referred to as 'Orientalism'.

Orientalism

Orientalism as a system of scholarship first emerged in the early fourteenth century with the establishment by the Church Council of Vienna of a number of university chairs to promote an understanding of Oriental languages and culture. The main driving force for Orientalism came from trade, inter-religious rivalries and military conflict. Knowledge of the Orient cannot, therefore, be separated from the history of European expansion into the Middle East and Asia (Kiernan, 1972). The discovery of the Cape route to Asia by Vasco da Gama in 1498 greatly extended the province of Orientalism, but it was not until the eighteenth and nineteenth centuries that detailed studies of Oriental societies were published in Europe. In Britain, the establishment of the Asiatic Society (of Bengal) in 1784 and the Royal Asiatic Society in 1823 were important landmarks in the development of western attitudes. Similar developments took place in France with Napoleon's Institut d'Égypte and the Société Asiatique in 1821, and in Germany an Oriental Society was formed in 1845. It was through these and similar institutions that knowledge of Oriental societies, studies of philology and competence in Oriental languages were developed and institutionalised. Although in common-sense terms the 'Orient' embraces an

ill-defined geographical zone extending from the eastern
Mediterranean to South-East Asia, Islam and the Islam
played a peculiarly significant part in the formation of we:
to the East.

Islam

Within the category of 'other religions', Islam has at least two major
distinguishing features. First, Islam as a prophetic, monotheistic
religion has very close ties historically and theologically with Christianity. It can be regarded, together with Christianity and Judaism, as a
basic variant of the Abrahamic faith (Hodgson, 1974). Secondly, unlike
other religions of the Orient, Islam was a major colonising force inside
Europe and from the eighth century onwards provided the dominant
culture of southern Mediterranean societies.

These two features of Islam raise the question: in what sense is Islam
an 'Oriental religion?' This deceptively simple question in fact goes to
the heart of the Orientalist problematic. If Orientalism addresses itself
to the issue of what constitutes the Orient, then it is also forced
ultimately to define the essence of Occidentalism. We might, for
example, take a number of Christian cultural attributes — scriptural
intellectualism, anti-magical rationality or the separation of the
religious and the secular — as constitutive of Occidentalism in order to
mark off the Orient. This strategy does immediately raise the difficulty
that Christianity, as a Semitic, Abrahamic faith by origin, could be
counted as 'Oriental', whereas Islam, as by expansion part of the
culture of Spain, Sicily and eastern Europe, could be regarded as
'Occidental'. The problematic religious and geographical status of
Islam was recognised by traditional Christian theology which either
treated Islam as parasitic upon Judaeo-Christian culture or as a
schism within Christianity. In Dante's *Divine Comedy*, the prophet
Muhammad is constantly split in two as an eternal punishment for
religious schism.

The problematic nature of Islam is not, however, merely a difficulty
within Christian theology. If the motivating issue behind Christian
Orientalism was the uniqueness of the Christian revelation with respect
to Islamic heresy, then the crucial question for comparative sociology
has been the dynamism of western industrial civilisation versus the
alleged stagnation of the Orient. Within Weberian sociology, the fact
that Islam is monotheistic, prophetic and ascetic raises important
difficulties for the view that Protestant asceticism performed a critical
role in the rise of western rationality. In *The Sociology of Religion* (1966)
Weber provided two answers to remove this difficulty for the Protestant Ethic thesis. First, while recognising that Muhammad's initial
message was one of ascetic self-control, Weber argued that the social

⌐ers of Islam were Arab warriors who transformed the original ⌐vation doctrine into a quest for land. Hence, the inner *angst* of Calvinism was never fully present in Islam. Secondly, the prebendal form of landownership in Islam resulted in a centralised state so that Islam became the ideology of a patrimonial structure and precluded the growth of urban asceticism (Turner, 1978a). This argument about social carriers and patrimonial power in Islam permitted Weber to treat Islam as a religion of world acceptance with a formal and legalistic orientation to questions of personal salvation (Freund, 1968). Since Islam presented no radical challenge to the secular world of power, it failed to develop a rational theodicy which would, in principle, have driven believers to a significant position of world-mastery. Islam, by legitimating the status quo, never challenged the political structure in such a way as to promote fundamental processes of social change.

Weber's treatment of Islam provides us with the accounting system that constitutes the basis of his comparative sociology of Oriental society, of which the central issue is a contrast between dynamic and stationary social systems. The task of Weber's sociology was to provide a historical account of the emergence of what he took to be the characteristic uniqueness of the West, namely the defining ingredients of rational capitalist production. These ingredients included rational (Roman) law, the modern state, the application of science to all areas of social life, especially to the technology of industrial production, the separation of the family from the business enterprise, autonomous urban institutions, an ascetic life-style which initially converted entrepreneurship into a 'calling' and finally the bureaucratisation of social procedures. These features of capitalist society were the institutional locations of a general process of rationalisation in which social relationships were increasingly subject to norms of calculation and prediction. The rationalisation of social life involved a continuous alienation of social actors, not only from the means of production, but from the means of mental production and from the military apparatus. The ownership of the means of economic, intellectual and milit⌐ry production are concentrated in bureaucratic, anonymous institutions so that, in Weber's view, capitalism became an 'iron cage' in which the individual is merely a 'cog' (Weber, 1965; Loewith, 1970). While the individual is subjected to detailed social regulation, rational law, bureaucratic management and applied science provide the social conditions for economic stability by which capitalist accumulation can proceed unhindered by moral conventions or by capricious political intervention.

In Weber's sociology of Oriental society, an accounting system is created in which the Orient simply lacks the positive ingredients of western rationality. Oriental society can be defined as a system of absences — absent cities, the missing middle class, missing autonomous urban institutions, the absence of legal rationality and the absence of private property (Turner, 1978b). In Europe, Christianity permitted cities to arise in which urban social relations were based on a universal faith rather than on particular tribal loyalties; in addition, European cities enjoyed considerable economic and political independence from the state (Weber, 1958). In the Orient, according to Weber, cities did not evolve organically as economic centres, but were imposed on the countryside as military and political sites of state control. The Oriental city did not provide a congenial environment within which an urban bourgeoisie could emerge free from unpredictable, *ad hoc* political control.

This analysis of the city, in turn, depends upon a basic contrast in Weber's sociology between the feudal structures of Europe and the prebendal organisation of land in the Orient. In feudalism, where individual land-rights are inherited by a stable system of primogeniture or limited partibility, land-owning knights enjoy a degree of political freedom from the feudal monarch in return for military service. In prebendalism, the prebend is a non-inheritable right which is controlled by a patrimonial state and therefore a stratum of cavalry is more directly subject to the royal household. Although some forms of private landownership do occur in prebendalism, legal ownership of private land is restricted in scope and there is a strong tendency for the wealthy to avoid risk-taking capital investments. Hence, in Islam, Weber thought that capital was frequently frozen in the form of investment in religious property (*waqf* property). Although property was subject to political interference, it was also difficult to obtain legal security because religious law was essentially unstable. It is consequently possible to imagine Weber's comparative sociology as an accounting system with 'rational law', 'free cities', 'urban bourgeoisie' and the 'modern state' in one column and '*ad hoc* law', 'military camps', 'state-controlled merchants' and 'patrimonial state' in the other. Weber does the work of translation from one set of social meanings to another context of meanings by a system of linguistic accounting in which Occidental categories have a privileged location.

It is often claimed that Weberian sociology represents a form of subjective idealism which unwittingly reproduces the contents of common-sense, bourgeois thought and that, by contrast, the historical materialism of Karl Marx penetrates the conceptual surface of bourgeois political economy to reveal the objective structures which ultimately determine social life (Hirst, 1976). This contrast is difficult to maintain in general terms, and particular problems arise with the commentaries of Marx and Engels on Oriental society (Turner, 1981a). In Marx and Engels's early journalistic writing on India, China and the

Middle East, we find the theoretical development of what has subsequently been referred to as 'the Asiatic mode of production' (Avineri, 1968). The point of this theoretical device was to contrast the socioeconomic stagnation of the Orient with the revolutionary character of capitalist society in which capitalists are forced to change constantly the technical basis of production in order to survive economically. The Asiatic mode of production is thus a form of social accounting which bears a close similarity to that employed by Weber.

Marx and Engels, forming their theory on the basis of utilitarian analyses of India and François Bernier's *Voyages* of 1710, focused their concern on the alleged absence of private property in land in Asia, where the state controlled the distribution of landownership. In some of the journalistic work, such as the article on 'The British Rule in India' of 1853 (Marx and Engels, 1972), Marx emphasised the importance of climate and geography in the desert regions of North Africa and Asia in the rise of the state which had important functions in the control of irrigation works. Because the state controlled the land in order to manage public irrigation systems, social classes based on the ownership of property could not emerge and instead the population was held in a condition of what Engels called 'general (state) slavery'. In the absence of social classes and class struggle, there was no mechanism of social change. Since the history of all societies is the history of struggles between classes, it followed that Asia 'has no history at all, at least no known history' (Marx, 1972, p. 81). In later works, such as *Grundrisse* and *Capital*, Marx shifted his attention away from the role of the state in irrigation to the nature of economic self-sufficiency of Asiatic villages as the ultimate explanation of Oriental stability. The outcome is still the same: the absence of radical changes in Asiatic social structure which, in Marx's terms, would count as historical change.

Weber and Marx adhered to rather similar accounting schemes to explain the presence of history in Occidental societies and its absence in the Orient. According to these schemes of translation, the Orient is a collection of gaps or a list of deficiencies — the absence of private property, the absence of social classes, the absence of historical changes in the mode of production. Since both Weber and Marx also adhered to the notion that state politics in the Orient were arbitrary and uncertain, their view of Oriental society may be regarded as yet another version of that more ancient system of accounting, namely, 'Oriental despotism'. The theoretical impetus for the analysis of despotic politics came from the development of the absolutist state in Europe, when philosophical discussions centred on the distinction between legitimate monarchy and arbitrary despotism. Thus, Benigne-Bossuet, instructor to Louis XIV, identified four principal causes of despotic rule; these were the absence of private property, arbitrary law, absolute political power and general slavery (Koebner, 1951; Stelling-Michaud, 1960). These causes of despotism were all evident in the imperial structures of Russia and Turkey. A rather similar position was taken by Montesquieu in *The Spirit of the Laws* in 1748 where he argued that despotism in the Asiatic empires was brought about by the absence of social institutions intervening between the absolute ruler and the general population, who were consequently unprotected objects of the ruler's passions.

Whether or not Marx eventually abandoned the concept of the Asiatic mode of production has subsequently become an important issue in Marxist theory and politics (Wittfogel, 1957). In recent years, a number of attempts have been made to jettison the concept by employing Louis Althusser's notion of an 'epistemological break' in the theoretical development of Marx's ideas. According to Althusser (1969), it is possible to divide Marx's works into distinctive periods in which the early idealistic humanism of the Paris manuscripts was eventually replaced by an entirely new scientific interest in the objective laws of the capitalist mode of production. On these grounds, it is possible to treat the concept of the Asiatic mode of production as a pre-scientific interest which Marx and Engels abandoned in their maturity. It has also been argued that, in any case, the concept is incompatible with the central element of the Marxist theory of the state as the product of a society divided along class lines. According to this view, class conflict is 'a condition of existence' of the state and, since in the Asiatic mode of production there are no classes, it is difficult to explain the existence of the state other than by vague references to 'climate and territory' (Hindess and Hirst, 1975).

Unfortunately, these attempts to extricate Marx from an Orientalist problematic simply bring in their train a series of additional theoretical difficulties. Once the Asiatic mode of production has been abandoned, it is then necessary to conceptualise all pre-capitalist modes of production within the rather narrow framework of slavery or feudalism, unless Marxist theory is prepared to admit new additions to the existing orthodox list of modes of production.

Judaism

Although Islam has traditionally been regarded as a schismatic version of Christianity or as an arid extension of Christian monotheism, Judaism has occupied a particularly problematic status in Orientalism. In the long history of Christian anti-Semitism, the Jews as rejectors and slayers of the Messiah were associated with deceit, cunning and trickery. The character of the Jew, the exclusion of the Jewish community and the involvement of Jews in trade and exchange became inextricably joined in western imagination. Jewish personality and usurious activity came to be synonymous. In Chaucer's *Canterbury Tales*, the Prioress describes an Asian ghetto:

> Where there were Jews, supported by the Crown
> For the foul lucre of their usury,
> Hateful to Christ and all his company.
> (Chaucer, 1960, pp. 185–6)

Two centuries later Shakespeare presented the prototypical characterology of the Jewish usurer in the figure of Shylock. Although Shakespeare pointed to the common humanity of Jew and Christian in Shylock's reply to Salarino ('If you prick us, do we not bleed? if you tickle us, do we not laugh?'), Shylock symbolises the rigidity of a merciless law, revenge and relentless usury. In a similar theme, the seventeenth-century Puritan poet, Andrew Marvell, wrote his satirical poem 'Character of Holland', in which the Dutch tolerance for the Jewish community was tied to the prominent role of Jews in the expanding maritime economy of Amsterdam. For Marvell, the proliferation of schism was the religious consequence of the expansion of exchange (Smith, 1973, pp. 86–7).

These literary sources embraced two contradictions in the relationship between Jews and Christians. Although the Jews had been forced into ghettos in the early part of the twelfth century, the Christian economy had become dependent on Jewish banking and finance. The Jewish-Christian relationship had peculiar ambiguities of dominance and dependence. Secondly, although Jewish ritualism and rites of circumcision were regarded as peculiar and primitive, Jewry was also the vehicle of money calculation and thereby of a form of rationality. The Jewish community combined irrational ritual and rational economy. These 'peculiarities' of Jewish identity eventually found expression in the sociology of Judaism via Hegel's philosophy of history and Marx's analysis of the 'Jewish Question'.

In September 1791 the French Assembly passed a resolution which gave Jews full political citizenship on the basis of a civil oath. Although this decision at one level solved 'the Jewish problem' by simply incorporating Jews within the polity, from the Jewish point of view assimilation also threatened to undermine a distinctive Jewish identity. While the Assembly's resolution was subsequently undermined by the anti-Semitic activities of the Terror, the French Revolution had the effect of dispersing the Jewish community throughout the major urban centres of France (Schwarzfuchs, 1979).

From the rationalist perspective, Judaism incorporated the universalism of monotheistic religion in denying the legitimacy of local gods and the particularism of its ritualistic definition of Jewish identity. It was this alleged paradox that formed the basis of Hegel's observation on

'Judaea' in which monotheistic unity had taken a decidedly exclusive direction. Judaism:

must necessarily possess the element of exclusiveness, which consists essentially in this — that only the One People which adopts it, recognizes the One God, and is acknowledged by him. (Hegel, 1956, p. 195)

This exclusive identity found its expression in 'the observance of ceremonies and the Law' which ruled out the development of self-conscious individuals. Instead, Jewish identity became attached to the family, to which the 'worship of Jehovah is attached' (Hegel, 1956, p. 197).

From the left-Hegelian perspective, the problem in Prussia was how to incorporate the Jewish community within the movement for social emancipation, especially working-class emancipation. The exclusion of the Jews from civil society had locked the Jewish population within a narrow range of social roles, so that the Jewish community was petit bourgeois in character. The solution outlined by the Young Hegelians like Bruno Bauer was that full political emancipation was to be achieved by the abandonment of religious exclusiveness on the part of both Christians and Jews. The ritual practices of Jews represented an obstacle to the development of a universalistic culture within which individual consciousness could be enhanced.

In his article on 'The Jewish Question' of 1843, Marx attacked Bauer's argument on the grounds that political emancipation was no real answer to the alienation which citizens experienced in the economic realm. In short, the Jewish problem could only be solved by a revolutionary transformation of the economy, since political enslavement was simply a manifestation of economic enslavement. In the course of this argument, however, Marx revealed a profound hostility to the political liberation of 'small nations' as an answer to the dominance of capitalism in civil society (Davis, 1965). At the same time, Marx, whose early views on money were in part shaped by a deep appreciation of Shakespeare's *Timon of Athens* and *The Merchant of Venice*, constructed his views of the political context of the Jews around the dual meaning of *Judentum* — commerce and Jewry.

In these early political pamphlets Marx thus gave further expression to the Hegelian paradox of the Jewish role in world history. In their capacity as merchant capitalists, Jews were part of that system of economic relations which promised, through the agency of capitalist production, to liquidate the particularities of national religious identity. However, the particularism of Jewish ritual which prevented their assimilation into Gentile society was pre-eminently an illustration of pre-capitalist traditionalism (Turner, 1978b).

Rationality

These debates about the nature of Jewish identity can be seen as part of a wider inquiry into the roots of western rational civilisation. Whereas classical western philosophy sought the roots of rationality in the Greek heritage, contemporary sociology has, under the auspices of German sociology of religion, located the technical rationality of industrial capitalism in the anti-magical vocation of Calvinistic Protestantism.

For Weber, Protestant asceticism contributed to the disciplined, this-worldly ethos of capitalist society by establishing vocational routines of hard work, calculation and practicality. This ethos emerged from the monotheistic and prophetic culture of Christianity, but if this argument holds for Protestant Christianity, then in principle it ought to hold for monotheistic, anti-magical Judaism. Weber's answer to this possibility was provided in *Ancient Judaism* (1952), where he argued, against Sombart's view (1962, p. 235) that Puritan views were 'more perfectly developed in Judaism, and were also of course of much earlier date', that Jewish ritualism prevented the full development of the rational potential of Old Testament monotheism. Although Jewish merchants had played a major role in commercial developments, they had not been crucial in the growth of rational capitalism:

The ultimate theoretical reasons for this fact, that the distinctive elements of modern capitalism originated and developed quite apart from the Jews, are to be found in the peculiar character of the Jews as a pariah people and in the idiosyncrasy of their religion . . . It is unquestionable that the Jewish ethic was thoroughly traditionalistic. (Weber, 1968, p. 614)

Like Marx, Weber thought that, of itself, the existence of merchants and banking facilities was not corrosive of traditional values and institutions. The drive for possessions, luxury and wealth was very widespread and prevalent in all human societies, but the decisive feature of rational capitalism was the pursuit of economic accumulation, disciplined and tempered by norms of calculation. In the case of Diaspora Judaism, the pariah-status of Jews and their exclusion from civil society had reinforced the religious particularism of the exclusive monotheism of Old Testament culture.

Although Edward Said has argued that there is a tenacious persistence within the Orientalist discourse by which Islam is reproduced in western analysis, it can also be said that the accounting scheme for understanding Judaism is equally persistent. Whereas Islam appears as a series of gaps, Judaism is represented as a system of contradictory combinations: usurious behaviour and traditional economics; a universal God and exclusive pariah membership; a rational anti-magical ethos and irrational practices. The problem of 'the Jewish Question' can thus be seen as a problem of locating Judaism at the intersections

of rationality/irrationality, universalism/particularism, exclusion/in-
clusion and of modernity/tradition. Within Orientalism, there are two
related discourses for Semites: the Islamic discourse of gaps and the
Judaic discourse of contradictions. In turn, these discourses point to
the question of capitalist origins.

The question which lies behind the accounting schemes of Marx and
Weber concerns the social origins of capitalism in western society and
its absence in Oriental society. This question carries with it all the
implications of the assumption about the uniqueness of the West, and
therefore a dichotomous contrast between the progressive West and the
stagnant East. There are two main theoretical strategies by which this
basic question can be avoided. In the first, the question of capitalist
origins in the Orient is inappropriate, because the prior existence of
European capitalism and the development of colonialism ruled out the
autonomous development of capitalism outside Europe. European
capitalism changed the global conditions for independent capitalism
elsewhere by creating a worldwide system of economic dependency
(Frank, 1972). The presence of capitalism in the Occident becomes the
explanation for the absence of capitalism in the Orient. In the second
strategy, it is possible to deny that capitalism has consistent social
characteristics or uniform consequences. Just as England, France and
Germany have unique developmental processes which cannot be sub-
sumed under the general label of 'capitalist development', so each
Oriental society is subject to individual, peculiar features which are
contingent and historical.

Although both strategies are in some respects theoretically attractive,
they are not without their own theoretical problems. The first solution
is still left with the question: why, then, *did* capitalism emerge uniquely
in the West? Any list of socio-economic causes to explain capitalism in
the Occident implies the absence of such causes elsewhere. Furthermore, it is not entirely obvious that a dependency theory or some notion
of 'underdevelopment' will account for the absence of autonomous
capitalist development outside Europe. The second solution would
appear to rule out any law-like statements about the general characteristics of capitalism conceived as an abstract model of society in favour of
empirical descriptions of particular developmental processes. The
outcome of both positions might be the notion that capitalism is a
purely contingent development. The alternative to Althusserian structuralism would be the position:

that industrialism was not written inevitably into the destiny of all agrarian
society, but only emerged as a consequence of an accidental and almost
improbable concatenation of circumstances which, it so happened, came
together in the West. (Gellner, 1980, p. 296)

However, it is difficult to see how methodological accidentalism could be accepted as a general basis for a sociology of capitalism, which attempts to provide causal statements about the necessary connections between social structures, while also recognising that empirically these connections may be very complex and subject to contingent variations. The conclusion must be that Weberian sociology, on the one hand, and structuralist Marxism, on the other, have not developed entirely satisfactory responses to the accounting procedures of Orientalism.

As we have seen, much of the debate about pre-capitalist modes of production in English-speaking Marxism was initiated by a new interest in the French philosopher Louis Althusser. The reception of Althusserian Marxism was in the context of various attempts to provide a structuralist explanation of economic processes which did not involve restrictive economic reductionism and to provide a scientific alternative to the Hegelian idealism of the humanistic Marx. It was not until this debate was well established that it became clear that Althusser's emphasis on the proper 'reading' of Marx's texts was part of a more general movement in French philosophy emerging from literary criticism, semiology and discourse analysis.

One of the crucial figures in the French context was Michel Foucault, whose analysis of the relationship between power and knowledge subsequently became important in the critique of Orientalism. Foucault's ideas are notoriously difficult to summarise, but one important aspect of his general position is that any extension of systematic knowledge also involves an extension of power relations in society, which is manifested in more subtle and rigorous forms of social control over the body. Foucault's argument thus differs radically from a conventionally liberal perspective in which the evolution of knowledge out of ignorance requires a similar political evolution of freedom out of oppression.

In the liberal view, the conditions for achieving knowledge through open debate involve fundamental political freedoms. For Foucault, the growth of penology, criminology, demography and other social sciences in the late eighteenth and nineteenth centuries corresponded to increasing political and social control over large masses of people within a confined urban space. More generally, these separate 'discourses' of the body constituted a dominant 'episteme' by which separate individuals could be categorised as different — as criminals, madmen, sexual perverts and so forth. All forms of language presuppose or create fundamental categories of sameness and difference, and the application of these categories is an exercise of power by which one social group excludes another. The growth of systematic reasoning can be measured or indicated by the growth of timetables, examinations, taxonomies and typologies which allocate individuals within a theoretical space just as Bentham's panopticon, the asylum, the classroom and the hospital administer bodies within an organised social space. Historically speaking, the growth of scientific psychiatry corresponded with the growth of the asylum (Foucault, 1967), the growth of penology with the prison (Foucault, 1977), the development of clinical medicine with the hospital (Foucault, 1973) and the discourse of sex with the confessional (Foucault, 1979).

Orientalist discourse

Within the perspective of Foucault's analysis of knowledge, we can now treat Orientalism as a discourse that creates typologies within which characters can be distributed: the energetic Occidental man versus the lascivious Oriental, the rational westerner versus the unpredictable Oriental, the gentle white versus the cruel yellow man. The notion of Orientalism as a discourse of power emerging in the context of a geo-political struggle between Europe and the Middle East provides the basis for one of the most influential studies of recent times, namely Edward Said's *Orientalism* (1978).

Orientalism as a discourse divides the globe unambiguously into Occident and Orient; the latter is essentially strange, exotic and mysterious, but also sensual, irrational and potentially dangerous. This Oriental strangeness can only be grasped by the gifted specialist in Oriental cultures and, in particular, by those with skills in philology, language and literature. The task of Orientalism was to reduce the bewildering complexity of Oriental societies and Oriental culture to some manageable, comprehensible level. The expert, through the discourse on the Orient, represented the mysterious East in terms of basic frameworks and typologies. The chrestomathy summarised the exotic Orient in a table of comprehensible items.

The point of Orientalism, according to Said, was to Orientalise the Orient and it did so in the context of fundamental colonial inequalities. Orientalism was based on the fact that we know or talk about the Orientals, whereas they neither know themselves adequately nor talk about us. There is no comparable discourse of Occidentalism. This is not to say that there have been no changes in the nature of Orientalism, but that these changes tend to mask the underlying continuity of the discourse. The early philological and philosophical orientations of Sacy, Renan, Lane and Caussin have been replaced by an emphasis on sociology and economics in the new programme of 'area studies', but much of the underlying politics of power remains.

Although Orientalism is an especially persistent discourse, Said believes that, given the changing balance of power in the modern world, there are signs of a new appreciation of the Orient and an awareness of the pitfalls of existing approaches. He thus pays tribute to such writers as Anwar Abdel Malek, Yves Lacoste and Jacques Berque and to the authors associated with the *Review of Middle East Studies* and the Middle East Research and Information Project (MERIP). These groups are both sensitive to the damaging legacy of Orientalism and to the need for new beginnings and different frameworks. Unfortunately, Said does not offer a detaiied programme for the critique of Orientalism or for the creation of alternative perspectives. To some extent, he is content with a general rejection of ethnocentric frameworks:

The more one is able to leave one's cultural home, the more one is able to judge it, and the whole world as well, with the spiritual detachment and generosity necessary for true vision. The more easily, too, does one assess oneself and alien cultures with the same combination of intimacy and distance. (Said, 1978, p. 259)

The problem of Said's attempted solution depends on how closely he wishes to follow Foucault's analysis of discourse. The point of the critique of official psychiatry, established clinical medicine and contemporary discourses on sex is not, for Foucault, to present alternatives, since these would simply be themselves forms of discourse. In Foucault's perspective, there is no, as it were, discourse-free analysis. Given the nature of the modern world, we are constrained historically to 'the patient construction of discourses about discourses, and to the task of hearing what has already been said' (Foucault, 1973, p. xvi). For example, Foucault's analysis of medicine does not propose an alternative medicine or the absence of medicine; instead he attempts an archaeology of discourse, of the historical layers that are the conditions of discourse.

An adherence to Foucault's perspective on discourse as a critique of Orientalism might, therefore, result in somewhat negative and pessimistic conclusions. The contemporary analyses of Islam and the Middle East to which Said approvingly alludes turn out to be themselves discourses, corresponding to shifting power relationships between West and East. The Orientalist premiss remains largely intact: I know the difference, therefore I control.

There may, however, be one starting-point which would be compatible with Said's universal humanism and Foucault's pessimism about discourse on discourses. It has been noted that language is organised in building-blocks of sameness and difference, but the main characteristic of Orientalism has been to concentrate on difference. In the case of Islam and Christianity, there is a strong warrant for looking at those aspects which unite rather than divide them, for concentrating on sameness rather than difference. We can then observe how common elements or themes are handled by Orientalist discourse as themes which are not 'really the same' or which in fact constitute departures and differences. As we have already commented, Islam and Christianity can be regarded as dimensions of a common Semitic-Abrahamic religious stock. They have also been involved in processes of mutual colonisation, having common traditions of Jihad and Crusade. In this sense, it is possible to refer to Islam as an Occidental religion of Spain, Sicily, Malta, Yugoslavia and the Balkans, and to Christianity as an Oriental religion of Syria, Egypt and North Africa. Islam and Christianity not only have important religious and geographical features in common; they also, to a large extent, share common frameworks in philosophy, science and medicine. Despite these overlapping cultural traditions, the general direction of Orientalism has always been to stress differences and separations. One particularly interesting illustration of this tendency is provided by the history of western philosophy.

Islamic science

Islam and Christianity as religions of prophetic revelation were not initially equipped to provide a philosophical framework within which to present and discuss the theological problems of orthodoxy. Furthermore, at an early stage they were both confronted by a powerful tradition of secular logic and rhetoric which was the legacy of Greece. The Aristotelianism which became the major Christian framework for the philosophical formulation of Christian beliefs was transmitted by Islamic scholars — Averroes, Avicenna, al-Kindi and al-Razi. Here, therefore, is an area of common experience and historical development, where medieval Christian culture was dependent on Islam.

The Orientalist response to this historical connection has been to argue that Islam was merely a medium between Hellenism and the Occident. Islamic scholarship neither contributed to nor improved upon the Greek heritage which eventually found its 'true' home in fifteenth and sixteenth-century European science and technology. The notion of an Islamic contribution to western culture was attacked, for example, in the nineteenth century by the French Orientalist and philosopher Ernest Renan. He argued that Islamic civilisation was incompatible with scientific advance:

All those who have been in the East, or in Africa, are struck by the way in which the mind of the true believer is fatally limited by the species of iron circle that surrounds the head, rendering it absolutely closed to knowledge, incapable of either learning anything, or being open to any new idea. (Renan, 1896, p. 85)

By extension, Renan suggested that science in Islam could and did only flourish when the prescriptions of orthodox theology were relaxed. One illustration of this position was Renan's sympathetic response to the Muslim reformer Al-Afghani, whose overt orthodoxy was matched by a covert, elitist rationalism. Finally, Renan claimed that the great majority of so-called Arab scientists and philosophers were in fact 'Persians, Transoxians, Spaniards, natives of Bokhara, of Samarcand, of Cordova, of Seville'.

This view of Islam as merely the sterile transmitter of Greek philosophy and science to European civilisation has subsequently been reaffirmed, although often with more subtlety and less prejudice. Bertrand Russell dismissively commented in his history of western philosophy that Arabic philosophy was not significant as original thought. A similar line of argument was taken by O'Leary in *How Greek Science Passed to the Arabs* (1969), where it was argued that Islamic philosophers were mainly important as translators of Greek culture. Although he recognised the importance of Muslim scientists in such fields as medicine, optics and chemistry, he treated Islamic thought as the property of a 'privileged coterie'.

The great attraction of seeing our philosophical, cultural and scientific inheritance as based upon Greek culture and of seeing Islam as simply a neutral vehicle for the transmission of those values is that it allows us to connect scientific freedom of thought with political democracy. The major contribution of Greek society to western thought was logical and rhetorical modes of argumentation, permitting the systematisation of debate and inquiry. These modes of analysis arose because of the need in the Greek polity for open, public dialogue. Once more, it is possible thereby to contrast the Oriental despotic tradition of closed, centralised authority with the Greek model of democracy requiring open, uninhibited discourse. The association of freedom and truth has thus become a central theme of western philosophers occupying very different positions within the political spectrum. Though in other respects in profound disagreement, there is an ironic agreement between Karl Popper and Jürgen Habermas that knowledge requires an open society. The problem with this emphasis on Hellenism and democratic inquiry is that it ignores the fact that Greek society was based on slavery and that the majority of the population was, therefore, precluded from these open debates between citizens.

The debate about the ultimate origins of Occidentalism and the connections between Islam and Christianity via Greek philosophy raises the question of whether the dynamism of western culture lies within a Christian legacy or in Hellenism. To illustrate the point of this observation it is enough to recall that, against writers like Werner Sombart in *The Jews and Modern Capitalism* (1962), Weber sought the origins of the ethos of modern society in Protestant asceticism, whereas Marx traced the secular/critical content of western thought back to Heraclitus. In general, those writers who are indifferent or critical towards Christianity are likely to underline the Greek roots of western society; in addition, they often take a sympathetic view of Islam as the basis for their criticisms of Islam. This position is characteristic, for example, of Friedrich Nietzsche. Thus, although Orientalism has so far been treated as a form of negative accounting that stresses the absences within Islamic society, it is also possible to detect forms of positive accounting which adopt certain features of Islam as the means of a rational critique of Christianity. The contents of Oriental society may thus not be the central issue for Orientalism, but rather it raises questions about the constitutive features of Occidental society. Whereas what we may call theistic Orientalism adopted Christian values as the counter-weight to Islam as a deviant religion, agnostic Orientalism treated Greek culture as the true source of western values, often incidentally treating Islam as a more rational form of monotheism than Christianity.

Hume and Nietzsche

It is possible to indicate the complexity of these relationships between Occidentalism, Orientalism and Hellenism in western philosophy by a brief comparison of Hume and Nietzsche. Although there has been much disagreement over the nature of Hume's philosophy of religion (Williams, 1963; Capaldi, 1975; Gaskin, 1976), it will be sufficient for this present argument to concentrate on Hume's celebrated contrast of the virtues of polytheism and monotheism.

In the *Natural History of Religion,* Hume argued that polytheism is the ancient religion of all primitive people and that monotheism developed later with the advance of rationalism, especially in the argument from design. Although there is this historical development from polytheism, there is also a constant swing backwards and forwards between these two types of theistic belief, since the vulgar and ignorant tend, in any society, towards polytheism. On the whole, the advantages to mankind of polytheism are greater than those arising from monotheism. The latter is associated with intolerance, exaggerated asceticism and abasement. When the gods are only marginally superior to mortal men, a more open, friendly and egalitarian attitude towards them is possible: 'Hence activity, spirit, courage, magnanimity, love of liberty, and all the virtues which aggrandize a people' (Hume, 1963, p. 68). The principal advantage of monotheism is that it is more 'conformable to sound reason', but this very fact brings about an alliance between theology and philosophy which, in turn, leads to a stultifying scholasticism.

Since Hume holds that Islam is a stricter form of theism than is Christianity with its trinitarian doctrine, it follows that Islam is 'conformable to sound reason', but this also means that Hume regarded

Islam as an intolerant, narrow religion. In regard to rationality, therefore, Islam is favourably contrasted with Christianity and, furthermore, Hume humorously refers to Islam as a means of illustrating the absurdity of Roman Catholic doctrines of the Eucharist. A Turkish prisoner was once brought to Paris by his Russian captor and some doctors of the Sorbonne decided to convert this captive to Christianity. Having been catechised and taken first communion, the Muslim prisoner was asked how many gods there were and replied that there were no gods, since he had just eaten Him! The point of this Hume illustration is to show that, although Said largely treats Orientalism as a negative accounting system, in the hands of a rationalist philosopher Islam can be used as a positive critique of the 'absurdity' of Christian doctrines.

This critical attitude towards Christianity was especially prominent in Nietzsche's philosophy. In *The Genealogy of Morals,* Nietzsche claimed that Christian morality had its social origins in the resentment of the Jews against their oppressors; the doctrine of turning the other cheek and altruistic love are in fact moral doctrines of a slave class giving vent to feelings of inferiority and suppression. Christian morality has its location in the psychological revolt of slaves against masters:

It was the Jews who, in opposition to the aristocratic equation (good = beautiful = happy = loved by the gods), dared with a terrifying logic to suggest the contrary equation, and indeed to maintain in the teeth of the most profound hatred (the hatred of weakness) this contrary equation, namely 'the wretched are alone the good; the poor, the weak, the lowly, are alone the good'. (Nietzsche, 1910, p. 30)

Nietzsche regarded the critical spirit of Socrates as the supreme root of true virtues of self-development, criticism and heroic independence. Although Nietzsche compared favourably the self-sacrifice of Socrates and Jesus for an ideal, he regarded Christianity as a system of conventional morality which destroyed individual creativity and critical thought (Kaufmann, 1974). It was from this perspective that Nietzsche came to see the slave morality of Christianity as the negation of the heroic virtues of Socrates and Muhammad. In the *Anti-Christ,* Nietzsche declared that:

Christianity robbed us of the harvest of the culture of the ancient world, it later went on to rob us of the harvest of the culture of Islam. The wonderful Moorish cultural world of Spain, more closely related to us at bottom, speaking more directly to our senses and taste, than Greece and Rome, was trampled down . . . why? because it was noble, because it owed its origins to manly instincts, because it said Yes to life even in the rare and exquisite treasures of Moorish life! (Nietzsche, 1968, p. 183)

Nietzsche's positive evaluation of Islam in general and of Islamic

Spain in particular cannot be readily understood in terms of Said's view of Orientalism, but it is comprehensible within a scheme of positive secularist Orientalism which employs Islam as the basis for a critique of Christianity.

Summary

The problems of translation and comparison, which lie at the heart of sociology and religious studies, have been implicitly resolved by the creation of accounting schemes that establish hierarchies of sameness and difference. In the study of Islam and Asiatic society, the dominant accounting procedure is Orientalism, which seeks to explain the nature of Islamic culture by negation so that Islamdom is constituted by its absences. In recent years the Orientalist tradition has been heavily criticised, but no radical alternative has yet emerged and, in terms of a pessimistic perspective on the nature of discourse, it is difficult to see how any valid alternative could emerge. The critique of Orientalism has largely neglected two possible routes out of the conventional discourse on the Orient. Alongside negative accounting schemes, there has also been a positive view of Oriental rationality on the part of secular philosophers, who have employed Islam as a mirror to indicate the absurdity of Christian faith; this option, however, is merely accounting in reverse.

Following Foucault's analysis of the archaeology of knowledge, Said has studied the various ways in which a persistent Orientalism has been founded on a contrast of differences, but a language of the Orient would also generate, in principle, an account of sameness. One solution to theological ethnocentrism, on the grounds, would be to emphasise those points of contact and sameness which unite the Christian, Jewish and Islamic traditions into mere variations on a religious theme which, in unison, provide the bases of our culture.

2 Social Cement

Nineteenth-century sociology of religion was itself a cultural manifestation of the social collapse of Christianity as a dominant institution in western society. The emergence of what promised to be a science of religious phenomena was ironically a measure of the diminution of religion's sociological significance. It is important, therefore, to understand the sociology of religion reflexively as an intellectual effect of precisely those social processes which a science of religion attempts to grasp theoretically. To write a history of the sociology of religion is in large measure to produce a treatise on religion in the modern world. Furthermore, the problem of religion in society is not, so to speak, an optional extra on the sociological curriculum, but a necessary area of inquiry for anyone who wants to understand the nature of the self, the bases of social relations and the limits of rationality. There is consequently a certain intellectual urgency about the sociology of religion which is experienced as a set of moral dilemmas. In particular, two questions have continued to dominate the subject: first, what is religion? and secondly, is it possible, either as an individual or as a society, to live without religion, or at least without a genuine substitute?

In the history of sociology of religion, these two naive questions often appear to be at odds with each other. If, with the progress of a scientific, urban civilisation, religion appears to be false intellectually, morally and socially, then the disappearance of religion as part of traditional human culture appears unproblematic. However, if religion as a social institution fulfils certain crucial social functions, then the collapse of organised religion as part of the social fabric acquires massive implications for social relationships. It was this problem, an apparent contradiction between the truth of religion and its social functions, which haunted the sociology of religion at its point of inception.

Of course, the crisis of religion in nineteenth-century Europe was not a problem peculiar to the discipline of sociology. Indeed, it found its early and formative expression in certain areas of philosophy and theology; we shall, for example, be obliged to deal in subsequent arguments with the whole legacy of Hegel (Plant, 1973) and Feuerbach (Galloway, 1974) on Marx's attitude towards religion (Ling, 1980; Miranda, 1980). In this introductory comment, however, we may note that the general catastrophe of Christian culture in Europe was most powerfully signalled by Friedrich Nietzsche's prophetic utterance that 'God is dead'.

In *The Gay Science* of 1882, Nietzsche presented the moving account of the madman in the market-place whose failure to find God leads eventually to the painful inquiry: 'Do we smell nothing as yet of the divine decomposition?' (1974, p. 181). The same theme was repeated more simply in *Thus Spake Zarathustra*, where the Wanderer is amazed to discover the Saint's ignorance as to the demise of God (Nietzsche, 1933, p. 5). Nietzsche's philosophical stance with respect to the eruption of a Godless society in Europe had certainly been anticipated by intellectuals like Arthur Schopenhauer who, in the *Neue Paralipomena*, had noted that the nineteenth century was an epoch in which religion was 'almost entirely dead'. Nietzsche's bitingly ironic style was also based on Heinrich Heine's *History of Philosophy and Religion in Germany*, in which Heine asked whether the bell had been heard which announced the last sacraments of a dying God (MacIntyre, 1967a, pp. 218-19; Stern, 1979, p. 144). The end of God's dominion was frequently proclaimed in nineteenth-century Germany, but Nietzsche's Godless theology has a singular and lasting significance for the sociology of religion.

Nineteenth-century thought

In the history of nineteenth-century thought, it is often suggested that there was a broad division between those philosophers who regarded religion as an obstacle to rational progress and those who treated religion as a necessary canopy protecting the individual and society from the chaos of dislocated values. More specifically, sociology can be seen as a conservative response to the social disruptions brought about by the French Revolution and the process of industrialisation; sociology identified a range of social institutions (the family, community, Church and school) which was functionally important for the preservation of society (Nisbet, 1967). At a more general level, the emergence of sociology itself was crucially influenced by the debate which raged over the role of the 'nonrational' in human conduct. Religion was either conceived as a principal vehicle for nonrational forces in individual behaviour or as an insurance against the impact of instinctual life on social arrangements (Bellah, 1970b).

It is generally held that the sociology of religion became possible when the philosophical questions as to the truth of religious doctrines were decisively replaced by sociological questions as to the social effects of religious practices (Goode, 1951). The significance of Nietzsche's Godless theology for the sociology of religion rests in its ambiguous position in this transition from problems of validity to problems of social effects. Nietzsche very clearly recognised the conflict between positivistic science (particularly of the Darwinian variety) and the stability of social meanings, the threat of an administered society to individual values and the impact of social differentiation on conventional moralities. Nietzsche created an intellectual space within which Max Weber's concept of capitalism as a disenchanted reality could appear and thereby also provided much of the thematic unity of the sociology of religion within the Frankfurt school (Siebert, 1976/7 and 1977/8).

Nietzsche and the death of God

What is immediately striking about Nietzsche's parable of the madman in the market-place is not that it denies the existence of God, but merely asserts that God is no more. Nietzsche does not claim that supernaturalist presuppositions are false or that religion is an illusion. We have to understand Godless theology as asserting that belief in God and the forms of life which would be compatible with that belief are no longer genuine options. Although Nietzschean philosophy is typically couched in psychological or even physiological terms, his account of the problem of Christianity is formulated as an issue in the sociology of belief.

It is useful to distinguish between Nietzsche's views on Christ, Christianity and Christian belief (Hollingdale, 1973, p. 186), but here I shall be primarily concerned with his analysis of the debility of Christian belief and practice in mid-nineteenth-century Germany. For Nietzsche, Christian belief had lost credibility; it had become mere 'malicious false-coinage' (Nietzsche, 1968, p. 150), and yet Christian doctrine was still preached and the label 'Christian' still had social currency. The conclusion which Nietzsche drew from this peculiar circumstance was that the presence or absence of Christian belief no longer had any significant social consequences for life in modern society. The statesman, the judge, the soldier and the patriot professed Christian belief, while being 'practical anti-Christians'. The death of God, which marks the loss of commitment to absolute values and the crisis of modern culture, is not, however, welcomed with any enthusiasm by Nietzsche and is not an occasion for celebration. The news of God's demise was, after all, proclaimed by a madman, since the loss of God involves a loss of purpose and meaning. Nietzsche's own insanity, solitude and wandering were thus to exhibit the crisis of culture which his philosophical fragments set out to dissect. The point of Nietzsche's philosophy was not to justify nihilism, but to avoid it and, in particular, to counteract the 'unbearable loneliness' which followed the 'terrible news' of the missing God.

Nietzsche's reluctance to embrace the Godless society was based on his inability to accept the implicit optimism of Darwinian evolutionary thought and his conviction that the modern state could not be legitimated. Nietzsche stood against the comfortable abandonment of

Christianity and the uncritical acceptance of the positivistic rationality which he thought were epitomised in Ernest Renan's *Vie de Jesus* (1863) and David Strauss's *Das Leben Jesu* (1835). Strauss, having accepted Darwinian science, continued to accept conventional ethics as if positivistic science had no implications for the moral conduct of individuals in society. Renan, 'that buffoon in psychologics' (Nietzsche, 1968, p. 141), and Strauss, 'the author of an ale-house gospel' (Nietzsche, 1979, p. 85), did not realise that the death of God meant that all previous forms of life required revaluation and that neither Darwin nor German philistinism could plug that metaphysical gap.

Nietzsche drew two lessons from evolutionary theory. The first was that, since everything is changing, there can be no absolute truths, but only certain claims which have a perspectival validity. The truth-claims of both science and religion are interpretations of reality which depend upon subjective presuppositions. The difference between science and religion is that the 'factual' discoveries of the former cannot be the basis for values concerning the meaning of reality. In short, our perspectival knowledge of empirical reality does not provide any guidance as to what we ought to do. The second lesson was that Darwinism has the effect of robbing the natural world of purpose. The theory of natural selection meant that the structure and process of natural phenomena were the product, not of a teleological purpose, but of purely fortuitous changes and circumstances. The untenability of supernatural presuppositions and the Darwinian world of blind nature meant that the natural and the social world were without purpose or meaning. This 'terrible news' had only dawned on those who were out of their senses.

This combination of circumstances had major implications for the social and political organisation of European societies. The general crisis of modern society was that there were no universal values which would provide the basis for political commitment to the state and which could provide the groundwork for communal consensus within society. Modern society lacked any intricate legitimation and thus the relationships between social groups within society were based on Darwinian conflicts between subordinate and superordinate classes.

Nietzsche, like Hegel, took the Greek city-state as his principal criterion for a critique of German politics. The evolution of European society meant, of course, that any notion of a return to Greek forms of political organisation was romantic and utopian. However, an analysis of the Greek *polis* would provide for what Nietzsche regarded as an appropriate 'genealogical' inquiry into political life. The virtue of the Greek state was that it generated a political space within which citizens could compete in argument just as they struggled physically in games and warfare. The contest (the *agon*) provided healthy means by which antagonists could compete to produce a viable political culture and robust human specimens. The external struggle of individuals within the game created the conditions of internal stability within Greek political space. Social stability and individual development were productively conjoined by these game-like practices (Strong, 1975). The unity of private interest and public order was gradually undermined by certain social and intellectual developments. The division of labour, for example, made individuals increasingly dependent on each other and the specialised, fragmented individual could no longer function as an autonomous competitor. The process of democratisation also contributed to the levelling of overspecialised citizens.

In the modern world, however, this decay of the state is obscured and disguised by the rise of nationalism, which creates an artificial meaning and significance for political life. A state which is maintained by nationalist ideology does not create a political arena within which citizens can mature morally and culturally. Nationalism is merely an instrument of political domination devoid of public, normative legitimacy. Hence, in *Thus Spake Zarathustra*, Nietzsche identified the nationalist state as 'the new idol' which is founded on lies and violence, driving its citizens into herd-like servility. The loss of certainty and conviction in religious assumptions and in natural law, which Nietzsche graphically regarded as deicide, resulted in cultural relativism with widespread, momentous effects: the loss of political legitimacy, the collapse of social consensus, the insanity of the solitary individual and the absence of purpose in natural phenomena. The consequence was that modern people inhabit a world where 'everything is false, everything is permitted' (Nietzsche, 1967a, fragment 602).

Nietzsche thought that the crisis of European culture provided conditions for the generation of new forms of moral authenticity, of which his own philosophical standards constituted a starting-point. Nietzsche did not, however, get beyond an announcement of the need for moral revaluation. In the absence of this 'revaluation of all values', modern society is the product of contingent conflicts under the dominance of the nation-state. It was for these reasons that Nietzsche treated the collapse of the credibility of religious belief as the most significant event of modern history. In this respect, Nietzsche's Godless theology outlined the major themes of the sociology of religion which came to fruition in Weber's condemnation of modern society as an 'iron cage' in *The Protestant Ethic and the Spirit of Capitalism* (1965) and in Peter Berger's discussion of the 'crisis of credibility' in modern cultures (1969).

Crisis of religion

The crisis of religious belief was widely experienced among the nineteenth-century intellectual stratum. It was poignantly expressed in literary form in the history of Robert Elsemere's transition from Anglicanism to agnosticism through a rationalist unitarianism (Ward, 1888; MacIntyre, 1969b). The fictional crisis of Revd Elsemere closely parallels the actual biography of the Reverend Professor William Robertson Smith (Black and Chrystal, 1912), whose perspective on religion combined German biblical criticism, anthropology and evolutionary theory. After a protracted battle within the kirk over Smith's articles on the Bible in the *Encyclopaedia Britannica* (in 1875), Smith was eventually dismissed from his chair in Hebrew at the University of Aberdeen for his alleged indifference to the authority and uniqueness of the Christian gospel. Smith's anthropological treatment of religion, which was eventually presented comprehensively in his influential lectures from Marischal College under the title *Lectures on the Religion of the Semites* (1889), attempted to reconcile relativism and evolutionary theory with adherence to Protestant Christianity.

The implication of biblical criticism and anthropological inquiry was that the meaning of religious beliefs and symbols were dependent on their social and cultural context; the 'truth' of religion appeared to be relative and specific rather than universal. Furthermore, in primitive society religious belief was relatively unimportant in relation to religious practice. In order to understand the world of the Arab bedouin or the Jewish tribes of the Old Testament, we have to concentrate primarily on their rituals, customs and religious practices, for it is the religious rite which embodies and gives expression to beliefs; these 'beliefs' have in any case yet to achieve articulate theological expression. In the Semitic culture of the Middle East, for example, it was the sacrifice which in ancient times formed a social bond between God and man and which, as a result, bound the individuals of the tribe together in a common pact of blood. To inquire into the nature of the sacrificial beliefs of these tribes would be to miss the crucial sociological function of the practices of religious sacrifice. In the totemic meal, the consumption of the sacred totem created a social relationship between the individual and sacred powers, while also confirming the social covenant of the tribe.

Such an analysis gave rise to the implication that the Christian Eucharist was in essentials no different from the totemic meals of the most savage societies and that the taboo which protected the Host had to be considered on the same plane as the taboo surrounding the primitive totem. The Victorian fascination with the taboo had radical implications for Christian belief (Steiner, 1956). Smith attempted to solve this anthropological threat to religious conviction by arguing that Christianity had evolved away from such primitive practices by spiritualising the whole problem of holiness. Whereas primitive people falsely equated sin with uncleanness and holiness with hygiene, the sacred in Christianity had taken on a completely spiritual and other-worldly significance. Hence expiation and communion were not aimed at the physical life of people, but at strengthening the spiritual bond between the individual and God. Ritual practices were now relatively unimportant in relation to questions of individual belief and intention; subjectivity had replaced adherence to external practices.

William Robertson Smith's theoretical endeavour to reconcile anthropological relativism with a commitment to Christianity by radically separating primitive and Christian religion gave rise to a protracted debate, which ended with his dismissal from Aberdeen. Whether evolutionary notions of hygiene and purity can be maintained within Smith's theoretical schema appears doubtful (Douglas, 1966). More important for the theoretical development of the sociology of religion was that the crises in Smith's interpretation of the Old Testament generated a range of influential issues and problems in the study of religious phenomena. Smith's approach to religion became particularly ,important for subsequent developments in French sociology and especially for the group of scholars associated with Emile Durkheim and *L'Année sociologique*. Although Smith's analysis of sacrifice had a direct and specific importance for the French anthropologists (Hubert and Mauss, 1964), his definition of religion as practice provided the basis for Durkheim's sociology of religion.

By way of summary, we can say that in Smith's anthropology religion is constituted by its practices, the social effects of which are to bind individuals together through participation in sacred meals. In primitive society:

Religion was made up of a series of acts and observances, the correct performance of which was necessary or desirable to secure the favour of the gods . . . Religion did not exist for the saving of souls but for the preservation and welfare of society . . . Ancient religion is but part of the general social order which embraces gods and men alike. (Smith, 1889, pp. 29–33)

The relationship between this definition of religion by reference to social practices and social integration and Durkheim's definition in *The Elementary Forms of Religious Life* is particularly close:

A religion is a unified system of beliefs and practices relative to sacred things, that is to say, things set apart and forbidden — beliefs and practices which unite into one single moral community called a Church, all those who adhere to them. (Durkheim, 1961, p. 62)

We cannot fully appreciate the significance of these definitions without some general notion of the conception of religion which dominated secular science in the nineteenth century. Pre-Durkheimian views of religion can be said to have been grounded in three fundamental assumptions; namely, individualism, intellectualism and positivism (Goode, 1951). Religion was conceived to be a property, indeed uniquely the property, of the isolated individual; the social significance and social consequences of religion were generally ignored. Religion was seen to be the intellectual response of the individual to natural phenomena, the finitude of human life or the meaning of subjective reality. Religion was primarily a cognitive phenomenon, a system of propositions, which aimed to provide explanations of reality by reference to supernatural entities. Finally, since positivist science was taken to be the only criterion of rationality and truth, the explanations of reality which were contained in religious beliefs were necessarily false.

Thus, religion arose out of the theoretical efforts of individuals to make sense of the world. This perspective took no cognisance of the role of emotion, symbol or ritual in social relationships and ignored the social consequences of religion for the organisation of societies. The nineteenth-century positivist perspective was clearly illustrated, for example, by Edward Tylor's definition of religion in *Primitive Culture* as 'the belief in Spiritual Beings' (1891, p. 424). Religion was the product of theoretical inferences on the part of 'ancient savage philosophers' and these inferences were, in the light of subsequent developments in positive science, false (Turner, 1971). The emphasis on the social effects of religious practices in the social anthropology of Smith and Durkheim represented a major theoretical departure from these individualistic, rationalist suppositions.

Durkheim and the forms of religion

Although Durkheim wrote extensively on religious issues in reviews, articles and books (Pickering, 1975), he depended on the analysis of secondary ethnographic material to develop his own theoretical position. This dependence on ethnographic sources was particularly important in his principal volume on the sociology of religion — *Les Formes élémentaires de la vie religieuse. Le système totémique en Australie* of 1912. This study of the fundamental forms of religious activity as a social phenomenon was and remains the centre of philosophical debate in sociology (Seger, 1957). *The Elementary Forms* is normally conceived by commentators as an analysis of the social genesis of mental categories; it has, therefore, to be read alongside *Primitive Classification* (Durkheim and Mauss, 1963), which was an essay on 'collective representations'.

According to Durkheim, his sociology of religion had three principal objectives. The first was to analyse the simplest known religion, namely, aboriginal Australian totemism, in order to determine the elementary forms of religious activity. By 'elementary', Durkheim did not mean historically original or primary, but rather those forms which were structurally basic and persistent. The second purpose of his study was to locate the genesis of 'the fundamental notions of thought or the categories'. For example, Durkheim argued that such basic categories as time, space and causality arise from forms of social organisation rather than from individual experience and inquiry. Such concepts are 'collective representations' and the authoritative force of these concepts is social; our 'ways of thinking' are ultimately 'ways of living' or social institutions, rather than biological or psychological phenomena (Lukes, 1973b, pp. 436-45). The third aim of his analysis of totemism was to establish generalisations about universal nature and functions of religion in all social relationships.

Against the individualistic and cognitive interpretations of Tylor, Max Müller and James Frazer, *The Elementary Forms* set out to show that religion does not consist of belief in spirits or gods, but rather religion is founded in a categorical distinction between a sacred world in opposition to a profane realm. Although it is possible to conceive of a religion which denies the existence of supernatural personalities (as in Theravada Buddhism, for example), all religions are characterised by a dichotomy between the sacred and the profane. It is this division which is:

> the distinctive trait of religious thought: the beliefs, myths, dogmas and legends are either representations or systems of representations which express the nature of sacred things, the virtues and powers which are attributed to them, or their relations with each other and with profane things. (Durkheim, 1961, p. 52)

Religious beliefs and rites are 'social facts' in Durkheim's sense (1938), since they exist independently of individuals, are external to the individual and impose certain ways of thinking and acting on individuals. The crucial theme of Durkheim's sociology of religion was, therefore, the existence of the sacred/profane dichotomy and the social effects of the practices relating to religious categories. His illustration of the social nature of religious categories from the ethnography of the Arunta tribe of Australian aborigines is particularly striking. Hunting and seed-gathering tribes which inhabit arid territories or deserts are forced to subdivide and to disperse in order to secure an adequate food supply. The periodic ritual practices which draw the tribe together and reassemble its constituent clans and families have a number of important social consequences for the collectivity. In addition to re-affirming tribal mythology and tradition, religious practices create strong emotional states (a collective effervescence, to use Durkheim's terminology), re-establishing and cementing social relationships within the tribe. The continuity and existence of the Arunta as a social collectivity depends, therefore, on adherence to certain religious practices. In order to grasp the exact nature of Durkheim's contribution to the theory of social integration, it is important to understand precisely the relationship between religious beliefs and ritual practices.

In principle, thought (religious beliefs) and action (religious ritual) are sharply distinguished, but Durkheim argued that, in practice, doctrine and rite are closely connected. Although the exact relationship between religious belief, ritual and experience remained unclear in Durkheim's sociology (Turner, 1971/2), Durkheim postulated a dialectical relationship in which the cult was dependent on the rite, but the rite was also the embodiment of the beliefs. At a more fundamental level, Durkheim's whole theory of the sacred presupposed a radical divorce between belief and practice. Durkheim rejected the whole notion that religion was founded on a philosophical error; he argued that, if religion was false, it could not have survived throughout human history. Religion was, by contrast, the expression of something basic, real and enduring. From a sociological perspective:

there are no religions which are false. All are true in their own fashion — all answer, though in different ways, to the given conditions of human existence. (Durkheim, 1961, p. 15)

There is, in short, a concrete, real and persistent referent to religious symbols which explains the continuity of religious practice and the resilience of religious belief. The real referent of religious symbols, which is external to individuals and survives the death of individual practitioners, is not the totem or the god, but society itself. It is society which possesses the supra-individualist authority, continuity and externality to impress awe and obedience on the solitary individual.

Two major sociological assertions follow from Durkheim's argument that the real, objective phenomenon behind religious symbolism is not god but society. First, it opens up a significant gap between belief and practice, since the subjective awareness of individuals concerning the explicit referent of religious symbolism, the god, is not in fact the real object of the symbol and the rite. Secondly, Durkheim's Arunta illustration suggests that it is collective involvement in religious practices rather than consensus over religious beliefs which creates the conditions for social integration.

We might suggest, therefore, that Durkheim's *Elementary Forms* represented an anthropological reflection on the etymology of the concept of 'religion', which, from the Latin *religio*, means 'to bind together'. Religion is also the control of men by the establishment of rules (*regulare*) which create mutual obligations, cementing social relationships. Religion provides that regime (*regere*) by which the individual body and the body politic are controlled and ordered. If religion can be regarded as a set of binding rules, then we have to pay special attention to the connection between belief and practice. We have to consider the question: can society be organised around and bound together by collective practices, irrespective of or in the absence of collective beliefs? To suggest an answer to this question, we will have to consider an earlier study of Durkheim's which first appeared in 1893, namely, *De la division du travail social: étude sur l'organisation des sociétés supérieures*.

Durkheim's sociology as a whole has frequently been interpreted as an attempt to solve the so-called Hobbesian problem of order; Durkheimian sociology was thus the heir of social-contract theories in which the conflict of interest between the individuals is resolved by the existence of a government which guarantees the contractual relations between citizens. It was assumed, primarily by Talcott Parsons (1937), that Durkheim's contribution to this classical philosophical problem of social order fell into two distinct phases. In the first, that is, in *The Division of Labour in Society* (1964), Durkheim located the sources of social stability in a set of objective constraints existing outside the individual. In the second, in *The Elementary Forms* (1961), social order begins to find its roots in the internal subjectivity of the individual. Thus, the meaning of constraint changes from the external and objective to the internal and subjective.

Within Parsons's perspective, Durkheim's early commitment to a positivist version of science and his aim of creating a social science of moral life resulted in a conception of 'moral constraint', which precluded notions of individual intention or individual subjectivity. Moral institutions were external, objective and restraining; they did not enter into individual consciousness in the form of guilt feelings or altruistic beliefs. Within Durkheim's positivist methodology, there is no difference, in principle, between moral constraint and physical constraint; the moral order is a sort of social gravity.

In Durkheim's study of religion towards the end of his life, there was a distinctive theoretical shift since, according to Parsons, social order now resides in the fact that the external moral order, the *conscience collective*, has become part of individual subjectivity via the linking mechanism of religious ritual. For Parsons, Durkheim's analyses of the social functions of ritual establish the basis, not just for a sociology of primitive religion, but for the understanding of the bases of social order in all human societies. Every society has to possess certain collective beliefs and general values which come to have normative significance for individuals through the agency of certain powerful rituals. From this perspective, Durkheim laid the foundation, not only for Parsons's own theory of social integration through socialisation and internalisation (Parsons, 1951), but on the broad-stream of American sociology (Parsons, 1973). In order to support this interpretation, as a minimum it has to be shown that *The Elementary Forms of Religious Life* substantially replaces *The Division of Labour in Society* and that every society requires a common culture, a *conscience collective* and a system of *représentations collectives*. These arguments are unwarranted for reasons which were originally developed in *The Dominant Ideology Thesis* (Abercrombie *et al.*, 1980). The nub of this argument with respect to Durkheim and the social functions of religion is that it is difficult to transfer arguments concerning religion in simple societies to contemporary capitalist societies for reasons which Durkheim himself acknowledged. If it is possible to generalise any of Durkheim's findings, it may be that the concept of 'practices' has a wider scope than that of 'common beliefs'.

In *The Division of Labour*, Durkheim made a distinction between two forms of social coherence, that is, between mechanical and organic solidarity. In simple societies characterised by mechanical solidarity, social order is based on the absence of a complex differentiation of social roles, the absence of individualism and doctrines of individuality and by the absence of cultural variations and divisions. Social cohesion between individuals and groups exists because there is an overarching *conscience collective*, a dense network of shared symbols and rituals, and the institutions of repressive law serve to uphold common sentiments and to punish deviations from group values. With increasing urbanisation and with a more extensive division of labour, mechanical solidarity begins to collapse and is gradually replaced by a new principle of organic integration. The development of social classes and specialised occupational groups has the effect of weakening and undermining common values and collective rituals. Although the *conscience collective* still exists in the *sociétés supérieures*, it became weaker, more abstract and less imperative. Labour mobility, urbanisation and social differentiation cut at the roots of tradition and diminished the force of common sentiments. These processes are necessarily conjoined since 'the authority of the collective conscience is . . . in large part composed of the authority of tradition' (Durkheim, 1964, p. 291). The social basis of the new society is located in the reciprocity created by an advanced division of labour and by a new, restitutive principal of law which underscores the forms of economic exchange in industrial society. Contrary to normative interpretations of Durkheim, it would appear that contemporary societies can be integrated around forms of economic dependency and legal restraint; common beliefs and rituals now appear to be residual and ineffective.

Most sociologists of religion have, however, clung to the notion that every society requires a system of common beliefs which legitimates existing social arrangements and that these general beliefs and practices are inescapably religious. Belief in the ubiquity of social cement is almost a professional hallmark among sociologists of religion. Justification for this belief from the sociological classics is often sought in the closing passages of Durkheim's *Elementary Forms*. Although Durkheim was not significantly influenced by Nietzsche (Lukes, 1973b), *The Elementary Forms* concluded by raising the crucial problem of Nietzsche's Godless theology and, in one sense, appealed for a radical 'revaluation of values':

the old gods are growing old or already dead, and others are not yet born. This is what rendered vain the attempt of Comte with the old historic souvenirs artificially revived: it is life itself, and not a dead past which can produce a living cult. (Durkheim, 1961, p. 475)

The problem was that the social structure of modern society appeared to be incompatible with a dense, dynamic and effectual *conscience collective*, but:

There can be no society which does not feel the need of upholding and reaffirming at regular intervals the collective sentiments and the collective ideas which make its unity and its personality. Now this moral remaking cannot be achieved except by the means of reunions, assemblies and meetings where the individuals, being closely united to one another, reaffirm in common their common sentiments; hence come ceremonies which do not differ from regular religious ceremonies, either in their object, the results which they produce, or the processes employed to obtain the result. (Durkheim, 1961, pp. 474-5)

There are major difficulties with the conclusions of Durkheim's sociology of religion as an attempt to generalise from the ritual practices of aboriginals to the universal functional requirements of any social system. There is, particularly in Durkheim's sociology of knowledge, a marked 'tendency to argument by *petitio principii*' (Needham, 1963, p. xiv). No society can exist without common ceremonials which reaffirm common sentiments and beliefs; the universal functions of ritual presuppose the existence in society of common sentiments, but it is the existence of these phenomena which Durkheim's thesis has to establish. In so far as common sentiments exist, their presence could be explained in terms of Durkheim's theory of individual economic reciprocity from *The Division of Labour* in society. There is some indication in Durkheim's sociology of religion of a rather different causal argument, which takes the form:

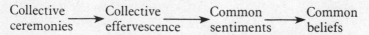

Collective ceremonies → Collective effervescence → Common sentiments → Common beliefs

In general such an interpretation of the origins of common beliefs in society has not found favour with sociologists, because it appears to depend on some notions about 'crowd psychology' in the tradition of Gustave Le Bon (1895) and Gabriel Tarde (1901). It also takes us back to the possibility that societies may be held together by the social cement of common practices without any underpinning in general values; the implication is that in a secular society the coupling between beliefs and practices is broken.

The answer to the specific problem addressed by Durkheim — how can economic self-interest and destructive egoism be socially contained in a society without a *conscience collective* and in circumstances where economic reciprocity often breaks down under the impact of class struggle — was eventually found under tragic and brutal circumstances in 1914. If Durkheim's initial sociological interests had been generated by the Franco-Prussian War in 1870, they were prematurely brought to a conclusion in the First World War.

In the crisis of wartime, there appeared to be an abundance of those common sentiments which had been diminished by the division of labour. Although they were clearly written under exceptional circumstances, Durkheim's influential pamphlets on the war — *Who Wanted the War?* and '*Germany Above All*' — referred confidently to new sources of common values and national commitment. His pamphlet on German expansion was basically an extended critique of the political philosophy of Heinrich von Treitschke in which the state, as an institution based on a monopoly of force, could not be subjected to a higher moral authority, especially in international relations. Durkheim complained that in Treitschke's treatment of the state the goal of political domination could be used to justify any means; these principles of power-politics rode roughshod over Christian idealism and natural justice. Treitschke thought that civil society was a terrain dominated by conflicting wills in opposition to the unity and harmony of the state; Durkheim, however, asserted that, by uniting together in society, people:

became conscious of the groups they form, from the simplest to the most elevated, and thus those social sentiments which the State expresses, defines and regulates, but which it assumes to exist, come spontaneously into being. (Durkheim, 1915, p. 30)

The state cannot, he claimed, rule against the wishes of its citizens and cannot be based simply on coercion in defiance of 'a universal conscience and a universal opinion' (Durkheim, 1915, p. 45). What was missing under peaceful circumstances, namely, a vital sense of national community, appeared to be generated by the exceptional circumstances of international conflict. The consequences of the national emergency were:

to revive the sense of community, to render it more active and make the citizens more accustomed to combine their efforts and subordinate their interests to those of society. (Lukes, 1973b, p. 554)

Having originally argued that social cohesion on the basis of collective beliefs was impossible in a differentiated society, Durkheim appears to have drifted towards the notion that collective ceremonies were necessary for the reaffirmation of common sentiments. In the absence of traditional religious ceremonies and beliefs, Durkheim identified nationalist sentiments and national ceremonial as the main roots of social cohesion. In short, Durkheim 'seems to have moved toward a civil-religion solution' (Robertson, 1978, p. 152) of the individual/society relation.

In the context of Durkheim's criticisms of Treitschke's power-politics, this identification of civil religion as the social cement of industrial capitalism is somewhat ironic. For example, Durkheim (1915, p. 45) criticised Nietzsche as the harbinger of the doctrine that the German state is the superman of history. In fact, Nietzsche was specifically hostile to German nationalism, condemned Treitschke in *Ecco Homo* (1979), identified the national state as the 'new idol' and rejected nationalism as a betrayal of European culture. For Nietzsche, the modern state cannot be legitimated on the basis of national values, and nationalism was a false attempt to cover up the fact of political decay. Of course, the notion that 'civil religion' could come to provide a basis for social solidarity in the absence of a Christian *conscience collective*, generating common sentiments to cement the nation-state together, did not originate with Durkheim. It was, for example, employed by Rousseau (1973) in Book 4 of *The Social Contract* of 1762. Having emerged within the context of the instability of French world war, the concept of 'civil religion' came to have particular pertinence in American political life.

Civil religion
In the treatise on the social contract Rousseau had argued that Christian spirituality rendered it unfit to serve as a civil religion; Alexis de Tocqueville, however, in the two volumes of *Democracy in America* (1946) which appeared in 1835 and 1840, claimed that Christianity was the vital basis of democratic politics in America. Having shaken off absolutism and religious intolerance in Europe, the religion of the settlers and migrants in American society could be accurately described as 'a democratic and republican religion' (de Tocqueville, 1946, p. 229). For historically contingent reasons, Christian religion in America had come to be modelled around the structure of secular politics. The separation of state and church, the absence of an established religion, the emphasis on freedom of conscience and the institutionalisation of religious freedoms meant that the organisation of the innumerable sects and denominations was paralleled to the democratic competition of parties within the political sphere. Withdrawn from overt political conflicts, religion provided a base-line of beliefs and manners so that

'by regulating domestic life it regulates the State' (de Tocqueville, 1946, p. 233). Religious organisation was not only homologous with politics, religion provided much of the ritualism and symbolism of the turning-points in American history. In short, Christianity functioned as the unrivalled civil religion of the new republic and 'religious zeal is perpetually stimulated in the United States by the duties of patriotism' (de Tocqueville, 1946, pp. 236-7).

The Tocquevillian thesis that the structural differentiation of American society and its democratic politics were directly matched by religious belief and thought became the basis of most subsequent commentaries on America's civil religion in the sociology of religion. It formed the principal theme of Parsons's view of the evolutionary development of Christianity towards American denominationalism (Parsons, 1963) and its influence was equally evident in Sperry (1946), Niebuhr (1949) and Williams (1965). However, the *locus classicus* for the whole debate on the civil religion in America remains Will Herberg's *Protestant, Catholic, Jew* (1960), which first appeared in 1955.

In providing an explanation for the 60 per cent increase in church membership between 1926 and 1950, Herberg presented his argument within the context of the differential response of immigrant generations to their own and host cultures. The central concepts for understanding these cultural responses were formulated in terms of self-identification and social location. Emigration to the United States jettisoned the majority of migrants out of traditional village life into a society which was mobile, individualistic and culturally plural. In some respects they had experienced the transition from mechanical to organic solidarity and the loss of a localised *conscience collective*. Although the economic problems of mere survival were dominant issues for the first-generation migrants, there was the additional problem of transplanting and conserving their traditional, ethnic culture in the New World. It was the regressive attempt to establish village and ethnic links within the new community that marked the first stage of Americanisation. Given the paramount problem of communication in a migrant, multilingual society, immigrants inevitably converged into language groups. The migrant church no longer functioned as the focus of village culture, but rather became the main vehicle for the maintenance of language and ethnic culture in a defensive capacity. The church as the principal articulator of 'old country' interests provided the new migrant with familiar institutions of self-identification and social location.

The response of second-generation migrants to host and ethnic cultures was far more ambivalent. The second generation was American-born, yet still migrant and partially assimilated. At home they followed the interests and spoke the language of their immigrant culture; at school and at work, their interests were American and their language English. A number of solutions for this cultural schizophrenia were adopted by these marginal communities. Some sectors of the second-generation communities were able to exploit their marginality by acting as mediators between the host and immigrant communities. The great majority of the second-generation immigrants, however, found their cultural strangeness an obstacle to social mobility and successful assimilation. A necessary condition of social advancement and acceptance was Americanisation. This segment of the second-generation community, therefore, responded to their social marginality by rejecting their ethnic culture and, since the ethnic church was a bastion of immigrant traditional, country culture, this also required a rejection of the religion of their parents.

With the emergence of a third generation, the situation of assimilation and social location was once more fundamentally transformed. The third generation felt American, spoke its language and had no sense of foreignness. Yet they still had an acute problem of self-identification and social location in an impersonal, mobile society. They possessed neither the community and religious links of their grandparents nor the politico-ethnic interests of their fathers. For the third generation, religious identification became an optimal choice, largely because American society expected the immigrant to modify all aspects of his ethnic culture without necessarily abandoning his church. Yet the continuity of religion into the third generation is deceptive. Just as the immigrant was assimilated into society by a process of Americanisation, so religion underwent a similar cultural accommodation. One facet of religious transmutation was that the multifarious sects and denominations became socially defined as Protestant, Catholic or Jewish. There was thus a process of cultural standardisation, since these three labels were regarded as socially and religiously equivalent. The religious definitions were thus regarded not so much as theological as social. The church had become a social community in which people married, raised their children and discovered their leisure pursuits. The three great communities of American life did not represent three institutionalised forms of a basic Judaeo-Christian faith so much as three divisions of the 'American Way of Life'.

The American Way of Life is not an epiphenomenon of Christianity, but a separate and independent religion with its own beliefs, rituals and saints. There is, however, some degree of cultural diffusion between the two religions:

It should be clear that what is designated under the American Way of Life is not the so-called 'common denominator' religion; it is not a synthetic system composed of beliefs to be found in all or in a group of religions. It is an organic structure of ideas, values and beliefs that constitutes a faith common to

Americans and genuinely operative in their lives, a faith that markedly
influences, and is influenced by the 'official' religions of American society.
(Herberg, 1960, p. 77)

In its political guise, the American Way of Life stands for the Constitution, democracy and individual freedom: on the economic side, it
represents *laissez-faire*. Above all, the civic religion espouses individualism, pragmatism and personal activism. In brief, the American
Way of Life may be aptly described as a secularised Protestant Ethic:

as a kind of secularised Puritanism, a Puritanism without transcendence,
without a sense of sin or judgment. (Herberg, 1960, p. 81)

The sense of optimism and emphasis on this-worldly activity and
discipline in the civil religion can thus be regarded as 'the derivatives
of a religious regulation of life' (Weber, 1961, p. 313) which had
originated in the asceticism of the American sects.

The social dominance of religion in American culture and its salience
in the political sphere appear to challenge the assumption which was
widely shared by nineteenth-century social scientists that the advance
of urban industrial society would necessarily bring about increasing
secularisation. As a number of contemporary writers have observed
(MacIntyre, 1967b), the Herberg thesis does provide a means of
reconciling the expectation of increasing secularisation with the facts of
public adherence to religious institutions and beliefs in the United
States. The theoretical reconciliation takes the form of asserting that in
America Christianity has survived industrialisation at the cost of its
traditional theological content. The appearance of public support for
Christian institutions — baptism, marriage, Sunday school and
worship — masks a profound diminution and transformation of the
content of religion. The churches come to fill the role of social clubs and
communal gatherings for mobile, alienated, urban middle classes
(Whyte, 1956); at the national level, Christianity could play an important part in the American stance against atheist communism in the
cold war. There is evidence of a trend away from orthodox Christian
belief (Stark and Glock, 1968), but this situation is combined with
adherence to religious practice and institutions which operate alongside
loyalty to the flag, attachment to Independence Day rituals and
emotional commitment to such sacred places as the Arlington National
Cemetery. The system of beliefs which lies behind these national
practices becomes relatively unimportant in relation to the social
functions and effects of the quasi-religious rituals of the civil religion.
The Christian religion survives in the context of a secular society
because it continues to produce that crucial social element without
which the pluralistic and conflictual society of North America could not
survive.

There have been many criticisms of the Herberg thesis and major objections to the data on which the argument ultimately rests (Argyle, 1958; Stark and Glock, 1965; Demerath and Hammond, 1969); the implication in this debate that American Christianity is a defective, surrogate religion has, however, received its main challenge from Robert Bellah's article 'Civil religion in America' (1970a) and, as a result, the whole problem of religion in a Godless society has been kept to the forefront of sociological inquiry into the nature of industrial society (Cutler, 1968; Richey, 1974).

Bellah's argument has been that the American civil religion is separate and distinct from official Christianity, but also that it possesses 'its own seriousness and integrity' (Bellah, 1970a). Although there is also an overlap between Christianity and the civil religion, the symbols, beliefs and rituals of the American Way of Life have emerged and evolved as responses to crises and turning-points in American history. These major events were primarily the Revolution, the Civil War and the entry of America in the twentieth century into global power-politics, especially in Vietnam. The civil religion is also overlaid with the themes of sacrifice, martyrdom and restoration in the deaths of Abraham Lincoln and John F. Kennedy. Its sacred scriptures include the Declaration of Independence, the Constitution and the Gettysburg address. In Bellah's terms, therefore, the civil religion is not just a vague or general veneer which religion has cast over the shoulders of nationalism — it is a religion with content, substance and particularity which provides a moral challenge rather than a comforting sop to national feeling.

` Bellah's defence of the validity of civil religion has to be understood alongside his epistemological position, which he developed in an article on 'Christianity and symbolic realism' (1970b). Whereas Durkheim had argued that there are no religions which are false, Bellah more strongly asserts against reductionism that:

religion is a reality *sui generis*. To put it bluntly, religion is true. (1970b, p. 93)

Symbolic realism
Symbolic realism invites us to take religion seriously and, in particular, to recognise the ineradicable importance of symbols and practices in human life. Symbolic realism is thus a contemporary solution to the nineteenth-century catastrophe of the death of God, in which religion was seen to be simultaneously necessary and false. By shifting attention towards symbols and practices as essential to the human condition, Bellah can embrace religious institutions as genuine (as a reality *sui generis*) without faltering intellectually over the stumbling-block of religious truth-claims. We might thus summarise Bellah's perspective under the slogan: God is dead; long live religion!

On closer inspection, it turns out that symbolic realism fails to answer the perennial problem of reason in relation to revelation; it fails to tell us what religious symbols symbolise and therefore avoids the issue of who or what it is that forms the subject of religious practice. For the symbolic realist, it is the fact of worship itself, the practice of religion, which constitutes religious phenomena in spite of the absence of theistic beliefs (Turner, 1972a). The notion that *homo religiosus* is one who takes practices rather than beliefs seriously is provided by Peter Berger's assertion: 'It is in worship that the prototypical gesture of religion is realized again and again.' (Berger, 1969, p. 109).

In this context, it is useful to make a distinction between two functions of symbolism. Religious symbols may embody or condense moods, feelings and values, but symbols may also refer to specific places, persons or events in history. The sign of the Cross in Christianity condenses moods of sacrifice and passion, but it also refers to the specific crucifixion of Jesus of Nazareth. The implication of the arguments of sociologists like Bellah and Berger is that religious symbols can be regarded as almost exclusively condensational rather than referential. By treating Christianity and the civil religion as primarily sets of condensational symbols, symbolic realism offers a method of avoiding the fact that at least traditionally Christians have understood their own symbolism as both expressions of mood and summaries of religious and historical facts. By directing attention away from the truth-claims of religion as to the eternal significance of historical events, symbolic realism conjoins rational man with religious society.

An appreciation of the social value of religion and its therapeutic importance for the individual brings the rational actor to opt for religious practice without commitment to the truth or falsity of religious beliefs. Symbolic realism, which offers a defence of Christian commitment, may paradoxically turn out to be a powerful restatement of American secularity. The symbolist argument against reductionism may be a natural counterpart to the American emphasis on religious practice as essentially beneficial, with or without the traditional beliefs which ultimately explain those practices. It has been frequently argued that Americans believe in religious practice rather than in traditional Christian orthodoxy: 'The faith is not in God but in faith: we worship not God but our own worshipping' (Herberg, 1960, p. 84). This commitment is an ironic reformulation of Durkheim's reductionism in which the object of religious symbols and practice was society itself. Furthermore, the notion that religion is 'a good thing' has become basic to American popular piety, which has slowly come adrift from the traditional Christian bases of belief and practice. Symbolic realism can operate as a justification for religion *per se*, regardless of content, in the same way that President Eisenhower's much-quoted observation:

Our government makes no sense unless it is founded in a deeply felt religious faith, and I don't care what it is

served as a legitimation for theological indifference to the cognitive content of religion. Practice makes perfect, even where the beliefs themselves may be rather remote or dubious. The argument here is that Bellah's symbolic realism is ironically the intellectual counterpart to the situation where Protestant, Catholic and Jew become equivalent labels, not for religious communities, but of social identification with the American polity.

Public rituals

In British sociology and anthropology, similar theoretical developments were taking place in contemporary debates over the importance of collective rituals in public life. For example, in the article by Shils and Young (1953) on 'The meaning of the coronation', it was argued that the coronation affirmed the nation's moral values; the ceremony was a 'national communion' which united British society around the symbols and rituals of monarchy. The national communion did, of course, assume the successful integration of the British working class within the political system. Similar arguments were advanced in favour of the investiture of the Prince of Wales (Blumler *et al.*, 1971), which was seen as an act of strengthening and legitimating family solidarity and national awareness. In a more comprehensive fashion, it has been suggested that industrial society is pulled together by a diverse ensemble of secular rituals such as the football cup final, cricket test matches, Guy Fawkes' Night and miners' gala parades (Bocock, 1974).

Although Durkheim's analysis of totemic practices in simple societies was an impressive contribution to our knowledge of the social mechanisms of religious practice, belief and experience, it is difficult to see how the analysis of religion as social cement can be fully satisfactory with respect to modern society. Even in its amended form as a 'civil religion', the notion of a sacred canopy embracing contemporary society is not wholly convincing. In the absence of conventional, overtly religious beliefs common to all sections of society, sociologists have focused on rituals, ceremonies and national practices as the binding force in industrial society. One problem with these Durkheimian perspectives on rituals as elements of social integration is that the vagueness of the concept 'ritual' permits a facile transition from the religious to the secular plane.

The concept of 'ritual' as any regular, repetitive, standardised activity of a non-utilitarian character is thus broad enough to embrace the most diverse collection of activities from changing the guard at Buckingham Palace to Memorial Day, from the opening of Parliament to saluting the flag. There is, in principle, no method of restricting the list of rituals which could count as part of the civil religion; unfortunately the diversity of the examples does not appear to carry any theoretical embarrassment for advocates of the efficacy of civil religions. Given the vagueness of the concept, it would indeed be difficult to know what to exclude (Goody, 1977).

The civil-religion argument does suffer from a common methodological difficulty which it shares with all arguments relating to the notion of a dominant culture. It equates social prevalence with cultural dominance, confusing frequency with social effects. A strong thesis about a dominant culture or civil religion would have to show that the beliefs and practices in question played a necessary part in the maintenance and continuity of a social system. It cannot be assumed that beliefs and practices which are publicly available necessarily have significant effects in the upkeep of crucial social processes and social arrangements. Most civil-religion arguments or arguments concerning nationalism are weak theories which point to the presence of certain allegedly common practices and suggest that these have integrative consequences. With respect to such ceremonies as the Royal Wedding, Independence Day celebrations or the coronation, one can show that these have social effects in the trivial sense that people are involved in them at various levels, but one has to go further to demonstrate that these rituals have specific effects on the stability of capitalist society. From the existence of communal rituals, one cannot make the assumption that these are functionally necessary or that they perform the functions ascribed to them. On existing evidence, the civil religion is at best loosely and only periodically connected with the reactivation of a problematic *conscience collective*, but the precise connections between these common sentiments and the structural arrangements of industrial society is inadequately specified.

Nationalism and the *conscience collective*
The sociological treatment of civil religions from Durkheim onwards provides ample illustration of the problems that also attend those theories which attempt to discover in national sentiment a parallel to religious enthusiasm. Both Marxists and sociologists have seen nationalism as a form of *conscience collective* over-riding the divisions of capitalist society, an ideology masking the naked conflicts of economic interest (Bottomore, 1979). Despite the apparent prevalence of nationalist beliefs in the political life of capitalist societies, the exact nature of the link between nationalism and capitalism has remained a matter of dispute.

There exist a number of general arguments about the significance of the nation-state and nationalist ideology in the development of capitalist economies (Poggi, 1978) and about the role of nationalist movements as responses to imperialism (Smith, 1971). The nationalist sentiment which concerned Durkheim does, however, often appear to be a short-term consequence of rather specific, historically contingent events; it is often difficult to produce any important general statements about the importance of nationalist rituals and emotions with respect to the necessary conditions of an industrial society. Disenchantment and disillusion with the First World War as marked in the poetry of the period, for example, would have to be set alongside the initial enthusiasm of patriotic commitment.

There is thus ample room for methodological dispute, but there are equally important theoretical issues at stake. The debates about the civil religion, the Herberg thesis, the *conscience collective* and so forth are ultimately directed at a basic issue in social philosophy, namely, the relationship between consent and coercion, consensus and conflict in social life. Parsonian sociology and American structural functionalism have, in various ways, been criticised for exaggerating both the extent and importance of value consensus in society (Dahrendorf, 1968). However, Marxist theories of capitalist society are confronted by the mirror-image problem of explaining the absence of revolutionary, proletarian politics in the core regions of the western world (Mann, 1973). The presence of nationalist beliefs and sentiments among the working class is often thought, at least in part, to explain this peculiar state of affairs. There is an assumed parallel between the religious, particularly millenarian, movements of the feudal Middle Ages and the irrational upsurges of fascism and nationalism in the twentieth century (Cohen, 1957).

The issue of nationalism as a surrogate religion is instructive in this context. Nationalism may appear to fulfil functions of social integration in certain crisis periods, such as that which obtained in France between the Franco-Prussian War and the end of the First World War, but nationalism may also be socially divisive within an ethnically or culturally diverse political collectivity. For example, European politics in the 1970s were dominated by political threats to the unity of centralised nation-states under the impact of regional and separatist movements. Nationalist and cultural politics in Ireland, Wales, Scotland, Brittany and the Basque regions threatened to cripple conventional politics (Nairn, 1975). Within a longer time-scale, British politics have always been fragmented along religio-nationalist lines, separating the Catholic and Celtic fringe from the Protestant centre (Hechter, 1975). When nationalist sentiment serves to define a political boundary against an external enemy in a war situation, it may have the intra-social effects noted by Durkheim; but when nationalist feeling sets off a reactive wave of separatist politics within an existing political system, then nationalism is socially corrosive. Since nationalist movements are often closely related to religious differences, as in Scotland (Turner, 1981b) or Canada (Coward and Kawamura, 1977), religion can have a role in consolidating social and economic divisions. Religious rituals may not so much preserve the social fabric as embody its internal conflicts (Lukes, 1975).

Conclusion

There are three major objections to be raised against the assumption that religion — either in the form of a civil religion or in an amalgamation with nationalism — can act as the social cement of modern society in the same way that it supposedly bound traditional societies together. First, it does not provide a genuinely satisfactory solution to the problem of class and class conflict in industrial society. The whole Durkheimian tradition in the sociology of religion can be criticised because it:

nowhere confronts the possibility that religious beliefs are ideologies, which help legitimate the domination of some groups over others. (Giddens, 1978, pp. 103-4)

The empirical evidence points to significant religious differences between social classes in terms of religious affiliation, style and practice. Denominational differences follow the fractures within the national class structure (Niebuhr, 1929) and at the local level provide the cultural contour of class politics within the city (MacLaren, 1974).

Secondly, as with any theory of common culture, there is a tendency for sociologists to neglect alternative conditions of social cohesion, as they exaggerate the effects of religious decline on social stability. Societies are held together not simply or even primarily by common beliefs and ritual practices, but by a multitude of 'material' factors — force, economic coercion, economic dependency, legal compulsion, economic scarcity, habituation and the exigencies of everyday life. Societies can continue to operate with relatively high levels of conflict, disaffection and indifference to norms in combination with pragmatic acceptance of values. The social cement is constantly eroded and swept away by these circumstances without any ultimate descent into *anomy* and social chaos.

Finally, although sociologists of religion have emphasised the social functions of religious and secular practices — coronations, national ceremonies, historic festivals — in modern society, they have failed to pay attention to that range of disciplinary practices of which Michel Foucault, Nicos Poulantzas and Louis Althusser have written so eloquently.

These three issues — class and religion, social control and disciplinary practices — form the basis of subsequent chapters and serve to generate a new range of perspectives within the sociology of religion.

3 Social Opium

In contemporary Marxism there is a marked tendency to diminish the materialist content of historical materialism while upgrading those aspects of Marx's thought in which culture and superstructure are in the foreground. In 1932, the publication of Marx's 'Economic and philosophical manuscripts' (which were written in 1844) served to illustrate the importance of the concept of alienation in Marx's work (Ollman, 1971). The publication of the 1857-8 notebooks (the *Grundrisse*) in Germany in 1953 pointed to the complexity of Marx's project for a critique of political economy, of which *Capital* (1974) was merely a section. The *Grundrisse* (1973) also indicated the continuing influence of Hegelian philosophy after Marx had apparently settled accounts with Feuerbach and the German idealist tradition. A number of writers have also stressed the significance of the argument in *Capital* concerning the 'fetish of commodities' as the essence of historical materialism (Lukács, 1971).

This appreciation of the humanism of Marx has often been conjoined with a depreciation of the effect of Engels on the theoretical content of historical materialism. The notion that the development of human society could be understood in terms of mechanistic laws of social motion and the existence of 'half-positivist, half-Darwinian interpretation of Marx's thought' are to be blamed on 'Kautsky, Plekhanov, and above all to Engels' (Berlin, 1978, p. 90). Thus, Engels's attempt in the speech at the graveside of Marx to make a specific comparison between Darwin's discovery of the 'law of development of organic nature' and Marx's discovery of the 'law of development of human history' (Engels, 1975b) is, within the humanist interpretation of Marx, fundamentally misguided. The emphasis on the anthropological humanism of Marx's thought has had important implications for the incorporation of Marxism into the sociology of religion.

Critique of Christianity
According to certain commentators on the biographical development of Marx's thought (McLellan, 1973), there were significant changes in Marx's attitude to Christianity. Starting with youthful acceptance of the truth of traditional Christianity, Marx came to abandon theistic belief on the basis of criticisms developed in, for example, Ludwig Feuerbach's *The Essence of Christianity* (1953). Towards the end of his life, Marx's critique of religion focused primarily on the political

functions of religion, especially as an ideology of the state. The principal target of Marx's critique:

was directed against the *use* of Christian religion by the socially and economically exploitative Prussian state for its own ends . . . Protestantism was a religion well suited, by its own nature, for such use by political rulers, for its ideas had a particularly close correspondence with the condition of man in a capitalist society. (Ling, 1980, p. 16)

If this type of interpretation is adopted, then it is a short step to the suggestion that Marx was mainly a critic of institutionalised Christianity and its political corruption. Since Christianity contains within itself a critique of politics, the implication is that Marx's thought is not only compatible with radical Christianity, but a necessary consequence of the Christian oppositional tradition. Marx has, therefore, often been treated as a secular prophet fulminating against the evils of capitalism and the complicity of the Church, just as the Old Testament prophets were scandalised by the worship of false gods (Parsons, 1964; Olssen, 1968).

More recently, a detailed examination of the publications, letters and notes of both Marx and Engels has led researchers to the conclusion that they 'saw their communism as a conscious continuation of authentic Christianity' (Miranda, 1980, p. 240). Although Marx's philosophical anthropology gave him a sensitive insight into the importance of religious consciousness in human life, some writers have detected a 'tendency' in Engels's work 'to describe religion at times as a direct expression of class interests' (Birnbaum, 1973, p. 21). Engels's lapses into reductionism were further exaggerated in Kautsky's *Foundations of Christianity* (1925) and in Bernstein's highly deterministic interpretations of historical change. The insistence on the scientific status of Marxism in the period of the Second International overshadowed Marx's humanistic perspective and meant that 'religion was depicted as a reflection of class interests, as a direct means of class domination' (Birnbaum, 1973, p. 22).

The argument presented in this chapter rejects any attempt to dilute the historical materialism of Marx and Engels, but also denies the importance of the alienation theme and fetishism in classical Marxism. It is equally important to avoid the conventional characterisation of Engels as merely 'mentor and glosser' (Carver, 1981, p. 73). In their principal analyses of religion, Marx and Engels did typically adopt a reductionist, class-theoretical perspective. Exegetical efforts to deny or obscure this fact are misguided. Equally, attempts to promote the 'humanist Marx' have been largely indiscriminate in their selection of texts to prove the point. Letters, newspaper articles, schoolboy essays, political pamphlets and large-scale publications have been pressed into service with little respect to their textual significance. Marx's own view that his journalism was 'muck' (Marx and Engels, 1956, vol. 28, p. 592) has not detracted commentators from lavishly selecting from his *New York Daily Tribune* articles.

There is, therefore, much to commend Althusser's view that there is a definite shift away from Feuerbachian, communalist humanism in Marx's work after 1845. This epistemological break with humanism contains three necessary elements: the development of a new range of concepts relating to the analysis of social formations and modes of production; a critique of all forms of philosophical humanism; the definition of humanism as a type of ideology (Althusser, 1969). Although Althusser's periodisation of the works of Marx is not without difficulties, it does have the merit of drawing attention to the uneven and heterogeneous nature of Marx's *oeuvre*. If we apply Althusser's notion of the epistemological break in Marx's development to the question of Marx's analysis of religion, we would be forced to conclude that the commentaries on religion in the period of his Feuerbachian humanism are fragmentary, slight and inconsequential.

My argument is that anyone who wants to understand the classical Marxist view of religion has to turn to Engels rather than to Marx. This classical interpretation emphasised the importance of religion in relationship to the development of modes of production and class conflicts. To provide support for this materialist position, it will be necessary to demolish the themes of alienation and fetishism as possible foundations for a Marxist sociology of religion. This demolition clears the ground for my presentation of Engels's analysis of religion as the outer garment of class interest. Such an interpretation of Marx and Engels may appear 'vulgar' in riding roughshod over the alleged humanism of Marx, but it does have the merit of differentiating Marx from other nineteenth-century theorists and of reaffirming Marx's historical materialism.

Marx's materialism
Marx's allegedly humanist interpretation of human alienation and the embodiment of human estrangement in the beliefs and practices of religion is contained in the famous section 4 ('The fetishism of commodities and the secret thereof') in volume I of *Capital* (1974), in which Marx employs human estrangement in commodities as an analogy for human estrangement in supernatural relationships. It is often held that the basis of Marx's materialism is the view that the social world and, to some extent, the natural world are effects of human practical activity ('labour'). The social institutions of the world that people inhabit — the family, village, church, factories and clubs — are the products of countless acts of labour. Unlike other animals, men have to produce

their material means of subsistence and so they occupy a material, cultural and technological environment which is inherited from history, but which is unambiguously a human product.

It is this emphasis on practical activity as transformative labour which distinguishes Marx's materialism from the abstract, static materialism of Feuerbach (Korsch, 1970). Through labour human beings not only in history transform themselves, but they also come to shape and subdue nature through the medium of technology. Man is dialectically part of nature, but also transforms the natural world through his natural capacities (Schmidt, 1971). Marx's concept of man as *homo faber* was, as Marx acknowledged, based on Giambattista Vico's view that human beings develop themselves through their own labour. These features of Marx's thought can be illustrated in a quotation from *Capital* which succinctly draws together the themes of labour, technology, nature and religion:

as Vico says, human history differs from natural history in this, that we have made the former but not the latter. Technology discloses man's code of dealing with Nature, the process of production by which he sustains his life, and thereby lays bare the mode of formation of his social relations, and of the mental conceptions that flow from them. Every history of religion, even, that fails to take account of this material basis, is uncritical. It is, in reality, much easier to discover by analysis the earthly core of the misty creations of religion, than, conversely, it is, to develop from the actual relations of life the corresponding celestialised forms of those relations. The latter method is the only materialistic, and therefore the only scientific one. (Marx, 1974, vol. 1, p. 352)

Although human beings create the world they inhabit, they often appear to conceive, experience and occupy that human world in a manner which appears to contradict their own creativity and productivity. There is a disjunction between 'the actual relations of life' and 'the celestialised forms' in which those productive relations are grasped. Marx's attempt to move scientifically from concrete relations to these heavenly forms is contained in the analysis of the fetishism of commodities in capitalist exchange relations.

In the conventional interpretation of the fetishism section of *Capital*, it is argued that, although social relations are constituted by practical activity, they come to assume a natural thing-like character; social relations become reified by assuming an autonomy and independence outside human activity. Reification occurs in an exchange economy because the social character of labour, production and exchange is obscured by the fact that the producers do not come into social contact with one another until they meet in the market-place to exchange their commodities. The social quality of the producer's labour only appears in the exchange of commodities. To express this reification of commodities, Marx employs religious terminology and supernatural metaphors:

A commodity is therefore a mysterious thing, simply because in it the social character of men's labour appears to them as an objective character stamped upon the product of that labour; because the relation of the producers to the sum total of their own labour is presented to them as a social relation, existing not between themselves, but between the products of their labour . . . it is a definite social relation between men, that assumes, in their eyes, the fantastic form of a relation between things. In order, therefore, to find an analogy, we must have recourse to the mist-enveloped regions of the religious world. In that world the productions of the human brain appear as independent beings endowed with life, and entering into relation both with one another and the human race. So it is in the world of commodities with the products of men's hands. (Marx, 1974, vol. 1, p. 77)

There is in this passage, therefore, a pronounced Feuerbachian theme. Just as the social character of commodity production appears as part of the natural world, as relationships between things, so the supernatural order which is equally the product of mental labour appears to rule above and independently of human beings. Marx finds in religion the perfect analogy of commodity reification.

One implication of this fetishism theory is that the greater the penetration of the economy by commodity-exchange relations, the wider the scope of fetishistic forms of conceptualisation. The expansion of the capitalist mode of production should, therefore, coincide historically with an intensification of fetishistic thought. Certainly, the categories of political economy and the 'forms of thought expressing with social validity the conditions and relations' of the production of commodities reify the specific characteristics of capitalist activity to stand for the nature of humanity as such. The historically specific circumstances of capitalist production are taken to be laws of nature. The production of commodities is surrounded by 'magic and necromancy' (Marx, 1974, vol. 1, p. 80).

Marx was also concerned in the concluding pages of the fetishism of commodities discussion to bring out a striking relationship between the ahistorical individualism of Robinson Crusoe, who has been so frequently the protagonist of bourgeois economic virtues, and the isolated individual of Protestant theology. In a passage which also illustrated his literary preferences for metaphors of reflection, he asserted that:

The religious world is but the reflex of the real world. And for a society based upon the production of commodities, in which the producers in general enter into social relations with one another by treating their products as commodities and values, whereby they reduce their individual private labour to the standard of homogenous human labour — for such a society, Christianity with its *cultus* of abstract man, more especially in its bourgeois developments, Protestantism, Deism, &c., is the most fitting form of religion. (Marx, 1974, vol. 1, p. 83)

Protestant individualism was thus the 'celestial form' which reflected the 'actual relations of life', but this reflex was also a concealment which covered the social nature of all practical activity. The real nature of human labour could be disclosed, not by a vigorous programme of re-education, but by changes in the social relations within which people are situated. To cite the preface to the *Critique of Political Economy*, it is the location of men in definite social relationships which determines the nature of their consciousness, and not their subjective consciousness which determines their social existence (Marx, 1971, p. 21). The subject awareness of individuals can, therefore, only be transformed by an upheaval in their social relationships. The religious reflex of these concrete social interconnections between men will disappear when the relations of 'every-day life offer to man none but perfectly intelligible and reasonable relations with regard to his fellowmen and to Nature' (Marx, 1974, vol. 1, p. 84). The disappearance of religious illusions hinges finally on the disappearance of commodity exchange within the capitalist mode of production.

There are three separate dimensions to Marx's alleged humanism which bear directly on the analysis of religion within a Marxist perspective. In the alienation motif, the estrangement of people from nature, society and themselves finds its heavenly expression in the separation of sinful humanity from the loving God. In the reification theme, the social character of human labour becomes objectified and obscured in forms of thought which picture the world as determined by immutable laws. Divine laws and laws of nature give permanent expression to these ahistorical, reified conceptions of the ethical context of human labour. Reification has the ideological functions of concealment by presenting that which is contingent and changeable in social life as enjoying the force and immutability of necessary laws of nature. In fetishism, by contrast, certain supernatural powers are granted to things (the totem or fetish) which, in reality, belong to social relationships. The ideological function is one of illusion rather than concealment (Abercrombie, 1980, p. 86).

These three functions — alienation, reification and fetishism — were prefigured in the Hegelian–Feuerbachian tradition which had profoundly influenced Marx in the 1840s, when Marx had claimed that the criticism of religion was the starting-point for all political and economic opposition in Germany (McLellan, 1970). The location of the fetishism of commodities doctrine in the first volume of *Capital* has thus been taken as persuasive evidence of certain continuities in Marx's thought and also as an indication of a permanent Hegelian influence (MacIntyre, 1969a; Avineri, 1970a; Singer, 1980).

Leaving the issue of philosophical continuities in Marx momentarily in parenthesis, the fetishism/reification theory has been widely influential in sociological studies of religion, law and knowledge in contemporary capitalism. It provides the basis for Peter Berger's analysis of consciousness (Berger and Pullberg, 1966) and for his perspective on religion as a 'sacred canopy' which shores up the anomic, shifting social world by clothing it with an aura of thing-like facticity and natural stability (Berger, 1969). The notion of fetishism has also played a prominent role in the development of Marxist theories of law. In capitalist society, there is a parallel between commodity fetishism and legal fetishism in which the form of law and the abstract, impersonal, legal subject develop alongside the abstract, formal character of bourgeois economic categories (Pashukanis, 1978). The form of the legal subject as an abstract, individuated possessor of rights is a necessary requirement of a capitalist system of production where the economic subject is the capitalist with ownership and management functions. Juridical discourse creates the subject as the owner of himself and therefore as a possessor of property, 'that is, by virtue of being the representative of himself *qua* commodity' (Edelman, 1979, p. 70). The subject in law is constituted or 'interpellated' by the law itself just as the subject in religion is formed through a recognition of an imaginary master which hails man out of darkness.

The theoretical employment of the fetishism of commodities argument from Marx's *Capital* in contemporary Marxism has allowed commentators to present Marx's ideas as necessarily opposed to technological determinism, Darwinistic science, mechanical materialism and teleological historiography. In short, it is necessary to distinguish between historical materialism and natural materialism (Sohn-Rethel, 1978). There are two basic arguments to be developed against these interpretations of Marxism. The first is that the fetishism of commodities theory does not provide an adequate general theory of ideology. The second is that basic concepts for a materialist analysis of society — social class, class conflict, exploitation and mode of production — are displaced in favour of a philosophical anthropology which is grounded in timeless concepts — reification, objectification, alienation — which ultimately presuppose some commitment to 'the essence of man'. My intention here is to restate a Marxist sociology of religion based on the notion of class and class interest through an analysis of the works of Engels. Unfortunately, as it stands, Engels's class-theoretical account of religion turns out to be inadequate. It is possible, however, to reformulate the theory to provide an analysis of religion as the ideology of dominant classes.

The fetishism of commodities argument suffers from a number of serious limitations which render it inadequate as a general theory of ideology or, more specifically, as a perspective on religion in capitalist society. One basic problem is that the argument will only work adequately in the context of an economy where all members produce commodities independently for market exchange. Fetishism emerges because separate, autonomous producers can only meet in the market to exchange. Thus, the arguments presented by Pashukanis and Edelman concerning fetishism in jurisprudential thought do not appear to be particularly relevant to monopoly capitalism where ownership and management are to some extent separated. Separate economic individuals do not exchange commodities in the market because the impersonal corporation tends to replace the capitalist individual and the capitalist family. In monopoly capitalism, the coincidence of the human, economic and legal subject begins to break down and consequently the theoretical assumptions of the fetishism thesis lose their pertinence (Hirst, 1979). In the sociology of law, the fetishism theory could not explain major differences in the form of law in different capitalist societies. There are, for example, important variations between English and Scots law, despite the common commodity structure of the British economy. In a similar fashion, the continuity of religion in monopoly capitalism and variations in the religious traditions of different capitalist societies could not be explained in terms of the fetishism of commodities and the reification process. The fetishism thesis, which in many respects is the hallmark of humanist Marxism, does not exhaust the various forms which ideology may assume and it does not provide us with an account of the specific content of ideological systems (Abercrombie, 1980).

The principal weakness of the fetishism thesis is, however, that it does not develop any specific conception of the apparatus of transmission by which beliefs are distributed within a society. It is important to develop the notion of an ideological apparatus intervening between economic circumstances (commodity production and exchange) and the consciousness of individuals (ideology). There has to be some notion of institutional mediation between the specific claims about exchange generating fetishistic thought and the more general idea that fetishism characterises the whole society (Abercrombie, *et al.*, 1980). This lacuna in the fetishism theory is particularly problematic in Lukács's treatment of reification in bourgeois society:

> But it is important to notice that this domination has virtually no institutional apparatus whatever. It is simply 'pure ideology' — the unseen rays of a hidden centre of the universe — commodity fetishism . . . Lukacs' whole account of bourgeois ideological domination is reduced to the invisible emanations of reification from commodities, which radiate out to bleach the consciousness of the inhabitants of capitalist society. (Stedman-Jones, 1971, pp. 48-9)

The Lukácsian theory of ideology fails to consider 'the transmission of ideology through various sets of institutions and practices with their own specificity and internal contradictions' (McDonough, 1978, p. 41). A theory of ideology must contain an account of the apparatus of ideological transmission, otherwise it is forced back on the vague notions of emanations and reifications.

Engels on religion

Since the fetishism thesis is inadequate as a general theory of ideology and consequently of religious beliefs, it is appropriate to turn to what might be considered a more conventional position, that is, to an account of religion couched in terms of class, economic interest and the mode of production. In this section, I want to argue that it was Engels, not Marx, who provided an unambiguous, detailed and historical-materialist explanation of the nature of religion in class societies. Engels was not, therefore, merely an exponent of Marx's theories; he made specific contributions of his own to such areas as military sociology (Henderson and Chaloner, 1959), the family and reproduction (Engels, n.d.) and historical sociology (1968). More importantly, it turns out that Engels was the only theorist in classical Marxism, with the exception of Kautsky (1925), who made a substantial contribution to the history of Christianity in the transition from feudalism to capitalism (1965) and to the sociology of religion (1975a). If we want a definite Marxist statement of the nature of religion on capitalism, it is to Engels, not Marx, that we have to turn. The reason for this is that Engels did not attempt to explain religion in general by reference to universal anthropological needs of the human species (à la Feuerbachian materialism); he did not ground religion in some notion of commodity exchange and the reification of consciousness (à la Lukácsian sociology). What he did achieve was the application of historical materialism to religious phenomena within the context of the specific conditions of working-class politics in the middle of the nineteenth century.

Marx and Engels, whether separately or jointly, regarded historical materialism as an original perspective on history and society. Marx's own statement of this new approach to historical and social analysis was presented in the preface to the *Critique of Political Economy* of 1859, in which he asserted that the anatomy of civil society had to be found in political economy, that is, in the 'mode of production of material life'. The transformations of the mode of production have direct consequences for the nature of consciousness so that the contradictions in the material base of society are reproduced in the contradictions and conflicts of ideology:

Just as one does not judge an individual by what he thinks about himself, so one cannot judge such a period of transformation by its consciousness, but, on the contrary, this consciousness must be explained from the contradictions of material life, from the conflict existing between the social forces of production and the relations of production. (Marx, 1971, p. 21)

In his famous letter to Josef Weydemeyer in 1852, Marx confessed that he had not discovered the dominance of class relations within the structure of bourgeois civil society; his contribution had to be sought in his argument that the existence of classes was tied to specific developments in the mode of production, that the class struggle results in the dictatorship of the proletariat and that this dictatorship is finally resolved within a classless society (Marx and Engels, 1963, p. 45).

Engels was equally specific about the nature of historical materialism; it refers essentially to a method of historical analysis:

which seeks the ultimate cause and the great moving power of all important historic events in the economic development of society, in the changes in the modes of production and exchange, in the consequent division of society into distinct classes, and in the struggles of these classes against one another. (Engels, 1975a, pp. 23—4)

The analysis of history could *not* start with the problem of conscious individuals, with the politics of the royal household, with religious beliefs or with changes in ideology. Historical materialism started with a simple fact that people in society 'must first of all eat, drink, have shelter and clothing' before they can engage in other activities like 'politics, science, art, religion, etc.' (Engels, 1975b, p. 16).

Any interpretation of Marx and Engels which suppresses the centrality of economic production and class conflict in their sociological analyses in favour of notions of fetishism, reification or alienation obscures the fundamental components of historical materialism. It is interesting, therefore, to note that, in the section from *Capital* on the fetishism of commodities, Marx admitted that it is only in capitalism that the economic base determines that 'material interests preponderate' throughout the social structure. In the Middle Ages it was Catholicism, and in classical Greek or Roman society it was politics, that 'reigned supreme'. No one should imagine, however, that in the Middle Ages people could:

live on Catholicism, nor the ancient world on politics. On the contrary, it is the mode in which they gained a livelihood that explains why here politics, and there Catholicism, played the chief part. (Marx, 1974, vol. 1, p. 86)

It is the economic base that determines which dimensions of the social structure (religion, politics, ideology and so forth) will be dominant. The political and social importance of Catholicism should not detract from the fact that people 'must first of all eat' or, as Marx put it, gain a 'livelihood'.

Marx's materialist commentary on religion, although interesting, was undeniably brief. It is, therefore, to Engels's historical studies that one must turn for an elaborate analysis of religion in terms of modes of production and class relationships.

Dominant ideology thesis

By way of prefatory remarks, it is important to realise that Engels's *Peasant War in Germany* (1965) was written in the summer of 1850 against the background of the 1848 revolutions and counter-revolutions which had prematurely halted Germany's bourgeois transformation. The pedagogic function of this historical study was to show that the peasants' defeat of 1525 and the workers' defeat of 1850 pointed to the precocious nature of the class wars of the respective periods. The weakness of the peasantry in the sixteenth century forced them into class alliances which resulted in significant advantages for the feudal princes. The weakness of the workers in the nineteenth century also resulted in political alliances between the bourgeoisie and *Junkers* which had important reactionary implications for the development of German history (Henderson, 1976, vol. 2).

The theoretical function of the study was to pinpoint the weakness of 'the German Ideology' which regarded the conflicts of the Middle Ages as nothing more than theological controversies. Engels's task was to demonstrate that the 'so-called religious wars' of the Reformation period 'involved positive material class interests' (1965, p. 41). In writing of the relationship between religious belief and class interest, Engels employed the vocabulary of concealment, disguise and shrouding. Class relations were 'clothed' in the language of religion, and the demands of the various classes were folded in a 'religious screen'. The reasons for this relationship of concealment are not difficult to discover. Since the Church monopolised mental production through its educational institutions, forms of social and political domination were necessarily expressed through the medium of religious language and ritual.

In *The German Ideology* Marx and Engels (1974, p. 64) had argued that the class as the 'ruling *material* force of society is at the same time its ruling *intellectual* force'. A similar 'ruling ideas' model is produced in Engels's perspective on the nature of religious beliefs in the Catholic Middle Ages, namely, that the dominant class which controls the means of mental production can generally insure that subordinate classes experience the world and conceptualise their place in that world through the mental categories of the dominant ideology of the ruling class (Abercrombie and Turner, 1978, p. 153). It also follows that even oppositional movements will couch their hostility to the prevailing system of exploitation in terms of these dominant categories. Since the dominant ideology was formulated in terms of religious concepts, opposition to that ideology typically found expression in religious forms. Revolutionary struggles against feudalism were fought out in terms of 'mysticism, open heresy, or armed insurrection, all depending on the conditions of the time' (Engels, 1965, p. 42). Both Marx and

Engels referred, for example, frequently to the materialist and critical views of the 'divinely inspired' Jakob Boehme (Ling, 1980). However, the language of religious opposition was not the essence of social conflict, but merely its outer garment. Thus, the opposition of the urban burghers to the wealth and luxury of celibate clergy in terms of an ideal of religious simplicity taken from primitive Christianity has to be seen as one manifestation of the economic struggle between the towns and the Church. It was the nature of the economic relations and the dominance of clergy over the apparatus of mental production which account for the fact that 'opposition to feudalism appeared only as opposition to *religious* feudalism' (Engels, 1965, p. 44).

If religion was the linguistic cloak of class struggles in the Middle Ages, then Engels's metaphor of language and covering garments would have to contain the notion of regional dialects, in that different classes employed very different religious symbols and idioms. For example, the political themes of the Old and New Testaments give rise to very different, typically incompatible, principles of government and state legitimacy. With the Lutheran Bible in their hands, the German peasantry had a powerful source of political ideology which could condemn present social arrangements in terms of the promise of a New Jerusalem. However, from the same biblical material it was possible to extract 'such a veritable hymn to the God-ordained authorities as no bootlicker of absolute monarchy had ever been able to extract' (Engels, 1965, p. 52). The opposite end of Lutheran principles of *de facto* legitimacy was occupied by Thomas Munzer's conception of the kingdom of heaven as a kingdom in this world based on communal property, democratic political control and classlessness. To inflame the passion of the masses, Munzer had to use 'the forceful language that religious and national delirium put into the mouths of the Old Testament prophets' (Engels, 1965, p. 116), because this religious language was the only means by which Munzer could reach the consciousness of his followers.

Although there was a common religious ideology in society, there were important class variations in the use of this ideology. Thus, although religious asceticism was an important general conception of individual moral behaviour, the meaning of asceticism took very different forms in the bourgeoisie and proletariat. Proletarian asceticism can be a protest against aristocratic luxury and it may have some political functions in mobilising subordinate groups against exploitation, but it cannot be a permanent moral code of such groups since they have too little to renounce. By contrast, religious asceticism among urban burghers had a very distinctive significance 'whose entire secret lay in *bourgeois thrift*' (Engels, 1965, p. 64).

There is no indication in Engels's study of the peasant revolts in

Germany that his analysis of religion presupposed any notion of the theoretical importance of concepts like fetishism, reification or alienation. This conclusion receives further support from consideration of Engels's studies of religion and the working class under conditions of capitalist production. Engels's analysis of Christianity in the nineteenth century focused on a paradoxical relationship between religion and bourgeois capitalism. On the one hand, there were certain basic economic and social changes in capitalist society which tended to undermine the social dominance of religious beliefs and institutions. On the other hand, the bourgeoisie, at least in England, recognised that religion was the most important mechanism for securing the acquiescence of the urban proletariat. Like King Canute, the English bourgeoisie faced a tide of secularism which it could not control, but which threatened the foundations of its political authority. The bourgeoisie supported religious revivalism, religious education and moral reformism because:

the people must be kept in order by moral means, and the first and foremost of all moral means of action upon the masses is and remains — religion. (Engels, 1975a, p. 38)

For the English bourgeoisie there appeared to be an obvious connection between the loss of religious authority, the growth of science and working-class revolts. The growth of working-class opposition in France appeared to be joined to the growth of secularism. Faced with such political dangers, the bourgeoisie lent their support to religion in a rearguard ideological battle.

Engels was convinced, however, that the religious props of bourgeois political control would necessarily collapse with the changes taking place in the economic organisation of English capitalism. In providing the reasons for that conviction, Engels offered a precise statement of the base/superstructure metaphor which was outlined by Marx in the preface. Engels's argument took the following form:

If our juridical, philosophical, and religious ideas are the more or less remote offshoots of the economical relations prevailing in a given society, such ideas cannot, in the long run, withstand the effects of a complete change in these relations. (Engels, 1975a, p. 39)

Fundamental changes in the relations of production in capitalist society were bringing about a complete transformation of civil society; these changes would eventually work themselves out in the more remote regions of ideology and religious practice. These geographical images of ideological relations constantly emerged in Engels's comments on the nature and role of the superstructure. The implication was that certain forms of belief and practice — such as accountancy, management studies or Taylorism — stand in close proximity to the economic base and hence change rapidly with economic developments. Other forms of belief— aesthetics, religion, principles of chess strategy — are 'more or less remote' from the economy and changes in these features of culture may not correspond closely to changes in the relations of production. Thus:

The further the particular sphere we are investigating is removed from the economic sphere and approaches that of pure abstract ideology, the more shall we find it exhibiting accidents . . . in its development, the more will its course run in a zig-zag. (Marx and Engels, 1955b, p. 466)

Alternatively, Engels conceptualised this problem in temporal rather than spatial terms by suggesting certain delays in the effect of economic on cultural phenomena in his notion of determination 'in the last instance'. The relationship between base and superstructure is a complex one, taking the form of a dialectic rather than causal interconnection. Although the superstructure may under certain conditions enjoy a relative autonomy, in the last instance, as Engels noted in his letter to Joseph Bloch in 1890, 'the economic movement finally asserts itself as necessary' (Marx and Engels, 1955a, p. 275). Although Marx and Engels constantly modified the notion that the 'legal and political superstructure' arises from 'the economic structure of society, the real foundation', they never abandoned the basic proposition that the structure of the mode of production is the anatomy of civil society.

Engels's theory of religion presents all the major difficulties of the dominant ideology thesis. His primary view of religion is that it formed the dominant ideology of the feudal period or, more precisely, religion provided the thematic content of the dominant world-view of medieval society under conditions of feudal property relations. Religion was the dominant ideology because the clergy and religious institutions were strategically located at the apex of the means of cultural production, or 'mental production' as Marx and Engels expressed it in *The German Ideology*. Because the ideology of the ruling class had a religious character, the total ideological system of the society was also religious. The world-view of the subordinate class was thus infected, so to speak, with this dominant religious outlook, and consequently the dominant and subordinate classes of feudal society were incorporated in this common ideology. The effect of religious incorporation was to inhibit the revolutionary consciousness of the peasantry. The reasons for this inhibitory action of religion on subordinate classes are not entirely clear in Marx and Engels's treatment of Christianity. On the whole, religion appears to have a narcotic impact on revolutionary consciousness, as Marx suggested in his critique of Hegel's *Philosophy of Right* in 1844:

Religion is the sigh of the oppressed creature, the heart of a heartless world, just as it is the spirit of a spiritless situation. It is the opium of the people. (Marx and Engels, 1955a, p. 42)

Religion directs working-class opposition and resentment against this world on to the next world or, as in millenarianism, to a distant period in the future. Class hatred was thus projected into the next world as a form of moral revenge as in the Beatitudes. Domination over the rich and the proud in the next world is the compensation the poor receive for their resignation in this life.

If the dominant ideology thesis is presented in a stark, unqualified form as a theory of class incorporation through indoctrination, then it becomes extremely difficult to explain or even recognise the facts of peasant resistance to feudal exploitation. Engels did frequently conceptualise religious ideology in a mechanistic and instrumental fashion, which suggested that the dominant class consciously utilised religion to mystify and control the peasants in feudal society and the workers in capitalism. The subordinate classes are kept in check by 'moral means'. The idea that ideology involves one class doing something, mystifying for example, to another subordinate class was also present in Marx's opium metaphor. The working class are dependent on the narcotic effect of religious promises; the religious drug is controlled and distributed by the dominant class through its intelligentsia, because the dominant class controls the means of mental production and circulation. However, Marx and Engels emphatically stated their argument in *The Communist Manifesto* that the history of human society is the history of class struggles. The ideological inhibitions of peasant opposition which result from religion cannot, therefore, be permanent; the peasantry cannot be totally saturated and satiated by the narcotics of the Church. Although the peasants did periodically revolt against feudal conditions, the dominant ideology was so powerful that even their opposition was expressed through the medium of the dominant religious ideology. Opposition was religious opposition: namely, mysticism, heresy and millenarianism. Even bourgeois opposition to feudal conditions typically assumed a religious language and idiom:

the religious imprint in revolutions of really universal significance is restricted to the first stages of the bourgeoisie's struggle for emancipation from the thirteenth to the seventeenth centuries and is to be accounted for not, as Feuerbach thinks, by the hearts of men and their religious needs but by the entire previous history of the Middle Ages, which knew no other form of ideology than religion and theology itself. (Engels, 1976, p. 31)

At a later stage, the bourgeoisie came to adopt an ideology which was more closely matched to its class position and this ideology was constituted by 'juristic and political ideas'.

Within this dominant ideology thesis, Engels and Marx assume that the principal classes of any society fall within the same general framework of beliefs. Both authority and opposition are expressed through the same ideological medium. Where these classes share the same set of ideological presuppositions and where the revolutionary potential of the subordinate class is held in abeyance by the narcotic of religious membership, it is often difficult to distinguish between the Durkheimian conception of religion as a social cement and the Marxist metaphor of religion as a social opium. Despite their very different assumptions and approaches, the idea that, through ritual, religion integrates the social group by reaffirming common values has the same analytical status as the idea that religious ideologies unite divergent social classes behind the garment of religious institutions and beliefs. Both types of theory are faced with the perennial difficulty of explaining the existence of conflict, opposition and revolt within societies which apparently have dominant ideologies. There is the additional difficulty in Marxism of reconciling the dominant ideology thesis with the economic argument that the principal condition for the subordination of the worker in capitalism is the separation of the worker from the means of production. The worker's acceptance of his situation within capitalism, at least in the early stages of capitalist development, is produced by the fact that he has to work to eat; in theory, ideological subordination is secondary to the economic compulsion which follows from the worker's dependence on market demand for labour.

Class and ideology

Marx and Engels did, however, have an alternative theory of ideology which related ideological beliefs directly to class position rather than to the monopoly of mental production under the exclusive surveillance of the dominant class. Whereas the dominant ideology thesis as expressed in *The German Ideology* suggests that each mode of production will have a common ideological structure embracing all classes, the class-theoretical view of beliefs which emerged in the preface to the *Critique of Political Economy* implies that each distinctive class will possess an ideology which directly gives expression to class interest. Each mode of production will give rise to at least two significantly separate ideologies corresponding to the class position of subordinate and superordinate classes. That is, where the first theory argues that religion forms the basis of social integration as either social cement or social opium, the second theory points to religion as the principal source, especially in feudalism, of *class* solidarity. These theories are, to say the least, in tension, since a high level of class solidarity is not compatible with a high level of integration within the social system (Turner, 1977a). It is difficult to conceive of the existence of general social values in a society split by social classes which are divided not only by contradictory class interests, but also by class-based ideologies.

The class-theoretical view of ideology in Marx and Engels arose out of the theory that it is 'social being that determines consciousness' and was illustrated frequently by Engels's observations of the nature of class relationships in nineteenth-century capitalism. In Marxism, the most important aspect of 'social existence' is a person's location within the class structure, since the social experience of labouring is crucial in shaping interests, attitudes and expectations. In more collective terms, each class, by virtue of its particular position in the stratification system, generates for itself through the stratum of class intellectuals a culture or ideology which gives conceptual expression to the material conditions of existence of that class. Thus, each class exudes its own distinctive system of beliefs, the precise nature of which is moulded by class interests. In 'The Eighteenth Brumaire of Louis Bonaparte', Marx gave cogent expression to this form of argument:

Upon the different forms of property, upon the social conditions of existence, rises an entire superstructure of distinct and peculiarly formed sentiments, illusions, modes of thought and views of life. The entire class creates and forms them through tradition and upbringing. (Marx and Engels, 1968, pp. 117—18)

The theory suggests that, at least in early capitalism, one would expect to discover a deep fissure in the cultural system of society separating the dominant and subordinate classes. Such a cultural fissure was detected by Engels in the ideological separation of classes in nineteenth-century Britain:

The bourgeoisie has more in common with every other nation of the earth than with the workers in whose midst it lives. The workers speak other dialects, have other thoughts and ideals, other customs and moral principles, a different religion and other politics than those of the bourgeoisie. (Engels, 1968, p. 124)

Although the bourgeoisie control the means of mental production, the existence of the dominant ideology is undermined by the contrary effect of 'social being'. There is thus an apparent contradiction between religion as the 'ruling ideas' of society and a society in which 'social class determines consciousness' and where each class expresses class interest through its own religiosity.

There are broadly two solutions to this apparently contradictory situation in which the same religion simultaneously unifies the social system around a set of core values and expresses the separate interests of contending classes. The first solution is to see religion as a social mechanism which satisfies the psychological needs of different classes. The second solution treats subordinate class-consciousness as a split consciousness.

According to the first perspective, it is argued that religion satisfies the need of the dominant class to feel that its privileged social position is legitimate; however, the same religion, or some version of it, gratifies the need of subordinate groups for consolation in this world or revenge in the next. As a narcotic, religion is the expression of human misery, but it is also a reaction against human suffering ('the expression of real distress and the protest against real distress'). When religious movements against this-worldly injustice fail or are crushed by military repression, they turn towards a solution in the next world or in some indeterminate future. Studies of millenarian movements in the Mediterranean (Hobsbawm, 1963) and cargo cults in South-East Asia (Worsley, 1970) provide useful illustrations of this argument. In general, religion provides solace and comfort for the poor, directing their attention away from political solutions to mundane exploitation. This is why, at least in Germany, Marx and Engels thought that criticism had to begin with the criticism of religion. Religion had the double function of compensating the suffering of the poor with promises of spiritual wealth, while simultaneously legitimating the wealth of the dominant class. One solution to the apparent contradiction of class solidarity versus social integration is thus to argue that by legitimating wealth and compensating for poverty, religion unified society while also giving expression to separate class interests. Religion is thus the social cement of the total society, while being the social opium of the class structure.

Problem of theodicy
This is the classical Marxist explanation of religion in terms of social class ('social being determines consciousness'); however, what I have referred to as the 'mechanism theory' of religion is very widespread in the sociology of religion and the sociology of knowledge. Even those theories which were allegedly fashioned in opposition to crude Marxist reductionism typically present a mechanism theory of religious belief. Some indication of the presence of such a theory can be obtained from a consideration of the role of the concept of 'theodicy' in sociology (Turner, 1981a).

The term 'theodicy', meaning a justification of God's goodness despite the existence of evil, was first systematically employed by Gottfried Leibniz in an essay of 1710 to demonstrate the rationality and morality of the universe. In Leibnizian theodicy, God had created the best of all possible worlds, in which evil, though an expression of the plenitude of reality, did not predominate over goodness and justice. Furthermore, evil often taught morally useful lessons by highlighting or exaggerating our enjoyment of good things. Illness teaches us the great pleasures of our natural health; in short, God turns evil into a means for achieving moral wisdom. Leibniz's essay was dedicated to Queen Sophie Charlotte of Prussia and it has been regarded as a cynical attempt by Leibniz to gain royal support for a philosophical doctrine which legitimated the status quo. The existence of inequality, the power of the state and the affluence of the monarchy can all be conveniently justified by reference to the doctrine of 'the best of all possible worlds'. The theodicy of Leibniz comforted the Queen of Prussia: her serfs continued to experience privations, while she enjoyed the benefits of royal birth in the knowledge that this situation was right and proper in the scheme of her Creator (Russell, 1945).

The concept of theodicy became part of the sociological tradition via Nietzsche's response to the attempts of Kant and Hegel to formulate a philosophical answer to the theological problem of evil. Nietzsche came to locate the problem of evil and theodicy firmly in the history of social groups, especially in the conflict between slaves and masters. For example, Christian morality is a morality of weakness that has its roots in Jewish resentment, the anger of a pariah group against dominant outsiders. Notions of moral goodness are thus grounded in group conflict, particularly in resentment against dominant aristocratic classes. The historical conflict between masters and slaves found its cultural expression in the opposition between moralities of honour and those of humility. Aristocracies develop ideological conceptions of value in terms of their own strength, wealth and prestige; they typically regard themselves as especially chosen to enjoy the fruits of this world. The morality of subordinate groups tends to be the obverse, since they define the worldly as the profane. What in the aristocratic world is 'virtuous' becomes 'evil' in plebeian society. The superordinate theodicy of happiness justifies secular dominance in this world; subordinate theodicies of suffering explain present misfortune in terms of future recompense.

Nietzsche located these dualistic theodicies in the Jewish experience of exile and diaspora, and in the feeling of *ressentiment* which coloured the psalmist's concepts of revenge and justice:

The Jews achieved that miracle of inversion of values thanks to which life on earth has for a couple of millennia acquired a new and dangerous fascination — their prophets fused 'rich', 'godless', 'evil', 'violent', 'sensual' into one and were the first to coin the word 'world' as a term of infamy. It is in this inversion of values (with which is involved the employment of the word for 'poor' as a synonym of 'holy' and 'friend') that the significance of the Jewish people resides: with *them* there begins the *slave revolt in morals*. (Nietzsche, 1973, p. 100)

Christianity inherited and elaborated these anti-values of slavery so that its emphasis on pity, mercy and charity was the product of weakness and resentfulness. The moral point of Nietzsche's 'natural history of morals' is to show that there is no virtue in merciful actions which emerge from a position of weakness. The genuinely moral person merely laughs 'at the weaklings which think themselves good because they have lame paws' (Nietzsche, 1933, p. 108).

Nietzsche's views on the Christian theodicy of suffering were not entirely original. His contrast between yes-saying and no-saying philosophies, between Dionysianism and Apollinian ethics were anticipated by Heinrich Heine, who also influenced Marx's attitude to Jewishness and politics (Lilge, 1960). Nietzsche's specific contribution was to provide a critical social psychology of group moralities, thereby laying the foundations for a dynamic sociology of knowledge.

Weber

It is possible to detect in Weber's sociology of religion a strong tendency to reduce religious beliefs to the interests and social psychology of classes, despite Weber's overtly critical views on Marx and Nietzsche. He rejected Marx's social-opium theory and Kautsky's view in *Foundations of Christianity* (1925) that the prophets were leaders of plebeian revolutions. By contrast, Weber in *Ancient Judaism* (1952) emphasised the social isolation of the Yahwistic prophets who spurned the psychological need of the masses for magical compensation. Weber also thought that Nietzsche's notion of *ressentiment* had a limited value in comparative religion, since, for example, Buddhism was 'the most radical antithesis to every type of *ressentiment* morality' (Weber, 1966, p. 116).

Although Weber overtly rejected this reductionist interpretation of religious beliefs, he did in practice characteristically employ a model of religion in which the content of religion could be directly related to systems of social stratification. In particular, Weber's sociology of religion was dominated by the basic dichotomy of theodicies of privileged and non-privileged groups. In privileged social groups, particularly those dominated by warriors, there is little propensity for a religion of salvation and compensation based on a sense of personal unworthiness. The sense of individual value, which high social status confers, is incompatible with a religion of collective *Weltschmerz*. Dominant social groups tend to be indifferent to religions of personal salvation from sinfulness, because such belief systems embrace religious humility as a virtue, a notion which is 'remote from all elite political classes, particularly the warrior nobles' (Weber, 1966, p. 85). These groups do not require much from religion beyond simple prayers for military victory. However, the religiously indifferent dominant class may fully recognise the political importance of religion as a cultural bromide of the subordinate classes. Such is historically the attitude of prestigious bureaucracies. The Roman bureaucracy of antiquity adhered to a social-opium viewpoint:

The bureaucratic class is usually characterized by a profound disesteem of all irrational religion, combined, however, with a recognition of the usefulness of this type of religion as a device for controlling the people. (Weber, 1966, p. 89)

The German officer corps of Weber's time also held the view that orthodox Christianity 'constituted the best fodder for the recruits' (Weber, 1966, p. 90), but bureaucratic support for the religion of the masses (*Volks religiosität*) found its epitome in the Confucian ethic. Although it was Hsun Tzu rather than Confucius who developed the agnostic humanism of the master to its fullest expression (Dawson, 1981, p. 44), Weber's conclusion that the Confucianism of the Chinese patrimonial bureaucracy 'was indifferent to religion' (1951, p. 146) has remained largely unchallenged.

Although the privileged strata of bureaucrats and warriors were either indifferent to religion or approached religion as a source of divine legitimation of their mundane good fortune, the disprivileged were drawn to religion for relief and recompense. The psychological requirements of the overprivileged — 'this psychological reassurance of legitimacy' (Weber, 1966, p. 107) — stand in reverse relationship to the ethic of compensation which is associated with the underprivileged — their 'particular need is for release from suffering' (Weber, 1966, p. 108).

Weber outlined a variety of responses to suffering which he treated as constitutive of the basic differences between the world religions. The theories of individual merit in Hinduism and Buddhism, as formulated in the karma-samsara doctrine, had the consequence of justifying inequality in this world by treating injustice in terms of personal failings in previous incarnations. At the other extreme, Weber located the collectivist theodicy of the Old Testament prophets for whom the tribes of Israel were a chosen people, bound to a jealous God by a sacred covenant. In Christianity this tension between religion and 'the world' in Jewish prophecy partly reappeared in the contradiction between the ethic of brotherly love and the presence of political violence in the state. Within all these religious traditions, Weber thought that the poor would periodically seek emotional compensation in ecstatic rituals, the services of holy men, miracles and orgiastic release in the sort of Dionysian cults which found their adherents in the marginal groups of classical society (Gouldner, 1967). In Christianity, however, the anti-magical nature of the Protestant tradition meant that, according to Weber, religious resentment frequently found an outlet in millenarian–messianic protests against this-worldly oppression so that religion was inextricably bound up with the history of European class relationships.

Contemporary views
This view of theodicies of compensation and legitimation can also be detected in the sociological analyses of Karl Mannheim, E. P. Thompson, Peter Berger and Thomas Luckmann. The dichotomisation of world-views by class position was, for instance, notably

prominent in Mannheim's study of *Ideology and Utopia* (1960). Ideological systems of belief are prevalent among dominant groups because their class consciousness prevents them from adequately perceiving aspects of their social context which might undermine their social dominance. The beliefs of oppressed groups are also typically 'situationally incongruous', but their ideological outlook is utopian in that they perceive only those aspects of their social context which promise immanent change and revolutionary transformation. Mannheim was in practice more interested in the history of utopian mentality which attempts to transcend the given social reality than with the ideological world-view which aims at social stability. Mannheim's study focused, therefore, on the rise and fall of various utopian mentalities from chiliasm to communism; these utopian mentalities have common themes of social opposition and are the product of 'social strata struggling for ascendency' (Mannheim, 1960, p. 187). Mannheim's account of the development of utopian thought through the history of Christianity followed Nietzsche's 'natural history' of morals because Mannheim argued that Christianity is 'primarily intelligible in terms of the resentment of oppressed strata' (Mannheim, 1960, p. 40).

In contemporary sociology of religion, the theme of dichotomous theodicies has once more arisen through Peter Berger's interest in religion as a 'sacred canopy'. Berger (1969) divides theodicies into those of happiness, which explain and justify the prevailing system of social inequality, and those of suffering, which provide solace making misery more tolerable. Following Weber, he provides a typology of theodician beliefs ranging from the individualist theories of rebirth through the dualist assumptions of Zoroastrianism to the violent chiliasm of the Anabaptists. Although collectivist theodicies of revenge and restoration that appear in the monotheistic traditions of Christianity and Islam may periodically threaten to destroy the status quo, most radical theodicies tend towards resignation or pathetic aspiration of some spiritual kingdom of just recompense. Because the millennium does not appear and 'the Madhi turns out to be but another all too mundane ruler' (Berger, 1969, p. 70), this-worldly radical theodicies are typically converted into conservative other-worldly doctrines. The transition in Iranian religious history of the radical Babis into the pacific Baha'is in the nineteenth century is one obvious illustration of this change in theodicy (Berger, 1957). Despite occasional revolutionary outbursts, the general function of the religions of the oppressed is to provide a solatium to those whom the Creator appears to have so conspicuously forgotten.

Summary
In this chapter I have outlined a number of theories of religion which

treat religious beliefs as part of the dominant ideology of a society and which argue that the principal function of such an ideology is to provide a social opium for oppressed social classes. The social structure is integrated, not by a common social cement, but by the narcotic effect of religion which diminishes the revolutionary potential of subordinate groups.

The theory of social opium typically runs into the difficulty of accounting for the presence of social conflict, especially of social movements whose radical aspirations are fired by religious imagery of revenge, return and restoration. This problem is particularly marked in Marxist views of religion, which want to argue that each class produces its own class consciousness while also arguing that there is a dominant ideology that overcomes separate class interests. The principal solution to these troublesome empirical issues is to argue that religion is a social mechanism which legitimates power for the dominant class and which compensates for the suffering of the underprivileged.

A second type of solution to this apparently contradictory situation might be to argue that most subordinate classes have a 'split consciousness', in that they simultaneously produce their own view of the world and inhale the religious atmosphere produced by the dominant culture of the dominant class. The culture of peasants, workers and underclasses will typically be an unstable mixture of indigenous beliefs and imported beliefs from those classes or their representatives which control the means of mental production. The conventional interpretation of working-class beliefs normally assumes the presence of a divided consciousness (Parkin, 1972; Mann, 1973). In the religious history of Britain, the various 'labour sects' of the nineteenth-century working class illustrate this curious blending of cultures in so far as they combined a working-class emphasis on the mobility of labour, mutual help and collective sentiments with a middle-class ethic of asceticism, individualism and achievement (Hobsbawm, 1963).

Unfortunately, these various attempts, both in orthodox Marxism and in mainstream sociology, to provide a class-theoretical, social-opium theory of religion tend to encapsulate the main theoretical difficulties of the dominant ideology thesis. These can be summarised thus. (1) They fail to provide a convincing account of the nature of the apparatus of ideological transmission by which beliefs are circulated in a society organised into distinct classes. (2) Consequently they exaggerate the degree to which the subordinate class actually adheres to the dominant ideology, while simultaneously neglecting the effect of ideology on the dominant class. (3) They overstate the importance of ideological incorporation, while failing to understand the importance of coercive forms of control. (4) The nature of the class structure is typically portrayed as a dichotomous system of stratification, whereby the two theodicies nicely conform to the privileged and disprivileged classes.

Although subsequent chapters are highly critical of all the assumptions of the dominant ideology thesis as it emerges in the study of religion, this book as a whole adheres to a decisively materialistic view of religion. The principal argument here is that in the dominant class one basic function of religion has been to protect the flow of property in a system of primogeniture by providing moral control of women and offspring. When the forms of property changed in the nineteenth century, religion shifted away from moral uniformity to pluralism.

Before considering religion as a system of control over female bodies — a theory which was prefigured in Engels's *The Origin of the Family, Private Property and the State* (n.d.) — there is another economic analysis of religion which we must consider seriously. The theory of religion as an exchange system works at two levels, as a system of transactions between men and gods and between religious leaders and disciples. The first level was introduced into the anthropology of religion in the nineteenth century in the form of a debate concerning totemic feasts and has been developed subsequently by Claude Lévi-Strauss. The second level is occupied by Weber's theory of virtuoso and mass religion in which the religious virtuosi are supported by the productive labour of the masses in exchange for charismatic gifts.

These theories of control and exchange conceive religion as inextricably bound up with the materiality of the world. In particular, it is difficult to produce a theory of religion without providing a theory of health, since religious salvation is historically tied to notions of physical well-being. In order to produce a sociology of religion, we will consequently have to consider various processes by which human bodies are produced, reproduced and exchanged.

4 Religion as Exchange

Religious universalism

The form of social relationships between lay people and religious specialists has been a perennial preoccupation of the sociology of religion. Status inequalities within the religious world appear to be as persistent and universal as they are in the secular sphere. In most religious traditions, lay people tend to assume the status of second-class citizens because they lack the skills, training, magical powers or charismatic endowments of full-time religious personnel and professional religious leaders. Although women tend to provide the bulk of religious followers, men dominate the higher echelons of religious organisations because they are not contaminated by menstruation and childbirth, are not confined to the domestic hearth, or because they possess superior rational knowledge of divine powers (Christian, 1972).

The religious hierarchy of grace largely reflects the division of the world into sacred and profane, which Durkheim (1961) thought was the axial distinction in the religious world-view. Lay people are, by definition, constantly involved in routine, everyday activities in secular employments which are necessary to produce food and reproduce people. The superior status of religious charismatics depends on their clear detachment from that grinding reality of domestic labour and lifelong employment. This social detachment from the profane world may be denoted by a variety of social insignia — clerical dress, tonsures or rabbinical clothing — and by peculiarities of status, most notably seclusion and chastity. These features are marks of the unequal distributions within human communities of religious grace, charisma or *baraka*.

The existence of religious stratification stands in a paradoxical relation to the formal doctrines of prophetic, monotheistic, biblical religions, that is, to Christianity, Islam and Judaism. At a formal level, the doctrinal core of these Abrahamic faiths is grounded in a radical universalism by which people are children of God regardless of their peculiar distinguishing marks of sex, ethnicity, age and social origin. Although Yahweh had a special relationship with the tribes of Israel, he was not a local, tribal God. In principal, a covenant with Yahweh was available to all peoples. In a similar fashion, Islam proclaims an egalitarian and universal call to a life of responsibility and acceptance. The world 'Islam' is derived from the Arabic root *salama*, which means both surrender and contentment or peace. A 'Muslim' is anyone who has fundamentally accepted divine revelation and will, so there is a sense in which Jews and Christians are 'Muslims'. In this inclusive meaning, any creature who lives according to divine laws is a 'Muslim' (Nasr, 1966; Watt, 1969). Since the Koran as revelation is addressed to humanity, classical Islam developed a profound opposition to religious inequalities within the religious community; the absence of an ecclesiastical, sacerdotal leadership is one illustration of this 'democratic' principle. In Christianity, the universality of Pauline theology found its expression in the doctrine of a 'priesthood of all believers' or a community of the faithful. It has been claimed (Weber, 1958) that the egalitarian ethos of Christianity played a major part in the urbanisation of European societies, because it meant that cities could develop on the basis of a common creedal adherence. Christianity thus contributed to the detribalisation of Europe, permitting the emergence of a strong urban coherence and civil autonomy. In these Abrahamic faiths, the fatherhood of God implied an egalitarian brotherhood of man, but ironically hierarchical religiosity, especially in the form of saintship, became a persistent feature of the social structure of these religions.

The Abrahamic faiths can be conceptualised sociologically in terms of a pendulum between ecumenical egalitarianism and localised hierarchies. The doctrinal thrust of these monotheistic religions is towards a fraternal equality, but their sociological form is towards permanent, hierarchical inequality. To some extent, all universalistic religions will experience the organisational dilemma which Ernst Troeltsch designated as the central conflict between Church and sect within the Christian gospel in his classic study, *The Social Teaching of the Christian Churches* (1931). The Church is an institution which embraces the whole nation in a hierarchical structure, where membership depends on birth rather than on conversion. The cost of social universalism is a relaxation of standards of orthodoxy and practice, and a tolerance of minimal forms of commitment. Church adherence thus tends to be formal and institutionalised through objective rites of baptism and confirmation. Within the Church, there is a rigid distinction between the laity and the priesthood, in which the latter have a monopolistic hold over sacraments and doctrine. Sects, by contrast, do not aspire to be 'popular' institutions, but exclusive communities of saints. The truth of the gospel they preach is widely available within the community of the elect, but inaccessible to the state and society as a whole. Sects require legal and political tolerance from the state, but within its own religious boundaries the sect requires discipline, control and rigorous criteria of membership. Sectarian groups thus achieve the goal of doctrinal and practical orthodoxy at the cost of influencing the nation. In this sense, Church and sect are alternative solutions to the contradiction between religious purity and social influence.

Church—sect typology

The debate concerning Troeltsch's church—sect typology has become the hallmark of classical sociology of religion. The typology became closely associated with various explanations of religious change, since it can be argued that sects, especially those with an evangelistic attitude towards the larger community, tend, by successfully converting new members, to develop into churches (Wilson, 1959). In British religious history, the development of Methodism from a conversionist sect into a denomination provides one illustration of this social process, but even this example is somewhat controversial since it can be claimed that early Methodism was a religious order inside Anglicanism and not a schismatic sect (Hill and Turner, 1971). The typology continues to be a focus of sociological discussion, despite periodic requests for its conceptual demolition (Eister, 1967) or reformulation (Robertson, 1970).

It is interesting to note that, although Weber frequently used the terms 'sect' and 'church' in his sociology of religion, his analyses of the relationship between religious professionals and laity, religious groups and society, or sacred and profane rested on a rather different theoretical model of religion as a system of exchange. In the copious footnotes which accompanied *The Protestant Ethic and the Spirit of Capitalism*, Weber made frequent reference to the fact that Troeltsch had already covered many of the issues relating to Protestant sectarianism. Weber commented, however, that, whereas Troeltsch was concerned mainly 'with the doctrines of religion', he was 'interested rather in their practical results' (1965, p. 188). A persistent criticism of the Troeltsch typology has been that it retains a theological rather than sociological problematic. Weber's own typology of religious forms depended upon a covert economic analogy that the relationship between gods and men, and between saints and laity required an exchange of different forms of wealth.

Virtuoso—mass religion

This implicit parallel between economic and religious exchange systems formed the basis of Weber's typology of virtuoso—mass religiosity, which Weber employed in a wide variety of religious and cultural settings. This typology in Weber's sociology has been strangely neglected as a perspective on social relationships involving exchange and inequality.

An exception to the general neglect is to be found in Guenther Roth's employment of the notion of 'ideological virtuosi' in his analysis of modern revolutionary movements (Roth and Schluchter, 1979). Roth notes, in my view correctly, that an essential feature of all virtuoso leadership is its complete separation or relative autonomy from direct labour and economic employment. The majority are always forced to adhere to this-worldly material interests in order to survive; neither businessmen nor workers characteristically produce a systematically ethical view of reality:

Instead, religious and ethical creativity has typically been found among what Weber calls groups without direct economic interests — rentiers of various kinds and marginal groups of intellectuals outside the dominant status groups, whether they were declassed, petty-bourgeois, quasi-proletarian, or pariah. (Roth and Schluchter, 1979, p. 155)

At least in principle, virtuosi could be separated from mundane labour under a variety of distinctive circumstances, such as unemployment, retirement, patronage or private means. On these grounds, there is no reason why religious virtuosi (that is, persons committed to a full-time and single-minded adherence to a set of religious principles) would also be a social elite.

This notion appears to be the starting-point of Weber's commentary on religious stratification, namely, that the unequal distribution of charisma (as between the virtuosi and the mass) is not correlated with the unequal distribution of secular wealth. In short, charismatic stratification and secular stratification do not correspond. Although Weber started out with this premiss, there are good reasons for believing, independently of Weber, that sacred and profane systems of stratification will intersect empirically. Furthermore, there are indications in Weber's own analysis that his view of religion involved the assumption that there is an exchange relationship between the virtuosi and the mass. The religious elite has to exchange the benefits of charisma for various forms of payment and tribute in order to maintain their separation from labour and the market-place. The sacred status of charismatic virtuosi rests on the secular labour of the laity. Weber regarded this system of religious inequality, based on unequal exchanges of charismatic blessings for earthly tribute, as a universal dimension of world religions, embracing such diverse elements as the *bhakti* piety of Hindu cults, sainthood in Catholicism, the monks of Hinayana Buddhism and the Sufi saints of Islam.

The common basis of these diverse forms of supererogational piety lies in the 'empirical fact' that people are 'differently qualified' from a religious point of view; charisma is a sort of 'talent' which, like red hair or musicality, is not equally distributed in human groups:

The sacred values that have been most cherished, the ecstatic and visionary capacities of shamans, sorcerers, ascetics and pneumatics of all sorts, could not be obtained by everyone. (Weber, 1961, p. 287)

In most circumstances, various forms of 'intensive religiosity' tend to result in 'a sort of status stratification in accordance with differences in charismatic qualifications' (Weber, 1961, p. 287). This religious stratification by charisma as a kind of spiritual prestige is to be measured along a continuum between pure virtuosity and mass religiosity. Because the majority of the population is permanently immersed in the demands of everyday survival, the mass cannot cultivate what little religious 'talent' they may possess by extra religious practices, contemplation or ascetic devotions. The mass is forced into a kind of dependence on a religious aristocracy who develop their religious abilities on behalf or instead of the mass. Although the drive for salvation and personal meaning may be very widespread, only a minority through innate talent and effort will attain the ultimate goals of religious mysticism or asceticism, because the majority has to deal with pressing needs of survival. Religious systems, despite their egalitarian doctrines, tend towards pyramidal structures of status inequality. Wherever religion is based on 'a systematic procedure of sanctification', one finds that religious 'rebirth' will be limited to an inner circle of adepts:

rebirth seemed to be accessible only to an aristocracy of those possessing religious qualifications . . . The earliest Christian sources represent these religious virtuosi as comprising a particular category, distinguished from their comrades in the community, and they later constituted the monastic orders. In Protestantism they formed the ascetic sects or pietistic conventicles. In Judaism they were the *perushim* (*Pharisaioi*), an aristocracy with respect to salvation which stood in contrast to the *am haarez*. (Weber, 1966, pp. 162—3)

There are thus two general features of Weber's virtuoso/mass typology as an orientation towards the analysis of practices of religious sanctification. First, human populations are universally stratified in terms of layers of charismatic proclivities. Second, there will be strong pressures among ordinary religious followers to diminish and reduce virtuoso religious demands in order to create a match between the demands of everyday existence and the demands of religious salvation. The pendulum swing in Troeltsch's typology between church and sect finds its equivalent in Weber's virtuoso/mass typology in the relationship between the purification of religious traditions by virtuosi and the accommodation or acculturation of 'great traditions' to the mundane practicalities of local conditions. Organised religion is forced to secure a compromise between elite and mass religiosity:

With the exception of Judaism and Protestantism, all religions and religious ethics have had to reintroduce cults of saints, heroes or functional gods in order to accommodate themselves to the needs of the masses . . . Islam and Catholicism were compelled to accept local, functional and occupational gods as saints, the veneration of which constituted the real religion of the masses in everyday life. (Weber, 1966, pp. 103—4)

In Christianity and Islam, there have been periodically strong puritanical reactions to saint worship combined with an emphasis on religious egalitarianism, the effect of which would be to rule out the intermediate role of charismatic saintship. Although religious elites are drawn towards a concentration on virtuoso standards, they remain dependent on lay tribute, contributions and levees. The demands of charismatic saintship remain outside the capacities of the religiously disprivileged, and this situation of underachievement provides the context for religious affiliation and discipleship. The laity performs necessary labour for religious personnel, without which religious charismatics could not enjoy an independence from the market-place. In return, the laity receive the religious blessing of the elect's charisma, typically in the form of health, fortune and longevity. There is, however, a paradoxical contradiction between the health flowing from charisma and the wealth generated by secular employment.

As cultural categories, the sacred and the profane are mutually exclusive. The sacred in society, according to Durkheim's formulation, refers to persons and phenomena which are set aside and protected by custom and ritual from the possibility of profane contamination. Like Rudolf Otto's account (1929) of the holy as the essential focus of religious experience and activity, Durkheim's category of the sacred points to that reality which transcends the individual and the momentary by embracing the collective and the extraordinary. The profane world is merely a residual category of the trivial and the ordinary which dominates everyday reality. The core of the profane world is simply the world of work, production and domesticity.

Although the profane and the sacred thus stand in profound opposition, the virtuosi who embody the sacred in the life of society are typically forced into a parasitic dependence on the labour which is carried out in the profane world. The labour of the laity provides the means by which extraordinary religious talent can be cultivated and trained without involvement in secular routines. In this respect, the religious hierarchy tends to parallel the secular system of stratification. To give this paradox a different formulation, the interests of laity and virtuosi are mutually exclusive. In principle, the virtuoso aims for enlightenment, release, mystical union or personal salvation. The interests of the mass are organised around mundane needs and issues, primarily health and wealth. Through the religious division of labour between those who labour in this world and those who labour for the next, these contradictory interests can be satisfied:

a deep abyss separates the way of life of the layman from that of the community of virtuosos. The rule of the status groups of religious virtuosos over the religious community readily shifts into a magical anthropolatry; the virtuoso is directly worshipped as a Saint, or at least laymen buy his blessing and his magical powers as a means of promoting mundane success or religious salvation. As the peasant was to the landlord, so the layman was to the Buddhist and Jainist bhikshu: ultimately, mere sources of tribute. (Weber, 1961, p. 289)

The less people are involved in the burden of labour, the more they are available for elite or prestigious religious positions. Although there is evidence to suggest that the religious elite is typically recruited from the secular elite, it also follows that retired or elderly persons are more likely than young, employed workers to adopt demanding religious duties and functions. For example, in Buddhist villages the elderly, especially widows, become *upasaka*, that is, lay persons who form a village elite because they can fulfil more Buddhist religious duties than young men (Obeyesekere, 1968).

Max Weber's sociology of religion was largely organised around the problem of the drive for personal salvation, the directions of salvational paths and, finally, the accommodation of this salvational quest to the practical exigencies of daily life. The corner-stone of these studies was Weber's analysis of the quest for personal salvation in Calvinism, which was ultimately realised in this-worldly callings in business and entrepreneurship (Roth and Schluchter, 1979). Weber's sociology of world religions remained incomplete at the time of his death in 1920. His analysis of Judaism, for example, in *Ancient Judaism* (1952) was, in fact, less concerned with the direction taken by the Jewish salvational quest than with the social background of pre-Diaspora prophecy and with the ritual consequences of the pariah status of post-Diaspora Jewry. Similarly, Weber's commentaries on Islam (Turner, 1974a) and Catholicism (Fanfani, 1933; Nelson, 1969a) were obviously programmatic. Consequently, Weber's virtuoso/mass dichotomy invites substantive elaboration and exploration. Weber's virtuoso/mass typology has been applied elsewhere to the hierarchical charismatic structure of early Wesleyan Methodism (Turner, 1981a). In order to demonstrate the range of Weber's model, two contrasted forms of elitist spirituality — Hasidic Judaism and Sufi Islam — provide informative examples.

Hasidic Judaism

Although Wach (1971, p. 336) associates virtuoso religion with ascetic denial of mundane reality, both Hasidism and Sufism represent mystical alternatives to the formal rationality of the Torah and the Koran. Hasidism, in particular, is to be interpreted as an eighteenth-century mystical movement against the social conditions which characterised *shtetl* society in eastern Europe. Hasidism, founded by Rabbi Israel ben Eliezer (1700—60) and known as Baal Shem Tov (the 'Master of the Good Name'), was in part a product of the grinding poverty experienced by the Ukrainian and Polish *shtetl*. The misery of Jewish ghetto existence was reinforced by pogroms and by the failure of Jewish millenarianism at the time of Sabbattai Zevi (1626—1716), the 'false Messiah' of European Jewry. In response to the social crisis engendered by the collapse of the millenarian expectations, educated Jews fell back upon an increasingly rigid interpretation of the Torah, while the poor and uneducated were drawn to the simplicity and emotionalism of Hasidic practice and belief. Whereas millenarianism pointed to a redemption in the future, Hasidism (or Chasidism) affirmed the joy of the present, the consolations of everyday life and the spiritual value of the ordinary people, the *Am-haaretz* (the 'people of the soil').

Although Hasidism has been regarded by the rabbinate as a heterodox or revolutionary movement, in many ways the teachings of the Baal Shem Tov (or 'Besht' from his initials BST) were an attempt to formulate an integration of the traditional principles of Halachah and Haggadah, external practice and internal piety (Epstein, 1959). Hasidism taught that ecstatic redemption could be achieved by the ordinary mass of people, without special training and qualifications, since the way to God was through joyous, fervent prayer. The movement thus presented an egalitarian doctrine of this-worldly redemption, which did not require a denial of or flight from the ordinary world of work and family life. Hasidism was a spiritual road out of the misery of the *shtetl* for the ordinary man whose lack of special training traditionally limited his access to the higher culture of the Torah and whose life precluded total adherence to rabbinic ritual, which only an elite could normally attain.

Hasidic doctrine affirmed the immanence of God in the world, both human and natural. Consequently, the everyday world of human existence, including work, sleep, food, drink and sexuality, was touched or infused with God's loving presence. The Hasidic response to this God-suffused reality was neither one of ascetic denial or mystical flight, but one of celebration in the form of chanting, dance and festival. The dancing of the ecstatic Hasidism came to be regarded as an antinomian threat to the orderly, rational world, over which the scholarly rabbinate had presided and which had been the principal defence of Judaism against dilution and accommodation. The Hasidic community thus came to be regarded with fear and hostility on the part of the *Mithnaggedim*, who, under the leadership of Elijah ben Solomon (1720—97), reaffirmed the traditional place of the Torah against charismatic inspiration in the life of the Jewish community.

There were, of course, ample grounds for the suspicions of the *Mithnaggedim* that the Hasidim were practitioners of magic and religious orgy. In their view, Besht was part of a series of Baale Shem (Masters of the Name), whose knowledge of the name of God gave them magical powers and the capacity to perform miracles. Enlightened, educated Jews of the nineteenth century looked on Hasidism with considerable embarrassment:

it could hardly attract liberal western European Jews who were on their way to full emancipation and to greater participation in Western European culture.

Hassidism appeared to them much too superstitious and obscurantist a movement of ignorants, too intensely fervid, emotional, irrational and mystical, though comforting for the masses. (Shmueli, 1969, p. 10)

It was not until the optimistic expectation of political and social emancipation for European Jewry had itself collapsed in the aftermath of fascism that Martin Buber's sensitive reappraisal of Hasidism (1956) paved the way for a more positive interpretation of Hasidic doctrine.

Hasidism emerged as a popular, egalitarian religion of the poor, which provided a spirituality consistent with the demands of everyday life, but it rapidly acquired the hierarchical features of all genuinely charismatic movements. The structure of Hasidism around inequalities in charismatic abilities is illustrated by the religious differences between *hasidim* ('the pious') as followers, the *Zaddikim* (helpers) and the *Rebbe* (teacher or leader). Whereas the Baal Shem Tov had believed that the prayers of the ordinary folk were as efficacious as those of the most exalted, his followers, especially Dov Baer of Meseritz (1710–72), taught that only the *Zaddik*, the wholly righteous, could approach God directly. The common people were too enmeshed in the cares of everyday life to pray with the necessary concentration and devotion. The *Zaddik* consequently became religious intermediaries who, through their prayers and righteous example, secured the blessings of God on behalf of the common mass. These earthly and heavenly blessings were achieved by the *Rebbe* for the inner circle of the *Zaddikim*, not through their superior learning, but by charismatic authority which eventually was passed from father to son as the possession of charismatic lineages.

Although the charisma of the *Rebbe* was an intensely personal possession, the leader gathered around him a community of followers, bound together by common allegiance, practice and belief. These nineteenth-century Hasidic communities of eastern Europe were focused around the 'court' of individual leaders, whose patriarchal household became the location of pilgrimage and festival. Within this court, the *Rebbe* was withdrawn from the cares of ordinary existence through the financial support of his followers, who in return were recipients of religious blessing and secular comfort. Followers sought advice, relief and consolation from their 'own' *Rebbe*, whose teaching and practice did not necessarily interfere with the official rabbi, who retained juridical power in the exercise of the Law. The hallmark of each *Rebbe* was the development of a special technique or way, the *derekh*, by which the *Rebbe* approached God in order to secure blessings to satisfy the needs of his followers. The metaphor of the way, which is common to both Hasidism and Sufism, implied differences in the religious abilities of fellow travellers and so Hasidism eventually embraced the notion of levels of religious attainment:

The concept of grade or 'level' is the basis of the Tsaddik's position among his followers. He is the one who through his own mystical efforts, through his descent from and spiritual relationship to the great teacher Baal Shem or his disciples has attained the highest level a mortal can reach, the 'level' of an intermediary between God and His sinful unfortunate children — the people of Israel. (Zborowski and Herzog, 1962, p. 168)

Like saints in Roman Catholicism, the *Rebbe* intercedes between his people and God, pleading their cause and prompting divine forgiveness. Out of this pleading emerged the concept of God, not as the harsh Father who imposed Exile as a punishment for transgressions, but as a divine figure of compassion, tenderness and mercy.

These inequalities of charisma between leader and followers also contained a necessary element of social exchange. The ordinary Hasidism needed the *Rebbe*, because their mundane existence precluded the achievement of higher religious levels; however, a *Rebbe* without followers was not a true *Rebbe*. In order to withdraw into the privileged life of the court and to provide his poor followers with financial help in times of crisis, the *Rebbe* depended on gifts and aid from disciples. The communal life of the court was organised around frequent celebrations, requiring food and drink to enhance the enjoyment of the dance. These celebrations eased the sorrows of the Hasidim and were also an expression of the religious joy of the community. The greater the celebration, the greater the status of the *Rebbe*. The dances and drinking sessions required considerable communal outlay in goods and cash. The *Rebbe*'s mediation or help was noted by payment of a 'redemption' (*pidyan*), paid to the *gabai* who negotiated appropriate payments for the services of the *Rebbe*. The growing wealth of the *Rebbe* and his family thus paradoxically became a social indicator of the spiritual standing of his particular court.

This exchange relationship between leader and follower was ultimately recognised as a religious principle in the teaching of the Hasidic leaders. The relationship between the *Zaddik* and the people:

is compared to that between substance and form in the life of the individual, between body and soul. The soul must not boast that it is more holy than the body, for only in that it has climbed down into the body and works through its limbs can the soul attain its own perfection. The body, on the other hand, may not brag of supporting the soul, for when the soul leaves, the flesh falls into decay. Thus the zaddikim need the multitude, and the multitude need the zaddikim. (Buber, 1956, p. 7)

Thus Hasidism contained a religious principle of mutual respect through exchange; however, it also expressed a sociological principle of religious stratification in that manual labour was recognised as incompatible with the virtuoso religious life: intensity of prayer was not possible in conjunction with intensive labour. This articulation of religious and secular stratification was even maintained in the transplantation of Hasidic communities to the urban ghettos of North America.

The Hasidic community of Williamsburg, for example, is stratified into six distinct levels or religious classes depending on their frequency and intensity of religious practice, and these strata are signified by special forms of clothing. Social standing in the community is also indicated by the emotional intensity with which rituals are performed:

> The greater the number of rituals and the more intensely they are observed, the greater the esteem accorded a person. The rites, rituals and the elements necessary for these performances are prescribed by law. But the law does not indicate the mannerism, the body movement, the emotional ecstasy, the joy or sadness that accompany the performance. Since these expressions are not specifically prescribed, they are completely Hasidic in character. (Poll, 1969, p. 60)

Although the whole Hasidic community is thought to enjoy higher status than assimilated Jews within American society, within the community itself those Jews whose behaviour approximates the standards set by the *Rebbe* have higher status than merely marginal adherents. The *Rebbes*, who form the core of the community, exhibit Hasidic standards in every aspect of their lives and, although their authority derives from their relationship to God, they are held to be direct descendants of prestigious Hasidic lineages. Religious mobility within the community is possible for those prepared to adopt more intensive religious life-styles, but increasing religious activity has important consequences for secular behaviour and involves certain economic costs.

Greater religious activity requires a certain freedom from direct economic labour, but it also requires greater expenditure on religious goods and services. Therefore, there is a strong correlation between religious and economic practice. Hasidic Jews prefer self-employment, typically in small, owner-occupier shops, which permits greater involvement in religious activities and hence greater social status. In general, a Jew:

> automatically becomes more religiously active as soon as his occupation makes such increased activity appropriate. Or a person may choose a certain occupation because it gives him more time and opportunity to be religiously active. (Poll, 1969, p. 117)

Alternatively, a person may seek employment as a religious functionary. The implication of these various occupational choices is, however, perfectly clear — low occupational status is directly associated with low religious status.

Although the *Rebbe* provides the normative core of the community and contributes in a vital way to the maintenance and continuity of Hasidism in a secular environment, the *Rebbe* is dependent on his 'congregation' for support or, more exactly, he is part of an important exchange of worldly for religious goods. This exchange is expressed in the language of duty and privilege, since it is a religious obligation to share one's secular wealth with a holy man who is regarded as a pillar of the community. This principle applies generally to religious services so that the circumciser (*mohel*) receives a payment, not for the actual act of circumcision, but because he is a person who is worthy of support. The continuity of this form of stratified religion depends significantly on the success of the Hasidic community in a secular, urban environment: namely, on the ability of Hasidic Jews to resist assimilation. In turn, the continuity of the community depends on the maintenance of a charismatic hierarchy as the exclusive vehicle of Hasidic values. Hierarchy and sociological continuity appear, therefore, to be mutually related in a functional circle of reinforcement.

Islam

Despite their long history of inter-religious conflict, Judaism and Islam share a number of common sociological features. They can be regarded as variations on a common theme of ethical prophecy, transcendental monotheism, divine revelation and communal salvation. In both, scripture and law as interpreted by scholars define the orthodox core of practice and belief, uniting believers into a community which has a teleological significance. It can, of course, equally be argued that the institutionalisation of this common theme and the impact of historical contingency on the development of these religions have produced a fundamental divorce in theological outlook. Whereas Islam was forged in the context of imperial expansion, exile and diaspora have shaped the tragic vision of Jewish expectations of return and restoration. The contrasted history of pogrom and conquest has fundamentally transformed the common theme into many detailed divergences, in particular the criteria of membership within the two religious communities (Yuval-Davis, 1980).

Despite these obvious differences, the situation of the unlettered believer in both systems is rather similar, in that the untutored have limited access to the scriptural core which ultimately defines holiness. In both Islam and Judaism, there is, so to speak, a common deviant subsystem. Whereas in Roman Catholicism saintship provides the normative model of religious orthodoxy, the radical egalitarianism of the central system precludes an official hierarchy of saints and prescribes a collectivity of scholars without sacerdotal functions. In consequence, Islam has been characterised as a dichotomous system catering for the separate needs of literate townspeople and illiterate tribesmen on the periphery of social and religious life (Gellner, 1969a). Urban Islamic piety is ascetic and puritanical, involving direct access to God through the Koran and without the mediation of holy men. In tone, this piety is rational and formal rather than emotional and spontaneous. The enduring characteristic of this form of religiosity is its profound hostility to the image so that calligraphy and non-representational art in the form of the floral or geometric arabesque were the dominant decorational mode of civic and religious architecture (Hodgson, 1964). The constituents of rural religiosity were diametrically opposed to the formally rational core of urban life-styles. For illiterate tribesmen, the holy man or marabout was the emotional embodiment of religion, which was hierarchically arranged in terms of lineage charisma. The mood of maraboutic religiosity was intense, colourful and personal, typically involving magic, divination and miracle-working (Westermarck, 1968).

It is not just that the tribesman requires the mediating religious services of the marabout or that the holy men offer counselling and health services. The saints of Islam in a tribal context traditionally mediated between contending tribes. Saints provide a crucial role of arbitration in inter-tribal disputes (Gellner, 1969b). Although the emphasis on scripturalism in official Islam provided the sociological setting for 'popular' Islam in the rural setting, there was also, especially in North Africa, a political context in segmentary rural society for the role of saint as tribal arbitrator. Any analysis of 'popular' Islam (Waardenburg, 1978) must make a distinction between the services provided by the rural, saintly lineages and the urban lodges (*zawiyas*). In the *bidonville* of North African cities, the popular religious clubs or lodges provide a setting within which the uprooted peasantry can find an emotional and supportive home; the popular *zawiyas* thus offer a form of ecstatic compensation for the deprivations of the shanty town and for detribalised social relations (Worsley, 1972). Contemporary movements towards national unification have been deeply hostile towards local saint cults, since magical forms of hierarchical religiosity have been associated with various forms of cultural colonial dependence. Puritanical revivals have been closely associated with nationalist ideology (Wolf, 1971). Whereas Hasidic religiosity in urban secular America has the function of maintaining a specific cultural identity, Sufism has provided a vehicle for preserving and fostering popular expressions of religiosity in relation to formal koranic Islam.

It can be argued (Turner, 1974a) that the saints of Islam have social characteristics which are the obverse of those which define 'saint' in the Roman Catholic tradition of western Europe. A saint in the Christian tradition is any person who has been proved acceptable to a papal court of inquiry, canonised and made the centre of an ecclesiastical cult.

Given the length of the canonisation process, saints are also dead. Furthermore, saints typically emerge from monasteries or nunneries, since the distractions of the everyday world are normally sufficient to rule out the common folk. Finally, since theological orthodoxy is a necessary feature of saintship, at least officially, saints are more likely to be recruited from the ranks of scholars and literate elites than from the untutored. The process of canonisation was thus an important feature of centralised, bureaucratic authority within the Church. The social-class background of Christian saints illustrates empirically the formal, definitional criteria of saintship (George and George, 1953—5). In Islam, these social connections between authoritative control and the labelling of saints are missing. Since the strict monotheism and egalit-arianism of Islam rule out the possibility of official saints, all mara-boutic roles must be, by definition, heretical. There are also important differences between the charisma of the Christian saint and the *baraka* of the marabout. Islamic Sufis marry and form holy lineages so that the term *baraka* can apply to both individuals and collectivities. The claim of descent from a holy person is thus an important part of the authority which an Islamic saint enjoys. The saints of Islam are thus typically unorthodox, popular, decentralised, and heirs of lineage charisma.

Although there are thus important cultural differences between Christian and Islamic saints, their religious styles are the products of unequal virtuosity. The historical roots of Sufism are located in religious protest against the secularity of Islamic society after the period of the early conquests on the part of 'high-minded ascetics' (Kritzeck, 1973, pp. 153—4). The term 'Sufism' itself is derived from *suf*, the undyed woollen garment of eastern ascetics. Their ascetic humility was later indicated by the adoption of a patched frock which was inherited by a novice on the death of the saint. A further indication of ascetic withdrawal from earthly splendour can be found in the terms which Sufis employed to describe themselves, namely 'the folk' (*al-qawm*) or the 'poor' (*al-fuqara*). Sufism was thus grounded in:

aversion to the false splendor of the world, abstinence from the pleasure, property and position to which the great mass aspires and retirement from the world into solitude for divine worship. (Ibn Khaldun, 1958, vol. 3, p. 76)

The asceticism, supererogatory practices and withdrawal of Sufi virtuosi are not, of course, possible for the great majority of the population. In exchange for the economic support which the laity offer saints, the virtuosi provide healing and advice to their audiences, which are recruited from women and the disprivileged, borne down by the mundane problems of illness, childbirth and old age.

There is also a process of religious selection, whereby the poor adhere to those religious orders or lineages which require the least commitment in terms of ritual practices and religious demands. Thus, the Jilaliyya order of ascetics is popular among women because the requirements of the order make the least impact on the daily routines of the household; by contrast, the Tijaniyya order is particularly demanding and therefore avoided by women who are heavily involved in domestic chores (Dwyer, 1978). The Tijaniyya order, one of the most rigidly ascetic of Sufi movements, tends to draw its membership from the rich and powerful sectors of the community (Abun-Nasr, 1965) in Morocco. The litanies of the Tijaniyya must be performed twice every day and they make difficult demands on the daily routines of peasants and workers. The result is that the lower social strata gravitate toward those orders whose ritual requirements most perfectly match their domestic and work routines; such orders as a consequence have low social status, precisely because they cater to the masses.

Economic payments to religious virtuosi may assume a variety of forms. Virtuoso withdrawal from the world may be achieved by a system of patronage in which a secular elite provides the means for religious personnel to practise religious virtuosity on its behalf. In medieval Christendom, for example, certain monastic orders were funded to pray for souls of the military feudal stratum, whose souls were in jeopardy as a consequence of their involvement in warfare (Rosenwein and Little, 1974). More commonly, an economically unproductive class of spiritual experts is financed by lay payments or fees and this results in the paradox that the virtuoso is maintained by the involvement of the mass in profane activity:

The contemplative mystic lives on whatever gifts the world may present to him, and he would be unable to stay alive if the world were not constantly engaged in that very labour which the mystic brands as sinful and leading to alienation from god. (Weber, 1966, p. 172)

The two alternatives to lay support are either forms of self-employment, as in the case of petty-bourgeois Hasidic shopkeepers, or systems of self-sufficiency off the land, which some Christian monastic communities have attempted. These two alternatives depend on the existence of a profane world of economic markets, commercialisation, systems of exchange and forms of credit. In contemporary western culture, the rural commune movement and other movements for an alternative society often require open or disguised forms of patronage, economic aid or welfare from the state, private supporters or inherited wealth (Rigby and Turner, 1972 and 1973).

One crucial feature of North African Islam is that the wealth which the holy lineages acquire is, in principle, redistributed to lay followers and disciples, especially to the poor and disprivileged. One of the social marks of *baraka* is wealth; it would be contradictory to be a poor marabout in possession of *baraka*, which is a property which generates physical health and economic well-being. The saint, therefore, stands at the crossroads of a complex process of economic exchange and distribution (Crapanzano, 1973).

Christianity

The analogy of economic and spiritual exchanges is clearly present in the language of *baraka*, but it was also prevalent in the Catholic conceptualisation of confessions of sins (Turner, 1977b). Christ's charisma which had poured out in his redemptive blood at Calvary was subsequently stored, not in a kinship system, but in the institution-alised grace of the official Church. In the thirteenth century, the doctrine of the Church as the 'Treasury of Merit' became fully artic-ulated and provided the theological basis for the issue of indulgences in compensation for penitential 'taxation'. The Church, acting as a charismatic bank, could issue notes to facilitate the exchange relation-ship between sin and penance, which were incorporated within the sacrament of penance. The fact that the centralised Church controlled the spread of charisma through the office of the episcopate thus prevented inflationary booms in the availability of charismatic wealth. These structural limitations on grace obviously at times created a situ-ation of scarcity which the black market of indulgences, as Chaucer's criticisms of the Pardonner suggest, developed to satisfy local demand.

The exchanges between the religious elite and the masses, which take the form of religious services in return for direct or indirect payments to maintain the virtuosi, are to be seen, however, as part of a much denser and more complex system of religious exchanges between gods and men. The charisma, *baraka* or *mana*, which is the root of virtuosi authority, is ultimately the gift of the gods to man as the basis of human wealth and plenty. Just as saints and disciples are bound together by various obligations resulting from their exchange relationship, so the notions of contracts and covenants between divine and human actors appear to be, in Durkheim's terms, an 'elementary form of religion'.

In *The Elementary Forms of Religious Life* (1961), Durkheim em-braced a theory of sacrifice first elaborated by William Robertson Smith in his *Lectures on the Religion of the Semites* (1889), where Smith argued that the sacrificial, totemic feast created a communal bond between the god and the tribe. Durkheim treated this social inter-dependence as a crucial feature of religious systems:

if it is true that man depends upon his gods, this dependence is reciprocal. The gods also have need of man: without offerings and sacrifices they would die . . . this dependence of the gods upon their worshippers is maintained even in the most idealistic religions. (Durkheim, 1961, p. 53)

Similarly, in the first page of Weber's *The Sociology of Religion* the existence of exchange and sacrifice is treated as a primary feature of religious behaviour. What Weber called 'the most elementary forms of behavior' are directed towards this world, namely, economic security, health, success and long life:

religious or magical behavior or thinking must not be set apart from the range of everyday purposive conduct, particularly since even the ends of the religious and magical actions are predominantly economic. (Weber, 1966, p. 1)

Weber treated the two principal elements of worship — prayer and sacrifice — as instrumental and rational actions directed at the manipulation or coercion of divine favour. In prayer, Weber suggested that there was a strong component of demand and recompense for religious actions performed in honour of gods. In sacrifice, Weber identified two essential features: namely, the coercion of divine personages and the establishment of a *communio* by ceremonial meals. In subsequent developments in anthropological theory, these perspectives on totemism and sacrifice have been modified and elaborated, first by Mauss (1920), Hubert and Mauss (1964) and Lévi-Strauss (1969). Although Mauss was critical of Smith's early theory of sacrifice, he retained the basic notion that various forms of exchange — potlatch, pledge, gifts and alms — between men, gods and nature create bonds of mutual obligation. The principle of charity in the Abrahamic religions was founded in the ancient notion that generosity was necessary to avoid the vengeance of the gods and that the consumption of wealth in useless sacrifices could more appropriately be given to the poor, widows and children.

Although in the 'higher religions' these overtly economic and instrumental features of exchange have been muted by altruistic ethical codes as the result of theological speculation, much of the basic symbolism and mythology of the Jewish and Christian traditions have their roots in problems of equality in exchange relations between men and gods. For example, it has been argued (Bakan, 1974) that one of the crucial themes of the Old Testament is the nature of paternity, namely, the processes of procreation and destruction. The knowledge that men played a part in the procreation of children conflicted with this notion of divine creativity, giving a godlike stature to fathers. Although men were creative, they were also mortal; God, by contrast, had the characteristics of destructiveness and immortality. The fact of paternity was, however, connected with three crucial problems. Patriarchal fathers were threatened by the possibility of filial disobedience and disloyalty; raising children in a harsh environment represented an economic danger to households; authentic paternity was difficult to prove, especially in the case of first-born children, and thus the legitimacy of heirs was always uncertain. There was, consequently, a strong social impulse towards infanticide, particularly in the case of first-born males:

The essence of Judaism and Christianity is the management of the infanticidal impulse resulting from these three factors, and a binding of the father against acting out the impulse. (Bakan, 1974, p. 208)

It is in this context that we are to understand the symbolism of baptism and circumcision, by which the 'children' of God the Father are recognised, incorporated into the community and saved from the sins of mankind. These rites of salvation — baptism and circumcision — are performed instead of infanticide by drowning and slaughter; they are ritual exchanges to the dark sin of murder. In Christianity, these rites were focused in the person of Christ, the sacrificial lamb, whose sacrifice cancelled out the debt of human sin against the merciful Father.

It is possible to argue, therefore, that the forms of exchange which are constituent of economic life in human societies provide the metaphors by which human actors conceptualise their relationship with the gods. As a general rule, one would expect that major changes in the modes of production within societies would be associated with equally significant changes in the theological conceptions of man–god exchanges. These parallels between economic and religious systems of exchange were certainly anticipated in the sociological analyses of Marx, Weber and Veblen. According to the mode of production, the god will take the form of a despot, a feudal lord or a capitalist employer. Thus Marx suggested that in the 'Asiatic land-forms':

A part of their surplus labour belongs to the higher community, which exists ultimately as a *person*, and this surplus labour takes the form of tribute etc., as well as of common labour for the exaltation of the unity, partly of the real despot, partly of the imagined clan-being, the god. (Marx, 1973, p. 473)

It can be argued that in Judaism the emergence of a centralised, monarchical government had an impact on religious conceptions of Yahweh, who was transformed from a god dwelling in the wilderness to a potentate with a heavenly court. The holiness of Yahweh and the lowliness of man was the religious counterpart to the political subjection of the ordinary citizen to centralised authority so that 'the concept of Yahweh's holiness imperceptibly becomes the concept of Yahweh's kingship' (Ling, 1968, p. 72).

One of the minor themes of Weber's sociology of religion can thus be seen as a study of how the emergence of capitalist relations of production revolutionised traditional, hierarchical conceptions of man-god exchanges within which the virtuoso–mass dichotomy was originally embedded. The hierarchical, quasi-feudal structure of virtuoso–mass interactions was itself a reflection of the hierarchical systems of social stratification in pre-capitalist society. These patterns of exchange were shattered by the emergence of capitalist production with the growth of social-class polarisation, which in turn had their impact on the modes of conceptualising man's interdependence with God. It is possible to illustrate this transition by considering the nature of God as portrayed in John Milton's *Paradise Lost*, located at the close of the feudal period, and John Wesley's sermon, the Good Steward (1768), delivered at the opening of the industrial, capitalist revolution. These two religious texts mark a profound transformation of conceptions of religious stratification in English religion.

The theodicy of *Paradise Lost* is couched in legal terms (Grierson, 1956); it is concerned with the transgression of divine law, the existence of human free will and God's juridical pardon. Waldock (1961) separates the problem of *Paradise Lost* into two issues: the fall of Eve and the fall of Adam; however, it is possible to see the theme of the poem as disobedience on the part of Adam and Eve, and the rebellion of Satan. The theme is one of rebellion by actors above their station in a 'great chain of being' that descends from God, through Christ the Messiah, the archangels, the angels, man and creatures. Adam and Eve, through an act of will, rise above their status through the unlawful seizure of knowledge; Satan attempts to maintain a feudal equality with the Son, thereby rejecting the heavenly distribution of powers. God's ways are justified to man by showing that crimes against just laws ought to be punished, given the existence of human will and responsibility.

The hierarchical character of this feudal conception of status is probably best illustrated by the narrative of the exaltation of Christ, Satan's rebellion and final defeat in Books 5 and 6. When God summons the heavenly host to hear His proclamation of Christ's rank, the 'Empyreal Host' arrives in the orders of a feudal army:

> Forthwith from all the ends of Heav'n appeerd
> Under thir Hierarchs in order bright
> Ten thousand thousand Ensignes high advanc'd
> Standards, and Gonfalons twixt Van and Reare
> Stream in the Aire, and for distinction serve
> Of Hierarchies, of Orders and Degrees.

In addressing this host, God assumes the role of a feudal king in declaring an unbreakable legal decree:

> Hear, all ye Angels, Progenie of Light,
> Thrones, Dominations, Princedoms, Vertues, Powers,
> Hear my Decree, which unrevok't shall stand.

Satan's rebellion begins with his rejection of God's proclamation of the Son of God as 'Messiah King anointed' which Milton explains in terms of Satan's envy and malice. The disobedience of Satan is again portrayed in feudal imagery as 'Affecting all equality with God' and Satan is described as 'the envier of his State'. The battles which occupy Book 6 are feudal struggles against dissident baronial forces, arranged against an omnipotent sovereign. After the triumph of Christ's armies, Satan:

> Fell with his flaming Legions through the Deep
> Into his place, and the great Son returnd
> Victorious with his Saints, th'Omnipotent
> Eternal Father from his throne beheld
> Thir multitude.

In *Paradise Lost,* the problem of theodicy is worked out through the medium of a narrative, involving a feudal reconstruction of the Genesis myth. Although the political struggle between English royal despotism and commercialised gentry provided the immediate context of Miltonic poetry, the language of *Paradise Lost* was feudal and therefore already archaic. It was nevertheless immediately comprehensible to an audience which understood the language of feudal rebellion.

Over a century later, Wesley's sermon on the Good Steward, delivered at Edinburgh in May 1768, offers a radical, different exchange analogy of the relationship between man and God. Wesleyanism clearly incorporated a variety of metaphors of exchange between sinful men and the merciful deity. Charles Wesley's hymns were, for example, frequently expressive of mystical devotion to Christ as a sacrificial offering. The language of totemic sacrifice appeared in such verses as:

> Arise, my soul, arise,
> Shake off thy guilty fears;
> The bleeding Sacrifice
> In my behalf appears.

However, equally important in Wesleyan hymnology and theology was the presence of commercial analogies of sin and recompense in which God took the form of the just banker. In Protestantism, there was, for example, a popular comparison of the weight of human sin with the growing national debt (Ling, 1966). Although wealth was regarded in Wesleyan theology as a secularising influence, Wesley employed the parable of the Good Steward to illustrate the essential character of the exchange relationship in religious behaviour. Money was treated as one of the paramount gifts of God to His worthy stewards. In addition to the necessities and convenience of life, God:

has committed to our charge, that precious talent, which contains all the rest, money; indeed it is unspeakably precious, if we are wise and faithful stewards of it. (Wesley, 1825, vol. 1, p. 639)

Given the importance of this talent, at our deaths we will be called to 'give an Account of our Stewardship', just as busy shopkeepers in this world have periodically to provide systematic accounts of their debits and credits. Wesley criticised two uses of money: namely, expenditure on luxuries and hoarding. On the day of the heavenly account, God asks whether that 'comprehensive talent, money' was employed in:

supplying thy own reasonable wants, together with those of thy family; then restoring the remainder to me, through the poor, whom I have appointed to receive it. (Wesley, 1825, vol. 1, p. 646)

This exchange relationship of stewardship was very far removed both from the Catholic analogy of a centralised treasury and from the feudal imagery that dominated Milton's *Paradise Lost*. On the one hand, it corresponded to the egalitarian and individualistic themes of Wesleyan Arminianism (Semmel, 1974). On the other hand, it accorded closely with the rational economic ethic of urban commercial classes, whose life-style fostered a conception of God as a just and systematic provider of talents.

Summary
It has often been argued that Protestantism was its own grave-digger; the rational ethos of radical Protestantism has the unintended consequences of reducing the scope of sacred persons, places and events in the everyday life of the believer. One result of this inherent potentiality for secularisation is that the 'immense network of intercession that unites the Catholic in this world with the saints and, indeed, with all departed souls disappears as well' (Berger, 1969, p. 111). The biblical images of God, furthermore, as the Good Shepherd, the majestic King and the sacrificial Lamb, which had a salience in pastoralist economies and centralised empires, lack an affinity with the life-style of urban workers. Against a background of urban secularisation, the ideologies of democratic participation, achievement and credentialism undermine the conditions which traditionally fostered a virtuoso ethic in religious practice. The growth in the division of labour produced, according to Durkheim, a new principle of redistributive justice, compatible with the metaphor of God as the Just Employer of human stewards.

The popular religious styles of the mid-twentieth century have, however, been very far removed from these traditional, hierarchical forms of religion. The religious dimension of the 'expressive revolution' of the 1960s emphasised spontaneity, personal experience and immediate feelings; these religious styles were critical of structure, hierarchy and formal organisation. Under the impact of this counter-cultural ethic, which was expressive of a modern 'liminality' (Martin, 1981), there was little scope for the traditional, supererogatory virtues of ascetic practice.

For some sociologists of religion, the modern ethic of 'doing your own thing' outside the traditional confines of organised religion (Bellah, 1964) may be a reflection of consumer culture and narcissism, but the process by which religious behaviour became highly personalised and religious phenomena diffused through social interaction was identified much earlier by sociologists at the turn of the century. In the cultural context of the modern world, religious activity:

which formerly manifested itself through the development of more adequate dogmatic contents, can no longer express itself through the polarity of a believing subject and a believed object. In the ultimate state of affairs towards which this new tendency is aiming, religion would function as a medium for the direct expression of life. (Simmel, 1968, p. 23)

Simmel thought that religion would become the 'tonality' of modern life; however, an alternative argument is that religion, at least traditional religion, has become uncoupled from the principal economic structures of industrial capitalism and is diffused to peripheral, interstitial regions of personal and social life. In this respect, there is a strong parallel between Troeltsch's analysis of the demise of the church—sect dynamic of Christianity and Weber's virtuoso—mass dichotomy. Troeltsch argued that, with the collapse of the universal church and the dominance of modern capitalism, his typology was not relevant to contemporary societies. For Troeltsch, the primary form of modern religiosity was mysticism, by which he meant privatised religiosity. In a similar fashion, Weber argued that the realities of modern existence precluded heroic religion and virtuoso prophecy; the religious style had to be performed *'in pianissimo'* (Weber, 1961, p. 155).

Religion and economy

In conceptualising the social functions of religion in human societies, sociologists of religion have either approached religion as a form of social cement that creates a bond between potentially antagonistic individuals or as a form of social opium that suppresses the conflict of interests between antagonistic social groups. On both accounts, religion functions to preserve social cohesion (Wilson, 1982). An alternative functionalist treatment of religion argues that religion is a primary institution of social control in social relationships. One common objection to functionalist explanations in sociology generally draws attention to the vagueness and absence of substantive content in functionalism (Merton, 1957). In order to define the nature of religious functions for social life, it is important to provide more precision and historical grounding to the notion of social control.

One theme of this chapter is that historically religion has been important for the distribution and control of property in society and it has performed this function by providing beliefs and institutions which are relevant to the control of instinctual life. More precisely, religious teaching on sexuality has facilitated the control of children by parents and women by men. The relationship between religion and the requirements of property can, in fact, never be drawn as tightly as this formulation would suggest.

In the present argument, however, attention is drawn to the crucial role of Christian moral teaching on sexuality and family life to the development of property relations in European society. This relationship is normally introduced through an analysis of the impact of asceticism on capitalist relations of production through the work, in particular, of Max Weber. I shall argue that this treatment of the connection between religion, the body and the economy is too selective by showing that religion has been historically fundamental to the solution of four basic social problems: namely, restraint, reproduction, registration and representation. This chapter is consequently directed towards an exploration of the Hobbesian problem of order, which I interpret as the question: how is the human body controlled? In order to introduce this issue, it is instructive to compare the perspectives of Friedrich Engels and Max Weber on the institutionalisation of human sexuality within the system of economic production.

It is significant that, in attempting to provide a definition of the 'materialist conception' of history, Engels saw the reproduction of human beings as a fundamental dimension to the production and reproduction of 'immediate life'. This process has a twofold character. First, there is the production of the means of subsistence (tools, food, clothing and shelter); and secondly:

the production of human beings themselves, the propagation of the species. The social institutions under which men of a definite historical epoch and of a definite country live are conditioned by both kinds of production: by the stage of development of labour, on the one hand, and of the family, on the other. The less the development of labour, and the more limited its volume of production and, therefore, the wealth of society, the more preponderatingly does the social order appear to be dominated by the ties of sex. (Engels, n.d., pp. 6-7)

The role of ideology in society, especially religious teaching on sexuality and family life, is to secure the social conditions by which this reproduction of human bodies can take place. In Engels's treatment of the historical development of the family, the monogamous marriage was closely connected with the emergence of private property and the subordination of women by men. The importance of monogamy was that, when combined with a system of primogeniture, it safeguarded the inheritance of private property within the family and concentrated domestic wealth within a limited range of kin. The socio-economic significance of monogamy:

is the begetting of children of undisputed paternity, this paternity being required in order that these children may in due time inherit their father's wealth as his natural heirs. (Engels, n.d., p. 100)

For Engels, therefore, the traditional marriage was essentially a contractual relationship, enforced by religion and law, to secure the stable transition of property between generations. Within this marriage of convenience, men typically adhered to a double standard in seeking romantic, sexual pleasure outside the home, while insisting on sexual loyalty and chastity for their wives and daughters. In this respect, Engels argued that the institution of prostitution and the prevalence of adultery were necessary by-products of a property system organised around contractual monogamy.

Within this family system, religion played a rather complex role. In the Middle Ages, the teaching of the Roman Catholic Church was ideologically important in supporting the stability of monogamous, contractual unions. However, Engels thought that the emphasis given by the Reformation to individual freedom of choice and conscience was not compatible with a system of arranged marriages. The Reformation principle of freedom of conscience was combined with the individualism of the bourgeois class and together began to undermine the forms of parental control which had been dominant under feudalism.

Marriage remained class marriage, but, within the confines of the class, the parties were accorded a certain degree of freedom of choice. (Engels, n.d., p. 133)

Engels's attempt to conceptualise the relationship between biological and economic reproduction within the monogamous unit was an important contribution to the development of a materialist theory of the functions of religion as an agency of social control. His characterisation of that relationship has, however, been greatly refined by subsequent historical research.

One problem in Engels's approach was that the relationship between Catholic teaching on sexuality and the economic requirements of property conservation was far more contradictory. We need to distinguish between the lay system and the ecclesiastical norms of married life (Duby, 1978). Although the Church's teaching on the sanctity of marriage did contribute to conservation of land within the feudal family, the notion of marriage as an indissoluble union created difficulties for landowners in cases where the wife proved to be barren or merely produced female offspring. There was, therefore, in the lay conception of marriage a strong need for repudiation of wives, and husbands were able to achieve this aim by allegations of incestuous union. Careful manipulation of the Church's categories of unlawful marriages on the grounds of incest was thus a common practice and eventually forced the Church to redefine the limits of appropriate marriages within the kin. With this modification of Engels's formulation of the connection between marriage, religion and property, it is possible to argue that religion played a major part in the social control of women and therefore of the distribution of private property.

Although in general terms the treatment of patriarchalism and patrimonialism was fundamental to Weber's political sociology, his commentary on the relationship between the family and the economy was underdeveloped. In volume 1 of *Economy and Society* (1968), Weber discussed various aspects of the relationship between descent groups and property, specifically considering land and women as forms of wealth. In addition to establishing a range of formal concepts for the analysis of the economy, Weber was concerned to deny any simple evolutionary view of the development of familial systems from matriarchy to abduction to patriarchy. In general, he denied that any simple causal mechanism could explain the diversity of linkages between kinship systems and forms of property. However, Weber thought that, in order for rational calculation of economic behaviour to develop in capitalism, it was necessary for the family to be separated from the economy; the family unit as the principal source of economic accumulation was treated as a primarily pre-capitalist characteristic of western societies. Weber thus suggested that the necessary components of capitalist development were:

the separation of household and business for accounting and legal purposes, and the development of a suitable body of laws, such as the commercial register, elimination of dependence of the association and the firm upon the family, separate property of the private firm or limited partnership, and appropriate laws of bankruptcy. (Weber, 1968, vol. 1, p. 380)

Weber's treatment of the separation of family and economy is characteristic of his general approach to the nature of capitalist society, namely, that such a society requires conditions of 'exact calculation'. Thus, in the introduction to *The Protestant Ethic and the Spirit of Capitalism* (1965), Weber argued that the rational pursuit of economic accumulation by capitalist means required precise calculation and this calculation was only possible on the basis of a separation between household and enterprise, on the basis of formally free labour and finally on rational law and reliable administration. Indeed, the rational ethos of capitalist society 'is to-day essentially dependent on the calculability of the most important technical factors' (Weber, 1965, p. 24). This calculation of labour and the rational organisation of enterprises were threatened by the irrationality of instinctual life and above all by sexuality. It is this conflict between rational calculation and irrational gratification which provides the theoretical site for Weber's analysis of the impact of Protestant asceticism on the rise of capitalist relations of production.

Religion and sexuality

In a comparative perspective, religious orientations to human sexuality have occupied a variety of positions along a continuum between total denial and orgy (Taylor, 1953). In *The Sociology of Religion*, Weber made a basic distinction between mystical flight from sexuality and ascetic mastery of instinctual life, but it was the latter religious orientation that concerned him most. Since the sexual urge is a paramount human drive, Weber treated it as problematic for any sustained salvational quest:

Rational ascetic alertness, self-control, and methodical planning of life are seriously threatened by the peculiar irrationality of the sexual act, which is ultimately and uniquely unsusceptible to rational organization. (Weber, 1966, p. 238)

Both Catholicism and Puritanism attempted to deal with sexuality either by sublimation or by legitimating sexual intercourse in terms of rational reproduction of the species. For Weber, however, it was primarily within the Protestant sects that the surveillance of the body and mastery of its reproductive functions achieved a complete rational formulation. Much of Weber's sociology of religion was, consequently, concerned with the historical roots of sexual asceticism and, in the Protestant Ethic thesis, with the consequences of sexual control on the secular development of industrial capitalism. Calvinistic asceticism, by taking monastic spirituality into the secular world as an ethos of world-mastery, provided the social model for capitalist discipline of labour. The importance of labour and secular vocations for the control of sexual drives provided a key theme in Weber's analysis of the origins of capitalist rationality:

The sexual asceticism of Puritanism differs only in degree, not in fundamental principle, from that of monasticism; and on account of the Puritan conception of marriage, only as the means willed by God for the increase of His glory according to the commandment, 'Be fruitful and multiply'. Along with a moderate vegetable diet and cold baths, the same prescription is given for all sexual temptations as is used against religious doubts and a sense of moral unworthiness: 'Work hard in your calling'. (Weber, 1965, p. 159).

The notion that one of the unintended consequences of the Protestant Ethic was the discipline and surveillance of labour has subsequently become a standard assumption of historical and sociological research on the cultural characteristics of capitalist society. In Britain, it has been argued that, during the early decades of the Industrial Revolution, the Methodist chapels socialised the labour force into a culture of hard work, punctuality and teetotalism. Thus, for E. P. Thompson (1963), Methodism served a double function in the development of a reliable workforce. First, it produced disciplined labour by demonstrating that irrational behaviour (gambling, alcoholism and laziness) blocked the achievement of salvation. Secondly, Methodism made labouring bodies docile by offering religious compensation for the deprivations of urban conditions and for the routines of factory life in emotional conversions, collective rituals and chapel fellowship. Thompson's analysis of the social effects of British Methodism can be extended to show a parallel between ascetic discipline and managerial control.

In Antonio Gramsci's commentary on Taylorism and Fordism, it was claimed that Puritanism in America laid the foundations for the managerial discipline of labour by suppressing the 'animality' of man in the interests of rational enterprises. The peculiar feature of Puritanism was that it involved a self-discipline and personal coercion rather than ideological repression imposed by management. Puritanism brought about a rational control of the labouring body, defending it from the irrationality of erotic pleasure outside the workplace:

'Puritanical' initiatives simply have the purpose of preserving, outside of work, a certain psycho-physical equilibrium which prevents the physiological collapse of the worker, exhausted by the new method of production . . . It seems that the new industrialism wants monogamy: it wants the man as worker not to squander his nervous energies in the disorderly and stimulating pursuit of occasional sexual satisfaction. (Gramsci, 1971, pp. 303—4)

Like Engels, Gramsci argued that the distribution of hedonism and asceticism in industrial capitalism was significantly influenced by class position. While the worker was compelled to engage in bodily disciplines by the nature of his conditions of employment, the wives and daughters of industrialists were converted into 'luxury mammals' for whom the adornment of the body and the cultivation of female beauty were dramatic evidence of patriarchal wealth.

Engels's recognition of the importance of monogamy for capitalist accumulation and Weber's analysis of the impact of asceticism on the labour force can thus be regarded as aspects of a general position in social theory that has treated the subordination of instinctual gratification as a basic requirement of civilisation. This juxtaposition of instinctual happiness and social stability was fundamental to a critical philosophical tradition linking together Friedrich Nietzsche, Sigmund Freud and Herbert Marcuse. Thus, the claim that Christianity involved a considerable institutionalised denial of life, especially instinctual gratification, was a basic feature of Nietzsche's criticism of conventional moralities. For example, Nietzsche typically argued that Christianity:

allowed only two kinds of suicide, dressed them up with the highest dignity and the highest hopes, and forbade all others in a terrifying manner. Only martyrdom and the ascetic's slow destruction of his body were permitted. (Nietzsche, 1974, p. 185)

Christianity was:

life's nausea and disgust with life, merely concealed behind, masked by, dressed up as, faith in 'another' or 'better' life . . . For, confronted with morality (especially Christian, or unconditional morality), life *must* continually and inevitably be in the wrong, because life *is* something essentially moral — and eventually, crushed by the weight of contempt and the eternal No, life *must* then be felt to be unworthy of desire and altogether worthless. (Nietzsche, 1967b, p. 23)

Against Christian morality, Nietzsche did not advocate unrestrained hedonism or a formless Dionysian enthusiasm for physical pleasures. He defined genuine or life-enhancing morality as 'self-overcoming' which required control and sublimation (Kaufmann, 1974). Given the existence of powerful sexual instincts, Nietzsche drew a distinction between the destruction of instinctual existence by emasculation and repudiation, on the one hand, and redirection and sublimation, on the other. Through redirection, the instincts could be aimed at spiritual and artistic growth; by contrast, repudiation created a society of moral weaklings. The importance of Nietzsche's criticisms of conventional ethical positions was found in the emphasis Nietzsche gave to the harmony of the physiological and psychological existence of humanity. Morality had thus to express and not repress physiology. It was for this reason that Nietzsche envisaged his philosophical investigation of morality as a physiological inquiry into the wholeness of human life (Hollingdale, 1973).

Nietzsche was deeply critical of the shallowness of bourgeois society, especially as it existed in provincial Germany, but he was equally opposed to the false belief that positivistic science could fill the moral vacuum created by the death-of-God. No moral comfort could be obtained from scientific advances, least of all from the evolutionary doctrine of Darwinism. Nietzsche's critical attitude towards scientific knowledge partly explains the problematic relationship between Freudian analysis of moral life and that offered by Nietzsche's critical physiological investigations. On the face of it, the concepts of resentment, repression, sublimation and industrialisation, which were basic to Nietzsche's 'revaluation of values', were also fundamental to scientific psychoanalysis (Anderson, 1980).

One basic issue in Freudian psychoanalysis was the tension between the critical implications of his therapeutic techniques and the conservative assumptions of his neurophysiology. Freud remained committed to neurophysiology as the basis of all psychological phenomena; the mind and its disorders could be explained in terms of an energy model of conscious and unconscious mental activity. It was this adherence to the primacy of natural science in establishing adequate criteria for a science of mental life that made his views on the relationship between instinctual life and civilisation so unstable. Freudian metapsychology, as a result, embraces both profoundly radical and conservative presuppositions (Breger, 1981). In the early sections of *Civilization and its Discontents*, Freud's argument concerning the contradiction between sexual happiness and the requirements of stability in civilian life expressed a conventional, masculine view of sexuality, aggression and rationality. Expressions of love, grief, dependence and affection were regarded as departures from masculine principles of reason and autonomy. In chapter 6, however, in the dichotomy between Eros and Thanatos, the discontents of civilisation were more clearly associated with male aggressiveness. Human misery was more definitely connected with aggression and with the internal punishments flowing from conscience and guilt. The discontents of advanced societies were no longer simply the product of unsatisfied pleasure principles, but were the outcome of sexual repression and punitive conscience.

The Freudian formulation of the relationship between society and nature, and between culture and instincts provided an important starting-point for writers within the Frankfurt school, or more widely within critical theory. The theoretical investigations of writers like Erich Fromm, Jürgen Habermas and Herbert Marcuse were directed at the reconciliation of Marxism and Freudianism (Jay, 1973). Marcuse, for example, rejected the relativistic implications of Nietzsche's death-of-God philosophy in defending the trans-social role of rational inquiry which could result in valid knowledge of social life. He was equally critical of Marx's uniform emphasis on human labour as the ground of all value and as the distinctive attribute of human organisation. For Marcuse, all labour was alienating and, even under socialist conditions of production, had to be regarded as 'a burden'.

Marcuse also criticised the pessimistic implications of Freud's opposition between happiness and civilisation, by arguing that sexual repression is only necessary in a situation of scarcity. In a Malthusian crisis, repression of sexual pleasure might be rational in the interests of social survival, but in capitalism the widespread employment of modern technology removed the threat of starvation. Modern societies are thus characterised by a 'surplus repression' which defends authority from critical and radical inspection. The radical potential of sexuality is thus restrained and sexual exploration confined to after-work periods, where instinctual pleasures can be exploited by the leisure industry. The consequence is that 'the libido becomes concentrated in one part of the body, leaving most of the rest for use as the instrument of labour' (Marcuse, 1972, p. 49). Whereas Freud had argued that happiness and civilised existence were incompatible, Marcuse thought that this situation only obtained in conditions of scarcity. Eros was no longer the source of our discontent, but the unifying principle of nature and society (Geoghegan, 1981).

Problems of human corporality

In these introductory observations, the connection between sexual repression, Protestant asceticism and capitalist production has been treated as a linking theme in contemporary analysis of the systematic relationship between personality and economy. There are obviously important differences between these theories; Marcuse's social theory stands in sharp contrast to the deep pessimism of Weber and Freud (Kolakowski, 1978, vol. 3). The common element in these positions is, however, their association of ascetic disciplines of the body and the managerial practices of industrial societies. They are also united in an implicit theory of secularisation, in which the religious practices of the monastery were transferred to the factory floor.

Although the study of the transplantation of asceticism into secular practices represents an interesting contribution to the sociology of religion, the conceptualisation of the secular body in sociology as such is somewhat narrow. Although sociologists are familiar with the

Hobbesian problem of order, that is, the social basis of stability and cohesion in society, we also need to analyse the Hobbesian problem of human corporality. The argument of this chapter is that religion is fundamental to the whole problem of the reproduction and regulation of human bodies in social space. The role of religion in society has to be considered in terms of four dimensions of this Hobbesian problem.

A	B
Volume (time)	Interior
Reproduction	Restraint
Intercourse	Instincts
Population	Physiology
Malthus	Freud
D	C
Density (space)	Exterior
Registration	Representation
Integration	Intimacy
Polis	Publics
Rousseau	Goffman

The theories of asceticism in Weber, Freud and Marcuse were largely directed towards the problem of instinctual restraint of the individual within the confines of social order. This type of theory is relevant to what might be termed an 'interior-body problem', and thus with the relationship between physiology and sociology. In character, this perspective tends to be individualistic, being concerned with interior psychological satisfactions and physiological drives within the framework of social pressures towards conformity. Individual guilt and conscience are treated as the principal mechanisms by which personality and society achieve complementarity. The question of the interiority of the isolated body is very different from the exterior problem of the body in its public setting. The exterior body can be conceived as the medium through which feelings and emotions are expressed, but these expressions have to assume a socially acceptable form, if they are not to disrupt the normal flow of interpersonal actions. The exterior-body problem is not one of restraint, but of normative representation.

In addition to the problems of restraint and representation, it is possible to conceptualise two separate issues of the plurality of bodies in time and space. The classical Malthusian debate centred on the rates of population growth in relation to the availability of food and land, and regarded moral restraints (such as celibacy and late marriage) as the most appropriate social responses to the reproduction problem. For the sake of convenience, I have approached this Malthusian debate in terms of the volume of bodies in time. The second may be considered as the problem of managing populations in space by methods of surveillance, especially registration, recording and individuation.

The Hobbesian problem of corporal order as a question of the management of human bodies can thus be organised under four subsystem categories: restraint, representation, registration and reproduction. Religion has historically been fundamental to these four societal tasks. In etymology, 'religion' derives from *religio* (bond or obligation), but is also related to *regulare* (rule) and *ritus* (ceremonies). In this chapter, religion is thus regarded as a system of bonding and binding through which human bodies are controlled and disciplined. Within this framework, secularisation can be regarded as the transfer of religious disciplinary practices to the secular domains of the polis.

Diet

Dietary practices in both ascetic and mystical spirituality have a long history in most branches of Christianity. They provided one of the principal means for the control of the inner body, releasing the spirit from the cloying presence of the flesh. Dietary asceticism was clearly important in the tradition of the virtuosi in the early Church and was later systematised in such treatises as Ignatius Loyala's *Spiritual Exercises*. Historical studies of religious disciplines often overstate the transitions in religious life brought about by the Reformation by suggesting that Protestantism abandoned the entire gamut of Catholic devotional and spiritual techniques (Black, 1902). Rather than rapid transitions in meaning and practice, the history of dietary discipline shows instead the gradual adoption of diet for secular ends, such as health, efficiency and fitness. The contrast between Catholic and Protestant dietetics in this evolutionary progress was somewhat insignificant. Both Catholic and Protestant approaches provided the basis for a shift away from renunciation of bodies to the utility of bodies. We can, therefore, treat the dietary timetable as part of the emergence of disciplines which converted bodies into productive utilities. For example, in *Discipline and Punish*, Foucault observed that:

These methods, which made possible the meticulous control of the operations of the body, which assured the constant subjection of its forces and imposed upon them a ration of docility–utility, might be called 'disciplines'. Many disciplinary methods had long been in existence — in monasteries, armies, workshops. But in the course of the seventeenth and eighteenth centuries the disciplines became general formulas of domination . . . The historical moment of the disciplines was the moment when an art of the human body was born, which was directed not only at the growth of its skills, nor at the intensification of its subjection, but at the formation of a relation that in the mechanism itself makes it more obedient as it becomes more useful, and conversely. (Foucault, 1979, pp. 137—8)

The growth of disciplines was thus an expression of the relationship of knowledge and power to bodies in social space. The dietary timetable, alongside developments in medical science, psychology, penology and social science, can be seen as a process of rationalisation which promoted a new productivity of bodies.

The dietary timetables which became popular in the seventeenth and eighteenth centuries were based on the premiss that Christians had a religious responsibility for the care of their bodies. The abuse of the body in the form of gluttony was seen to be equivalent to suicide, in that it curtailed the normal expectation of life. The fashion for diet thus emerged among the aristocratic rich who were prone to obesity and concern for appropriate diets expressed a religious anxiety about the impact of intemperance on life expectancy. The achievement of good life and health came to be a sign of inner religious value; dietary management assumed a close, intimate proximity between religious salvation and physical health. In Britain, for example, the medico-religious publications of George Cheyne, especially *The English Malady* of 1733, provided the central components of the aristocratic life-style. Cheyne contrasted the traditional, rural occupations of the gentry with the overcrowded, urban life-style of the London elite. Sickness was most common among:

the Rich, the Lazy, the Luxurious, and the Unactive, those who fare daintily and live voluptuously, those who are furnished with the rarest delicacies, the richest foods and the most generous wines, such as can provoke the Appetites, Senses and Passions in the most exquisite and voluptuous Manner. (Cheyne, 1733, p. 49)

The aristocracy within the urban environment of London were being destroyed by luxury, inactivity and over-consumption. Cheyne's remedy was dietary management, exercise and restraint which, in controlling the passions, would promote long life, sanity and moral rectitude.

The theoretical basis of Cheyne's regimen was derived from Descartes's mechanistic model of the body and from the medical rationalism of the Leiden school. Descartes and Harvey provided the basic model of the body as a hydraulic machine, but this iatromathematical tradition was combined with the religious notion that dietary management was performed in the service of God, in that men have a caretaker duty towards their bodies. Cheyne's dietetic ideas can be traced back to the *Hygiasticon, or the right course of preserving life and health unto extream old age* of 1634 of Leonard Lessius (1554—1623) and to the *Trattato della vita sobria* of 1558 of Luigi Cornaro (1475—1566). The *Trattato*, which was translated into English by George Herbert in 1634, was directed towards the Italian nobility and presented a critique of the 'bad customs' of aristocratic society and, more generally, of decadent Italian society. The social malaise was the result of:

the first, flattery and ceremoniousness; the second, Lutheranism, which some have most preposterously embraced; the third, intemperance. (Cornaro, 1776, p. 14)

Cornaro conceptualised the discipline of diet within an exclusively spiritual framework as a protection against the natural temptations of the flesh, regarding 'Divine Sobriety' as pleasing to God. Cornaro's treatment of 'violent passions' provided a basis for the religious practices of George Herbert and his community at Little Gidding and for Cheyne and his aristocratic clients.

Although Cheyne wrote principally for the London elite of gentry, professional men and scholars, his dietary regimen eventually reached a far wider, popular audience through the preaching and practice of John Wesley and the Methodists. In his *Primitive Physick or an Easy and Natural Method of Curing Most Diseases* of 1752, Wesley showed himself to be familiar with and appreciative of Cheyne's regimen of milk, vegetables and seeds as a cure of insanity, obesity and melancholy. Wesley had commended Cheyne's 'Essay of Health and Long Life' to his mother in 1724, commenting that it 'is chiefly directed to studious and sedentary persons' (Telford, 1931, vol. 1, p. 11). Wesley also wrote to the Bishop of London suggesting that, although abstaining from wine and flesh was not a doctrinal requirement of orthodox Christianity, diet and restraint were clearly compatible with it. By following Cheyne's regimen, Wesley claimed that he had been:

free (blessed be God) from all bodily disorders. Would be to God I knew any method of being equally free from all 'follies and indescretions'. But this I never expect to attain till my spirit returns to God. (Cragg, 1975, vol. 2, p. 345)

There was, therefore, an 'elective affinity' between the Wesleyan ascetic calling in the world and the dietary regimen of George Cheyne. Diet offered a method of controlling those passions which impinged upon the rational organisation of life and threatened the religious vocation.

One can also suggest a relationship between the requirements of stable production and a disciplined workforce in competitive capitalism and dietary management of rational bodies. The control of the inner body produced, as it were, a dietary ethic which was compatible with the spirit of capitalism. Cheyne's discipline of aristocratic bodies was transferred via Wesley's *Primitive Physick* to the social surveys of the nineteenth century which were specifically concerned with the abuses of working bodies (alcoholism, prostitution and insanitary conditions) in the urban environment of capitalist society. There were important economic and political reasons for improving the health of the working class through regulation of sanitation, diet and education.

This new emphasis on the discipline of the body through the national efficiency movement in Britain coincided with a concern for the health of schoolchildren. As Foucault has argued, the chapel, the school and the factory became centres of regulative practices by which urban populations could be subject to scientific surveillance. These regulative practices were, however, grounded in a secular rather than religious language of the body. They also implied a new metaphor of the body as a political economy of reproductive life. The sixth edition of the *Handbook for Attendants of the Insane* of 1913 captures this new metaphor precisely, by arguing that the human body is 'simply a bank account of loss and gain, of waste and repair . . . [the insane] have overdrawn and are overdrawing their bank account' (Clark, 1913, p. 41). Dietary control of insanity required a monetarist policy of discipline and cut-backs. These changing metaphors of the body, the calculation of calories, the rise of dietetics and the new regimes of nineteenth-century asylums are clearly relevant to Foucauldian analysis as an account of the intimate relationship between forms of power and modes of discourse.

Although there were major shifts in the culture of the body in the Victorian period, there were also important continuities of the traditional religious discourse of diet. The Revd H. Newcomb's *Christian Character: a book for young ladies* (1862) was representative of a particular type of mid-nineteenth-century moral instruction. The book offers a complete guide to young ladies in society who are to have pleasant personalities and pleasing manners. Newcomb remains of interest because he clearly connects religion with physical health:

A healthy and vigorous state of the body is important to a high degree of usefulness. The services which God requires of us, as labourers in his vineyard, are such as to call for vigour of body and strength of mind. A feeble state of health, other things being equal, must be a hindrance in the divine life. (Newcomb, 1862, p. 160)

In order to achieve this 'degree of usefulness', Newcomb recommended attention to health as a Christian duty, regularity of habits, two hours per day for exercise in the open air, concern for the quantity and quality of food and 'to glorify God in eating and drinking' (Newcomb, 1862, p. 173). In the bibliographical appendix to this text, Newcomb commended in his 'course of reading' for young ladies the works of Cornaro as a basic guide to Christian health. Although a conventional religious literature was thus part of the health education of Christian homes, the dietary norms of Cornaro and Cheyne were being replaced within the wider community by a new political economy of the body.

Whereas eighteenth-century dietary programmes were expressed through the language of religious duty, nineteenth-century dietetics grew out of the debate about urban management, efficiency and the fiscal problems of incarceration for deviants. In science, thermodynamics replaced the ancient discourse of humours; digestion and equilibrium as asceticism and labour were united in factory discipline. The problem of the longevity of the aristocratic body was replaced by the search for labour discipline and effectiveness.

In the twentieth century, the traditional procedures for the control of the inner body in the form of passions have been partly replaced by a contemporary interest in the external body. The Hobbesian problem of restraint has given way to the question of representation, that is, to gestures, presentations of self, and exterior symbols of status and personality. The commercialisation of the body and the narcissistic personality have transformed dietary regimen into a quest for, amongst other things, sexual happiness and self-enhancement. The culture of narcissism (Lasch, 1980) can be taken as an indication of this shift from the regimen of interiors to the representation of self through the external body.

Gestures

In Foucault's account of disciplines, the moral order of the asylum under the control of reformers like Pinel and Tuke was organised around a system of paternal authority and the internal conscience of the inmates. The external social order rested ultimately on the 'court of conscience' within the individual and was institutionalised in confessional practices (Hepworth and Turner, 1982). By contrast to the organised rationality of penological space, the sociology of interpersonal, symbolic exchanges in contemporary western societies is deeply problematic.

One theme of modern sociology is that the secularisation of the exterior body is to be measured in terms of a deritualisation of gestures whereby the stable world of formalised honour has been superseded by social instability, encapsulated in Goffman's concept of 'the presentation of self in everyday life' (1969). This process can be seen as a transition from honour to dignity, that is, as the transition from a society in which the value of the individual is located in social positions, such as the gentleman-knight, to a society where individual worth is socially free-floating as 'human dignity' (Berger, 1973). The *persona*, developing out the Etruscan culture of masks, was originally external and separate from the self (Mauss, 1979). The modern conception of 'the person' as the unity of body, self and conscious will emerged out of the integration of the Roman law context, with its notions of personal legal rights, and of the Christian notion of moral consciousness. The concept of 'the person' was eventually shorn of its ritual and legal setting to emerge as pure subjectivity. There was, however, a large area of potential conflict between the Christian notion of the subjectivity of the soul and the classical emphasis on honour. Personal value within the culture of the European courts was inextricably bound up with the concept of 'civility', which was primarily focused on the nature of the norms of body gestures within public space.

In *The Civilizing Process* Norbert Elias (1978) identifies Erasmus' *De civilitate morum puerilium* of 1530 as the main location for *civilité* in European societies. This treatise on pedagogy discussed a variety of social settings in which 'bodily culture' was important, especially at banquets, amusements and festivals. Erasmus expounded at length on the problems of nose-blowing, belching and farting in public. For example, eating with three rather than five fingers was the mark of a knight. Although Erasmus' treatise contains much traditional advice on manners, the sixteenth-century *civilité* gradually replaced existing ideas about courteous behaviour. Situated in a transitional period between feudalism and the absolutist monarchies, Erasmus was representative of an independent, humanistic tradition.

With the disappearance of the feudal 'courtoisie', there was a new emphasis on the importance of social observation and a greater interest in the status implications of clothing and dress. Observation of oneself and others in social settings became increasingly significant, if gestures were to take on their appropriate meanings. The new culture of civility was observant and sensitive to public displays of social manners. In the transitional world of the treatise, there was considerable mixing of social groups and an anxiety over personal presentation as the more rigid codes of feudal honour became obsolete. These codes of civility permitted strangers and people of different rank to mix socially without conflict or embarrassment. Observation and scrutiny of men in public, not tied together by kinship or communal obligations, were aspects of the new sensitivity to external decorum, where personal reputation came to depend on the refinement of gestures.

Etiquette can thus be seen as a feature of social maintenance that creates a stable social space which is both impersonal and convivial. Indeed, the conviviality between strangers was made possible by the existence of rules of impersonality. This civility of strangers was precisely the moral world celebrated by Rousseau and also the world destroyed by the cosmopolitan culture of the crowded city. Familiarity between urbanised citizens results in a decline of impersonal *civilité* as people become exposed to the gaze of others in a culture which elevates intimacy to a primary value. The Rousseauist critique of city life provides the immediate context of Richard Sennett's analysis of the secularisation of urban space and the collapse of civic impersonalism in *The Fall of Public Man* (1974). Sennett's approach to the problem of contemporary representation is based on the paradox that any increase in intimacy entails a decrease in sociability. The impersonal tradition of *civilité* discouraged public intimacies in favour of communal solidarity and sociability between strangers. Secular urban society has created a cult of personal intimacy which attempts to define the nature of public space by denying any value to impersonal rules of public conduct. The imposition of intimacy and subjectivity on the public domain results in the 'fall of public man' and the emergence of a new personality in narcissism. As Durkheim noted, the collapse of an objective sense of a common sacred cosmos creates a social vacuum which the expressivity of spontaneous representations and subjective individualism attempts to fill. In Sennett's sociological critique, the result is 'the tyranny of intimacy'.

This analysis of the crisis of representation in modern urban cultures can be seen, to some extent, as a restatement of the notions of 'other-directedness' and 'the lonely crowd' (Reisman 1961). In a society without a common agreement on *civilité*, social actors 'make out' and avoid embarrassment by the employment of a variety of interactional tactics. The new rituals of micro-engagements have no location in a sacred order and are largely spontaneous, emergent adjustments to the contingencies of everyday interaction. The social order of contemporary societies is thus contradictory. On the one hand, there is the emphasis on intimacy and subjective spontaneity in interaction. On the other, there is the growth of bureaucratic control and registration. The intervention of the state in late capitalist society results in an extension of disciplinary practices through the detailed registration of bodies; at the same time, in interpersonal relations the traditional code of *civilité* is constantly undermined by the search for individualism in expressive encounters. In order to understand this contradiction, it is important to contrast what Foucault refers to as the problem of 'the body of individuals and the body of populations' (1980, p. 172), that is, the restraint and representation of individuals versus the reproduction and registration of populations.

Symbols of paternity
Within the anthropology and history of religions, there has been a traditional concern with the relationship between patriarchy, paternity and religious symbolism (Goody, 1962). In large measure the institutions of kinship exchange, exogamy and incest taboo reflect a permanent tension between the importance of stable transmission of

property between generations and the permanent possibility of illegitimacy. Both the Old and New Testament, for example, gave prominence to the issues of paternity and inheritance in the biblical imagery of the Tree of Knowledge and the creative God. The fact of male involvement in the biology of human reproduction was to some extent compromised by the dangers of filial disloyalty, the economic burden of children and the possibility of inauthentic paternity (Bakan, 1974). Since the precise duration of gestation was uncertain, there were special anxieties surrounding first-born offspring and hence strong social pressures towards infanticide, buttressed by the constraints of economic scarcity. In biblical symbolism, circumcision and baptism came to represent alternatives to child murder by slaughter and drowning. The eucharistic sacrifice was, in this interpretation, a transference of parental guilt for the institution of infanticide.

In any society organised around male dominance, male inheritance and primogeniture there is a corresponding social need to question the importance of women in the physiological reproduction of men and an ideological pressure to enhance the unique importance of the male semen in the generative act. Medical conceptions of the reproduction of men have thus played a crucial role in theological speculations about sexuality. For example, one of the most influential medieval texts on human generation was Giles of Rome's 'De formatione corporis humani in utero' (Henson, 1975), which overturned the Galenic two-seed theory in favour of the creativity of the male seed. The female womb came to be regarded as a suitable vessel within which the male seed was solely responsible for the creation of men. The Church inherited the Aristotelian doctrine of female inferiority and the Pauline doctrine of sexuality as a threat to male spirituality. Women, as a secondary creation out of Adam's rib, were regarded as a monstrous threat to personal piety and to family stability (Maclean, 1980). Although, in theoretical medicine, the role of women in reproduction was persistently denied, in practice the importance of women in the reproduction of men as inheritors of family property could never be wholly excluded. Given the medico-religious view of the irrationality of female sexuality, the legitimacy of offspring was a perennial uncertainty.

These anatomical and theological viewpoints produced a powerful ideology of sex in which the economic requirement that female fertility should be carefully controlled was reflected in the theory of female hysteria. It is difficult to argue that the theory of hysteria was simply a product of economic requirements of property transmission in feudalism and early capitalism, since the notion of female hysterics can be traced back to the Egyptian Kahun Papyrus of 1900 BC. In the Egyptian medical treatises, one finds a discussion of hysterical disorders resulting from the displacements of the womb. At a later stage, the theory of the wandering womb was replaced in Galenic medicine by the idea that seminal putrefaction was the cause of hysterical behaviour in women (Veith, 1965). In the seventeenth and eighteenth centuries, female hysteria was analysed in terms of 'melancholia' and 'English madness' by Richard Burton and George Cheyne. In the nineteenth century, the investigations of Charcot and Freud pushed the analysis of hysteria towards the problem of repressed sexuality. As Breuer and Freud tersely commented in their 'preliminary communication' of 1893, 'hysterics suffer mainly from reminiscences' (Freud and Breuer, 1978, p. 58).

Although there were major changes in the theory of hysteria, the treatment of hysterics and the basic notion that hysteria had sexual origins remained constant for many centuries. The therapeutics for hysteria involved actual or simulated sexual intercourse; it was commonly observed that hysteria was particularly common among divorced or single women. The treatment almost invariably recommended early marriage and regular pregnancy. This continuity of practice, despite shifts in theory, points to continuities in the social and economic roles of women as reproducers of men — and consequently of property. Victorian theories of hysteria thus indicate a continuity of marriage practices from feudalism to capitalism, by which men controlled female sexuality through medico-religious doctrines in order to organise the transmission of property from father to son.

Religious controls on female behaviour were thus crucial for the concentration of land in feudal estates, but the ideological emphasis on reproductive legitimacy continued into the period of early capitalism. The importance of family funding for nascent capitalist enterprises in the absence of adequate long-term loan facilities underlined the importance of the role of primogeniture in the intergenerational conservation of wealth. The religious grounding for the control of reproduction disappeared in late capitalism with the growth of institutional investment, the reorganisation of capital financing and the separation of ownership and control of industrial property. The real importance of the separation of family and economy is to be located in the decline of private family capitalism in western societies in the middle of the twentieth century; this separation lies behind the relaxation of divorce and inheritance laws in a variety of matrimonial causes acts from the late-Victorian period onwards. The secularisation of familial ideology is thus an outcome of long-term changes in the dominant mode of production in industrial societies.

The ideology of male creativity and female chastity and hysteria was directed at the dominant class of property-owners, and had little relevance to either landless peasants or property-less wage labourers. These groups were regarded as being incapable of love, chastity or virtue. They remained, as Gramsci noted, within the 'realm of animality'. The reproductive activities of subordinate groups only came to the attention of dominant classes in the crisis of the demographic transition which accompanied capitalist accumulation in the early decades of the nineteenth century. In north-western Europe, celibacy and late marriage, necessitated by the structural absence of viable household units, partially explained the stability of populations (Andorka, 1978). When these structural limits on the reproduction of subordinate groups began to crumble under the impact of improved conditions of urban employment for young people, the importance of moral constraints on sexual activity was clearly perceived. For Malthus, human populations had to opt for late marriage and family limitation, if famine and pestilence were to be avoided. Classical political economy thus incorporated a number of anxieties about time and space. Nature had restricted the space available for human populations, since sexual happiness, as it were, competed with land. These conceptions of natural limitations were expressive of the deep anxieties which lay behind Malthusian pessimism and Benthamite doubts about the possibility of continued economic advancement (Wolin, 1961).

The problem of the reproduction of bodies in north-western Europe was settled eventually neither by famine (except in the cases of Ireland and northern Scotland) nor by moral restraint and voluntary celibacy. The stabilisation of the multiplicity of bodies resulted from a wide variety of social changes: the spread of contraceptive devices; improvements in the productivity of land and labour; a new emphasis on domesticity and child management; the development of new standards of middle-class prosperity; outward migration. With these social changes, sexual happiness became detached from the traditional Christian notion that the only justification for sexual gratification of the body was in reproduction. This secularisation of eroticism was not, however, simply a matter of decline, but involved a transference of norms of religious practice into the secular arena, where they became attached to new goals of personal fulfilment. Whereas monastic bodies were trained, disciplined and dieted to produce athletic but celibatarian persons, contemporary bodies are disciplined to achieve public norms of sexuality. The reproduction of bodies in time has been replaced, as a social issue, by the representation of sexuality in personal encounters.

The 'accumulation of men'
The reproduction of bodies through time was thus part of the metaphysical anxiety that informed classical political economy. Although the problem of bodies in space, especially the urban density of populations in nineteenth-century Europe, was fundamental to early social philosophy, it has been neglected as a linking theme in the work of

Rousseau, Durkheim, Lévi-Strauss and Foucault. The epistemological, philosophical and political contributions of these four writers have been frequently discussed, and their reflections on 'the accumulation of men', to use Foucault's phrase, represent a significant input into the Hobbesian problem of populations.

In Rousseau's philosophy, for example, solitariness as an absolute value was a major feature of his perspective on nature, education and religion. For Rousseau, urban crowding was held to undermine proper self-respect (*amour de soi*), because men became too dependent on the opinion of others and lapsed into selfish-love (*amour propre*) (Cassirer, 1954). In the discourse 'On the origin and foundation of the inequality of mankind', Rousseau contrasted the independent savage ('Solitary, indolent and perpetually accompanied by danger') in a state of nature with civil man in populous cities. The former was motivated by self-love and was the arbiter of his own actions, but he was not necessarily predatory since he also possessed natural compassion or pity. Pity was mankind's 'only natural virtue' but it was diminished in the transition to civilisation. Paradoxically, the more men live in the company of others, the more selfish their actions become and the more denuded of pity. Rousseau's argument was summarised in the proposition that 'In proportion as the human race grew more numerous, men's cares increased' (1973, p. 77).

The conflict between the solitary mind and the populous city, between nature and civilisation, was part of the dispute between M. d'Alembert and Rousseau over the nature and role of the theatre in the modern state. Rousseau contrasted the social consequences of the theatre in Paris and Geneva. In the French capital the citizens were already corrupted and therefore the theatre was part of the state policy to amuse men who have nothing better to do with their liberty. By contrast, in a small republic like Geneva, where the citizens were still relatively honest, the theatre must necessarily have a corrupting effect on public morality. The large city is:

full of scheming idle people without religion or principle . . . In Paris . . . everything is judged by appearances because there is no leisure to examine anything. (Rousseau, 1960, pp. 58—9)

Because all citizens were infected by selfishness, reputation rather than inner personal worth became the criterion of judgement for men and women. Rousseau thus argued that the theatre was perfectly adapted to a society which operated on the basis of reputational prestige. The theatre encouraged the introduction of luxury because there was a competitive relationship between wives to establish prestige through the adornment of their bodies. Within the crowded spaces of the city, familiarity breeds contempt.

These themes — the loss of self-respect and of civility — were dominant in Rousseau's final publication, the title of which was itself particularly revealing — *Reveries of the Solitary Walker*. These walks in part provided Rousseau with an excuse for autobiographical reflections, but they also constantly returned to the theme of how the pressure of the population in the public domain disrupted the natural harmony between mind and nature. Rousseau's social philosophy can thus be regarded as an inquiry into the organisation of populations within an urban space where the public civilities of Geneva collapsed under the weight of selfish actions and reputation. Numbers and presentation of selves were linked together within the contemporary polis (Sennett, 1974, pp. 118—19).

The relationship between Rousseau's social philosophy of natural man and Lévi-Strauss's structural anthropology is well known. Jacques Derrida (1976), for example, draws attention to their interest in the emergence of writing in human culture as a crucial step in the transition from animality to society. The chapter on 'A Writing Lesson' in Lévi-Strauss's *Tristes Tropiques* (1976) represents a central interpretation of the loss of innocence on the part of a pre-literate community. More directly, Lévi-Strauss in *Totemism* (1969) regarded Rousseau as providing the theoretical origins of modern anthropology in the question: how do men pass from nature to culture? Rousseau showed that 'every human mind is a locus of virtual experience where what goes on in the minds of men, however remote they may be, can be investigated' (Lévi-Strauss, 1969, p. 176).

Although this transition from nature is a major issue, it has to be seen in the context of Rousseau's concern with the problem of population pressures. Lévi-Strauss interprets the major thesis of Rousseau's discourse on human inequality as an investigation of the social consequences of demographic change. Thus, the transition from animality to society and:

from nature to culture depended on demographic increase, but the latter did not produce a direct effect, as a natural cause. First it forced men to diversify their modes of livelihood, in order to exist in different environments, and also to multiply their relations with nature. But in order that this diversification and multiplication might lead to technical and social transformations, they had to become objects and means of human thought. (Lévi-Strauss, 1969, p. 173)

In order for men to become 'objects' of thought, it is necessary to have writing which permits the exercise of power and control through means of recording, classification and registration of bodies in space.

There are three principal areas of theoretical contact between Rousseau and Lévi-Strauss. First, there is a romantic view of the solitary mind. Secondly, there is the realisation that population density produces an increase in the division of labour and corresponding changes in culture, particularly in writing and recording — a theme which was elaborated by Durkheim (1964) in *The Division of Labour in Society*. Thirdly, there is the assumption that the singular human mind reproduces internally the basic forms of myth and symbolism so that the central features of modern anthropology are addressed to Kantian philosophy.

These themes of romanticism, demography and cognition are clearly articulated in the autobiographical *Tristes Tropiques*. This study may be regarded as an extended reflection on the effects of western culture on primitive simplicity and especially a reflection on the social consequences of demographic change and urbanisation on aboriginal innocence. In his first encounters with the colonised islands of the West Indies, Lévi-Strauss remarks:

This was not the first occasion on which I had encountered those outbreaks of stupidity, hatred and credulousness which social groups secrete like pus when they begin to be short of space. (Lévi-Strauss, 1976, p. 33)

The quiet and solitude of the deep forests of South America contrast sharply with the human misery of the teeming cities of Europe and Asia. Indian cities, in particular, provide the ultimate expression of 'filth, chaos, promiscuity, congestion; ruins, huts, mud, dirt' (Lévi-Strauss, 1976, p. 169).

The dynamic density of populations in crowded urban space has important consequences. For Rousseau, it resulted in a loss of natural pity and self-respect. For Durkheim, the outcome was the death of the old gods, the decline of an extensive *conscience collective* and the growth of social solidarity based on restitutive law and reciprocal exchanges. For Lévi-Strauss, it brought about the demise of the natural order. For Foucault, the concentration of populations gives rise to the social sciences, directed at the control of docile bodies through the secular practices of registration and bureaucratic records.

If Foucault's epistemological work represents analyses of knowledge/power, his historical inquiries centre on body/society. The object of these investigations is the emergence of discursive and non-discursive practices by which the human body is organised and controlled within social space. The organisation of vagrant, unemployed bodies provides part of the central theme of *Madness and Civilization* (Foucault, 1967); the supervision of docile bodies within Bentham's panopticism is the critical issue of the second half of *Discipline and Punish* (Foucault, 1979); the centralised gaze of clinic medicine and the hospitalisation of bodies constitute the motif of *The Birth of the Clinic* (Foucault, 1973); the sexuality of the body is the focus of *The History of Sexuality* (Foucault, 1981). For Foucault, Marxism has typically overlooked the materiality of the body and Foucault suggests that it would be 'more materialist to study first the question of the body and the effects of power on it' (Foucault, 1980, p. 58).

The 'accumulation of men' in European societies was associated with the proliferation of regimes and practices of control — timetables, taxonomies, examinations, drill, *dressage*, surveys, census forms, calculation and chrestomathy. It is the problem of expanding numbers of bodies within a restricted urban space which generates Foucault's employment of numerous spatial metaphors — terrain, horizon, landscape, site, domain, archipelago and position — in his analysis of social and conceptual organisation. One might extend this Benthamite problematic with one drawn from Malthus: the geometric expansion of populations had to be controlled, not simply through moral restraint, but through a moral calculus of surveillance and inspection. The discourses and practices of the nineteenth century developed a profound medicalisation of the body:

A 'medico-administrative' knowledge begins to develop concerning society, its health and sickness, its conditions of life, housing and habits, which serves as the basic core for the 'social economy' and sociology of the nineteenth century. (Foucault, 1980, p. 176)

It is for this reason that Foucault locates the origins of sociology, not in the works of Comte and Montesquieu, but in the practices of the medical profession. This explosion of registration was also part of Foucault's implicit analysis of the secularisation of European culture, in that the transference of monastic disciplines to the school and the factory was part of the new bio-politics of social order.

A similar line of argument dominates *The History of Sexuality*. Contrary to the view that the history of sexuality from Victorian times to the Freudian present is a history of liberation, Foucault argues that the modalities of sexuality in contemporary society are the product of a 'discursive explosion' that had its origins in the confessional literature of the seventeenth century. Out of the sacrament of penance and the discourse of the flesh in the Catholic confessional *summa*, there has emerged a scientific discourse of sexuality in biology, physiology, psychiatry and demography. These discourses were productive, not repressive, in creating new types of sexual behaviour and new categories of sexual deviance. This scientific discourse of the flesh is organised along two axes — individual desire and the dynamics of population. The issue of sexual surveillance first developed in the dominant class, but was rapidly extended to the reproductive capacities of subordinate groups. In the development of sexuality:

one of the primordial forms of class consciousness is the affirmation of the body; at least, this was the case for the bourgeoisie during the eighteenth century. It converted the blue blood of the nobles into a sound organism and a healthy sexuality . . . Conflicts were necessary (in particular, conflicts over urban space: cohabitation, proximity, contamination, epidemics, such as the cholera outbreak of 1832, or again prostitution and venereal diseases) in order for the proletariat to be granted a body and a sexuality. (Foucault, 1981, p. 126)

Having acquired sexuality, the irrationality of the proletarian body had to be surveyed by a regime of strict taxonomy and classification so that passions could be redirected into productive functions. The eroticism of the dance of death and the rape of life from previous periods was now 'carefully supplanted by the administration of bodies and the calculated management of life' (Foucault, 1981, p. 140). In this organisation of bodies, one might argue that secularisation equals classification or, in Weber's language, that one aspect of secularisation is that all areas of life become increasingly subject to bureaucratic control and scientific measurement.

The consequences of this accumulation of bodies are to be discovered in an extended mental and architectural specialisation in society. The need to organise sexuality promoted a massive intellectual division of labour in the social and medical sciences, while also stimulating a reconstruction of architectural space within the hospital, asylum, school and factory. These disciplines of the body were an 'anatomo-politics of the human body' and a 'bio-politics of the population' (Foucault, 1981, p. 139). The coherence of modern societies is achieved, therefore, not through a shared religious canopy of general values, but through a dense network of micro-disciplines which secure and control the production and reproduction of bodies. The disciplinary and regulatory control of populations operates through classifications, typologies and categories, which are embedded in panoptic practices and bureaucratic institutions. The surveillance of populations within this detailed urban space is secured through identity cards, licences, taxation codes, biographical details of age, place of birth and sex, insurance numbers, passports, number-plates and public credentials.

Although it is often argued that modern secular societies are characterised by individualistic ideologies, it would be more appropriate to argue that they paradoxically combine a bureaucratic surveillance of populations and an individuation of bodies. Social individuation is the process whereby bodies acquire precise location within a society through the allocation of definitive marks; it is on the basis of this individuation that the interpellation of subjects by ideology is possible (Hirst and Woolley, 1982, p. 135). Such processes of individuation by bureaucratic means have to be differentiated carefully from individualism, as a critical doctrine of individual rights, and from individuality, as a theory of human creativity (Weintraub, 1978). The integration of contemporary societies is the effect, not of civil religion or value consensus, but of the dull compulsion of registration and economic constraint.

Summary

In this chapter, an examination of the body in society has provided a new perspective on the traditional theme that one of the functions of religion is the achievement of social control. The conventional issues of social integration and social control can be treated by reference to four dimensions of human corporality — the body of individuals (interior and exterior), the body of populations (time and space). By extension, social systems are geared to the solution of four 'system problems' — reproduction, restraint, representation and registration.

In the process of secularisation, various forms of moral restraint, internal disciplines of asceticism, external rituals of public control and public codes of representation are transformed and transferred into secular practices of dietary control, narcissism and intimacy. With these changes in interpersonal intimacy, there was a corresponding elaboration of the apparatus of social control. Regulative panopticism emerged as a new principle of organisation of mass society. The intimacy of the private world is conjoined with detailed regulation of public space.

Behind these developments, there was a long historical process in which sexuality and the family were separated from the basic forms of economic accumulation and ownership. In order to understand these structural changes, it is important to examine in more detail the relationship between religion and property in the transition from feudalism to capitalism and the growth of individualism from religious concepts of the individual to legal concepts of corporate identity.

6 Feudalism and Religion

Secularisation

Nineteenth-century theories of industrialisation were also theories of secularisation. It was thought that the transition from rural to urban societies had broken the hold of the Church over society and the control of religious ideas over the minds of men and, more importantly, over women. The development of European societies was seen to be divided chronologically into ages of faith and ages of secularity; this cultural division coincided with that deep fissure in the structure of western society, namely, the transition from feudalism to capitalism. For Saint-Simon, the 'feudal–theological system' was being replaced by a new order based on the industrial classes and positivist science. In the industrial–scientific system, the government of men would be transformed into the administration of things (Taylor, 1975). In Auguste Comte's positivist philosophy, medieval society, characterised by the dominance of the Catholic Church and militarism, was being rapidly overtaken by a new system in which scientists and industrialists would assume dominant social roles (Aron, 1968, vol. 1). By the time of Herbert Spencer, the military/industrial contrast had become 'a richly embroidered common-place' (Peel, 1971, p. 193) among dissenting liberals. The notion that secular society was necessarily conjoined with industrial development was thus part of a wider preoccupation with social progress (Sklair, 1970).

We can, in fact, distinguish a majority and minority view on social evolution and progress in nineteenth-century philosophy and social science. In the majority view, the collapse of the old military/theological system creates a general crisis in social organisation and human consciousness. Under appropriate political circumstances, however, an industrial/secular society creates greater social welfare by improving the productive base of society and creates greater social freedom for the individual. In the minority view, the benefits resulting from industrialisation are not only precarious, but costly. Urban industrialisation had destroyed a settled world of rural communities, in which men were securely located in a unified social, natural and spiritual reality. The social and geographical division of labour had radically dislocated that unity, and the apparent autonomy of individuals from more traditional institutional moorings did not necessarily result in greater existential certainty and happiness. This nostalgic view contrasted the artificiality of modern social relations with the natural, 'organic' structures of traditional society, a contrast made famous by Ferdinand Tonnies in his study of community and society (*Gemeinschaft* and *Gesellschaft*) (Freund, 1979).

More generally, there was a distinction in German philosophy between *Zivilisation* (the outward, superficial manners of an industrial society) and *Kultur* (the inward, genuine culture of individuals). The minority view of the impact of industrial development in Germany assumed a profoundly pessimistic perspective of the consequences of secular industrialism. The traditional Christian culture of Europe was dead, but, in the absence of authentic culture, uprooted man was alienated and estranged. Philosophical opposition to Darwinistic optimism and national confidence found violent expression in Nietzsche's analysis of the death of God and nihilism as the consequences not simply of industrialisation, but of western history. This thematic *Kulturpessimismus* underscored Weber's critique of bureaucratisation in both capitalism and socialism (Merquior, 1980) and was reflected in Heidegger's analysis of the loss of authentic existence in the transition to a society based on competition and credit.

The issue of secularisation thus divides sociology into two camps: one that treats secularisation as a loss of faith and authenticity; and another that regards secularisation as a gain in personal freedom and autonomy. The language employed to describe these changes in western culture and society is itself often indicative of these metatheoretical assumptions. For example, MacIntyre in *Secularization and Moral Change* (1967b, p. 12) refers to the 'destruction of the older forms of community' by rapid urbanisation. With the transformation of the countryside by industrialisation, the working class was:

torn from a form of community in which it could be intelligibly and credibly claimed that the norms which govern social life had universal and cosmic significance, and were God-given. (MacIntyre, 1967b, p. 15)

The loss of community entails the loss of moral coherence; it is this 'destruction' of the moral community which triggers off the decline of religion, since, for MacIntyre, religion is always an expression of the moral unity of a society.

Modern moral systems lack that universality and significance which was enjoyed by pre-secular thought rooted in the moral integration of society. The result is that factual questions about the nature of God and morality can no longer be raised in modern society, because the universe in which those questions make sense has disappeared. Atheism ceases to be an option, because theism has no specific content. In this context, Christianity becomes mythology, adherence to which is personal and optional (MacIntyre and Ricoeur, 1969).

The loss of community means that it is difficult to discover any coherent moral existence; this applies equally to Christianity and Marxism. For MacIntyre, the sociological limitations on Christian beliefs also impinge on Marxism, since the secular values which Engels anticipated have not emerged — at least not yet. We can note that the validity of MacIntyre's account of secularisation depends upon the truth of two propositions. The first is that pre-modern society, specifically pre-industrial society, possessed a moral unity which was expressed through a common cosmology and theology. Secondly, this common world-view meant that there were general agreements as to the nature and purpose of this life, agreements which rendered moral commitments binding and authoritative. MacIntyre's argument has, in short, to diminish, although not to deny, the role of social divisions in pre-industrial societies in order to enhance the notion of moral community. This chapter is primarily concerned to show that these two factual claims cannot be substantiated.

Marx and Engels on social change

In general, Marx and Engels lacked this pessimistic and nostalgic view of social change; they had more in common with Comte and Saint-Simon than with Nietzsche and Weber. Marx's areligious optimism about industrial change has, of course, been frequently denied. Although it has been claimed that there exists a 'conscious and basic identity between authentic Christianity and Marx's movement' (Miranda, 1980, p. 229), it is difficult to deny that Marx saw secular industrialisation as necessary and progressive. Marx was perfectly aware of the devastating effects of factory life on the working class and globally of the cruel consequences of colonialism, but he had none of the nostalgic feeling for rural, religious cultures which is characteristic of the implicit anti-industrialism of the Marxism of Georg Lukács (Stedman-Jones, 1971). Marx's sociology is typified by a strong hostility to peasant society, to rural culture and to the stationary societies of Asia (Turner, 1974b). For Marx, Christian belief blocked the development of genuine proletarian consciousness; the 'criticism of religion is the premise of all criticism' (Marx and Engels, 1955b, p. 41), but opposition to religion has to be more than simply a theoretical opposition. Marx assumed that taking religion seriously diverted attention from the real issues of political and economic struggle. Because social being determines consciousness, the struggle of the proletariat takes place at a material not cognitive level. Marx's own opposition to religion was intensified in later Marxism, as Lenin's views on religion unambiguously demonstrate:

Religion is one of the forms of spiritual oppression which everywhere weighs down heavily upon the masses of the people, overburdened by their perpetual

work for others, by want and isolation. . . Those who toil and live in want all
their lives are taught by religion to be submissive and patient while here on
earth, and to take comfort in the hope of a heavenly reward. (Lenin, 1965, p. 7)

Arguments that either Marx or Marxism are not fundamentally
atheistic are not easily entertained.

What Marx and Engels shared with Saint-Simon was the assumption
that the transition from feudalism to capitalism involved a radical break
in the history of Christianity. Although Marx and Engels occasionally
suggested that Protestantism was the form of Christianity most suited
to the bourgeoisie, their general position was that capitalist development broke the hold of religion over society. Capitalist industrialisation
inevitably produced secularisation. In Marx's account of religious
change, it is not, however, simply the case that changes in the economic
base of society produce direct changes in the social superstructure.
Recent interpretations of the base/superstructure metaphor have paid
close attention to a crucial passage in *Capital* where Marx discussed the
connection between Catholicism and feudalism. Marx distinguished
between modes of production in terms of the dominance of politics,
economics and religion in social life:

that the mode of production of material life dominates the development of
social, political and intellectual life generally . . . is very true of our own times,
in which material interests preponderate, but not for the middle ages, in which
Catholicism, nor for Athens and Rome, where politics reigned supreme. In the
first place it strikes one as an odd thing for anyone to suppose that those
well-worn phrases about the middle ages and the ancient world are unknown to
anyone else. This much, however, is clear, that the middle ages could not live on
Catholicism, nor the ancient world on politics. On the contrary, it is the
economic conditions of the time that explain why here politics and there
Catholicism played the chief part. (Marx, 1974, vol. 1, p. 85)

According to Marx's historical materialism, in every epoch it is obvious
that people have to reproduce their economic conditions of existence in
order to survive. Writing to Kugelmann in 1868, Marx said that every
schoolboy knows that a society which did not reproduce the conditions
of production as it produced could not last above a year (Marx and
Engels, 1955b, p. 209). Every society must, in addition to producing,
reproduce its relations and forces of production. These fundamental
economic requirements determine the general character of society — its
politics, ideology, institutions and culture. Why, then, does Marx note
that religion in feudalism and politics in classical civilisation 'reigned
supreme'?

In attempting to resolve the traditional problems of the base/super-
structure metaphor in which the economy determines 'in the last
instance' and the superstructure has 'relative autonomy', writers like
Louis Althusser and Nicos Poulantzas have attempted to separate the

notions of 'domination' and 'determination'. Thus, a social totality is composed of a number of different structures or 'instances', but these are all determined by the economy. The economic base determines which element of the superstructure is dominant in a social formation. In fact, these superstructural elements can be 'conditions of existence' of economic production. The relationship between base and super- structure is not simply one of interaction or 'elective affinity'. For example, in capitalism the legal superstructure (particularly laws of property and contract) is a necessary requirement of economic activity. Although ideology has different functions in each mode of production, in general ideology is a necessary dimension of any society, if people 'are to be formed, transformed and equipped to respond to their conditions of existence' (Althusser, 1969, p. 235).

As we have seen, societies must both produce and reproduce. The reproduction of the forces of production includes not only machinery and equipment, but labour power. The reproduction of labour power involves the provision of shelter and food, but crucially it involves the development of skill and 'of its submission to the ruling ideology of the workers' (Althusser, 1977, p. 127). Thus, the reproduction of the conditions of production requires the intervention of the super- structure of law, politics and ideology.

The apparatus by which this requirement is provided can be divided into the 'repressive state apparatus' (RSA) and the 'ideological state apparatus' (ISA). The former is in fact the state itself, which is composed of the police, army, prisons and civil service. There is a multiplicity of ISAs — educational institutions, the Church, the press, artistic associations and the family. Social formations can be distin- guished in terms of the dominance of these elements and by their combination of repressive and ideological systems. In pre-capitalist societies, the Church was the dominant ISA and provided a great variety of educational, ideological and cultural services, which fostered submission to existing social arrangements. The growth of capitalism differentiates these functions amongst a variety of institutions, but, according to Althusser, it is the school/family couple which is now critical for the reproduction of labour. We can now express Althusser's account of the dominant/determinant distinction as:

Social formation	*Structure in dominance*	*State apparatus*
Ancient	Politics	RSA/ISA undifferentiated
Feudal	Religion	Church/family
Capitalist	Economic	School/family

In order to give Althusser's abstract statement of the base/super-structure problem some empirical content, we can turn to an account of the dominance of religion in feudal society by Nicos Poulantzas in *Political Power and Social Classes* (1973). According to Poulantzas, in capitalism the economy is both dominant and determinant, because the economic situation of the property-less labourer forces him to surrender his labour power; no 'extra-economic factor' is required to achieve this economic control of capital over the worker. The skill of the worker has to be developed by the ideological apparatus of various educational institutions, but the economic subordination of labour is secured by the separation of the worker from the means of production. In feudalism, however, the peasant had a certain economic independence from the landlord, albeit a precarious and uncertain independence. Peasants did not have feudal immunity and their claims on the land were not fully guaranteed in law. They did, however, have some possession of land and labour. In addition, there were customary rights to pasture, common grazing, wood-gathering and produce within the village commune. The peasants thus were to some degree self-sufficient because they had a measure of control over the means of production of their own subsistence. In feudalism, the peasant was not entirely separated from the means of production and the subordination of the peasantry had to be brought about by 'extra-economic factors', that is, by ideological and political control.

This specification of Althusser's discussion is still conceptually imprecise. There are a variety of ways in which the notion of ideology as a 'structure in dominance' could be interpreted. The dominance of religion in feudal Europe might require that peasants were indoctrinated by religious beliefs, the effect of which was to render peasants docile and submissive. Alternatively, it may be that religious institutions were functionally necessary for the continuity of feudal arrangements. In the first formulation, there is the implication of conscious manipulation of religion by the dominant class to secure the subordination of peasants. In the second, it would be possible to state Poulantzas's argument in terms of the unintended consequences of actions which have functional effects upon a social system. A third possibility would be that ideology in feudalism is crucial for securing legal titles to land on the part of a dominant land-owning class.

These three possible interpretations indicate a basic division in Marxist accounts of ideology which are either class-theoretical or mode-theoretical (Abercrombie *et al.*, 1980). We can either analyse religion as part of the dynamic of class conflicts, in which one class manipulates religious beliefs in order to bring about the subordination of workers, or we can attempt to conceptualise religion more abstractly as a general condition of the reproduction of the mode of material existence. Both Poulantzas and Althusser have attempted to analyse the nature of various modes of production without reducing ideology to number plates on the backs of social classes and without treating ideology as simply beliefs held by individuals. For Althusser, the 'individual' is the bearer of certain socio-economic functions whose place in society is determined by ideology. It would, therefore, be inconsistent with their position to interpret the 'dominance' of ideology in subjective terms as the dominance of certain beliefs in the consciousness of individuals.

We can consider this distinction between the dominance of certain structures in society and the dominance of beliefs in individual consciousness by turning to an analysis of feudalism in the work of Barry Hindess and Paul Hirst (1975). They clearly reject the implication that the concept of 'dominance' in Althusser's rendition of the base/ superstructure metaphor refers to the ideological subordination of people. They argue that the concept of structural dominance in historical materialism cannot be interpreted as political domination of one person over another; such an interpretation is a retreat from an analysis of the structure of social relations to an investigation of subjective interaction between persons. The ideological/political structures of feudalism are requirements of exploitation, not of subjective incorporation of peasants:

the separation of the producer from the means of production, the condition of exploitative relations of production, depends upon political/ideological conditions of existence. The feudal economy supposes the intervention of another instance in order to make the conditions of feudal exploitation possible. (Hindess and Hirst, 1975, p. 232)

In feudalism, although landlords had legal titles to land, peasants had a degree of effective possession. Peasants were, however, controlled by landlords because the lords determined the size of plots of land occupied by peasants, regulated the conditions of re-tenancy and controlled certain means of production, in particular drainage and mills. The class struggles of feudalism were fought over these conditions; they were fundamentally conflicts over rent, tenancy, access to land and other means of production. Because the landlords did not have complete economic control over peasants, ideological/political factors played a dominant role in the subordination of the peasant class.

As an explanation of the dominant role of ideology and politics in feudalism, these structuralist theories in modern Marxism are not entirely satisfactory. There are two issues (one minor and one major) which we can consider in relation to the debate as to the centrality of religion under feudal conditions. The first is that the specificity of the religious dimension in the ideological structure tends to disappear in the conflation of ideology and politics in the notion of the 'extra-economic factor'. In attempting to situate the 'political/ideological instance' within feudal societies, Hindess and Hirst do not suggest why Catholicism in particular provided conditions of existence for economic exploitation. Would any form of Christianity have had the same effects? In treating religion as part of the ISA system, it is political force itself which plays the principal role within the 'extra-economic factors' which were necessary for social reproduction. The traditional notion of the superstructure becomes, in practice, specified as 'political conditions'.

Secondly, in attempting to provide a scientific analysis of ideology as a set of 'material practices' which have definite consequences on the social structure, Marxists have wanted to erase the notion that ideologies consist of false beliefs in the consciousness of social actors. More specifically, Althusserian Marxism treats the human subject as simply the bearers or supports of structural arrangements (Larrain, 1982). Such an erasure is, however, too drastic. It is still important in Marxist sociology to ask whether these 'supports' do in fact internalise dominant beliefs and appropriate the dominant culture as subjectively legitimate. It may turn out empirically that, whether or not human subjects adopt dominant beliefs, their social location is so closely determined by political and economic circumstances that they have little choice with respect to alternative forms of behaviour. Compliance makes domination easier, but a class which has a virtual monopoly of force, both economic and political, may survive considerable cultural dissent and political apathy. It is clear from Marx's own statements about the dominance of Catholicism in the Middle Ages that the dominance of ideology included the dominance of certain beliefs in social activity. It would be odd, to say the least, for Marxists to argue that the dominance of religion in feudalism could be established independently of whether anyone believed in religious values. Historical materialism does not rule out asking whether in feudalism religious beliefs and practices either directly influenced behaviour or indirectly constrained behaviour. When Marx and Engels claimed that 'The ideas of the ruling class are in every epoch the ruling ideas' (1965, p. 61), we have to assume that they meant the functions of dominant ideologies assume the presence of certain beliefs. When Lenin said:

The proletariat of today takes the side of socialism, which enlists science in the battle against the fog of religion, and frees the workers from their belief in life after death by welding them together to fight in the present for a better life (1965, p. 8)

we have to assume that he meant that belief in life after death actually inhibited the development of proletarian politics. Such naive questions as 'Did they believe that?' are not, therefore, an entire travesty of classical Marxism.

The debate about the secularising consequences of capitalism comes to hinge crucially on the existence in feudalism of a 'moral community' within which religious beliefs could be taken seriously. To show that Catholicism was a dominant ideology in feudal Europe, we have to show that both landlord and peasant were embraced by religious beliefs, the effect of which was to aid the reproduction of exploitative relations. The expression 'to aid' is used here deliberately, because part of my argument is to show that the relationship between economy and ideology can never be tightly drawn; the effects of religious beliefs in feudalism were empirically confused, contradictory and diverse. Furthermore, religious commitments had very different consequences for different social classes; their prominence and salience have to be isolated for different social classes.

Within contemporary sociology of religion, there is a clear division between those sociologists who argue that feudal Europe was dominated by a religious world-view and those who argue that feudal Europe was not 'an age of faith' (Goodridge, 1975). The first treats the history of religion under capitalism as a history of attrition in which, from a position of social dominance, the Church withers away under the impact of urbanisation, social differentiation and modernisation. For convenience, we can call this the attritionist theory. The second position holds that, since Christianity was never successful in incorporating an incorrigible peasantry by extending its cultural control beyond the limits of the principal European cities, we cannot accept arguments about the secularisation of Europe; secularisation as religious decline must presuppose a prior dominance of Christianity and is, therefore, historically utopian (Martin, 1969). For convenience, we can call this position the atrabilious theory.

For attritionists, secularisation involves the erosion of religious institutions and beliefs from public life, relegating Christianity to the social fringe and to personal privatised experience. With the development of industrial capitalism, social functions previously performed by the Church are differentiated and taken over by secular institutions, operating on the basis of empirical knowledge and oriented towards secular goals. For atrabilious theorists, in medieval Europe the great mass of the population was excluded from the civilising culture of the Church and exiled to cultural regions dominated by magic, superstition and error. The modernisation of society does not mean that the mass acquire elite culture, because their lives are now organised around the superficial pleasures of popular culture. To call such interpretations atrabilious is to indicate their pessimistic orientation; genuine religion, like authentic culture, is incapable of extensive dissemination and

requires careful cultivation and protection. Just as the authentic orthodox culture of the Church, as the principal agent of western civilisation
against barbarians, was never socially dominant, so the articulate
rational culture of contemporary society is a minority interest. Below
the thin layer of modern enlightenment, there is a subcultural world of
heresy, superstition, magic and vulgarity.

Attritionist theory

In Britain, the best defence of the attritionist theory has been presented
by Bryan Wilson. In an early definition of secularisation, Wilson (1966,
p. xiv) claimed that this 'meant the process whereby religious thinking,
practice and institutions lose social significance'. The secularisation
process is to be measured in terms of declining Church membership,
the loss of ecclesiastical prestige, the disappearance of religious control
of education and the encroachment of secular knowledge in the private
and public domain. In later definitions of secularisation, the basic
notion that secularisation involves a loss of social significance for
religious institutions has not been changed, but the dimensions of the
process have been amplified.

Secularization relates to the diminution in the social significance of religion. Its
application covers such things as, the sequestration by political powers of the
property and facilities of religious agencies; the shift from religious to secular
control of various of the erstwhile activities and functions of religion; the decline
in the proportion of their time, energy and resources which men devote to
super-empirical concerns; the decay of religious institutions; the supplanting,
in matters of behaviour, of religious precepts by demands that accord with
strictly technical criteria. (Wilson, 1982, p. 149)

Secularisation in fact is not just a process within society but a change of
society, namely, a transition from a rural, stable *communitas* to an
urban, technical society.

This view of secularisation can be subject to a number of criticisms.
It can, for example, be objected that the prevalence of cults, particularly among young people, is evidence that modern society is not
dominated by technical rationality and that the need for a religious
purpose to life is a permanent feature of human existence, independent
of major changes in the socio-economic organisation of society. In
Wilson's view, such cultic movements among the young are peripheral,
ephemeral and individualistic; they do not, like the traditional sects,
attempt to change society, but only to induce individual adaptation
to rational society through meditation, mysticism or private rituals
(Wilson, 1976). Cultic groups are not counter-cultural, but acultural,
appealing to marginal social groups whose social commitments to
family or work are minimal. Such groups as the Divine Light Mission
and Hare Krishna are not evidence against the secularisation thesis;

rather, they are massive confirmation that religion in industrial society survives mainly as an eccentric private disposition.

Western societies have, of course, experienced a number of major religious revivals in the period of industrialisation, which would suggest that secularisation is not a simple pattern of institutional decline. These movements can, however, be seen as 'the diffusion of religious dispositions among a section of the population previously religiously unsocialized' (Wilson, 1982, p. 152). Thus, Methodism in recruiting sections of the urban working class to its ranks provided the religious basis for a disciplined workforce, and in this respect Protestant revivalism may have the unintended consequences of promoting conditions of secularisation. The waves of revivalism, furthermore, tend to diminish in terms of their social significance. The line from Methodism to Salvationalism to Pentecostalism to Charismatic Renewal is a cultural line that traces this sociological diminution. Globally there is, then, an exchange relationship in which, in return for the export of Protestant revivalism to the Third World, we import a mixture of Oriental cults and mystical paraphernalia. This exchange produces a gap in the cultural balance of trade, since Oriental cults do not contribute significantly to the transformation of western society, whereas revivalism in the Third World has a number of positive functions. The result is that European societies no longer possess a unifying moral culture as the platform of religious adherence; instead industrial society relies on an 'impersonal, fundamentally amoral rational order' (Wilson, 1982, p. 164), periodically supported by coercion and constraint.

Atrabiliousness

An alternative to the attritionist position has been systematically outlined by David Martin, whose objections to the conventional view of secularisation fall under three headings. First, Martin argues that the secularisation thesis has to assume a backward-looking utopian view of medieval Christianity in which people were 'really' religious. The secularisation myth has to take certain elements of Catholicism in the eleventh to the thirteenth centuries as the norm of true religion, from which all subsequent divergence can be taken to define the secular. These normative elements are:

the temporal power of the Church, extreme asceticism, realism in philosophy, and ecclesiastical dominance in the spheres of artistic patronage and learning. (Martin, 1969, p. 31)

This norm will not serve as a valid sociological criterion, because it is partial and selective. Secondly, the secularisation thesis adheres to an 'over-secularised concept of man' in contemporary society, which minimises the continuity of pre-modern consciousness — magic, superstition and irrational belief — into so-called rational, technical society. Modern society has not witnessed 'any increase in generalized scepticism', but 'remains deeply imbued with every type of superstition and metaphysic' (Martin, 1969, p. 113). Finally, the political significance of Christianity has varied enormously between the pluralism of North America, the Catholic/Protestant dualism of Northern Ireland and the cultural monopoly of Catholicism in Italy (Martin, 1978b). Religion continues to exhibit remarkable strength in those situations where politically disprivileged groups turn to religious differentiation and difference as a cultural rallying point (Martin, 1972). The secularisation process, in so far as it exists, is certainly not uniform or unilinear. David Martin, of course, doubts that 'secularisation' is a valid sociological concept, precisely because there is uncertainty over whether Europe was ever significantly Christianised. Christianity in the past may have been much weaker than commonly assumed, whereas Christianity in the present may be much stronger than attritionists normally suggest (Martin, 1967).

As perspectives, attritionism and atrabiliousness are apparently incompatible. In defence of the former, it can be argued that the notion of a 'rational society' does not assume that superstition and magic have wholly disappeared. The dominance of rationalism in society:

means that principally there are no mysterious incalculable forces that come into play, but rather that one can, in principle, master all things by calculation. This means that the world is disenchanted. (Weber, 1961, p. 139)

A society which is organised in terms of 'means–ends rationality' routinely depends on a 'political economy of regulation' (Mitnick, 1980) to achieve dependable administrative goals, rather than on divination by oracles or traditional pronouncements or charismatic revelation. Such a society can exist alongside widespread superstition and magical practices in the populace. Furthermore, as Wilson suggests, the debates about secularisation and de-Christianisation have to be regarded as somewhat separate issues. Against the attritionist position, it is difficult not to agree with David Martin that the historical evidence suggests that the mass of the population in pre-modern times was indifferent to any form of religion. In pre-modern times, the rural hinterland of Europe lay outside the civilising influence of the Church, but also outside the influence of supernaturalist belief; this pre-Christian population was primarily concerned with a pre-eminent problem — survival.

These two apparently contradictory perspectives are clearly not the only possible accounts of secularisation (Shiner, 1966; Luckmann, 1967; Robertson, 1970; Acquaviva, 1979), but they clearly bring into focus the controversy that surrounds the issue of an 'age of faith'. The argument of this chapter is that these two perspectives are not incompatible, but actually require each other in order to produce a general theory of secularisation. The themes of attrition and atrabiliousness refer to the cultural organisation of societies conceived as a unity; they are theories of the general culture of societies.

When we begin to ask how religious dominance relates to social classes in particular, rather than to societies as a whole, we can see how these apparently contradictory positions actually imply each other. The attritionist position is empirically valid in the sense that, for the dominant class, religion had an essential function in the organisation of social behaviour; the atrabilious position is also empirically valid in that the peasantry was largely excluded from the religious system of the dominant class. Subordinate classes periodically inverted the symbolism of orthodox Christianity to provide the ideological basis of protest, but in general they lived in a cultural terrain devoid of dominant Christian symbolism. In this interpretation, secularisation means that religion lost social significance in the cultural orbit of the dominant class, because religion became separated from the economy with fundamental changes in the organisation of property. In order to understand the importance of religion in feudal society, we have to examine the impact of religion on the dominant class rather than on society in general. Religion under feudal conditions was not especially significant in the subordination of peasants, but it played a crucial role in the economic and social organisation of the land-owning class. To grasp this socio-economic role, it is important to consider the effects of Catholic Christianity on the familial, sexual and generational organisation of property.

Family strategies in feudal society

In pre-modern societies which combined primogeniture with monogamy and feudal tenures, the wealth of landlords depended crucially on the survival of male heirs, a successful marriage policy and the absence of intra-kin conflicts. This familial strategy was a precarious exercise. Mortality rates tended to be high for aristocratic males in the context of militarised feudalism; daughters and wives typically outlived sons and husbands, creating social pressures for the remarriage of widows, female infanticide and polygamy. Infertility, infidelity and over-production of daughters were particularly threatening to the preservation and concentration of land in the household unit under the dominance of patriarchal nobles. The micro-politics of familial inheritance were also profoundly influenced by demographic changes and consequently by the availability of land. A system of primogeniture in a period of population growth creates a surplus population of young males without rights to land; conquest and territorial expansion is one 'solution' to such a situation. It has been suggested, for example, that at least one causal factor in the outward expansion of the Vikings from the ninth to the tenth centuries was the presence of a surplus male population (Brøndsted, 1965). Another possible resolution of over-production in aristocratic families was the creation of religious foundations which siphoned off surplus sons and daughters.

The problems of property distribution under conditions of primo-geniture and monogamy can be illustrated by consideration of a recent study of the Saxon nobility in the tenth and eleventh centuries (Leyser, 1979). The Ottonian aristocracy of early medieval Saxony was pecu-liarly beset by the difficulties of producing male heirs. Their lives were dangerous, hard and short. Early marriage for aristocratic daughters was offset by high rates of infant mortality and death during confine-ment. Great nobles were frequently killed by rivals, followers and even servants. Furthermore, the Slav and Polish wars severely depleted the ranks of the Saxon nobility. Given the dangers that surrounded the lives of noblemen, it is not wholly surprising that women survived longer than men. Although there was a clear preference for sons to inherit the land of fathers, women could acquire property in the absence of a male claimant. In Saxony, there is evidence that noblewomen thus accum-ulated considerable wealth.

Yet it is also clear that the position of wealthy unmarried widows was insecure. They had to face the unremitting pressures and challenges of their *co-heredes* — their own and especially their husband's kin who did not acquiesce in their control of so much *predium*, enhanced as it was by dower-rights. (Leyser, 1979, p. 62)

In order to protect themselves from these social pressures, wealthy widows commonly founded religious houses to gain immunity from their kin.

The presence of unmarried girls in the aristocratic household was a particular problem. Their numbers were occasionally reduced by female infanticide, but the establishment of nunneries also permitted lords to shift the burden of responsibility for girls on to a religious institution. Noble girls were thus protected from the incestuous inter-est of their kin, but also from:

the intrusion of strangers and worst of all unequals, especially slaves. Savage penalties awaited the latter and the offending women but the former could saddle head of families with unwanted feuds . . . To read the penitentials of the early middle ages suggests that there was something like an unending promis-cuity crisis in the habitations of the laity — noble, free and serf — and not the laity alone. (Leyser, 1979, p. 64)

The transfer of daughters to religious establishments provided one means by which this promiscuity crisis could be contained. Saxon lords also secured the benefits which flowed from the prayers and good works of their female kinfolk. The worldly success of men outside the protective wall of Saxon nunneries was advanced by the spiritual activities of women, extracted from the domestic politics of noble production. The importance of religion in this society was not to act as an 'extra-economic factor' in the exploitation of serfs, but to contribute to the resolution of dilemmas in the reproduction of the dominant class.

The promiscuity crisis of noble families in Saxony assumed similar dimensions in other regions of feudal Europe in later centuries. The delicate balance of family structure, inheritance and land may well have been adversely influenced by the rise in the European population from the tenth to the thirteenth centuries. The demand for land in thirteenth-century England was particularly acute, making landed widows particularly attractive as potential spouses (Postan, 1972). The Black Death (1346—50), which reduced the population of Europe by one-third, brought about a rapid, if gruesome, change in the land : labour ratio (McNeill, 1979). With or without the constraints and contingencies of demography and disease, the problem of the reproduction of the aristocratic feudal household was widespread in Europe, given the precarious position of male heirs within the domestic unit.

The basic elements of the aristocratic marriage and family system are particularly well exposed by Georges Duby's study of twelfth-century France (1978). Since marriage was a treaty between two feudal households, marriages were typically arranged by the heads of household. There was also a preference for endogamy, since cross-cousin marriages enhanced the amalgamation of property that had been separated by previous marriages. This endogamy tended to produce alliances which were, from the Church's point of view, incestuous. There were strong reasons for regulating the sexuality of women, since either pre-marital promiscuity or adultery seriously jeopardised the production of legitimate male offspring. In general, the Church's teaching on sexual restraint and fidelity adequately supported the material interests of the dominant class in its search for concentrated ownership of land. Landlords were, however, forced to manipulate the regulations concerning incest as a pretext for the repudiation of barren wives — a procedure which the Church strongly opposed.

Given male primogeniture, there was a problem in relation to younger sons who could not marry aristocratic women without some claim to land, and surplus daughters for whom suitable partners could not be secured. These 'youths' were forced into sexual alliances with peasant women and concubines or adopted careers in war and monastic seclusion. It has been argued that these landless males became the principal bearers of the culture of Courtly Love (Lewis, 1936), which expressed in fantasy the sexual dilemmas of their social location in terms of adulterous unions with noblewomen. Their lives provided a sharp contrast to the expectations which governed the lives of the male heirs. The first-born male had to display the principles of chivalry, which emphasised chastity before marriage, honour and courage. The offspring of sexual alliances between 'youths' and household concubines tended to produce 'a kind of pleasure reserve within the house itself' (Duby, 1978, p. 24) in contrast to the productive sexuality of the male heir.

In *The Dominant Ideology Thesis* (Abercrombie *et al.*, 1980) it was argued that the Courtly Love tradition was a form of deviant sexuality, which emphasised the nature of marriage as a treaty between households. Romantic sexuality existed outside wedlock and pointed to the importance of legitimate unions for the consolidation of property in land. The teaching of the Church on the nature of sexuality contributed to the conservation of property and, although Courtly Love was a threat to medieval notions of chastity and fidelity, these love poems may have paradoxically reinforced the norms of marriage by recognising its contractual nature. There is, however, an alternative interpretation of Courtly Love which more directly supports the argument that Catholicism was the dominant ideology of the dominant class and that Catholic teaching on sexual morality in the Middle Ages clearly supported the conservation of property for the land-owning nobility.

The view that Courtly Love literature positively advocated sexual promiscuity is seriously challenged by D. W. Robertson (1980), in whose analysis Courtly Love provided a social criticism of the destructive consequences of unbridled passion. Texts illustrative of Courtly Love — such as Andreas Capellanus' *De amore* or the *Roman de la rose* — have to be read as ironic, humorous investigations of the folly of human sensuality. In a more serious mood, Courtly Love poetry suggested that lecherous desire was destructive of the highest virtues of medieval society — honour and chivalry. Unlawful sexual alliances undermined the social hierarchy which was seen as essential to social stability. The argument of Chaucer's *Troilus and Criseyde* was that:

passionate popular outbursts were an inversion of the natural order of sovereignty in the commonwealth. They boded ill for Great Troy and New Troy alike . . . if the state succumbs to the passions of the people, disregarding its ordered hierarchies in the pursuit of self satisfaction, it is, in effect, worshipping Venus and subjecting itself to Fortune. (Robertson, 1980, p. 271)

Christian restraint of passion was necessary for the good of the commonweal, whereas paganism in celebrating the pleasure of Venus corrupted the natural order of society. In this interpretation of Courtly Love, the poetic critique of licence worked alongside Catholicism in preserving the monogamous marriage system and the legitimate distribution of property via virtuous women.

The argument of this chapter is, therefore, that Catholic views of sexuality and family life provided a necessary ideological prop for a system of primogeniture as a vehicle for property distribution. Religious houses and celibacy provided mechanisms for coping with the undesirable, but inevitable consequences of such a system of inheritance, namely, surplus sons and daughters. Adherence to primogeniture was, of course, variable within European societies; in some regions, partibility was common and adequate provision was made for younger sons and daughters (Goody, Thirsk and Thompson, 1978). The English aristocracy was, however, noted for its rigorous adherence to inheritance by primogeniture. Although the norm of primogeniture distinguished Europe from other continents, within Europe it was the case that England became notorious for its rigid application of the principle of impartible inheritance. The threat of disinheritance was thus a powerful weapon in the politics of English aristocratic life (Macfarlane, 1978, p. 88). The social and political dominance of the English aristocracy was seen to depend upon:

strict settlement; efficient but conservative estate administration; subordination of personal choice to financial advantage in the selection of marriage partners; avoidance of addiction to horses, cards, dice and women; and a prudent policy of family limitation. (Stone, 1973, p. 160)

Although the moral problems of impartible inheritance were anxiously debated in England between 1500 and 1700, the political advantages of primogeniture were clearly recognised. During the Commonwealth, for example, it was argued that the stability of the political order hinged on the continuity of wealthy families, which in turn depended on a system of primogeniture. If the religious supports for impartible inheritance were crucial for the continuity of feudalism, they also played an important role in the emergence of capitalism. In the eighteenth century with the development of 'strict settlement' (Habakkuk, 1950), younger sons excluded from landed property sought social advancement in urban professional careers, especially in law and commerce. Primogeniture thus drove aristocratic but landless sons into capitalist roles and cemented the alliance between the traditional aristocratic class and the emergent bourgeoisie. The Protestant Ethic provided an ideology well-matched to the material interests of this stratum of urbanised aristocrats, seeking their fortunes in urban commerce.

Religion was the dominant ideology of the feudal period in the sense of providing important social functions for the land-owning class. It was an aid in the control of sexuality, especially of women, in the interests of the regular distribution of property and of the concentration of land within the noble class. Religion also provided supernaturalist backing for the concepts of chivalry and honour as constraints on unrestricted violence and conflict (Rosenwein and Little, 1974). Religious houses provided a spiritual guarantee of the success of male property-owners, but they also compensated for the sin of warfare and destruction.

These functional contributions of religion to the feudal social system had very little relevance to subordinate classes. Feudal society was not, as MacIntyre and others suggest, a unified social totality; there was a deep and permanent rift between lords and peasants in terms of power, culture, wealth and religion:

> the lines of division between the feudal landlords and the rest of society were cut more deeply and were more fixed than all other divisions in medieval society. From this point of view medieval England was a highly stable and wholly polarized two-class community wherein a much elevated class of feudal magnates and knights was confronted with a much inferior mass of rural humanity. (Postan, 1972, p. 174)

These lines of division ran deeply throughout European feudal society. Throughout Europe, the *popolani* were mere clods, devoid of sentiment, culture and even humanity. The peasantry was separated from lords by language, breeding, culture, ritual and symbol; the rift was periodically spanned by intermediary groups, such as lawyers, but this social mobility only served to reinforce the great divide. Feudal society was clearly divided by class divisions, but these can be defined subjectively as a divide between people (lords) and subhumans (serfs). Feudal Europe can thus be conceived as a collection of cultural islands within which orthodox, literate, articulate Christianity survived among the ruling class and a cultural hinterland, dominated by heresy, pre-Christian belief, superstition, magic, indifference and deviance, within which the peasantry existed as a subcultural unit. It was not until the early part of the thirteenth century that the Church made a serious effort to incorporate this deviant hinterland.

Confession

The fourth Lateran Council in 1215 was a major turning-point, not only in the history of western Christianity, but in the development of the social structure of European societies. The provisions of the Council have to be seen in the context of the Church's struggle against the Albigensian heresy and, more generally, against the continuity of peasant folk religion, magic and superstition (Ladurie, 1980). The objective of these thirteenth-century reforms was to create a residential clergy which was literate and celibate. The parochial clergy, once educated and disciplined, were to win over the great mass of the rural population which still existed in a state of pagan indifference to Christianity. In Languedoc and other remote regions of Christendom, the peasants 'were as allergic to culture as they were to the Reformation, and to the rudiments of lay learning as they were to the revival of sacred learning' (Ladurie, 1974, p. 162).

In reforming the clergy and converting the laity, the Lateran Council made regular confession an obligation on the laity and, to this end, encouraged the development of confessional manuals for the use of parish priests. The Council also required that doctors should request confessors to hear the confession of dying patients (Clarke, 1975). In addition, the Council sought to improve the frequency and quality of sermons; bishops were responsible for the appointment of suitable preachers and for the content of sermons (Robertson, 1980, p. 116). In his summary of the effects of the Council, Foucault argues that the confession became one of the principal institutions for 'the production of truth' in western culture:

> with the resulting development of confessional techniques, the declining importance of accusatory procedures in criminal justice, the abandonment of tests of guilt (sworn statements, duels, judgments of God) and the development of methods of interrogation and inquest, the increased participation of the royal administration in the prosecution of infractions, at the expense of proceedings leading to private settlements, the setting up of tribunals of Inquisition: all this helped to give the confession a central role in the order of civil and religious powers. (1981, p. 58)

The confession of the laity provided an internal investigation of conscience which could be linked to the external operation of public order. The effect of confession, in this argument, was to legitimate the authority of the priest, and it also provided a bridge between subjective guilt and objective power. The sacrament of penance was, in a world of heresy and witchcraft, an instrument of social control, designed to incorporate the laity within the dominant culture of the Church (Tentler, 1974).

How successful, however, was confession in providing an effective system of social control? There is certainly clear historical evidence that there was considerable lay opposition to the coercive nature of confession and priests experienced difficulties in bringing their flock to the confessional (Lea, 1896; Zeldin, 1970; Turner, 1977b). Over the centuries following the Council of 1215, penance declined in severity and the growth of commercialised indulgences provided means of avoiding the full impact of the sacrament of penance. If confession had a moral impact, it was prominent and persistent more among the nobility than among the peasantry. Within the peasant class, women were probably more significantly exposed to the Church's teaching on sexual impurity and to the benefits of regular confession than was the case for men. In the remote regions of European Catholicism today, in rural Spain for example, it is still the case that the 'culture of guilt', which is associated with the confessional, is a dominant feature of the lives of women (Christian, 1972). More sophisticated, urban Catholics may be able to 'shop around' for a lenient priest to provide a confession tailored to their particular circumstances (Valentini and Meglio, 1974).

The argument that the reforms brought about by the Church in the medieval period often had rather limited consequences in spiritualising the culture of subordinate groups and for integrating remote regions into the dominant, literate culture of the towns gains additional support from evidence of persistent rural and regional adherence to folk, pre-Christian and deviant traditions. The areas where Albigensianism took root were in later periods also characterised by witchcraft crazes, Protestantism and, in the case of south-west France, Occitan regionalism. Witchcraft in the sixteenth century was particularly prevalent among the poor communities of the European highlands, forests and remote areas, where the Church had little significant control (Trevor-Roper, 1967; Delumeau, 1969; Ladurie, 1974). The English peasantry and urban poor in the sixteenth and seventeenth centuries also exhibited widespread indifference to official Christian institutions and a continuous commitment to folk religion, witchcraft and demonology (Thomas, 1971). The public festivals and rituals of the official Church were often not so much occasions for displaying loyalty and commitment, as periods for renewing subcultural values and modes of opposition. The feast of fools, Mass-bouffe and Mass-farce were occasions for inverting the official symbolism of the Church to give expression in satire of social protest. Utopian villages, the land of Cockaigne, the golden past and the millennial dream provided critical, but fictional, alternatives to the actual deprivations of social life (Grans, 1967).

Feudal societies were deeply conflictual and class divisions were sharply marked by differences in language, dress, culture and religion. If religion was 'dominant', then it played an important role in the economic and political organisation of the land-owning class, but it cannot be suggested that the peasantry was significantly controlled by Christian belief and institutions. Whether or not it is possible to argue that the peasant was still in some sense 'religious' is dubious. As Weber wrote (1966, p. 1), the religious orientation of the ordinary rural folk was to this world in the search for security and prosperity. To include magic, indifference, hostility to religion, folk belief and superstition under the heading 'religion' is to make the concept empty of any precise content.

The atrabilious view, that the secularisation thesis is invalid, if it presupposes a period prior to industrialisation in which the mass of the population was systematically incorporated within Christian/religious institutions, is valid. Christianity did, however, play a crucial role for the nobility and subsequently for the urban industrial capitalist. The attritionist view is thus also correct in the specific sense that industrialisation brought about a society in which the Church no longer had a dominant position in public life. The weakness of the Church in feudal times was that, despite the development of the confessional, regular sermons and an educated clergy, it did not possess a powerful apparatus for the transmission of its culture to an illiterate, exploited population.

In general, the rural hinterland remained outside the world dominated by literate Christianity. The Reformation and Counter-Reformation are thus paradoxical in that they represent both a major effort to incorporate the poor and the illiterate within the institutional space of religion and a set of processes which point towards secularity. Although Arminian Protestantism, in destroying the old sacramental structure, placed greater emphasis on the literate believer and achieved considerable evangelical success among the poor, Protestantism divided the elite and provided the faithful with skills which could also be put to secular, political ends. Traditional carnivals became occasions for massive social conflict in a society divided, not only by class and region, but by Protestantism and Catholicism (Ladurie, 1981). Although Protestant revivalism among the rural and urban poor can be seen as the transmission of religious beliefs among social groups 'previously religiously unsocialized' (Wilson, 1982, p. 152), it also contributed to the fragmentation of a society in which class differences were marked by religious practice and belief. However, the society which Protestantism and capitalism replaced was also a society in which there was no common moral order.

7 Individualism, Capitalism and Religion

Sociological and historical studies of the social role of individualism in European societies are consistently ambiguous (Robertson and Holzner, 1980). Individualism is seen to be both the dominant ideology of capitalist society and a corrosive belief system which stands in opposition to collective and traditional modes of existence. Both Marx and Weber, for example, regarded individualism as the 'natural' complement of competitive capitalist arrangements by legitimating property rights. In addition, they thought that the Protestant Reformation was the seed-bed of political and economic individualism. In *Capital*, Marx noted in the discussion of the fetishism of commodities that:

> for a society based upon the production of commodities in which the producers in general enter into social relations with one another by treating their products as commodities and values, whereby they reduce their individual private labour to the standard of homogenous human labour — for such a society, Christianity with its *cultus* of abstract man, more especially in its bourgeois developments, Protestantism, Deism and etc. is the most fitting form of religion. (Marx, 1974, vol. 1, p. 83)

In the culture of competitive capitalism, the abstract Protestant believer was an extension of the isolated Robinson Crusoe of bourgeois political economy. Marx's treatment of Protestant individualism is thus not far removed from Weber's conception of Protestant man in *The Protestant Ethic and the Spirit of Capitalism* (1965). Although Weber recognised a difference between mystical and ascetic individualism, his sociology of salvation was primarily concerned with the latter. Thus, the strong opposition to emotion and ritual within the Puritan sects generated a 'disillusioned and pessimistically inclined individualism' (Weber, 1965, p. 105). In addition, their distrust of the religious comforts of human fellowship reinforced the isolation of the individual before God. In Calvinism, this was also associated with the disappearance of any reliance on the private confessional. The result was to strip man of any sacramental props in the quest for salvation.

In historical sociology, there is, therefore, a widely held assumption that the religious individualism that emerged out of Calvinistic theology and practice was 'the most fitting form of religion' for nascent capitalism in the seventeenth century. In Marxist terminology, individualism became the dominant ideology of capitalist society, conceived as a market within which countless independent individuals exercise rational choices (Goldmann, 1973). The civil society of capitalist relations is simply the product of the exchanges between autonomous individuals. The ideology of individualism serves to constitute individual subjects, separate them and then interpellate individuals as bearers of socio-economic functions (Hirst, 1979). Religious individualism is thus one version of an ideology which simultaneously separates and combines individuals within society (Hirst and Woolley, 1982, p. 120).

By contrast, rationalist individualism is often interpreted as destructive of social bonds and collectivist arrangements. As a political ideology, individualism is associated with opposition to established political practices. In *The Structure of Social Action*, Talcott Parsons (1937) argued that rational individuals would employ force and fraud to achieve their ends and consequently society could only exist if there were common values and standards which limited the impact of individual deviance. In the development of sociological theory, Parsons detected a marked trend away from utilitarian individualism in the social philosophy of Emile Durkheim, Max Weber and Vilfredo Pareto. The Parsonian analysis does, however, point to the complexity of the concept of 'individualism'. In both Durkheim and Parsons, individualism was closely identified with hedonistic egoism, a conception which was far removed from the Puritan tradition and from nineteenth-century romanticism.

These different conceptualisations of individualism do have one thing in common, namely, the identification of individualism with deviance, opposition and emancipation. In a more recent statement of the problem, Edward Shils (1981) treats hedonism and individualism as two emancipatory critiques of the growing rationalism and bureaucracy of contemporary societies:

Emancipationism here means that every individual should be free to gratify his impulses, that he should attain happiness, defined by his own desires, and that he should associate only with persons who are akin to him in spirit. (p. 303)

In this respect, individualism is corrosive of traditional arrangements in both politics and religion, being opposed to the restrictive weight of customary procedures and sacred practices.

As an ideology, individualism is not just a critique of contemporary social arrangements, but is employed retrospectively to criticise the past. The ways and customs of ancestors, from an individualist perspective, appear to be conformist, and thus superficial and conventional. Individualistic beliefs can become part of the struggle between groups, generations and classes to assert and legitimise innovatory practices and institutions. Individualism is part of a discourse which identifies discontinuity and difference. Theories of individualism typically specify a range of contrasts pinpointing the absence of individualism in other cultures. Oriental societies are said to lack any strong doctrine of the individual and the absence of individualism is further tied to political despotism and economic stagnation. In Hegel's philosophy of history, for example, 'Mahometan' was eventually overcome by fanaticism and fatalism (Hegel, 1956). In a similar fashion, Weber pointed to the absence of a genuinely individualist path to salvation in Islam, Judaism and Confucianism. In Islam, the norms of the warrior elite were decidedly collectivist and conformist. In Judaism, the pariah status of the Diaspora Jews encouraged ritualism and adherence to communal practices. It was only in Christianity that individualism could develop in the urban environment of medieval Europe. Western conceptions of individualism tend, therefore, to identify urban Puritanism as the catalyst of individual autonomy and as the background of capitalist individualism.

Individuals and individual rights

The concept of the 'individual' and the doctrine of 'individual rights' have played a major role in the development of western philosophy and political theory. In the nineteenth century, theoretical formulations of the individual/society contrast provided the context within which sociology as a distinctive discipline emerged. In the twentieth century, debates about 'epistemological individualism' and 'methodological individualism' (Lukes, 1973a) were fundamental to the philosophy of the social sciences as the neo-Kantian legacy of the German cultural sciences. In more recent times, the nature of 'the subject' in discourse analysis, the problem of human agency in structuralism and the constitution of 'economic subjects' in Marxist theory have brought the issue of individualism and the individual to the forefront of sociological inquiry (Giddens, 1979).

These analytical issues have been stimulated by a number of valuable empirical inquiries into the historical emergence of individualism in European societies (Macfarlane, 1978). Individualism can be said to have entered sociological theory at two levels, namely, in the formulation of the concept of 'society' and in the debate concerning the social conditions which are conducive to capitalist development. At the first level, we have to recognise that any theory of society will entail a theory of the individual, even where this theory denies individual autonomy in favour of a strong conception of social determination (Durkheim, 1938). At the second level, individualism provides an interesting test of theories of ideology, since individualism appears to be an oppositional ideology of rising social classes, a necessary ingredient of western culture and a system of beliefs which is peculiar to capitalist society. The causal linkage between individualism and the emergence of capitalism is unclear. The lack of clarity is surprising, given the general agreement which exists as to the importance of individualism for capitalism. In this chapter, it is the second issue — the connections between individualism and capitalism — which is important, but this consideration inevitably involves some discussion of the traditional individual/society issue.

In order to illustrate the importance of individualism as a theme in discussions of ideology, it is important to raise some general problems in theories of ideology. In order to simplify some of the complexity which surrounds this issue, it is convenient to suggest that any theory of ideology will have to consider three broad questions. First, it is necessary to take a position on the inevitability or otherwise of ideology in relation to the economic system. A system of beliefs may be either necessary to the functioning of an economic system or it may stand in a largely contingent relationship. In practice, it is difficult to distinguish this argument from some notion of the social triviality of beliefs for the continuation of a socio-economic system. A strong theory of individualism holds that a capitalist system *must* have notions of individual property, individual rights and so forth; a capitalist system could not continue without individualistic laws relating to trespass, ownership and inheritance. By contrast, beliefs about the rights of animals and the immorality of blood-sports have a contingent relationship to capitalism; they are merely inconvenient from the point of view of landlords. Although it is generally thought by sociologists that individualism is a necessary feature of the growth of capitalism, the exact relationship between these has never been adequately specified.

In this chapter, I shall critically consider *The Philosophy of the Enlightenment* (Goldmann, 1973) and *The Political Theory of Possessive Individualism* (Macpherson, 1962) to pinpoint the difficulty of showing that individualism is a necessary ideological condition of capitalist production. The broad answer suggested in this chapter is that individualism was important as a critical philosophy during the emergence of the bourgeoisie, but it is contingent in relation to capitalism, particularly late capitalism. Individualism is prevalent in capitalist societies, but it is difficult to move beyond this empirical observation to demonstrate in a more precise fashion that individualism is a necessary requirement of the capitalist mode of production.

The second broad issue for a general theory of ideology is to relate ideology to class positions and to determine how ideology brings about or maintains the subordination of classes. Whereas the necessity/contingency problem concerns ideology as a requirement of the mode of production, the major theories of individualism may be regarded as 'class reductionist'; individualistic beliefs are held to express or reflect the economic interests of the class of property-owners. The doctrine of individual rights, especially 'possessive individualism', is regarded as the ideological form of the rising bourgeoisie (Lukács, 1971). The weakness of class reductionism has been severely criticised, especially by Poulantzas (1973) who objected to the conception of ideology as a number-plate stamped on the back of classes. This approach also raises empirical difficulties (Abercrombie *et al.*, 1980) in respect of the impact of individualism on subordinate groups. Individualism may be a suitable oppositional ideology for private property against traditional feudal property in early capitalism, but it is difficult to imagine how individualism could have relevance to subordinate groups or how conceptions of private property could survive without modification in late capitalism, where there is considerable 'depersonalisation' of property (Scott, 1979). Beliefs about private property may 'fit' the needs of an emerging bourgeois class, but the nature of property rights and beliefs in late capitalism have not been adequately analysed by sociologists.

The third general question for a theory of ideology concerns the apparatus or mechanism by which ideological beliefs are transmitted between classes, groups or generations. In more traditional approaches, the mechanism connecting the individual to belief was seen in terms of drives, motivation or interests. In conventional Marxism, it was class interest which explained adherence to certain beliefs, but it is in fact theoretically and methodologically difficult to 'read off' ideology directly from class interest. The concept of 'interest' has a more specific and limited theoretical role than commonly ascribed to it in Marxist analysis. Furthermore, it is impossible to study the role of ideology for a social class without locating classes within the social framework, the general character of which is determined by the mode of production. Contrary to the view of Westergaard and Resler (1975), individualism does not have the same features or salience in late capitalism that it had in nascent capitalism.

Individualism as ideology

Any theory of individualism as an ideology will have, therefore, to provide some account of the connection between individualism, social classes, the mode of production and the institutional apparatus of transmission. In addition, there are difficulties in the definition of individualism. In a previous discussion of religion as social control, it was suggested that there is a common tendency to confuse individualism, individuality and individuation. This conceptual confusion can be illustrated from the work of Nicos Poulantzas, which draws attention to important relationships between 'private citizens' and the 'popular state'. In modern capitalism, the separate citizen has to be organised by the state under the unity of the popular will:

The specialization and centralization of the capitalist State, its hierarchical-bureaucratic functioning and its elective institutions all involve the atomization of the body-politic into what are called 'individuals' — that is, juridical-political persons who are the subjects of certain freedoms . . . The centralized, bureaucratized State *instals* this atomization and, as a representative State laying claim to national sovereignty and the popular will, it *represents* the unity of a body (people-nation) that is split into formally equivalent monads. (Poulantzas, 1978, p. 63)

This juridical-political ideology in constituting individuals means that the conflicts within society between classes are experienced as conflicts between persons, whereas the state has the fictive role of reorganising separate persons under the unity of popular political institutions (Urry, 1981).

In addition to this ideological process, Poulantzas locates individualisation in the organisation of labour by Taylorist principles in the large-scale production unit. The social division of labour, the fragmentation of skill and the specialisation of the labourer result in the atomisation of the worker. This social isolation of the individual subject develops alongside the specialisation of the human body as an 'appendage of the machine' in the capitalist enterprise. In suggesting an economic explanation of individualism, Poulantzas provides an important insight into the work of Michel Foucault.

In his historical studies of the growth of systematic knowledge and the coercive institutions of the modern age, Foucault treats the 'individual' as the product of disciplines and discourses. As social control became more detailed and precise, the individual became more differentiated and specialised by systematic discourses. Examinations, timetables, registers and records were external indicators of a process by which individuals were produced, recorded and controlled:

The individual is no doubt the fictitious atom of an 'ideological' representation of society; but he is also a reality fabricated by this specific technology of power that I have called 'discipline'. We must cease once and for all to describe the effects of power in negative terms: it 'excludes', it 'represses', it 'censors', it 'abstracts', it 'masks', it 'conceals'. In fact, power produces; it produces reality; it produces domains of objects and rituals of truth. The individual and the knowledge that may be gained of him belong to this production. (Foucault, 1979, p. 194)

The creation of deviant types of criminology, of psychiatric personality by psychology and of physical types of scientific medicine was part of the productive dimension of power/knowledge, but this construction was accompanied by the differentiation of human subjects under the bureaucratic regime of the school and the factory. The production of the individual by developments in knowledge and by the detailed organisation of social space is an exercise of power.

Poulantzas wants to appropriate Foucault's description of individualisation for an analysis of contemporary politics, but he attempts to locate this process, not so much in the growth of organised knowledge, but in juridical ideology and in the relations of economic production. The creation of 'individuals' is an effect of the increasing division of labour and the fragmentation of the labour process, which are requirements of commodity production in late capitalism. The role of the popular democratic state then becomes that of representing these atomised citizen-subjects through the medium of popular democracy. Capitalist societies are thus subject to two paradoxical processes — the separation of individuals by economic specialisation and the unification of citizens by the state representing the popular will. These processes are presented at an imaginary level by juridical individualism, which conceives subjects as separate but equal.

These sociological discussions tend to confuse three separate issues — individualism, individuality and individuation — which have different implications for the stability of capitalist societies. In terms of preliminary definition, I shall take individualism to be a doctrine of individual rights, which may be expressed in a variety of religious, political, economic or legal forms. The origin of this doctrine is conventionally associated with Calvinistic Protestantism, which transformed notions of conscience and rationales of conduct by replacing sacramental methods of expiation, especially the confessional, with the individual 'court of conscience' (Nelson, 1968 and 1969a). This individualistic conception of the contractual nature of man and God, with its bleak emphasis on individual responsibility for action, has been treated as the precursor of political and legal individualism in the treatises of Hobbes, Locke and Bentham. The peculiarity of Calvinist individualism was, of course, its combination of an active ethic with a distinctly pessimistic interpretation of human sinfulness. Calvinist individualism was thus very different from the rationalist individualism of the Enlightenment and the more optimistic individualism of political economy:

Founded upon a crushing sense of sin, and a pessimistic condemnation of the world, without colour or emotional satisfaction, it is an individualism based upon the certainty of election, the sense of responsibility and of the obligation to render personal service under the Lordship of Christ. (Troeltsch, 1931, pp. 589—90)

The point about individualism, in both optimistic and pessimistic moods, is its critical and dissenting character. The individualised conscience was a challenge to the institutionalised sacraments of Roman Catholicism, especially against the Treasury of Merit and the ecclesiastical monopoly of grace. Economic individualism undermined the customary economic relations of feudalism (Goody *et al.*, 1978). Legal individualism was a challenge to the 'sinister interests' of the traditional aristocracy which constrained the political representation of the bourgeoisie.

Individualism is thus a doctrine of rights. For example, in Locke's theory of property rights anyone who joins or transfers their labour with natural phenomena or some object has a claim over that object. A man who grows a crop and mixes his labour with nature has a property right over the produce (Becker, 1977), but this theory does not necessarily involve some notion of personality, subjectivity or individual development. Individualism in its Lockean form was concerned with the character of the external relations that connected individuals to the economy and the society; it involved a discussion of the origins of that dense network of rights and duties that formed the structure of civil society. Individualism as a bourgeois doctrine of individual rights to property was less concerned with the interior cultivation of the person, which is the domain of individuality.

The contrast between individualism and individuality formed part of the crisis of the empiricist tradition in utilitarianism, which was expressed in the biographical crisis of J. S. Mill. The Benthamite calculus of pains and pleasures, which provided the principle of Mill's education, resulted in Mill's depression of 1826, from which he recovered by reading the poetry of Wordsworth and Coleridge. Poetry provided the framework within which Mill could explore his own subjective interior — an opportunity denied by the positivist rigour of Benthamite individualism (Packe, 1954). Individuality is therefore a romantic theory of the subjective interior of persons, which is concerned with the growth of sensibility, taste, consciousness and will. What individualism and individuality have in common is their critical, protesting character.

Although individuality as a doctrine owes much to the critique of utilitarianism, it was most consistently developed within the German philosophical tradition, but this also stemmed from the German pietist and mystical Christian stream. From Hegel onwards, the aphoristic writings of Nietzsche and Kierkegaard (Thulstrup, 1980) turned against the systematic Hegelianism of the time to produce ethical notions that gave a primacy to individuality. In Nietzsche's later writings, the authentic personality involved the transcendence of conventional moral standards by the individual who has fully realised his personality and potential. Although this conception of individuality is critical, it is also elitist; it is a concept which has a strong appeal to isolated and alienated intellectuals, cut off from the mainstream of university employment and middle-class culture. Nietzsche's superman ethic only makes sense when contrasted to the world of the conformist mass, off whom the virtuoso intellectual is forced to live. Nietzsche's emphasis on celibacy and withdrawal is indicative of this elitist isolation, which is illustrated by the narrative importance of mountains in Nietzsche's philosophical stories of supermen. Bourgeois individualism and elitist individuality are thus distinctive concepts (Weintraub, 1978).

Individuation

If individualism and individuality are doctrines concerning the organisation of the self and society in terms of maximising individual rights and personal autonomy, individuation is to be regarded as a set of practices by which individuals are identified and separated by marks, numbers, signs and codes. More precisely, individuation refers to the individuation of persons as differentiated bodies. The sociological issue of individuation bears a close resemblance to the question of identification in philosophy, where identity, consciousness and bodies are necessarily conjoined. The question 'Who are you?' is difficult to answer without reference to the identification of a body in space and time (Strawson, 1959).

Recent debates about ideology as the interpellation of subjects may thus be appropriately annexed to Weber's concept of bureaucratisation and Foucault's analysis of disciplines that require the separation and identification of persons as objects of control. Individuation is paradoxical in that, by making people different and separate, it makes them more subject to control. The theoretical issue is to decide whether these practices of individuation satisfy certain necessary political and economic functions within a given mode of production. In Chapter 5, it was argued that, although the apparatus for individuation in capitalist society is greatly extended, some form of individuation is necessary in any mode of production. However, individuation appears to be particularly important in societies where the state plays a dominant economic role. What is clear is that individuation has greatly increased in modern society, in which the facilities for information storage are very extensive:

A man of the sixteenth or the seventeenth century would be astonished at the exigencies with regard to civil status to which we submit quite naturally . . . But in our technical civilization, how could anyone forget the exact date of their birth, when he has to remember it for almost every application he makes, every document he signs, every form he fills in . . . and when he starts his first job he will be given, together with his Social Security card, a registration number which will double his own name. (Ariès, 1973, p. 13)

Although individualism may be an important doctrine in early capitalism for a bourgeois class intent upon reorganising property

relations, it retains its oppositional character and may decline in significance as an ideology of private possession in a society where the state
exercises a crucial role with respect to public investment and economic
development. What late capitalism does require, however, is an apparatus for individuating the mass of the population for purposes of control
and surveillance.

The relationship between individualism, individuality and individuation may thus be conceptualised in these terms:

Type	Focus	Mode	Origins
Individualism	Class	Opposition	Asceticism
Individuality	Elite	Critical	Mysticism
Individuation	Mass	Control	Monasticism

Thus individualism emerges out of the ascetic Protestant tradition with
its emphasis on autonomy, activity and responsibility; through the
philosophical debates over property and contract, this doctrine becomes relevant to an emerging class which expresses its political
opposition to the existing society through individualistic beliefs. By
contrast, individuality has more in common with the mystical tradition
in Christianity, with its withdrawal from social relations to the
development of a subjective interior. Withdrawal in this case also
involves a highly critical attitude towards conventional moralities and
conformity to traditional arrangements. Individuation is associated, by
comparison, with the surveillance of large populations by bureaucratic
means. In so far as individuation involves a detailed control of the body,
the disciplines of bureaucracy may have been prefigured by the monastic regulations of the Christian tradition. The monastery was the first
'total institution' of European Christendom, providing a model for
subsequent timetables and schedules of regulation.

Goldmann and Macpherson on individualism

Two separate issues have thus been identified. First, there are general
requirements which any theory of ideology must satisfy. Secondly,
there are specific issues raised by the sociological analysis of individualism. To illustrate the outlines of my argument, it is useful to
consider two classic accounts of European individualism by Lucien
Goldmann and C. B. Macpherson.

In *The Philosophy of the Enlightenment*, Goldmann (1973) wants to
provide a sociological explanation of what he regards as the seven
fundamental categories — the autonomy of the individual, contract,

equality, universality, toleration, freedom and property — of Enlightenment thought. The central feature of these categories is the autonomy of the individual who, with the growth of an urban market economy, becomes 'an independent element, a sort of monad, *a point of departure*'. Society in Enlightenment philosophy was thought to result from:

the action of countless autonomous individuals on each other and in response to each other, behaving as rationally as possible for the protection of their private interests and basing their actions on their knowledge of the market with no regard for any trans-individual authority or values. (Goldmann, 1973, p. 18)

It was this economic individualism which provided the basis for the characteristic world-view of European thought, namely, rationalism and empiricism. These systems of thought were based on the assumption that empirical knowledge of reality had its primary location within the individual mind, performing as an active recorder of the external order.

Goldmann seeks to relate these categories of thought, in particular individualism, to the development of the capitalist economy, one of the prominent features of which is the presence of markets for goods and services. Goldmann argues that his analysis is basically an application of Marx's treatment of the commodity form in volume 1 of *Capital*. In a capitalist economy, commodities are produced, not for use, but for their exchange value. An economy of this form requires markets in which the exchange value of commodities can be realised through unlimited transactions.

It is this character of commodity exchange in free markets that offers Goldmann a starting-point for his explication of individualist beliefs. For example, freedom of exchange requires the absence of social impediments to unlimited and open transactions. Prohibitions against exchange on religious, cultural or racial grounds constrain exchange in ways which are economically damaging. Economic exchange tends, therefore, to promote religious tolerance. The argument that freedom of the market and freedom of conscience develop simultaneously is vividly illustrated in Andrew Marvell's poem on the 'Character of Holland', which is frequently quoted in studies of the Dutch economy (Boxer, 1965; Smith, 1973). Marvell used the metaphor of exchange to describe the nature of religious tolerance which is created by trade:

Hence Amsterdam, Turk, Christian, Pagan, Jew,
Staple of sects and mint of schisms grew:
That bank of conscience, where not one so strange
Opinion but finds credit and exchange.

Market exchange requires the supporting notion that 'every individual appears as the autonomous source of his decisions and actions'

Goldmann, 1973, p. 20). Although individualism tends to develop among Protestant sects, the explanation of this growth is sought in features of an economy based on exchange value.

A similar position is taken by Macpherson, who links the doctrine of political individualism in Hobbes and Locke to the growth of capitalist relations in the seventeenth century, specifically to the rise of possessive property rights and markets. Individualism was 'possessive' because it assumed that every person was the proprietor of his own body and its capacities; society was simply the relations of exchange existing between such proprietors. However, Locke took for granted the existence of a working class which depended on wages to survive and that the working man was not a genuine citizen with full membership of the political system. There is thus a parallel between the Calvinistic distinction between the spiritual elect and the non-elect in relation to the Church and the property class and the property-less in relation to the State. The natural equality between individuals in nature is obliterated by the differentiation of property in society. In fact, civil society exists to protect the interests of men of property against the threat of the labouring classes. There was, then, an important collectivist element to Locke's political individualism:

> The individuals who have the means to realize their personalities (that is, the propertied) do not need to reserve any rights as against civil society, since civil society is constructed by and for them, and run by and for them. All they need do is insist that civil society, that is, the majority of themselves, is supreme over any government, for a particular government might otherwise get out of hand. (Macpherson, 1962, p. 256)

Locke's bourgeois individualism thus faithfully reflected the organisation of classes within early capitalism, where labour is formally free in the market-place, but radically unequal in terms of the ownership of the means of production. Although Locke's political philosophy was directly influenced by Calvinism, its dominant theme was 'one of the most versatile individualistic rationalism, purely utilitarian and secular in character, which can be abstracted as it stands from the religious setting of Locke's theory' (Troeltsch, 1931, vol. 2, p. 638).

In criticising the explanation of individualism in terms of the growth of exchange markets and private property, I shall concentrate on Goldmann's exposition. My criticism is divided into minor and major issues. Starting with certain technical difficulties in Goldmann's account, there is an issue of definition in his equation of 'market society' with 'capitalism'. Within a strict theoretical framework, the existence of trade areas or markets cannot be simply treated as equivalent to capitalist relations of production, since markets do not necessarily require the existence of capitalist producers, wage labourers, factory enterprises or the realisation of a surplus in terms of profit. The trade in luxury goods, elementary banking institutions and merchant classes pre-dates the rise of industrial capitalism, as Marx and Weber clearly noted. In any case, the notion of 'urban markets' is very elastic. For example, in the fourteenth century, the growth of the Florentine textile industry produced a new social environment which contradicted much of the existing teaching of the Church on morals and economics. The economic teaching of Bernardino of Sienna and Antonino of Florence can be seen as an attempt to restate the Catholic position on prices and wages in relation to the novel conditions created by economic change. Although they recognised the dangers of unrestrained pursuit of profit, they equally accepted the justification for private property and profit where business served a useful social function (de Roover, 1967). It is, therefore, all too easy to exaggerate the transition from scholastic to Enlightenment economic theory.

Another difficulty with the Goldmann thesis is that it remains unclear whether all seven categories of Enlightenment thought are equally relevant or necessary for unrestricted economic exchange. Following Weber's sociology of law, it is certainly the case that capitalists require legal security of private property and economic contracts, but they may be able to operate successfully in societies where criteria of universality and equality between individuals are only weakly developed or partly guaranteed in law. It may also be the case that capitalists *believe* that people are equal, while *treating* certain sections of the population, such as women, unequally. As we have seen in the case of Locke, Enlightenment philosophy may be highly ambiguous over the question of equality of rights. Finally, trade can take place between collectivities or companies rather than between economic individuals. There is no necessary reason for the economic subject to be a person and therefore individualism may be a contingent development in early capitalism rather than a requirement of capitalism as such. Quite simply, 'legal subjects are by no means exclusively human subjects' (Hirst, 1979, p. 13).

One major difficulty which Goldmann shares with other historians of individualism concerns the periodisation of ideologies of individualism. There is considerable disagreement as to when and where the doctrine of individualism is to be located in European development. In his study of Renaissance Italy, Burckhart, (1955, p. 81), comments that towards the close of the thirteenth century 'Italy began to swarm with individuality' in the bustling cosmopolitan culture of the northern cities. Devane (1976), by contrast, identifies the full flowering of individualism with the Reformation of the sixteenth century. Both Goldmann (1973) and Chenu (1969) situate individualism in the thirteenth century with the growth of urban markets. In the case of England, it has been suggested that:

ordinary people in England from at least the thirteenth century were rampant individualists, highly mobile both geographically and socially, economically 'rational', market-oriented and acquisitive, ego-centred in kinship and social life. (Macfarlane, 1978, p. 163)

The term 'individualism' in its modern sense dates from the English translation (1946) of Alexis de Tocqueville's *Democracy in America* of 1835, when it was perceived as 'a novel expression' (Williams, 1976, p. 136). Yet Arieli (1964) suggests that the European concept of individualism had certain negative implications of instability that had to be reformulated before individualism could become acceptable as an ideology in nineteenth-century America. Although these differences in periodisation suggest that individualism is not simply the effect of capitalist relations of production and exchange, they do not immediately rule out a close historical and sociological association between individualism and capitalism. Individualism was the product of early developments in urban markets, independent universities and the Calvinist theology of salvation; once nurtured in the social context of Protestant Europe, individualism subsequently became the secular ideology of an emergent capitalist class of property-owners.

It is plausible to show a relationship between the property interests of a capitalist class and the ideology of individualism, but it is much less plausible to demonstrate that the labouring class accepted individualistic beliefs or that working-class individualism had the effect of incorporating working people within capitalist society. In Locke's version of possessive individualism, the labouring class was largely excluded from civil society by virtue of its exclusion from property. More generally, it is not clear that the capitalist mode of production requires all seven categories of Enlightenment thought in order to be politically subordinated and incorporated. In the classic Marxist position, the separation of the worker from the means of production by force, the uncertainty of employment, the organisational difficulties of political opposition and the 'dull compulsion' of economic circumstances were sufficient to force the worker to sell his labour power without the additional factor of ideological incorporation. Although individualism may be an expression of bourgeois interests, the working class is more likely to espouse collectivist principles or to exhibit a consciousness which contains a mixture of dominant and subordinate beliefs (Parkin, 1972). In so far as individualism has pronounced ideological consequences, these will take the form of 'aiding' the dominant class as property-owners to exercise their economic functions of exchange. It is, however, important to recall the essentially dissenting character of individualistic doctrines which, against custom, legitimated claims to private property for the bourgeoisie in the period of its formation:

Individualism, therefore, might be taken up by groups of any kind which oppose the *status quo* and require ideological legitimation of their dissent. (Abercrombie, 1980, p. 62)

Once the political and economic situation of the bourgeoisie has been consolidated within the economy and in relation to the state, individualism may lose some of its salience as a legitimating principle.

If the specification of the connection between belief and class is problematic, then the relationship between belief and the mode of production is more so. It is not clear from Goldmann and other writers on individualism whether the capitalist mode of production is the cause of such beliefs, whether such beliefs are a necessary requirement of capitalist exchange or whether the two stand in a contingent relationship. Goldmann appears to take three rather separate positions: Enlightenment beliefs were the consequence of changes in the organisation of economic production and exchange; these beliefs were a cultural precondition which facilitated economic restructuring; there was an analogy between individual economic exchange and individual rational actors.

The problems raised by Goldmann's analysis are also present in most interpretations of Weber's *The Protestant Ethic and the Spirit of Capitalism* (1965): was the relationship between Calvinist belief and rational economic behaviour causal, contingent, analogous or one of 'affinity'? Arguments in Marxism about the fetishism of commodities turn out on close inspection to be ones of analogy. In Marxist theories of law, it is conventionally argued that capitalism requires certain legal supports for individual property-ownership. More abstractly, it is suggested that the legal subject has to be analysed as a legal expression of the commodity form:

If objects dominate man economically because, as commodities, they embody a social relation which is not subordinate to man, then man rules over things legally, because, in his capacity as possessor and proprietor, he is simply the personification of the abstract, impersonal, legal subject, the pure product of social relations. (Pashukanis, 1978, p. 113)

The abstract man of political economy is like the abstract man of legal theory, and both resemble the isolated abstract theological subject of Calvinism; the resemblance is explained by the fetishism of thought that is generated by the relations of exchange in commodity production. There are general difficulties with theories of legal individualism that attempt to extend Marx's notion of fetishism from *Capital* (Abercrombie, 1980), but there are additional questions relating to the forms of public property in late capitalism. It is not invariably the case that the legal and economic subjects are, as it were, invested in the human person. The fetishism argument has to identify capitalist property with individual property, whereas:

Corporate forms of capital are inassimilable to this coincidence of subjects (owning, possessing, calculating). Monopoly, in separating ownership and possession, legal subject and economic subject, dissolves the connections which are necessary to capitalist social relations proper. (Hirst, 1979, p. 119)

Legal individualism is, therefore, important in the early stages of capitalism, in legitimating capitalist property for individual possessors of private property, but in late capitalism it is difficult to see how individual claims on property are preconditions for corporate owner-ship. There may be a residual role for individualistic beliefs of this form in relation to the legitimation of private consumption. However, although consumerism may be a pronounced feature of late capitalist societies, this individualised consumption exists alongside a wide variety of collective consumption of national wealth.

Finally, in relation to Goldmann's argument, it is important to make a somewhat obvious distinction between beliefs and actions. For example, there is a clear difference between believing that people are equal and treating people as equals. A private capitalist may be ideo-logically committed to the doctrine of equal rights, but he may, in the daily organisation of his enterprise, treat women and children as un-equal by paying them less than men per hour. Contrary to Goldmann, it is not even clear that capitalist production and exchange requires egalitarian beliefs or practices; capitalism has been highly flexible in adjusting to a variety of systems of social stratification, including those based rigidly on race (Parkin, 1982, p. 96). Alternatively, it is possible that capitalists may privately believe that female labour is inferior to male labour, while being compelled by legislation, unionisation and the scarcity of labour to treat labour equally regardless of sexual differ-ences. There is no clear-cut relationship between belief and practice and this suggests a more complex version of the Goldmann thesis:

(1)   Capitalist behaviour ——➤ (2)   Social practice ——➤ (3)   Beliefs

The intervening variable (2) refers to such actions as treating people equally in practice, which provides the link between capitalist be-haviour (buying and selling) and belief (believing that people ought to be treated as equals).

Goldmann's thesis is primarily concerned with (3), that is, the articulate beliefs of Enlightenment philosophers concerning the auton-omy, rationality and equality of human beings. He attempts to argue that (3) is the result of (1), namely, that capitalist exchange relations produce or are analogous to rational conceptions of individual sectors. His argument does not show that beliefs about individualism and equality were present and effective in the behaviour of merchants and capitalists. The methodological problems for historical research that this distinction between belief and practice entails are rarely broached by the sociology of religion (Marshall, 1980).

An alternative view

The principal conclusions of this discussion are that individualism is associated with the development of urban exchange relations and the emergence of a class of owners of private property. Individualism flowed along two separate but related social channels. First, there was the pessimistic route of ascetic Calvinism, in which fallen man is isolated before God and stripped of any sacramental supports. Second, there was the more optimistic doctrine of rational individualism, which flowered among the intellectuals of the Enlightenment. Individualism starts therefore in dissent — the dissent of Protestants from Catholicism and the dissent of the bourgeoisie from feudal relations of property. Individualism has to be sharply distinguished from individuation. Possessive individualism becomes progressively less relevant to capitalist production as the form of property-ownership is transformed by the separation of ownership and control in late capitalism. Individuation as a method of social control becomes correspondingly more relevant in a society where the state extends its control over both economy and society.

It is now possible to extend this argument to consider the wider contribution of the sociology of religion to the study of modern individualism. This consideration can begin with two observations about Weber's sociology of religion, in particular about two gaps in Weber's contribution. First, Weber made little direct contribution to the formal analysis of the church–sect typology; instead, he was more concerned with paths to personal salvation in terms of asceticism and mysticism. This gap is in part explained by the existence of an exhaustive coverage by Ernst Troeltsch in *The Social Teaching of the Christian Churches* (1931). Secondly, Weber adopted a somewhat negative attitude towards mysticism, treating it as an emotional, often ritualistic, accommodation to the secular world. By extension, Weber had very little to say about the development of post-Reformation Catholicism. Weber's sociology of religion was thus organised around the impact of puritanical asceticism on the modern world. The importance of this observation is that mysticism, like individuality, is a highly individual form of dissent; furthermore, it has been argued that mysticism is prominent in contemporary forms of personal dissent from rational capitalism. In both respects, it is instructive to start with Troeltsch's treatment of church, sect and mysticism.

Troeltsch on individualism

The church–sect typology has been extensively discussed in the sociology of religion and equally extensive criticisms have been raised against its principal conclusions (Niebuhr, 1929; Pope, 1942; Wilson, 1959 and 1982). Briefly, sects are exclusive religious communities, which give special emphasis to their monopoly of religious truth, their democratic lay organisation and the denial of sacerdotal priesthood and sacramentalism. Sects have strict criteria of membership, typically through conversion, and as a result tend to be protest groups, drawing their membership from the disinherited and dispossessed. The church-type has the opposite set of characteristics, recruiting its membership by birth rather than conversion from a wider basis within the class structure. It treats the rituals of inclusion — baptism, confession, marriage and confirmation — as the principal roads to membership, which is inclusive and catholic, implying a lower level of definite commitment and attachment. Churches are thus organised around the principle of *extra ecclesiam nulla salus* — personal salvation resides within the ritual framework of the organised church.

The implication is that sects are the genuine seed-bed of individualism in opposition to the traditional, collectivist practices of the church. The church-type gives prominence to the objectivity of religious teaching and experience, encapsulated in time-honoured rituals of membership and exclusion; the sect-type emphasises the subjectivity of religious experience, encapsulated in the immediacy of the conversion experience itself.

This basic dichotomy in the sociology of religion has given rise to extensive typological variations in respect of religious societies (Turner, 1970), religious orders (Hill, 1971), cults (Campbell, 1972 and 1977) and denomination (Martin, 1962). From the perspective of the present argument, Troeltsch's argument that the church–sect typology was relevant to a context in which the established church had a national significance has a particular relevance. For Troeltsch, the oscillation of church and sect only applied to a context prior to secularisation when the church embraced the national population. In modern capitalism this oscillation of conformist church and dissenting sect has been replaced by the private, individual form of mystical commitment.

The oppositional and critical aspect of personal mysticism was an important element in Troeltsch's definition of this form of religion, which Troeltsch regarded as basically a living, inward experience of divinity. Mysticism is either indifferent to the external forms of religious worship or hostile to popular manifestations of religion, because the mystic perceives both to be superficial and artificial. The intensity of the mystical experience often produces ecstasy, possession and trance, which may then become sources of new beliefs and mysterious practices. For Troeltsch, mysticism was often connected with eroticism, since sexual excitement was used to stimulate religious ecstasy which, in turn, could be expressed through sexuality. Sufi themes of 'Come, fill the Cup, and in the Fire of Spring/The Winter Garment of Repentance fling' adequately illustrate this mystical dualism of flesh and spirit. This dualism was, however, also present in the Christocentric mysticism of St Paul and in the four gospels according to John the Divine with the symbolism of darkness and light. This dependence on allegory and symbolism is an inevitable feature of mysticism, because the mystical experience and consciousness are defined by their ineffability (James, 1929). In tracing mysticism back to the gospels of Christianity, Troeltsch was able to claim that mysticism, like the church-type and sect-type, had its origin in the theological outlook of the primitive church. The sociological character of mysticism radically distinguished mysticism as a type from both church and sect.

The sect separates individuals from the world, but binds them together in a tight fellowship and places strong expectations of conformity and adherence upon its members. For example, Wesley, who once described the Church of England as 'a rope of sand', placed great emphasis on fellowship and communalism; his bands and class meetings were intended to counteract the isolation of believers within the conventional church. Wesley appealed to the model of the primitive church to justify this overriding concern for the community of believers (Hill and Turner, 1971). The individualism of religious mysticism is very different from sectarian individualism, because it 'lays no stress at all upon the relation between individuals, but only upon the relations between the soul and God' (Troeltsch, 1931, vol. 12, p. 743).

Mysticism tends to be indifferent to those rituals which bind together the faithful into a community. It is committed instead to the conception of an invisible church that creates a purely spiritual union not apprehended by those who do not possess a mystical consciousness. Where mystics do establish religious groups and leaders, these communities tend to be very fluid, intimate and ephemeral. Mysticism is thus in opposition to formal dogmas and objective ecclesiastical organisations, but its oppositional character is elitist and in this respect Troeltsch's mystic/church dichotomy bears a close relationship to Weber's virtuoso/mass contrast. Thus, mysticism:

assumes in a very aristocratic way that the concrete forms of worship will continue to be the religion of the masses. It is its mission, however, to call the true children of God out of that external worship in order to lift them up into the Kingdom of God which is purely within us. (Troeltsch, 1931, vol. 2, p. 747)

Paradoxically, the mystical opposition to formal dogma and practice did not necessarily lead to secession so typical of sectarian religions. For the mystic, the external husk of ritual was simply irrelevant to the quest for salvation. Mysticism, as Troeltsch put it, 'lives on and in' other religious communities and groups, seeking to transform them by inward experience and subjective response to God.

In the history of Protestantism, mysticism had thus been largely exercised within the institutional framework of existing sects or churches, and was thus not entirely cut off from the broad tradition of western Christendom. With the decline of the Church as a national institution and the growing secularity of capitalist society, mysticism had become increasingly divorced from the mainstream of religion and predominantly an outlook of an educated elite:

the modern educated classes understand nothing but mysticism. This is due to the reflex action of the atomistic individualism of modern civilization . . . In its depreciation of fellowship, public worship, history, and social ethics this type of 'spiritual religion', in spite of all its depth and spirituality, is still a weakened form of religious life, which must be maintained in its concrete fullness of life by churches and sects, if an entirely individualistic mysticism is to spiritualize it at all. (Troeltsch, 1931, vol. 2, p. 799)

Troeltsch's treatment of the history of mysticism from its origins in Pauline Christianity through the Protestant sects to modern individualism has to be set in the context of philosophical debates in German culture, which, in turn, determined many of the theoretical parameters of German sociology. In particular, the typology of religious organisations in Troeltsch's socio-theology relates directly to the classical antinomies of German *geisteswissenschaften*. These antinomies are individual/society, subjectivity/objectivity, experience/knowledge and freedom/determinism (Robertson, 1978). Troeltsch's typology implicitly explored the problems of how individual experience and subjectivity related to the objective, deterministic structures of social organisation. The three types of religious organisation represent three modes of connecting religion to the world; to some extent, mysticism reconciled the dichotomy between sectarian subjectivity and ecclesiastical objectivity by providing a place for internal religious consciousness in the setting of church and sect. The mystic lived 'in and on' the objective and external forms of religion, transforming the individual and society in the crucible of experience.

Meaning and change

The problem of reconciling the antinomies of Kantian thought can thus be treated as a central motif of German social science. In *Meaning and Change*, Roland Robertson (1978) has traced this development through Hegel, Nietzsche, Kierkegaard, Simmel and Weber. However, the question of transcending the categories of Kantian epistemology was most critically outlined in the work of Georg Lukács (1971). In an argument that was not unlike the thesis presented by Goldmann,

Lukács treated the 'antinomies of bourgeois thought' as a manifestation of the reification of consciousness, which resulted from the nature of economic relations in capitalist society. In short, Lukács traced the characteristic dichotomies of bourgeois thought back to the fetishism of commodities produced by the forms of economic exchange in capitalist society. Kantian philosophy in particular, with its sharp division between the phenomenal and noumenal world, manifested the problematic of subjectivity and objectivity. The importance of Kant, in Lukács's estimation, was that Kant recognised the intractable nature of the separation of inner freedom and external determination by nature without offering any superficial resolution of this conflict. Nevertheless, Kantian man, like Robinson Crusoe, was wholly the product of capitalist conditions:

man in capitalist society confronts a reality 'made' by himself (as a class) which appears to him to be a natural phenomenon alien to himself; he is wholly at the mercy of its 'laws', his activity is confined to the exploitation of the inexorable fulfilment of certain individual laws for his own (egoistic) interests. But even while 'acting' hs remains, in the nature of the case, the object and not the subject of events. (Lukács, 1971, p. 135)

The divisions in bourgeois thought could not be resolved by transforming the divisions in bourgeois society, that is, by practical action. The solution to the philosophical dilemmas of the Kantian system was thus to be located in the revolutionary action of the proletariat. In changing the basic structures of capitalist economic relations through violent revolutionary action, the proletariat would liquidate the basic forms of reified consciousness. The proletariat would realise the unfolding of ths Hegelian Idea, not in contemplation, but in praxis.

Lukács's problem was, of course, that the actual consciousness of the working class in the early decades of the twentieth century did not exhibit the features of genuine consciousness of their revolutionary role; it did not even show any promise of the coming transformation. In the period leading up to revolution, it was the party which would have to act as the arbiter and mentor of revolutionary consciousness. Lukács did not seriously explore the problems of bureaucratic control of politics that dominated the political sociology of Weber and Michels; he could not admit that bureaucracy has a political logic and gains interests which are relatively independent of the economy. The bureaucratic consciousness may be thus as partial as the consciousness of the bourgeoisie.

The legacy of Lukács's search for a social group which would embody reason and overcome the antinomies of thought was reproduced in the Frankfurt school which, particularly in the philosophy of Marcuse, looked towards radicals, students, blacks and women as the spearhead of critical thought. Although at a theoretical level the critical

theorists attempted to resolve the individual/society paradox by reconciling Marxism and Freudian psychoanalysis (Held, 1980), at a political
level the absence of revolution drove them inexorably towards pessimism — and hence back to Weber's pessimistic view of the collapse of the
individual under the weight of technical rationality (Turner, 1981a).

The pessimistic theme of *The Protestant Ethic and the Spirit of
Capitalism* (Weber, 1965) was that the very forces of modern progress
that emerged out of Calvinism — rational thought, antipathy to magic,
an ascetic calling and individualism — in creating a capitalist society
came eventually to undermine freedom of conscience, liberalism and
personal autonomy. In capitalism, the very meaning of life was threatened by technical rationality, by science and by bureaucracy; socialism
did not offer an alternative, since industrial socialism would intensify
the process of control via the agency of the party bureaucracy. At the
end of the journey, started by Luther and Calvin, lay the iron cage of
capitalist society. It is particularly interesting that this dominant
metaphor of capitalist society should have been extracted by Weber
from John Bunyan's *The Pilgrim's Progress* of 1678 (Tiryakian, 1981).
The man, who was shut up in a dark room to repent his life of lust and
pleasure, described his condition as 'the iron cage of despair'. It was
this note of desperation in Weber's treatment of the individual/society
relation that clearly separated his position from that of early, rationalist
individualism (Hunt, 1981). Where Bernard Mandeville at the beginning of the eighteenth century had argued in his *The Fable of the Bees*
that individual vices of greed and avarice resulted in the public good of
economic progress, Weber's 'negative heterogony of purposes' (Stark,
1967) suggested that even human goodness, of which there is little,
must end in evil. Weber described himself as religiously unmusical, but
his version of the relationship between the individual and society had a
strong flavour of Calvinist pessimism. The only mode of existence for
the modern intellectual was an ethic of responsibility in the direction of
either a calling in science or politics. The mystical orientation of the
private individual was, for Weber, an unacceptable compromise in
relation to this world.

Because Weber thought that a religious calling in the world was no
longer possible, he sought a resolution of the individual/society complex in the calling of science and politics. These vocations were a form
of this-worldly asceticism by which we may face up to the seriousness of
life with some degree of rationality. Unlike Lukács's messianic expectations of revolutionary violence, Weber's approach is tentative and
modest. Weber's two speeches on 'science as a vocation' and 'politics as
a vocation' are thus to be seen as an attempt to provide an ethic which is
in tune with the disenchantment of capitalism — an ethic which locates
personal authenticity in the practice of science or politics. There is no

ultimate or transcendental legitimation for these choices, which can only find partial support in rational inquiry and serious commitment:

The tension between divine will and worldly order has been transformed into the tension between human will and social order, and the primacy of transcendence has been replaced by that of this world. The world view that has an elective affinity to modern society remains dualist, but it has lost its transcendental moorings — it is a world view of immanence. (Roth and Schluchter, 1979, p. 52)

Weber saw no alternative to the processes of individuation which were necessary in capitalist society for the routine control of populations and which progressively undermined individual differences. Individuation paradoxically separates and standardises persons in a system of bureaucratic control. Individuality could flourish, however, among an elite who seriously faced the challenge of secular society not by private mysticism and outdated faith, but in terms of a responsible calling in the world. The irony was that Weber's personal fate — mental illness and political failure — forced him to adopt a somewhat contemplative role in society, which thereby has a passive mystical dimension. The problem of individuality in Weber's sociology and philosophy was, as Robertson (1978) shows, part of the German cultural tradition, but it may also be the product of the contemplative isolation which has been the fate of intellectuals.

8 Religion and Political Legitimacy

The King's two bodies

Effigies

The chronicler Geoffrey le Baker records that King Edward II was murdered at Berkeley in 1327 by having a red-hot iron inserted in his anus; his body, suitably disembowelled and embalmed, was buried three months later in St Peter's Abbey Church at Gloucester on 20 December. His burial marked an important development in western mortuary practices, since his natural body was accompanied by an effigy bearing the symbols of regal authority. This custom of placing an effigy on the coffin of the king then became, particularly in France, an important feature of royal funerals.

The employment of effigies was simply part of the legal and religious tradition in which the king had two bodies — a natural body subject to death and a political body in which resided incorruptible sovereignty (Kantorowicz, 1957). The visible fiction of the effigy on the coffin replaced the invisible reality of physical decay within the coffin, thereby providing 'evidence' to the belief that the king can never die. Although Edward II as a person was incompetent and died a less than noble death, the principle of sovereign authority, competence and continuity was preserved in the fictional person of the king's effigy (Prestwich, 1980).

The problem of legitimating earthly power enjoyed by political institutions in terms of religious beliefs and symbols has a long and complex history. This problem is particularly acute in cultures dominated by Christianity, which is, in many respects, a somewhat apolitical religion. More precisely, the position of orthodox Christian theology in relation to political power is mixed. Early Christian theology regarded the power of imperial Rome in particular and political power in general as evil; Apocalypse of John bears testimony to such an anti-political orientation. The church as an institution, however, was forced to come to terms with worldly authority and this compromise was achieved through Pauline theology, in which the legitimacy of power is only secured 'by the grace of God'. Pauline theology provided the basis for the view that secular power is derivative of divine power and that secular rulers are thus representatives of supernatural authority. When Christian monotheism was subsequently combined with the Roman concept of emperorship, the symbolic power of the Roman rulers was greatly extended. In Christianised Rome, there was a tension between the development of Caesaro-papism, in which the emperor was divine and above the law, and Pauline concepts of 'by the grace of God', which implied a merely executive function for secular power in, for example, rooting out evil with force. These relationships between religion and politics can be considered in terms of Walter Ullmann's thesis that the emergence of European political theory was formed by the contrast between the descending and ascending principle of kingship (Ullmann, 1969 and 1975).

Ullmann's analysis of medieval politics is concerned with the issue of legitimacy, that is, by what agency is legitimate power to be exercised? Medieval society provided two entirely contradictory answers to this question in the descending theme (power descends from God) and the ascending theme (power ascends from the community).

The ascending thesis, which chronologically preceded the descending principle, was associated with the popular assemblies of the Germanic tribes as depicted in Tacitus' *Germania*. These tribal chiefs had no power other than that given to them by the community and its assemblies. Because the chief was a representative, there existed a communal right of resistance against rulers who abused their position:

Metaphorically speaking power ascended from the broad base of a pyramid to its apex, the king or duke. The popular assembly controlled the ruler's government and it was mainly as a court of law that the assembly worked effectively. This ascending theory of government may also be called the populist theory of government, because original power was anchored in the people. (Ullmann, 1975, pp. 12—13)

By contrast, in the descending theory the legitimacy of rulers has its origin in God and therefore the community has no genuine right of resistance and no power over the king. The ruler is seen to be responsible to God, not the people, and thus the descending principle can be called a theocratic theory of government. Power is distributed downwards through officials who remain responsible to the king rather than to the people whom they govern.

Under the impact of the Christianised Roman Empire, the ascending principle was driven out and did not re-emerge until the end of the thirteenth century. For Ullmann, the ascending principle anticipated, so to speak, the concepts of political consent and citizenship as the corner-stones of modern liberal theory, whereas the descending thesis, having in fact its greatest success in Byzantium, was the product of academics and clerics. The coronation of kings as a sacramental act, rather than the election of representatives, indicated the triumph of the clerical mind in the descending tradition of political legitimacy; anointing by the clerical hierarchy replaced the consent of the community in the production of legitimate rulers (Nelson, 1977).

The Ullmann thesis has been criticised for imposing a modern version of liberal constitutionalism on medieval political practice and for misinterpretation of, for example, Henry de Bracton's writings on kingship (Oakley, 1973). As an alternative to the picture of an oscillation between ascending and descending principles, it may be more appropriate to consider the development of medieval political thought in terms of an impersonalisation of power — that is, the separation of political authority from the person of the king. The notion of impersonal authority was thus preparatory to the growth of the state as a political abstraction, separate from the persons who happen to exercise political functions. Medieval political thought was thus not simply concerned with the source of legitimacy, but with the competence with which it was exercised. Debates about the sacred nature of kingship as the source of legitimacy were supplemented by new concepts of political and administrative competence:

The long process by which the personal, theologically conceived power of the ruler became impersonal and public led to new terms in discussions of political authority. The growth of new symbols of public power — 'crown', 'community of the realm', 'estate of king', and the suprahuman character of the anointed ruler — all reflected attempts to reconcile the older private view of kingship with the newer and more legally articulate public view. (Peters, 1970, pp. 19—20)

In the thirteenth century, theorists began to sharpen the distinction between unlawful competent rulers (*tyrannus utilis*) and lawful incompetent rulers (*rex inutilis*), which provided criteria for resistance to and deposition of kings (Wieruszowski, 1963). The concept of *rex inutilis* did not question the lawfulness of kingship as such; it directed attention towards the performance of government. Regardless of theoretical elaborations, throughout the medieval period kings were regularly murdered, deposed or forced to abdicate. In the case of Edward II, his deposition and murder was the end result of an incompetent reign, but the continuity of the realm was aided by the symbolism of the king's effigy and by the existence of a legitimate male heir to the throne. In order to understand this separation of person and power, we must return to an exposition of Kantorowicz's discussion of the king's two bodies.

Liturgical kingship

Tudor and Elizabethan jurists often adhered to decidedly mystical views of the king's two bodies; in fact, their christological orientation to the debate concerning the nature of the king's person had its origins in a treatise written around 1100 by an anonymous cleric from Normandy, who is conventionally known as the Norman Anonymous. Feudal writers were quite familiar with the complex interpretation of the secular and the religious. Bishops could be barons; churches exercised secular functions. The Anonymous extended this obvious mixture to the person of the king who, by consecration and anointment, was filled by *natura* and *gratia*. Just as Christ was the God–man, so Christian kings were *persona mixta*, having both secular and spiritual capacities. This sacral view of the nature of the king's person implied also an attitude of subservience and devotion on the part of subjects to their king. Political rebellion against the king was tantamount to heretical uprisings against God. Christ who was King and Priest was thought to be represented on earth by the king who also embodied these religious and political functions. This theory expressed the liturgical view of kingship that was prevalent between the ninth and twelfth centuries.

Changes which subsequently took place in theology involving a greater emphasis on the spiritual nature of Christ were reflected in theories of earthly kings:

there resulted the replacement of the more christocratic-liturgical concept of kingship by a more theocratic-juristical idea of government . . . There was a period of transition from the earlier liturgical kingship to the late-mediaeval kingship by divine right, a period, clear in its contours, during which a royal mediatorship, though strangely secularized, still existed, and during which the idea of royal priesthood was vested in the Law itself. (Kantorowicz, 1957, p. 93)

In this transition, the king was seen to be under the Law and subject to it, not out of necessity, but as a matter of free choice. Since the Law was the king's will, the relationship between Law and monarchy was a voluntary one. Another version of this legal context which fully conformed to the idea of *persona mixta* was to distinguish between Natural and Positive Law. The Law of Nature was independent and self-sufficient, whereas positive laws were the creation of kingdoms and courts, and consequently relative and subject to change. There was correspondingly an unchanging Justice throughout the universe which was inadequately contained within the justice of secular courts. The king came to be seen as the intermediary between Natural Law and Positive Law, between eternal Justice and the decisions of temporal courts. In the thirteenth century, the idea of the king as by grace the living image of God gave way to more abstract concepts of the monarch as the personification of Justice. The juxtaposition of nature and grace was replaced by the contrast between natural and human laws. Theological perspectives were gradually adapted to the administrative requirements of a secular state.

There were also changes taking place in the traditional notions of the 'mystical body of Christ'. The traditional liturgical concepts of the *corpus mysticum* were being given a sociological content as these concepts gained a new reference, namely, the 'body politic'. Whereas *corpus mysticum* had originally referred to the host in the Eucharist, it was gradually transferred to the body of the Church and finally to the wider society. These christological ideas were slowly becoming sociological.

This change had an impact on the two-bodies theory, because the king came to be seen as a private person and a public corporation. The king was a natural man, but also the immortal symbol of the national body and the political structure. To be a king the king no longer required the liturgical rituals which in the coronation 'made' him, as it were, an anointed, deified monarch. The 'little interregnum' between accession and coronation disappeared. The ceremonial of coronation remained, but it served political rather than ritualistic ends:

the king's true legitimation was dynastical, independent of approval or consecration on the part of the Church and independent of election by the people. (Kantorowicz, 1957, p. 330)

The continuity of power came to be guaranteed by the dynastic principle, but the separation of person and office, monarch and crown, individual and corporation was still necessary as part of the edifice of political stability. Above all, the king came to be the abstract symbol of authority and of *dignitas*. The continuity of the king's body was secured by lawful, dynastic marriage; the continuity of state, by the dignity which dwelt with the Crown.

Regicide

The force of the thesis of the king's two bodies as a principle of political legitimacy is seen in the 'royal utopia' publications which appeared after the interregnum and glorious revolution of the seventeenth century; these utopian schemes recognised that the harmony of society rested on the presence of a legitimate king as the head of the social body (Davis, 1981). More dramatically, the treatment of regicides demonstrates that an attack on the private person of the king is also a political assault on society, the king's public body. For example, on 28 November 1660 the body of Oliver Cromwell, who had died two years earlier, was removed from Westminster Abbey and, together with the corpses of Bradshaw and Ireton, was taken to Tyburn to hang on the gallows. Their heads were cut off and exhibited at Westminster Hall for a day (Ridley, 1977). Samuel Pepys with his usual earthiness marked the day by purchasing a hat for thirty-five shillings. An equally remarkable case was that of the regicide Damiens who, on 2 March 1757, was condemned to death by public execution. The flesh was torn from Damiens's body, burnt with sulphur, quartered and reduced to ashes.

This gruesome event forms the opening scene for Michel Foucault's *Discipline and Punish* (1979). Resting his argument on Kantorowicz's account of the king's two bodies, Foucault argues that the extent of the physical punishment given out to regicides is a measure of the importance of protecting society which is represented in the royal body. As political legitimacy became disassociated from the physical body of the king, there was a corresponding change in the nature and object of punishment. Under the two-bodies principle:

the body of the condemned man became the king's property, on which the sovereign left his mark and brought down the effects of power. Now he will be rather the property of society, the object of a collective and useful appropriation. (Foucault, 1979, p. 109)

Punishment of the body was replaced by the penalty of public works which indicated a collective interest in the condemned person and a concern for the moral lessons of punishment. With adherence to panopticism, penology became focused on docile, disciplined bodies rather than on the unpredictable agony of the scaffold. This reorganisation of penological institutions was thus connected with new disciplines of the body, but behind this dressage of the body there was the history and formation of the state — a history which Foucault deliberately neglects in favour of an analysis of the micro-politics of order. This history of the state is a necessary basis for any discussion of religion and political legitimacy, and this history of political power has to be seen in terms of the transition from feudalism to capitalism via the absolutist state.

Ideologies of legitimacy

It is characteristic of those texts which approach the issue of political legitimacy from a history of ideas perspective that they fail to show a concrete connection between the political structure of feudal society and its legitimating beliefs; furthermore, the audience at which these theories of monarchical authority were directed is not specified. It is clear, for example, that the doctrine of the king's two bodies was a powerful religious ideology of political legitimacy, but it is not clear which social classes accepted these doctrines as self-evident, normative and authoritative.

Kantorowicz (1957) cites the famous miniature of the Gospel book of Aachen of 973 in the Abbey of Reichenay as typical of the Christo-centric period of European civilisation (900—1100); the miniature shows the Emperor Otto II clearly connected with divine power, being an earthly representative of divine power. Who saw this miniature and how did they respond to it? Was the symbolism of the Aachen miniature directed at the dominant class or was it designed to incorporate the subordinate class? Who understood the complex symbolism of this artefact? These questions are not addressed by Kantorowicz and no clear answers emerge from this monumental study. The Aachen symbolism was in fact relevant to the dominant class itself. The ideological conflicts which existed behind these debates in the nature of kingship were conflicts within the dominant class and they hinged on one crucial problem: was the king a landowner alongside his barons or was the king a superior being whose existence guaranteed the authority of other feudal lords?

The central feature of feudalism in which these theories of political legitimacy arose was the struggle between local and central authority. European feudalism is thus most appropriately conceptualised as a system of 'parcellised sovereignty' (Anderson, 1974a). The relationship between lord and vassal was relatively egalitarian and highly personal, growing out of a political bond between men-at-arms. Below these feudal relations between lords, the peasantry were socially and politically excluded from this personal tie of comradeship. Feudalism thus had a strong tendency towards fragmentation into local dynasties which were weakly connected to centralised kingdoms. There were, of course, important variations across Europe; after the Norman conquest, English kings were relatively successful in imposing their authority over other landlords, but in France, the monarchy was somewhat ineffectual in relation to its hinterland (Duby, 1953).

The political ideologies of this system, as described by Ullmann and Kantorowicz, were neither necessary nor relevant to the normative incorporation of peasants. These political ideologies were addressed to the question of the king's relation to other landlords. Was the king *primus inter pares* or was he the supreme and sole origin of power and authority? The doctrine of the king's two bodies can thus be seen as an attempt to counteract the fragmentation of the feudal political order.

Ständestaat

These ideological and political relations were very different from the forms of association that emerged within the system of the Ständestaat. In representing the interests of the towns and the estates through the *parlements,* the Ständestaat challenged the personal, feudal authority of the king and his nobles. Within these urban polities, the concepts of corporate rights and franchises were developed by the university lawyers and were very different from the traditional notions of feudal immunity. In defence of these legal rights and expanding commercial interests, new military institutions, especially the urban militia, evolved and replaced existing feudal forms of personal military service (Weber, 1958). From the thirteenth and fourteenth centuries, the Ständestaat were the context for important developments in legal, political and administrative institutions:

In particular, the growing size of the towns and the fact that the distinctively urban social groups were committed primarily to economic pursuits . . . led to the formation of elected representative bodies that often 'governed' by enacting statutes — a momentous innovation. (Poggi, 1978, p. 55)

Throughout Europe, there were various 'solutions' to the see-saw political struggle between the monarchy and the Ständestaat, and thus between various forms of political legitimacy. The process of political centralisation was more decisive in France and Germany than in England, but, although the growth of centralisation and absolutism appears to be a defeat of local city autonomy, the absolutist state was important in creating certain administrative and political requirements for capitalism. The paradox of the absolutist state thus plays an important role in the transition from the personal legitimacy of the king to the impersonal legitimacy of law.

Despotism

The terms *despotisme éclairé* and *despotisme légal* were used in the 1760s to distinguish the enlightened absolutism of Europe, which acknowledged the existence of Natural Law and to which subjects submitted voluntarily, and Oriental despotism, which was illegal and involuntary (Hartung, 1957). The legitimacy of enlightened absolutism rested on its rational character in sweeping away local, particular impediments to commercial development by instituting universal criteria of administration, communication and economic transactions.

Although the absolutist state contributed to the demise of the system of estates, its relation to the traditional feudal aristocracy was contradictory:

For the apparent paradox of Absolutism in Western Europe was that it fundamentally represented an apparatus for the protection of aristocratic property and privileges, yet at the same time the means whereby this protection was promoted could simultaneously ensure the basic interests of the nascent mercantile and manufacturing classes. (Anderson, 1974b, p. 40).

Absolutism aided these classes by creating uniform systems of law, reducing internal restrictions on trade, protecting national industries by tariffs, supporting colonial enterprises and developing administrative rationality. With this expanding administrative apparatus, the absolutist period saw the growth of impersonal public law, which permitted greater precision and reliability. Although the absolutist monarchs acquired superhuman personalities as indicated by Louis XIV's title, *le Roi soleil,* the doctrine of the king's two bodies encouraged a separation between the personal body of the king and the abstract body of the state. Under absolutist polities, the state had become an instrument of public policy, organising the economy and the contours of civil society. In Europe, the adoption of Roman constitutional law, the growth of impersonal public law and the formal regulation of the civil bureaucracy represented an important political reorganisation of power in which the king was progressively detached from the state.

Hegel

The absolutism of the seventeenth and eighteenth centuries thus provides the backcloth for the full emergence of the capitalist mode of production and, in political terms, of philosophical debates concerning the relationship between the abstract state and the concreteness of civil society. The modern problem of political legitimacy is firmly located in the problematic linkages between the universal claims of the state and the particular claims of social classes within society. The doctrine of the universal abstract state found its apogee in the idealist philosophy of Georg Hegel, for whom the state resolved and transformed the egoistic and particular conflicts between individuals within civil society. It was in the state that separate individuals realised their freedom; the state was the embodiment of reason and universality, standing over the particularities and restrictions of civil society (Kolakowski, 1978, vol. I). In Hegelian philosophy, the divinity which once adhered to the king's body is transferred to the state itself:

For truth is the Unity of the universal and subjective Will; and the Universal is to be found in the State, in its laws, its universal and rational arrangements. The State is the Divine Idea as it exists on Earth. (Hegel, 1956, p. 39)

The notion that the state incorporates the historical development of reason and freedom provided a blanket legitimation for any particular state, in particular for the Prussian state. Hegel can, therefore, be criticised for providing a philosophical justification for *de facto* governments, such as the Prussian government of Frederick William III (Popper, 1945). From the point of view of the sociology of religion, however, it is possible to identify two major secular routes out of Hegel which lead into the contemporary problem of political legitimacy, namely, the Marxist critique and the Nietzsche/Weber perspective on the modern state.

Marx's objection is well known and can be briefly stated (Hibbin, 1978). Although there is considerable doubt as to the precise nature of Marx's theory of the state (Holloway and Picciotto, 1978), Marx did not believe that the state in capitalist society could transcend the social divisions which were the consequences of capitalist relations of production. The state, if not a direct instrument of the dominant class, at least worked in the interests of capital, in securing the relations of economic production and representing the political interests of capital. The state was not the 'phenomenon of the Idea', but the product of class relations at a definite stage in history. Thus, in his debate on the 'Jewish

Question', Marx argued that the Jews could not be liberated merely at the political level; genuine freedom could only result from radical transformation of the whole economic basis of society. The political alienation of people as private citizens had to be solved by a total transformation of the economic basis of society.

The Hegelian theory of the state failed to analyse the roots of political conflict in the anarchy of the capitalist economy (Mandel, 1969). Just as the separation of layman and priest represented in Catholicism a form of religious alienation, so the liberal state of the capitalist epoch constituted a political alienation separating the citizen and the private individual. The antinomies of bourgeois political philosophy — state/society, citizen/individual, public/private — were products of class contradictions in the anatomy of society. The state as such had no intrinsic legitimacy, being merely an instrument of political force which operated in the interests of the dominant class.

The solution to these contradictions had to be located in the transformation of the capitalist mode of production by the working class as a universal class. Whether Marx, in substituting 'proletariat' for 'state' as the rational principle of history, remained within the Hegelian problematic is not immediately relevant (Hyppolite, 1969). More importantly, Marx's critique of the Hegelian theory of the state provided a major opening for secular conceptualisations of power: law is the outcome of secular class conflicts and does not have its source in natural law or divine will.

Weber

The critical location in sociology of the problem of state legitimacy is the political sociology and sociology of law of Max Weber. To understand the difficulty Weber experienced in identifying the ground of political legitimacy in the modern world, we have to grasp the nature of Weber's relationship and dependence upon Nietzsche. For both, the political bankruptcy of contemporary politics, especially German politics, had its ultimate origin in what Nietzsche called the 'death of God', that is, in the radical devaluation of law and standards. Weber said that the intellectual honesty of a scholar could only be judged by his response to the questions posed by Marx and Nietzsche (Baumgarten, 1964). Although Weber's relationship to Marx has been endlessly dissected (Turner, 1981a), the continuity of his sociology with Nietzsche's analysis of modern nihilism has been seriously neglected.

Weber has been commonly regarded as the theorist of political legitimacy. The notion that power is legitimised by reference to custom and tradition, or to the charismatic claims of a personal leader, or to the legal-rational procedures of political administration is often regarded as

Weber's most important contribution to political sociology. Thus, we are told that:

No form of authority is satisfied with an obedience which is merely external submission on grounds of common sense, expediency or respect: it seeks further to arouse the members of the group to faith in its legitimacy, that is, transform discipline into adherence to the truth which it represents. Weber conceived of three types of legitimate authority. (Freund, 1968, p. 229)

These bland interpretations of Weber quickly run into a number of basic problems in his sociology of domination: Weber argued at both the practical and theoretical levels that the legitimation of state power in secular society was deeply uncertain. Any interpretation of Weber's view of legitimacy has to reconcile a number of contradictory trends in Weber's political sociology. Although it is certainly true that, in his formal analysis of power, Weber sought the roots of normative legitimacy in tradition, charisma and legal-rationality, Weber's analysis of German politics was more concerned with problems of class conflict and the struggle for state power than with the question of individual commitment to authority (Beetham, 1974). The specific crisis in Germany was that, because the modernisation of Germany had been brought about from above by Bismarck, the middle classes were lacking in political experience and organisation; there was consequently no social defence against the bureaucratic encroachment of the civil service into individual life. Germany thus lacked any creative political leadership, because political life was swamped by bureaucracy (Giddens, 1972).

In approaching Weber's sociology of legitimate domination, it is also important to separate out his analysis of intra-state politics, in which the search for normative validation is important, from his views on inter-state politics. Weber treated the relations between states as a matter of pure political struggle (*Machtpolitik*), so that in modern politics the international arena is unrestrained by normative regulation. These difficulties in interpretations of Weber have been recently identified by Frank Parkin (1982), who successfully outlines the key dimensions of Weber's political sociology. Despite Weber's interest in the formal properties of legitimacy, societies are seen to be 'held together not so much through contractual relations or moral consensus as through the exercise of power' (Parkin, 1982, p. 70). In protecting its territorial basis and in dealing with other states, this 'exercise of power' is particularly characteristic of the state as a social institution. Indeed, the state cannot be defined in terms of its ends, but only in the means which are specific to it, namely, the exercise of physical force.

Power is ultimately an exercise of coercion regardless of the social actor's perceptions of the legitimacy of power, but Parkin suggests that

Weber made a distinction between power in general and the more specific notion of domination. There are two sources of domination. The first arises from monopolistic control of economic resources in the market-place; economic domination does not require normative compliance and gives rise to what Marx referred to as 'the dull compulsion' of economic arrangements. The second source of domination arises from the monopolistic control over administrative offices and, in Weber's view, this ownership of the means of administration requires legitimation and compliance. Unlike power as such, administrative domination depends on obedience to commands. It is 'sociology of command' that produces the threefold distinction between traditional, charismatic and rational modes of legitimation. Although this sociology of command was fully articulated, it was not adequately supplemented by a 'sociology of compliance'.

Weber's sociology of legitimate domination was thus more concerned with the question of power from the point of view of dominant groups than with the question of submission from the perspective of the mass (Merquior, 1980). Parkin, however, suggests that Weber outlined the elements of a theory of compliance in the speech on 'politics as a vocation' and also in *Economy and Society,* when Weber noted that compliance to a command was achieved through:

empathy or through inspiration or through persuasion by rational argument or through some combination of these three principal types of influence of one person over another. (Weber, 1968, vol. 2, p. 946)

This sketch of a theory of compliance is the parallel to the fuller analysis of legitimate domination and produces an abstract model of the grounds of obedience:

Domination	Compliance
Tradition	Empathetic
Charisma	Inspirational
Bureaucratic	Rational

Compliance to the exercise of domination is thus a complex social phenomenon; the motivation for compliance is not simply a matter of the perception of legitimate commands from superiors, but may involve apathetic compliance, pragmatic acceptance, fear of possible punishment and simple expedience. It is, however, characteristic of Weber's sociology of industrial capitalism that the exercise of coercion is an essential ingredient of social order.

This discussion of typologies of command and compliance suggests, however, that Weber took a static view of the problem of legitimacy. It is well known that Weber thought that legal-rational domination and rational compliance had gradually replaced tradition and charisma as the principal basis of political control in capitalism, but we need also to bear in mind Weber's analysis of the fragility of legal-rational domination and the crisis of secular legitimacy. To grasp the nature of Weber's pessimistic view of modern politics, we have to bring his sociology of religion to the foreground. Once the crisis of politics and the crisis of religion are seen as a single theme in Weber's sociology, we can also understand the continuity of Weber's sociology out of Nietzsche's project of 1888 to overcome nihilism and Christianity by 'a revaluation of values'.

Nietzsche

The preoccupation with Nietzsche's *Kulturphilosophie* and *Lebensphilosophie* has overshadowed Nietzsche's contribution to political philosophy (Krell, 1981). In defending Nietzsche against the fascist reception of his analysis of will, his admirers presented his philosophy as radically anti-political in outlook. Discussions of Nietzsche's 'will to power' rightly locate 'will' and 'power' in the context of an analysis of individual growth, 'self-overcoming' and moral development. The 'will to power' includes political power, but is primarily concerned with individual existence (Hollingdale, 1973).

These interpretations of Nietzsche fail, however, to identify the importance of Nietzsche's criticism of modern politics and nationalism for a general assessment of his philosophy. Nietzsche's study of Greek society, his rejection of German nationalism and his hostility towards modern politics as a form of moral degeneration constitute a definite political stance. As with many nineteenth-century philosophers, Nietzsche used the Greek polis as a bench-mark for an evaluation of contemporary political life. Nietzsche recognised, of course, that rapid social change in Europe precluded any utopian return to Greek politics as a model for social organisation. However, Greek political discourse provided criteria for an assessment of political decline in contemporary Germany.

The importance of the Greek state for Nietzsche was that it provided a political space within which citizens could compete in argument. Like the Greek athletic contest, politics was an arena of the will to power. The conflict of political wills institutionalised violence and promoted the development of the best specimens of the species. Internal political stability and personal growth were possible because conflict was not repressed, but sublimated in games and warfare (Strong, 1975). The contest between antagonistic men in the *agon* of external wars and public games produced 'healthy' social and political results. The decay of Greek politics was the result of a reduction in the differences between individuals, dependence on slave moralities and the division of labour which made individuals merely specialised units within the social framework. This fragmentation and specialisation destroyed the pristine unity of public and private life in the ancient Greek polis.

In Christian Europe, this process of subservience is continued by adherence to the doctrine of political conformity in Paul's Epistle to the Romans. Lutheran Protestantism, despite its appeals to individual conscience, merely perpetuated a slave morality by demanding adherence to the secular state. In contemporary society, this historical decay of 'healthy' politics has been masked by an idolatrous commitment to nationalism. With the death of God, nationalism provides an artificial meaning for political engagements, disguising the profound decay of moral life in society. In *Thus Spake Zarathustra* (Nietzsche, 1933), the nationalist state is the modern idol, which is an instrument of repression to crush individuality and to promote slavery; the modern state breeds superfluous men. For Nietzsche, socialism was not an alternative to repressive politics. In *The Dawn* of 1881, Nietzsche complained that were socialism to triumph, socialists would place themselves in 'iron chains' and enforce a 'fearful discipline'. The only justification for the state was the promotion of 'overmen', that is, individuals who have not suppressed their instinctual drives, but directed them towards self-fulfilment. The death of God and the decay of politics required not a false nationalist idol, but a total moral break and the revaluation of life.

The secular state
There are a number of obvious parallels between Nietzsche and Weber in terms of their treatment of individuality versus political control (Fleischmann, 1964). Weber's defence of individuality against political conformity, his adherence to charismatic politics and his 'decisionist' argument in the ethic of responsibility bear a close resemblance to Nietzsche's notion of the 'overman', commitment to the individualist theme in Schopenhauer and Emerson, and primarily in Nietzsche's critique of the state as a blockage to self-overcoming. Weber's metaphor of modern society as 'an iron cage' and an 'army camp' is compatible with similar views expressed by Nietzsche.

Capitalism required administrative routinisation and calculation of performance within a detailed division of labour, thus preventing personal individuality; standardisation was inevitable unless people refused 'to be ruled like sheep':

In the American 'benevolent feudalism', in the so-called 'welfare institutions' of Germany, in the Russian factory constitution . . . everywhere the house is ready-made for a new servitude. It only waits for the tempo of technical economic 'progress' to slow down and for rent to triumph over profit. The latter victory, joined with the exhaustion of the remaining free soil and free market, will make the masses 'docile'. Then man will move into the house of servitude. (Weber, 1961, p. 71)

The complexity of the economy and the intervention of the state would create an insatiable demand for clerical workers, officials and administrators: the result was dominance by a 'caste of mandarins'. Against these trends of bureaucratisation and mass conformity, Weber looked for those social and political conditions which would protect individuality and cultivate 'the best that is in men, those physical and emotional qualities which we would like to maintain for the nation' (Bendix, 1966, p. 44).

Although it is possible to isolate certain similarities between the philosophies of Weber and Nietzsche, the most important aspects of this relationship can be summarised under two general headings — the secularisation of society and politics as naked force. Nietzsche saw the loss of transcendental values — the death of God — as the major turning-point of modern world history, the result of which was not simply the decline of conventional moral systems, but the eradication of moral significance for human life itself. The outcome of this terrible event is that we inhabit a social world in which 'Everything is false; everything is permitted' (Nietzsche, 1967a, section 602). Unlike the general run of nineteenth-century atheists, however, Nietzsche did not feel that the death of God was a cause for enthusiastic celebration. Although human freedom from subservience to the Christian God was a necessary precondition for personal authenticity, there were no grounds for believing that secularisation inevitably meant moral progress. Nietzsche's view of secularisation was very much bound up with his general rejection of teleology and more specifically with his hostility to the doctrine of progress associated with positivism and Darwinism.

For Nietzsche, history was simply the endless struggle of ingroups and outgroups for power, as expressed through the will to gain power and resentment; there was no necessary logic to this struggle, no Hegelian unfolding of the Spirit or positivist triumph of science. Nietzsche's treatment of classical Greece was typical of his general approach to historical problems. Against the conventional view of Greek harmony, Nietzsche saw Greece as a society torn by conflicting groups and traditions, but the resolution of these crises through an attempted merger of Dionysian energy and Apollinian form produced a dynamic cultural milieu for individuality. Nietzsche denied both the unity of history and the unity of mankind: decadence was, however, equally distributed through human civilisations.

Weber shared both assumptions about the significance of secularisation for the collapse of moral certainty and about the impossibility of the concept of historical 'progress'. Weber's speeches on politics and science as vocations are riddled with Old Testament metaphors about the loss of innocence and the effects of the Tree of Knowledge (rational science). Capitalism permits us to eat the Forbidden Fruit, but, in making the world less magical and more intelligible, it paradoxically makes personal life less meaningful. Weber was also clearly hostile to the notion of progress in general and to the specific suggestion that social science could determine unambiguous ends which we ought to follow. In political life, the consequence of rationalisation and secularisation was that the modern state, as an institution enjoying a monopoly of force, was stripped of any metaphysical, religious or supernaturalist legitimacy. In modern society, the divinity which once surrounded the king's body, the sanctity of natural law and the time-honoured legitimacy of national tradition, had collapsed, leaving a vacuum which formal rational law simply could not fill.

Legitimate domination
Weber's definition of the state is a direct guide to his view of political reality; from the point of view of political sociology, the state is:

a compulsory organization with a territorial basis . . . The claim of the modern state to monopolize the use of force is as essential to it as its character of compulsory jurisdiction and of continuous operation. (Weber, 1968, vol. 1, p. 56)

The issue of the legitimacy of domination, as we have seen in the discussion of tradition, charisma and legal rationality, is central to Weber's political sociology. In particular, the modern state, unlike the king's body, rests on rational grounds of legal legitimacy, that is, in:

a belief in the legality of enacted rules and the right of those elevated to authority under such rules to issue commands (legal authority). (Weber, 1968, vol. 1, p. 215)

Unlike charismatic and traditional authority, legal rationality as a principle of domination rests on correct adherence to administrative processes and decision-making criteria.

There is, however, in Weber's account of legality as a basis for legitimacy an inherent circularity. A rule is legitimate, if it is so regarded, and the basis of this acceptance is that it is correctly enacted by legitimate procedures. The state is legitimate, if it can in fact enforce legitimate rules. This circularity results from Weber's adherence to methodological neutrality with regard to the ends of the state and to legal positivism which expunged all consideration of substantive justice. The state is defined by its institutionalised means of procedure, not by its substantive character — 'Dictatorship and democracy, straw-berry and vanilla' (Parkin, 1982, p. 73).

In the sociology of law, as conceived by Weber, issues of substantive truth and justice can play no part in a science of legal regularities; the empirical regularities of law, not its normative significance, are the focus of sociology. Law is simply imperative command, backed up by organised violence and not a system of normative regularities, grounded in substantive value — such was Weber's reply to Rudolf Stammler's *The Historical Materialist Conception of Economy and Law* of 1906 (Weber, 1977).

Natural law

The problem for Weber's theory of the state, however, was that although legal rationality might legitimate the basis of command, it was inadequate as a principle of compliance. Weber recognised that the modern problem of political compliance was largely an effect of the collapse of natural law, which in itself was a consequence of the dual process of secularisation and rationalisation. Weber admitted that secularisation, the growth of legal scepticism and the socialist critique of law made it increasingly difficult to secure political compliance in industrial capitalism.

Weber's view of natural law was complex, since natural law in different social circumstances could either be the platform of political protest or the basis of legal integration of society. This may not be a contradictory position, since Weber wants to suggest that the natural-law tradition provided the basis for claims against society (as in the notion of 'natural rights'), legitimated exchange relations (in the natural rights of freedom to exchange) and, finally, provided an absolute backing for secular law, which was modelled on natural law. In Weber's view, western legal systems have undergone a progressive rationalisation in terms of systematic and formal features; arising in magic and revelation, laws:

proceed to increasingly specialized juridical and logical rationality and system-atization, sometimes passing through the detour of theocratically or patri-monially conditioned substantive and informal expediency. Finally, they assume, at least from an external viewpoint, an increasingly logical sublimation and deductive rigor and develop an increasingly rational technique in pro-cedure. (Weber, 1968, vol. 2, p. 882)

Natural law stands, as it were, midway between laws based on religious revelation and modern secular laws, which have formal precision, but lack the normative authority of prophetic laws. Natural law is based on norms which are not the product of legal enactment; their legitimacy is not derived from the 'due process of law', but from their teleological and immanent properties. The norms of a natural-law system provide:

the specific and only consistent type of legitimacy of a legal order which can remain once religious revelation and the authoritarian sacredness of a tradition and its bearers have lost their force. (Weber, 1968, vol. 2, p. 867)

Natural law derived partly from the Christian tradition, in which it was held that God had to conform to the laws of nature, and partly from the Enlightenment, in which the rights of the individual were part of nature. Natural law had historically a complex relationship to social classes, because it both legitimated the rights of individual property and the right to the produce of labour. However, it is evident that Weber thought that natural law enjoyed a 'dignity' and authority which are not characteristic of modern legal formalism. The decline of natural law has the effect of weakening the legal system as a basis for the legitimation of the state. Formal legality is inadequate as a system of inducing the compliance of the masses to the exercise of power.

The legal system thus develops as a neutral, technical procedure by which enactments are achieved routinely; its legitimacy depends on the fact that legal pronouncements are, in principle, not arbitrary or *ad hoc*. At the same time, the law is battered by the contradictory demands of social classes. Property-owners require legal security of ownership, legal dependability and the security of administration. By contrast, the working class require substantive justice and a reduction of their insecurity in the market-place. This class struggle produces two contrasted views of law as either a system of social regulation or a source of rights. Although the form of law becomes increasingly rational, the content of law is subject to sectional, class demands which arise from the anarchy of the capitalist market.

Capitalist society
The paradox of capitalist society is that, although the apparatus of command increases with the growth of systems of administrative surveillance, the bases of compliance are difficult to secure. In the nineteenth century, the working class acquired rights of citizenship, some of which arose from political struggle, whereas others were directly in the interests of capital. These citizenship rights include a diversity of claims for political involvement, educational improvement, welfare and medical provision (Marshall, 1950). The implication of these rights is that the working class can make extensive claims on the state, which have the effect of raising the level of taxation and public expenditure. Working-class rights of citizenship tend, therefore, to create a permanent inflationary movement within the capitalist economy (Goldthorpe, 1978). These claims may be periodically weakened or cut back by economic recession, stagflation or monetarism, but they have yet to be obliterated in the western capitalist democracies. Conflict is thus a permanent feature of the market-place and periods of relative

industrial peace are to be explained, not by the existence of normative consensus between management and labour, but in terms of coercive regulation:

regulation is, of course quite unstable. The webs of rules have little binding force, because there is no real consensus about the legitimacy of rules, which represent the ability of one party to impose its will on another. Consequently when it is advantageous to do so, or when the power balance shifts, both sides ignore the rules which they have endorsed, or at least tolerated. (Hill, 1981, p. 149)

The state in modern capitalist society thus has to secure the loyalty of citizens in terms of certain welfare benefits, but at the same time it must create favourable economic conditions for capitalist growth. These two activities of the state are not entirely compatible, because welfare contributions to citizens tend to undermine the profitability of *individual* capitalist enterprises, despite producing a healthy, educated workforce for capitalism in general.

These contradictory pressures between citizenship rights and profits are part of a more general problem which Jürgen Habermas (1976) has identified as a systematic crisis in capitalism in terms of economics, motivation and legitimacy. Although the state attempts to secure the loyalty of citizens by welfare, the competitive relationship between political parties tends to raise the expectations of voters for social benefits which the economy cannot provide. This gap between the expectations of the electorate and the performance of governments results in a long-term disequilibrium of political arrangements. In addition, the employment market cannot fully satisfy the expectations for stable, rewarding careers which are generated by the modern school curriculum. These legitimation and motivational crises are compounded by the absence of a culture with roots in general religious values. The state cannot depend upon religion or natural law as a basis of legitimacy. Bourgeois culture in capitalist societies:

was always dependent on motivationally effective supplementation by traditional world-views. Religion, having retreated into the regions of subjective belief, can no longer satisfy neglected communicative needs. (Habermas, 1976, p. 77)

Neither traditional Christianity nor the new religious movements have relevance to public issues of legitimating state activity, welfare distribution or the structure of the economy.

The state in modern society is, as it were, in a cleft stick because the political system has to justify the unequal distribution of rewards in the absence of general legitimacy. Economic inequality has to be legitimated in the context of high and rising welfare expectations. This legitimation deficit cannot be filled by ideological engineering because, in Habermas's view, ideologies are only successful, if they have a natural, unplanned quality. Cultural traditions 'remain "living" as long as they take shape in an unplanned, nature-like manner, or are shaped with hermeneutic consciousness' (Habermas, 1976, p. 70). There can be no administrative provision of systems of meaning. Political attempts to generate ideological commitment through the organisation of the educational curriculum tend to be self-defeating. Indeed, the requirement for planning in late capitalism undermines important elements of bourgeois ideology, such as privatised individualism.

Summary
We can now summarise this analysis of the relationship between religion and politics. Under feudalism, the concepts of divine kingship and the king's two bodies emerged through the political struggle between landowners. Religion provided the symbolic medium by which the dominant class conceptualised its political relationships. The integration of feudal societies was *aided* by a common religious system, but this was not a *necessary* requirement; the peasantry was excluded from political life and the massive military inequality between lords and serfs was normally sufficient to secure the continuity of feudal domin-ance.

The transition from feudalism to capitalism was marked by an increasing impersonalisaton of power, in which the sovereignty of the state was separated from the person of the king; in legal theory, the reception of Roman law provided a new basis for legality. The political opposition of the bourgeoisie to feudal relationships was ultimately legitimised by reference to 'Nature' and 'Reason', which guaranteed individual rights to property and freedom of exchange. In early capit-alism, the state was subordinate to the market and this situation was legitimated for the dominant class by utilitarian theories of individual ownership.

The crisis of late capitalism is the result of: (1) the entry of the working class as citizens into the political arena; (2) the inadequacy of the economy to satisfy rising expectations for welfare; and (3) the inability of legal formalism to provide a system of normative legitim-ation for continuing socio-economic inequality between formally equal citizens. Late capitalist societies are neither coherent nor integrated around a system of common values, but their continuity is secured by: (1) an extensive regulatory apparatus which has various legal, political and repressive elements; (2) the difficulty of maintaining political opposition; (3) welfare inducements which are pragmatically accepted; (4) passive political participation; and (5) the 'dull compulsion' of economic relations which creates social dependency, despite a general decline in the demand for labour which technological change produces in advanced capitalist enterprises. Political commitment to capitalism may be periodically, as it were, 'topped up' by nationalism or such collective rituals as coronations and presidential inaugurations. Despite claims to the contrary (Shils and Young, 1953), by the late Middle Ages the genuine liturgical significance of kingship at the centre of the coronation ceremony had been stripped of its constitutional importance (Kantorowicz, 1957, p. 329).

Capitalist societies do experience legitimation crises, but these are not fatal, since social continuity is secured by other means. Such societies can 'tolerate' extensive sexual, political and social deviance, while also generating movements for moral reform among middle-class audiences. The paradox of such societies is that a great diversity of cultural phenomena can assume a commercialised form, from youthful deviance to middle-class human potential movements (Stone, 1978). The transformation of rock protest and working-class Punk styles into commercial enterprises is probably the classic example (Frith, 1978).

In conclusion, religion has been historically an aid to the social continuity of politically dominant classes, but it is not a necessary requirement of capitalist societies. Political compliance can be secured, despite the absence of legitimate command.

9 Religion and Global Politics

Religion in modern society

In contemporary western societies, we find a great diversity of religious forms and practices, but it is possible to provide a general statement of the main sociological dimensions of the 'religious system'. The dominant Christian tradition, inherited from the pre-industrial period, has experienced a major shrinkage in institutional significance and social impact. In this sense, institutionalised Christianity has been secularised in terms of a decline in membership, adherence, wealth and prestige (Wilson, 1966 and 1982). The state can no longer be legitimated in terms of an overarching set of absolute values by reference to the divine right of kings or in terms of natural law. Education, welfare, medicine and law are institutional areas which are relatively separated from the churches and operate as public arenas under the general surveillance of secular government. The churches as specialised institutions have been relegated to the periphery of social life in providing certain optional rituals for baptism, marriage and death. The result is that 'personal identity becomes, essentially, a private phenomenon' (Luckmann, 1967, p. 97). Modern religious systems are thus privatised, flexible and essentially experimental, providing frameworks for the individual and adjustment to the contingencies of contemporary circumstances (Bellah, 1964).

At an organisation level, the attrition of the mainstream Christian churches and denominations provides the general context for amalgamations and an acceptance of dialogue and ecumenicalism. Ecclesiastical attempts to unite churches are grounded in a genuine theological vision of Christian unity, but they inevitably imply a diminution of specific commitment to religious traditions and a willingness to abandon definite adherence to cherished traditions. Paradoxically, efforts to resolve interdenominational differences produce intra-institutional conflicts which further undermine the social impact of the churches (Turner, 1972b). The impact both of secularisation and ecumenicalism varies considerably between denominations and it is possible to chart these variations as a continuum between the mainstream Protestant churches, which exhibit low levels of orthodox belief and commitment, and sectarian groups, which preserve a more traditional style of adherence to conventional Christianity (Glock and Stark, 1965; Stark and Glock, 1968). The general attenuation of religious belief and commitment proceeds alongside partial retention of faith on the part of small-scale sectarian institutions (Wilson, 1970a).

The paradox of modern religious culture is that this diminution of traditional Christian culture has been accompanied by a mushroom growth in marginal cults, especially by religious groups influenced by Oriental faiths (Glock, 1973; Zaretsky and Leone, 1974; Glock and Bellah, 1976; Richardson, 1977; Needleman and Baker, 1978). There is apparently a contradiction between the development of such marginal cults and the development of rational, secular, technological society, but, on closer inspection, it can be argued that the new religious movements provide a social milieu in which marginal or isolated individuals can find a meaningful context for their partial reintegration back into society. Such religious cults as the Divine Light Mission and Meher Baba serve to resocialise and integrate marginal adolescents, 'drop-outs' and drug addicts back into the conventional routines of employment, monogamous family life and education (Robbins, 1969; Marx and Ellison, 1975). The cornucopia of cults in contemporary society is thus not in fact evidence against secularisation, but confirmation of the trend of religious belief and practice towards social marginality and privatisation (Wilson, 1976). Cultic religious groups, like youth culture in general, have the effect of integrating marginal groups with low social commitments to work and family into the mainstream of social life (Eisenstadt, 1956).

The diversity of modern cultures and the absence of political constraint in the selection of life-styles have the characteristics of a pluralistic supermarket (Berger, 1969). Within the cultural marketplace, choices are not politically constrained and the selection of cultural life-styles is, in principle, limitless. One can opt for Buddhism on Monday, Zen on Tuesday, Sufism on Wednesday and have the rest of the week off. In the advanced democratic societies, there are no effective constraints on these personal options, provided they do not impinge on the day-to-day operations of the state's regulative bureaucracy. Such choices are purely private and entirely optional. It can also be argued that the diversity and pluralism of the cultural market compensates for the limitations and stringency of the workplace. Like alcoholism and sexuality, religious pluralism provides the spiritual counterpart to the rigidity of time and space on the factory floor. The new religious movements, however, recruit heavily from the white-collar strata and from the ranks of younger executives. Among such organisational men, the new religious fringe offers rewarding techniques of self-realisation and personal fulfilment; as such, they are updated versions of a secularised Protestant Ethic of achievement. The new religious movements can be seen as contemporary versions of the old inspirational American literature which promised personal success and material reward as a consequence of religious adherence (Schneider and Dornbusch, 1958).

The continuity of popular religion in opposition to the general trend of religious secularisation has been explained in terms of the modern search for community, whereby cults provide a social location for alienated individuals (Snelling and Whiteley, 1974). Such religious groups are also interpreted as a basic search for existential meaning in a society dominated by bureaucratic rationality and technology (Glock, 1976). Within a materialistic perspective on religion, this study has attempted to locate the diversity of modern religious forms within an economic context in which religious behaviour has become divorced from the system of property-ownership. Without denying the importance of such religious groups as loci of community and meaning, the possibility of new religious movements exists because conventional Christianity has been divorced from its traditional role in relation to the conservation and distribution of private property.

Now that institutions — banks, governments, companies and pension funds — rather than individuals and families provide the main source of finance for long-term investment, the need for moral control over wives, eldest sons and daughters is diminished. The ancient linkage between the body, property and family under the social regulation of religion has been broken in late capitalism by the rise of depersonalised finance, the separation of ownership and control, and the dominance of the multinational corporation (Bell, 1961; Scott, 1979). Expressed somewhat opaquely, in modern capitalism the economic subject is no longer a moral or religious subject, but merely an institution subject to a certain degree of legal regulation. Because the economic system does not depend on concepts of honour, chastity or chivalry to secure the distribution of resources, capitalism is not disrupted by high levels of divorce, filial disobedience or nymphomania. In capitalism, deviance typically assumes a commercialised form which is wholly congruent with the economic patterns of 'normal' culture. This is not to say that husbands do not prefer faithful wives, obedient daughters and loyal sons, while they themselves adhere to a double standard of sexuality. It is simply to argue that the capitalist economy is not dislocated when these patrimonial preferences are not realised.

Religion and social values
In the language of a more traditional sociology, there is no system of general values integrating either individuals or classes into the dominant culture of late capitalist society. It is true that in a society like Britain, where status differences between social groups are heavily etched by accent, schooling, taste and regional culture, religion continues to provide a degree of cultural coherence among dominant groups. In England, the traditional connections between Anglicanism,

club and school still serve as social marks of 'reliability' (MacIntyre, 1967b). In the old squirearchy, however, having a son at a prestigious university and a daughter in a rural commune would not be an unusual or disreputable combination. Communes themselves become alternative finishing schools. Conventional Christianity may serve as a feature of intra-group solidarity, but it no longer provides crucial economic functions for a land-owning class or expresses an underlying coherence of the moral community. Britain is, of course, peculiar in a variety of ways; it is one of the few modern industrial societies which is not significantly a migrant society.

In many 'new nations' religion has an important social function in the preservation of ethnic cultures and in the mediation between host community and migrant group. Although the establishment in Canada (Coward and Kawamura, 1977) and Australia aspired to maintain the alliance of Protestantism, loyalty and empire, their inherent diversity precluded the integration of commonwealth societies around a dominant religious value (Mol, 1972). In Australia, Anzac Day was a purely national, secular event and not a celebration of Protestant conceptions of imperial loyalty (Firth and Hoorn, 1979). The presence of substantial Muslim communities within the old commonwealth clearly restricts the impact of national symbolism in a specific religious framework (Abedin, 1979). It is equally difficult to argue that sport provides a vehicle for the expression of national sentiments in such diverse societies and that sport, therefore, operates as a 'secular ritual' which binds the society together with the force of a religion (Moore and Meyerhoff, 1977). Attachment to sport in commonwealth societies often serves to separate regions or classes, thereby giving expression to social conflicts which are not resolved at the level of the contest. In societies with great ethnic or cultural diversity, specific and exclusive attachment to particular religious traditions tend to diminish over generations. The third and subsequent generations *may* be attached to the wider community through the symbolism of the 'national religion', such as 'the American Way of Life' (Richey, 1974). These features of national integration are in my view minimal; the diversity and pluralism of industrial societies is not so much resolved by religion, as expressed and reinforced by it.

One institutional consequence of the pluralism of capitalist societies is that religious professionals no longer have a monopoly as spokesmen of the dominant culture. Historically, I have argued that the control of priests over the whole society was always limited, but what they enjoyed in pre-capitalist societies were exclusive cultural privileges within the dominant class. The traditional monopoly of the clergy over education, welfare, rituals of marriage and death, and their general prominence in culture has, according to Wilson (1966), been successfully challenged by the emergence of 'helping' or 'service professions', equipped with modern credentials. The clergy as a result have suffered a sharp decline in recruitment, qualifications, income and social significance, although there is evidence that their prestige remains relatively high. Although the demand for clergy at marriage ceremonies and funerals is still considerable, secular services have also grown, especially in relation to second marriages. Even in the service of the dead, the clergy now compete with qualified 'death specialists' (Huntington and Metcalf, 1979). It is possible, therefore, to consider the decline of the clergy as a dominant profession in terms of a general decline in social significance, but this perspective overlooks the main issue — the disappearance of the clergy as guardians of the spiritual world of the dominant class. The clergy as confessors of kings, spiritual directors of ladies and educators of young lords have disappeared with the replacement of the feudal family by the industrial capitalist and then by the board of directors.

Since secular society does not possess any general system of values to give absolute legitimacy to social, economic and political functions, the coherence of contemporary societies depends increasingly on a variety of regulative practices, economic restraints and ultimately force. In the workplace and in society as a whole, everyday reality comes to depend on the regular operation of bureaucracy and predictable administration which reduces social actors, in Weber's view, to 'little cogs' in the 'iron cage' (Krygier, 1979). Such an administered society is, of course, periodically punctuated by religious revivalism, charismatic movements and spiritual nostalgia, but such movements do not halt the trend towards secular modes of existence. The central paradox of secular society for the sociology of religion is, however, to reconcile the irreducible facts of secularisation with the centrality of religion, especially on a global scale, to political opposition in, for example, Russia, Poland, Iran, South America and Israel.

Religion and politics

In general, the relationship between religion and politics is shaped by the history of connections between majority and minority religious traditions. In this respect, we can conceptualise a social continuum between monopolistic religious frames (Italy) to pluralistic situations where there is no established church (America) with duopolies in which Protestantism and Catholicism exert a relatively equal influence over the population (the Netherlands). The nature of church/state relations and consequently the character of political opposition will vary considerably according to the overall context of religious monopoly, duopoly or *laissez-faire* (Martin, 1978).

Another important dimension of Martin's general theory of secular-isation centres on the issue of whether religion is seen by a population to have been imposed from outside or whether religion functions as a vehicle for national sentiment against outside aggression. For example, religious adherence is often associated with reactive, cultural national-ism against outside political control. In order to provide a framework for the analysis of religion in relation to political radicalism on a world scale, it is useful to make a distinction between intra-state conflicts and inter-state relations. The latter category includes situations in which an alien religion is imposed on a subject population as the result of colonial oppression; in colonial situations, religion may become the vehicle for national unification and liberation. The former category includes regional conflicts within a nation-state in which economic imbalance gives rise to the politics of separatism and regional identities are expressed through local religious institutions as the media of sub-cultural identities. In practice, such a neat distinction is difficult to maintain, since, for example, Scottish nationalists claim that Scotland is a separate nation under the tutelage of the centralised English state. Celtic nationalists would deny any distinction between intra-regional competition and inter-national struggles. For Celtic nationalists, there is little to choose between internal and external colonialism.

What both forms of colonial development share in common, how-ever, is that the absence or denial of regional or national determination is typically expressed and intensified through the medium of religious differences. Although there is ample sociological evidence for such reactive cultural nationalism, the employment of religious symbolism by national protest movements often involves profound transform-ations of religion, which, in the long term, have to be seen as further examples of secularisation. As an illustration of this argument, I shall first discuss the theory of internal colonialism in the British context and then extend the analysis to consider the 'politicity' of Christianity, Islam and Judaism within the context of global colonialism.

Internal colonialism
It has been suggested (Hechter, 1975; Nairn 1977) that the Celtic periphery of the United Kingdom is an internal colony of a powerful, centralised English state that has, over the last two hundred years, carried out a determined policy of cultural incorporation and Angli-cisation. The nationalism of the nineteenth and twentieth centuries can thus be seen as attempts to preserve the distinctiveness of Celtic tradition and society against the tide of the dominant English culture in the context of increasing regional economic imbalance (Webb, 1978).

The survival of Scotland's civil society — a separate legal, edu-cational and religious tradition — was particularly important in the political history of Britain. The union of crowns in 1603 and the incorporating union of 1707 obliterated the Scottish state, but preserved the essential institutions of Scotland's civil society. The union of Scotland and England had the peculiar effect of confirming and preserving the social distinctiveness of Scottish society. In particular, it ensured Presbyterianism as the dominant religious tradition and as the established church. In short, Scotland entered the modern period fully equipped with the 'marks' of nationhood (Gellner, 1964), except in one crucial respect — a separate language to unify the Highlands and Lowlands against English culture.

There is, therefore, much to commend the application of Hechter's internal-colonialism thesis to recent Scottish development, in which identification with a separate Presbyterian tradition became a principal basis for national opposition to cultural and political incorporation within the English system. In particular, the notion of 'Presbyterian democracy', with its emphasis on lay involvement in the kirk, was seen to contrast sharply with the educational and social elitism of English society. Presbyterian ministers, on the other hand, were frequently to the forefront of patriotic associations which sought to preserve the teaching of Scottish history in the schools and contributed significantly to the romantic revival of Scottish literature (Hanham, 1969). Although the industrialisation of Scotland in the nineteenth century pointed towards the emergence of a secular society and a radical working class, the importance of Presbyterianism to the Scottish identity kept the kirk at a central point in civil society. In this respect, it is possible to see a parallel situation in the dominance of the Welsh chapels in the politico-cultural organisation of Welsh regionalism (Williams, 1978). Hechter's thesis of internal colonialism fails, however, in one crucial respect, namely, that Scotland historically was constituted by two separate national identities, not one.

One issue confronting the arguments of Hechter and Nairn is that there is a core/periphery distinction *within* Scotland which is parallel to the problem of the external English core and Scottish periphery. Hechter's version of the internal-colonialism thesis has to assume that Scotland enjoyed a unified political and cultural history, devoid of significant internal divisions along class and regional variations. The thesis also has to present Presbyterianism as the exclusive and dominant vehicle of Scottish opposition to England's internal colonialism. Hechter's interpretation of Scottish society thus suppresses the fact that in the Highland region the Presbyterian established kirk was closely identified with repressive landlordism and that political opposition to landlords and Lowland society was articulated through the medium of Roman Catholicism, Jacobitism, the evangelical tradition of the Free Kirk and various forms of rural populism (Hunter, 1976).

Prior to the military destruction of Highland society in the eighteenth century, Scotland was clearly divided into two distinct societies with distinctive forms of political, social and religious organisation. The Highlands were organised around a clan structure, hierarchical chieftainship and a precise divorce from Lowland agrarian capitalism (Smout, 1972; Carter, 1974; Dickson, 1978.) Historically, the Highlands were Catholic or Episcopalian with a substantial admixture of Celtic, folk and pagan religiosity. Prior to eighteenth-century industrial changes, the marked Presbyterian individualism of the Lowlands had very little resonance in the *gemeinschaft* structures of the Catholic Highlands. By focusing his analysis on the cultural Anglicanisation of Scotland as a whole, Hechter neglects the cultural imperialism of such associations as the Scottish Society for the Propagation of Christian Knowledge, which treated the existence of the Gaelic tongue as a clear indication of pre-Christian superstition, antipatriotic popery and political sedition. It was only after the nineteenth-century Disruption that missionary Presbyterianism gained any foothold in the dissident Highlands.

Nationalism

Nationalism has typically to create rather than locate firm historical roots. In the selective process of backward-looking nationalism, cultural choices have to be made between a complex set of traditions, which are potential candidates for inclusion within the dominant political perspective. The organisation of a unified Scottish national identity has to choose between, at least in principle, whig or romantic interpretations of the national tradition. In practice, an amalgam of cultures is more likely as the final outcome of national identities (Brand, 1978). Although whigs are inclined to scrap traditional cultures as particularistic and quaint, romantics attempt to resurrect traditions which they regard as diluted by superficial accretions. The difficulty with Scottish nationalism has been that one crucial dimension of its indigenous, authentic past was Celtic and Catholic, but, since the eighteenth century, the basis of Lowland civil society was the network of Presbyterian institutions.

Although these historical divisions between Catholicism and Protestantism have been important dimensions within the political debate about Scottish national identity, they cannot be divorced from questions of social class and ideology. Presbyterianism provided much of the 'moral content' of nineteenth-century nationalism, just as Methodism in England contributed a pietist dimension to liberal politics (Hill and Turner, 1975); however, Presbyterian patriotism was closely associated with small-town politics, rural interests and a Pujadist distaste for large-scale bureaucracy. Presbyterianism formed a natural alliance with the Scottish National Party in the 1930s, but it is difficult to see how that alliance could be maintained in the context of the industrial central belt or in the Scottish new towns. Presbyterianism is increasingly less relevant to the politics of the Scottish National Party which, to achieve electoral success, has to break into the traditional working-class constituencies which are dominated by the alliance between Catholicism and the Labour Party. Religion becomes an anachronistic feature of Scottish nationalism. With the erosion of membership of the principal denominations in the urban centres of modern Scotland, the idea that the Church of Scotland can continue to act as a *volkskirche* is increasingly a sociological fiction. The fiction is compounded by the continuity of basic social divisions between the rural Highlands and the industrial Lowlands, Protestant and Catholic fissures in the working class, and by separate regional interests within Scotland.

Three conclusions may be drawn from this brief commentary on Scottish nationalism. First, the internal-colonialism thesis has a general plausibility in that in the Celtic subregions religion has played an important cultural role in differentiating peripheral regions from the English core state, but on closer inspection the periphery can often be further subdivided into a core and its exploited peripheries. Secondly, religion often plays a crucial role in the inception of nationalist identities and ideologies, but this very involvement often entails a radical redefinition of religion in the interests of short-term political requirements: religion survives on behalf of politics. Thirdly, it is never possible to analyse the survival of religion in secular society as simply a matter of regional protest against centralised politics without a parallel analysis of how religious commitments are fractured by class position, economic interest and party affiliations. One peculiarity of Scotland has been that, although the Church of Scotland has often been the means of cultural opposition to English penetration, it has also been in opposition internally to the folk traditions of the crofting community, Irish migrant radicalism and working-class Catholicism.

Despite these specific complications, it can be argued that the vitality of religion in secular society is often internally connected with the political functions of religion as the vehicle for minority protest, regional opposition and political criticism. The point of these observations is, however, to raise a more general issue, namely, the location of world religions within the context of inter-state conflicts. The oppositional role of religion within internal colonial conflicts is simply indicative of a variety of broader questions concerning religious vitality and colonialism on a global scale.

Politics and world religions

If the survival and vitality of Catholicism in Poland, Baptist sects in

Russia (Bourdeaux, 1968) or Mennonites in Canada (Epp, 1977) can be, in part, attributed to subjective experiences of deprivation and objective facts of political control of communities within a state, the militancy and maintenance of religious identities in a world context might also be seen as consequences of cultural responses to colonial control. However, to understand the militancy of Islam and Judaism, for example, we need to grasp the different forms of politics that developed within the Abrahamic faiths.

It is often assumed that there is a necessary gap between religion and politics, and we mistakenly adopt reformed Protestantism as the model of the politicity of religion in the separation of church and state. In his sociological commentaries on Buddhism, for example, Weber typically exaggerated the apolitical nature of Buddhist institutions (Tambiah, 1976). Weber's general argument was that any religion with a decisive emphasis on brotherly love would be forced to come to terms with the facts of political violence and, in particular, with the state as an institution with a monopoly of coercion. Weber thought of religions in terms of a continuum, with apolitical Buddhism at one extreme and Islam as a 'warrior religion' at the other. The politicity of religious perspectives was shaped, according to Weber, by the social character of the principal groups which, through history, had been the carriers of the world religions. In short, the distinctive character of various religions has been largely determined by the 'ideological carriers' who propagated different faiths. These ideological carriers can be summarised in the following manner:

In Confucianism, the world-organizing bureaucrat; in Hinduism, the world-ordering magician; in Buddhism, the mendicant monk wandering through the world; in Islam, the warrior seeking to conquer the world; in Judaism, the wandering trader; and in Christianity, the itinerant journeyman. (Weber, 1966, p. 132)

The rituals and theological content of religions are developed rationally by the professional interests of religious intellectuals, but the characteristic essence of world religions has been constituted by the life-style of their ideological carriers. This thesis was further specified by Weber in his analysis of 'the social psychology of the world religions' when he drew attention to the influence of 'formative periods' in the construction of religious perspectives. The basic presuppositions of world religions have been historically determined:

through the peculiarity of those strata that have been the carriers of the ways of life during its formative and decisive period. (Weber, 1961, p. 281)

The period of formation of world religions is thus seen to have a charismatic authority and prestige in relation to subsequent developments.

In order to understand the peculiar features of world religions, and their politicity in particular, we have to examine the total social environment in which religions had their inception, the specific characteristics of their ideological carriers and the formative events of religious movements (Turner, 1976). In religions, the 'decisive period' of early formation comes to have a normative authority over later evolution, so that religious history is often subjectively defined as a decline. In Islam, religious change is seen as a departure from the pattern of practice and belief established under the Four Rightly Guided Caliphs. The history of Judaism is measured against the golden age of the prophets and the tribal covenant with Yahweh. In Christianity, the 'primitive church' provides the basic criterion for the reformation of corrupt practices and heretical departures from tradition.

The separate developments and character of the Abrahamic faiths can thus be seen in terms of formative responses to the political framework within which they developed their pristine doctrines and practices. The socio-political contrasts are obvious. Islam developed in the interstices of the Sassanian and Byzantine empires and achieved theocratic hegemony within its immediate territory. Christianity was excluded from political influence by the dominance of Roman imperialism at Jerusalem, Alexandria and the Mediterranean:

Christianity for a time served in significant measure as the faith of the proletariat of the Roman Empire; whereas nascent Islam was the faith, and indeed the *raison d'être* of an entrepreneurial class. (Smith, 1957, p. 37)

The millenarian and messianic character of early Christianity meant that Roman political power was regarded as ephemeral and finite; Christian politicity was shaped by the belief that the community of believers was faced by the question of short-term survival in the interregnum between the crucifixion and the coming kingdom of God. By contrast, Islam was initially concerned with the problem of consolidating its political control, the extension of the House of Islam, and the perfection of a sacred community. In contrast to both Christianity and Islam, the history of the Jewish community was punctuated by the oscillation of covenant, exile and return: Babylonian and Egyptian exiles, the fall of Jerusalem, Diaspora, Holocaust and return. Although it is clearly important to maintain a sharp distinction between history and interpretations of history, between historical origins and normative foundations, it is possible to summarise Weber's model of the Abrahamic faiths in a tabular form (see p. 210).

We can see, therefore, that Weber attempted to characterise the theological and ritual content of these religions in terms of their ideological carriers and their foundation events. For example, Islam and Judaism incorporated a clear sense of the spatial dimension of their

Religion	Carrier	Context	Norm	Myth
Judaism	trader	exile	covenant	return
Christianity	journeyman	exclusion	community	restoration
Islam	warrior	conquest	caliphate	House of Islam

spirituality. In Judaism, the promise of the land and the return from exile are crucial dimensions of the covenant between God and people. With the Diaspora, the identity of the Jewish community was maintained by their ghetto-status, exclusion as a pariah group, ritual particularity and their ideological commitment to in-gathering of the community to the Holy Land (Weber, 1952). By contrast, Islamic triumphalism is associated with the creation of unity within the household of Islam and the defence of doctrinal coherence through inward struggle (the interior jihad) and outward conflict (the exterior jihad). Christianity, shaped by millenarian hopes of Christ's Coming, by the slavery of Rome and by its urban artisans and journeymen, developed a negative attitude to this world and especially to secular political power. Whereas Judaism and Islam depended on notions of sacred space, Christianity was theologically more concerned with problems of eschatology and sacred time. Furthermore, in Christianity this holy history (*Heilsgeschichte*) is measured by suffering, betrayal, fallen man, martyrdoms and crucifixions. The consequence is that:

the type of religious experience most favoured in Christianity is the personal acceptance of redemptive grace which is to transform the inward springs of life . . . The type of religious experience favoured in Islam is, then, the active personal acceptance of prophetic truth, which is to discipline and orient one's total life. (Hodgson, 1960, pp. 54 and 59)

Notions of personal guilt, sin and the theodicy of suffering, which are historically central to Christian theology, were largely underplayed in Islamic thought. In Weber's comparative sociology, therefore, Judaism and Islam were both more overtly politicised religions, with clear commitments to holy places, communal hegemony and the religious importance of God's promise to particular social groups through revelation and prophecy.

Ethnocentricism
Before discussing the relevance of Weber's model of religious politicity for modern politics, we need to consider the problem of the ethnocentric bias in Weber's approach. It is interesting to note, for example, the parallel between Nietzsche's account of the psychology of resentment and Weber's treatment of the social psychology of world

religions. For Nietzsche, the Christian emphasis on the moral merits of pity and charity towards enemies often masked an underlying hypocrisy. Christian pity grew out of the weakness of slavery and was based on an expectation of divine retribution and revenge in the next world. By contrast, Islam, which 'presupposes men', was destroyed by Christianity in Spain 'because it was noble, because it owed its origins to manly instincts, because it said Yes to life even in the rare and exquisite treasures of Moorish life' (Nietzsche, 1968, p. 183). It can be argued that both Weber and Nietzsche share a common commitment to what is in fact a Protestant conception of hypocrisy and a western view of the 'proper' relationship between politics and religion.

In sociological terms, there are further difficulties with the association of Judaism to 'pariah groups' and Christianity to slavery. There can be little disagreement that the social exclusion of Jews as 'a negatively privileged class' or 'pariah' was the sociological fate of Jewish ghettos in the classical and medieval period (Gregorovius, 1948). However, although the Jewish community remained distinct and separate, it often enjoyed considerable social and political protection from both Christian and Muslim authorities, because Jews provided essential social and economic functions. It has been argued (Shahak, 1981) that the Jewish community enjoyed its greatest degree of privilege and protection in strong feudal regimes, where the Jewish community mediated between monarch and peasantry. The privilege and prestige of Jewish communities occurred in pre-1795 Poland, the Iberian kingdoms of the fifteenth century, in the feudal principalities of eleventh and twelfth-century France, in the feudal kingdoms of Sicily and Naples, and in the sixteenth-century heyday of the Ottoman Empire. In this controversial view, Jewish privilege coincides with the exploitation of peasants by feudal lords in pre-modern social systems; this conjunction was one location of rural anti-Semitism in, for example, Poland and France. The peculiar combination of privilege and exclusion gave the Jewish communities, before the impact of Napoleonic reforms in Europe, the following social characteristics: (1) the absence of a Jewish peasantry with a concentration of professional and white-collar occupations; (2) dependence on royal powers for protection and patronage; and (3) an ideological opposition to the surrounding Gentile population. The subsequent attempt by Zionists to secure a territorial solution to the 'Jewish Question' involved the inversion of the *shtetl* social structure in order to create a Jewish working class (Borochov, 1937).

Weber's view of the social psychology of Christianity is also the view of Protestantism of itself and of other religions. Reformed Protestantism treats spirituality as devoid of any spatial referent to holy lands, shrines, cities or lands; it is pure religion, expunging all associations with religious objects (relics, bodies and sacral paraphernalia). Places of worship become simply auditoria for the disembodied Word, as the architecture of Victorian Methodism clearly demonstrates. There is also a definite dissociation between sin and sickness; the Protestant version of confession does not involve any washing of the body, fasting or other rituals of purity. In the modern period, Christianity in general has emphasised subjective commitment over practice and ritual, personal feeling over theological precision, and spiritual fellowship over festivals, community and ritual celebration. This version of Christian religion, which we might call 'cognitive reductionism' as the mirror-image of 'economic reductionism', is central to Weber's sociology of religion, informing his paradoxical view of Protestantism, in which personal spirituality had massive significance for the secular organisation of capitalist society. Thus, we have to temper the view of Christianity as spiritual, universalistic, deritualised and above spatial reference with the fact of crusade, holy shrines, healing saints, military chaplains and colonial evangelists (Kiernan, 1982).

Although Weber's model of comparative religions provides a range of critical differences between religions, it is equally possible to blur these differences by taking note of the martyr tradition in Shiism, the theme of religious suffering in Hasidism, the ethic of fraternity in Islam, and so forth. What can be defended in Weber's analysis is that the emphasis on spatiality and politicity in Judaism and Islam is relatively muted in Christianity. In Judaism, the covenant between God, people and land is an essential aspect of faith; in Islam, the spatial coherence of the household of religion is a necessary condition of correct religious practice. Furthermore, in Islam the pilgrimage to Mecca is one of the Five Pillars of Faith; the loss of Mecca would thus have massive consequences for the integrity of Islam. Although in Christianity the Holy Land, locations associated with the Apostles, shrines and holy cities are obviously important in day-to-day practice, they are not requirements of faith. It is this religious significance of space in Islam and Judaism which has contributed to the political militancy of Islamic and Judaic culture in the modern period of colonialism.

Islam
Between Napoleon's Egyptian expedition of 1798 and the death of Lord Cromer in 1907, the core regions of the household of Islam came under either direct European control or indirect mandatory supervision. The economic and military consequences of European control were far-reaching. In negative terms, indigenous enterprises collapsed under the impact of western commodities, which were imported under concessionary agreements. Agricultural land was converted to the pro-

duction of raw materials such as jute and cotton for export to western industrial societies; this brought about an alliance between Muslim landlords and western capitalists.

Societies such as Pakistan and Egypt eventually became predominantly mono-crop exporting societies with large trade deficits, which were in part the result of food-import bills. The long-term decline in raw-material prices reinforced the financial indebtedness that was brought about by modernisation programmes on technology, which was often poorly suited to local needs. In Egypt, for example, state expenditure on irrigation to increase cotton production was not matched by any real increase in revenue, because of the superior position of foreign merchants, declining cotton prices and the inefficiency of the state bureaucracy. Industrial enterprises in Egypt, established by Muhammad Ali, were unable to compete successfully with imported European goods, which had lower production costs (Owen, 1969). Similar developments occurred in Syria and Lebanon (Hourani, 1946), Turkey (Lewis, 1961), Pakistan and Bangladesh (Karim, 1956), in North Africa and Asia (Smith, 1957; van Nieuwenhuijze, 1958; Charnay, 1971 and 1980; Hodgson, 1974). The transformation of Palestine was traumatic and had radical, long-term consequences for relations between Islam and western societies (Migdal, 1980).

In addition to these economic and political challenges to traditional Islamic practices and institutions, Muslim leaders also felt threatened by the spread of western secularism, western educational systems and Christian missionary activity (Watt, 1969; Jansen, 1979).

Reform

In the history of modern Islam, it is often conventional to analyse the Islamic response to westernisation and colonialism as falling into two related, but distinct phases — Islamic reform and secular nationalism. European imperialism and Christian missionary activity created a critical intellectual and religious problem for Muslim leaders, namely, why Islam, as the final perfection of monotheism, was everywhere in decline and decay? The solution to the problem lay in the fact that pure Islam, the Islam of the formative period of the Four Caliphs, was an active, dynamic and rational religion, perfectly fitted to the needs of modern, technological society. This pristine Islam had, however, been overlaid by pre-Islamic folk and alien accretions which had obscured the genuine and authentic core of the religion of the Prophet. Paradoxically, the modernisation of Islam involved a return to its origins and the exclusion of alien additions from the conceptual and social space of the pristine faith (Hourani, 1962; Keddie, 1968).

In the initial phase of the Islamic response to European colonialism, there was a comprehensive emphasis on scripturalism, a commitment to this-worldly activism, an extensive social criticism of the folk religiosity of the Sufi orders and a movement to reform social institutions, especially education, law and the family (Adams, 1933; Wertheim, 1961; Wolf, 1971). Reformism aimed to sweep away the false attitudes of passivity, fatalism and mere imitation. Sufism, in particular, was blamed for the transmission of an irrational and passive ethic among the rural masses. The despotic governments of medieval Islam were also seen to be corrupting influences, diminishing the genuine participatory politics of early Islam. The reform of Islam, however, has been regarded by western observers as involving a subtle reinterpretation of traditional Islam, which made basic religious norms compatible with secular political concepts. The return to scriptural purity, in fact, was a redefinition of Islam, requiring a selective view of traditional beliefs and practices.

Scripturalism

In the second phase of Islamic reform, the attempt to legitimise social changes and new attitudes by reference to tradition was replaced by a more secular commitment to nationalism and national politics without the outward casement of religious assumptions. Scripturalism was thus an interlude between traditional society and the secular world of modern politics. Like Puritan reformism in Christianity, it is argued that Islamic scripturalism, with its emphasis on activity in this world and its hostility to magic and mysticism, unwittingly prepared the groundwork for the emergence of modern secular society:

Stepping backward in order better to leap is an established principle in cultural change; our own Reformation was made that way. But in the Islamic case the stepping backward seems often to have been taken for the leap itself . . . Islam, in this way, becomes a justification for modernity, without itself actually becoming modern. It promotes what it itself, to speak metaphorically, can neither embrace nor understand. Rather than the first stages in Islam's reformation, scripturalism in this century has come, in both Indonesia and Morocco, to represent the last stages in its ideologization. (Geertz, 1968, pp. 69—70)

Scripturalism acted as a social prism by which the traditional values of Islamic society could be refracted into modern secular society, but the process of refraction necessarily changed the content and function of traditional religion.

In this perspective, religion can serve major public functions in secular society as the channel for political opposition to colonialism, but the political importance of religion at the periphery only obtains in the early opening phases of nationalist rejection of western control. These processes of cultural change obviously vary between Islamic societies. In order to understand the complexity of the relationship between

Islam and modern politics, it is instructive to consider the recent history of Shiism in Iran.

Shiism

Shiism was originally the party of Ali (Shiat Ali) and claimed that Ali, the son-in-law and cousin of the Prophet, was the genuine successor to the Prophet who died in 632. Ali was also the father of the Prophet's daughter and father to the Prophet's male descendants, al-Hasan and al-Husayn. Ali was assassinated in 661; the Shiat Ali developed as the main oppositional force which rejected the legitimacy of the Sunni caliphate. The killing of Ali, al-Hasan and al-Husayn gave martyrdom, suffering and passion a central role in Shiite theology, worship and politics. Shiism developed a critical distinction between the unjust and illegitimate rulers of the world, on the one hand, and the pious legitimate ruler (imam), on the other. The history of human societies came to be seen as a cycle of hidden imams and revealed imams, under whose leadership the Islamic community would be led to victory or martyrdom (Lewis, 1967; Hodgson, 1974). Shiism possesses a built-in ideology of legitimate opposition which, once mobilised, can radically de-legitimise secular authority in favour of the coming imamate.

The institutionalisation of Shiism as the state religion under the Safavid dynasty in 1501 is, therefore, a paradox which has divided Shiite leaders into supporters and opponents of the Iranian state. The Shiite ulama has consequently had an unstable and uneasy relationship with the political apparatus, periodically becoming the focus of anti-government forces. This oppositional role of Shiite institutions within Iranian society achieved a new intensity with the growth of western influence in Iran and with the development of secularism under the Pahlavi shahs.

The recent history of Shiite opposition has been well documented (Keddie, 1966; Boyle, 1968; Algar, 1969; Halliday, 1979; Fischer, 1980). A brief outline of these developments will suffice to illustrate the complex role of Shiism in the development of Iranian opposition to external colonialism and internal repression (Turner, 1980). The background to religious opposition was the growth of concessionary treaties with Russia and Britain, which subordinated the Iranian economy to foreign imports. In response to economic decline, landlords increased rents on peasant holdings and land was further concentrated under the ownership of the land-owning class. The development of an autonomous Iranian bourgeoisie was limited by the penetration of colonial capitalism, the decline of local industry under the impact of foreign commodities, the absence of an adequate Iranian financial structure and, finally, by the preference Iranian merchants showed for investment in land rather than industry. Iranian merchants, in this dependent economic context, steadily became agents for Russian and British enterprises.

The modern period of Shiite opposition thus evolved in a situation of economic underdevelopment and can be dated from the Tobacco Uprising of 1890, following the award of a monopoly over the export and internal trade in tobacco to a British company. The monopoly had serious implications for a variety of social groups in Iranian society. In particular, tobacco-growers would come under foreign control, traders would be forced from the market and consumers would find their supplies contaminated by infidels. In response to this threat, the chief mujtahid declared that smoking tobacco under a foreign monopoly was against religion; this resulted in the concessionary monopoly being effectively broken.

The Tobacco Uprising forged an alliance between tradesmen, intellectuals and the ulama and was the first step in the movement for a constitution which would control the royal administration. The merchants and guildsmen called for a code of law, regular courts and a national assembly based on a limited franchise. These constitutionalists wanted to restrict the Shah's expenditure by directing the tax revenue to the treasury rather than to the Shah's personal budget, and they supported the establishment of a national bank. The movement for constitutional reform was, however, frustrated by the opposition of the Shah, the resistance of tribal leaders and Russian officials, and by the social disruption that accompanied the First World War.

The subsequent history of Iranian reform and social development has been dominated by two contradictory processes. First, there has been an increase in the state apparatus as the driving force behind the rapid industrialisation of the economy. The consequence of industrialisation was that Iran became increasingly dependent on foreign investment, skill and labour, which, in combination with high rates of inflation, alienated the Iranian working class and the unemployed urbanised masses who had been squeezed out of the countryside. These modernising shahs also lost the support of the ulama, who rejected the secularisation of the community which followed in the trail of industrial modernisation. Secondly, the goal of industrialisation was the creation of an independent, modern society with the capacity to exercise considerable autonomy in the field of international relations. Since industrialisation on the basis of oil revenues tended to suck in foreign goods, technology, expertise and labour, rapid economic development became increasingly incompatible with the aim of national autonomy.

The cycle of economic change, foreign dependency and social conflict became depressingly repetitive. In the reign of Reza Shah (1925—41), the secularisation of culture, development of railways, government control over industry and modernisation of the army was halted by indebtedness and the failure of his agricultural policy. The attempt by Muhammad Musaddeq's government (1951—3) to gain control over supply and refinery in the oil industry collapsed under the blockade of Iranian oil on the world market, the opposition of the Eisenhower administration and the disaffection of the Iranian bourgeoisie which was squeezed by the declining revenues from oil. In the 1960s and 1970s there was a marked economic change with the White Revolution in land reform and with the investment of oil revenues in the chemical, steel and fertiliser industries, but this rapid industrial development had the effect of exacerbating existing structural problems rather than resolving them. The social consequences of economic development under the regime of Mohammad Reza Pahlavi were to drive the peasants off the land through mechanisation and concentration of landownership, to reduce the employment of skilled and professional labour by the use of migrant foreign workers and to undermine artisans and small-scale business by foreign competition. The oil-price boom of 1973 also gave rise to bribery, corruption and racketeering. The consequence of social disruption was to unite a wide cross-section of Iranian society — students, workers, peasants, mullahs and industrialists — against the Shah's regime, and to bring religious opposition to the secular nationalism of the Pahlavis to the foreground of political struggle.

Religious opposition in Iran traditionally followed one of two directions (Fischer, 1980). When foreign intervention in Iran was particularly significant, religious opposition was expressed through attacks on ethnic and religious minorities, such as the Baha'is, who were accused of complicity with foreign powers. When the Pahlavis were engaged in a process of national consolidation and brought in measures to secularise traditional behaviour, such as dress or the social role of women, religious opposition was expressed directly at the state itself. Political and repressive actions by the Pahlavis against the religious leadership then reinforced the Shiite theology of martyrdom, in which pious men are destroyed by tyrannical kings. Religious festivals such as Ramadan became occasions for massive popular protest against the existing regime, and the murder of Mujtahids by SAVAK personnel served to remind the people of the cosmic drama of the betrayal of Ali and his sons. Weeping over martyrs was turned eventually into violent action against tyrants.

With the fall of Mohammad Reza Pahlavi on 16 January 1979, the covert divisions within the religious movement against the Shah began to assume increasing, and ultimately tragic, importance. Shiite theology can take either a radical direction or a profoundly conservative turn. This paradoxical bifurcation of perspectives was clearly encapsulated in the persons of Ayatollah Sayyid Ruhollah Musavi Khomeyni and Dr Ali Shariati (1933—77). Khomeyni emerged in the 1970s as the principal opponent of the Shah's secularising policy, which in practice meant massive foreign involvement in the Iranian economy. Although Khomeyni's opposition to the Shah was radical, it was in religious terms also very traditional. It has become increasingly clear that what Khomeyni sought to achieve was the re-establishment of the authority of the ulama over the people and the government, a return to the dominant role of the religious law (the *sharia*), the reassertion of the traditional role of women and, above all, the maintenance of the power of the religious leadership (the mullahs, mujtahids and ayatollahs) in controlling everyday behaviour in conformity to tradition (Jafar and Tabari, 1981). However, in asserting his special authority within the religious leadership, Khomeyni was involved in a process of redirecting Shiite theology towards a legitimation of the political status quo.

Writing from within a western Christian tradition, it is often rather difficult for us to understand properly the apparant absence of genuine clericalism, especially a sacerdotal priesthood in Islam. We might say that Islam has a clerisy, a literate class of mullahs and mujtahids, but not a clergy invested with sacred authority and liturgical power. In Iranian Shiism, an ayatollah (sign of God) is an influential, leading mujtahid, that is, a person competent to exercise rational interpretation (*ijtihad*) of the law. An ayatollah al-uzma is someone who is regarded as the leading mujtahid of his period. However, the imam is a leader with transcendental authority, descending from Ali and the twelve successors of the Prophet, whose coming will create the perfect Islamic community — the imamate. The imam is essentially messianic with a supernatural legitimacy and not simply an elected leader.

During the revolutionary struggle against the Shah, Khomeyni permitted his own supporters to refer to him as Imam Khomeyni and to interpret him as someone with supreme authority in matters of sacred law. The authoritarian role of Khomeyni was further indicated by his willingness to declare holy war (jihad) against those who opposed him within the Muslim community. Khomeyni claimed, therefore, not simply to be *primus inter pares* in respect of other ayatollahs, but a person with messianic authority. With the fall of the Shah and the liquidation of opposition to Khomeyni, Iran in the early 1980s thus moved rapidly towards a repressive theocracy in which opposition, especially from Kurds (Chaliand, 1980), is automatically defined as anti-Islamic.

The religious movement against the Shah was, however, also inspired by the democratic and progressive interpretation of Islam, which is to be found in the speeches and publications of Ali Shariati (1979 and 1980). Born in 1933 near Sabzavar by the Kavir desert, Shariati was educated by his father, a leading member of the ulama, and attended Mashhad University. In 1959, he went to Paris to study sociology and he was deeply influenced by Gurvitch, Sartre, Camus, Massignon and Fanon. After he returned to Iran in 1964, his lectures at Mashhad and Husayniya-yi-Irshad were periodically curtailed by harassment and arrest. He died in England under mysterious circumstances on 19 June 1977, and was buried in Damascus near the shrine of Hazrat Zaynab. During his brief lifetime, Shariati became the dominant intellectual force among the mujtahids and his continues to be the major Islamic alternative to Khomeyni's version of Shiite opposition.

From his study of western thought during his stay in Paris, Shariati came to argue that the analysis of mankind presented in Christianity, Marxism and existential humanism fell short of a genuinely humanistic perspective in which human beings are free, creative and active, but also exist in a living community. It was within Islam, once it was correctly understood and liberated from the control of authoritarianism and fatalism, that people would discover a philosophy which gave full weight to the historical importance of man as conscious, active and purposeful, and they would discover a political creed which was revolutionary and democratic. The materialism of western thought created a reductionist perspective on humanity and limited the spiritual consciousness of the individual. The true message of spiritual Islam, with its dynamic view of human agency, had been corrupted by political and religious authoritarianism. We know how Islam:

was reshaped under the Arab Caliphate, how it became a rationale for the acts of the most savage conquerors, and how in time it became a powerful cultural force, which, in the name of jurisprudence, scholastic theology, and Sufism, cast an aura of religiosity over the feudal order of the Saljuqs and Mongols and bound the Muslim people to the chains of predestination. The road to salvation was no longer mapped out through *tauhid*, pious acts and knowledge. Instead, it lay either through an inherited tradition of blind conformity, entreaties, vows and supplications; or else in flight from reality. (Shariati, 1980, p. 39)

In order to realise the goal of a free, progressive society, therefore, the people of Iran did not have to turn to the played-out philosophies of the West — Marxism and positivism. Muslims had to revive the true inheritance of their own religious tradition, but this revival would require revolutionary action to throw off the political control of misguided mullahs and repressive shahs, along with the whole canopy of fatalistic, conformist values.

Essentially, Iranians had to think for themselves rather than listen to the traditional leaders who preached imitation and submission. There were no fixed standards, since:

Man is a 'choice', a struggle, a constant becoming. He is an infinite migration, a migration within himself, from clay to God; he is a migrant within his own soul. (Shariati, 1979, p. 93)

The Iranian people as a whole had to accept the burden of this choice and the social responsibility that went with it. This psychological migration was an essential requirement of political change — 'Verily God does not change the state of a people until they change the state of their own selves' (Koran, 13:11).

Shariati's version of the problem of Islamic society — Islam is true essentially, but falsified by alien accretions — pointed backwards to the reformist philosophies of Muhammad Abduh (1849—1905), Rashid Rida (1865—1935), Rifaa al-Tahtawi (1801—73) and Jamal al-Din al-Afghani (1839—97). Islam is a rational religion, compatible with science and technology, but avoids the materialism and reductionism associated with western rationality. Islam is radical and egalitarian, without producing the inhuman consequences of materialist Marxism and social Darwinism. Shariati, however, gave many traditional religious notions in Islam a radical content. The migration (*hijra*) from Mecca to Medina that marked the beginning of Islam became a subjective struggle, expressing the struggle for self-realisation. The unity of God in the doctrine of *tauhid* was a political philosophy, spelling out the unity of classes and race against *shirk* (not as a denial of God's unity, but as discrimination in social relations).

In Shariati's reinterpretation of Marxism, God = the people (Allah = al-nas) in opposition to the king–owner–aristocracy. The message of the Koran, which begins with the name of God and concludes in the name of the people, is that rulership belongs to God, that is, to the people. The principle of *taslit* (empowering) in Islamic jurisprudence has been wrongly interpreted, according to Shariati, as a doctrine of individual property rights. Instead, the saying 'Property belongs to God' is equivalent to 'Property belongs to the people as a whole'. The doctrine of woman created out of man's rib as a justification for sexual divisions is also false. The term translated as 'rib' in fact means 'nature or disposition'; the story of Adam and Eve in fact means that woman was created with the same nature or disposition as man. Religious history was no longer a struggle between monotheism and polytheism, but between oppressors (polytheists) and oppressed (monotheists), pointing towards a society grounded in *tauhid*, a unity which only Islam could guarantee. Unlike Khomeyni's call for the re-establishment of the traditional status of the ulama, Shariati's message invited the people to think out their position, independently of traditional constraints and ossified institutions. In the process, the mujtahids gave the whole corpus of traditional, religious concepts a social and ethical content.

The continuity of Islam in a society like Iran can, at one level, be explained relatively simply. Shiism was a religious doctrine that embraced most sections of society and was, in particular, the ideological idiom of certain key groups — rural peasants, the urban working class and the unemployed subproletariat of Tehran's shanty town. In addition, Shiism was born as an ideology of protest and its martyrology was well suited to populist movements against foreigners, minorities and repressive governments. The mobilisation of Shiite ideology did, in its claim to return to the roots of Islamic theology, involve a reinterpretation and translation of pristine concepts. The overt unity of religious ideology and political practice within the opposition to the Pahlavis was, however, more apparent than real. The mujtahids of the left, inspired by the teachings of Shariati, sought a revolutionary reorganisation of the social structure along anti-capitalist lines and found their principal support among students, academics and professional groups. The reformists around Prime Minister Bazargan and Ayatollah Taleghani were supported by middle-class professionals, technicians and traders and attempted to develop an amalgamation of Shiism with western liberal ideas. The Islamic moderates associated with Ayatollah Shariat-madari had the support of the bazaar, the senior clergy and the Azerbaijanis; the moderates opposed the theocratic authoritarianism of Khomeyni's group. Finally, the Islamic conservatives under the leadership of Khomeyni have suppressed left-wing Islamic opposition and abrogated initial demands for regional autonomy and individual liberty which were crucial to the movement against the Shah.

Although it is possible to argue that religion often plays a crucial role in expressing political deprivation and, in the case of Islam, acts as a major critique of secular colonialism, the precise nature of that role will depend on the complex conjuncture of classes and political forces operating in a society at a given moment. The theme of martyrdom was particularly effective as a basis of opposition against the Shah, but whether Shiism can operate as a unifying ideology of a differentiated society like Iran, without substantial redefinition, is unlikely. Within Iran, Shiism is not relevant to the problem of Sunni minorities such as Kurds, Arabs and Turkomans or to such groups as Jews or Baha'is. Adherence to Shiism within the Muslim majority is also fractured by social divisions. The crisis of the 1970s produced a rather specific unity among a diverse range of groups in opposition to the Shah, but the attempt by Islamic conservatives to impose theocracy on Iran in the 1980s has once more welded opposition behind the themes of righteous suffering and martyrdom against a party that claims to be ultra-orthodox. Hence, the notion that religion acts as the social cement of peripheral groups experiencing either internal or international colonialism cannot be countenanced without considerable qualification. The social viscidity of religion is typically achieved by extensive reconstruction of traditional theologies and is characteristically short in duration, being rapidly overtaken by the divisive forces of class, ethnicity and region.

Judaism

In discussing the possibility of the survival of religion into secular societies as the vehicle for national or regional opposition by subordinated groups, the principal example for sociological inquiry would, however, have to be drawn from the political history of Judaism from the beginning of the nineteenth century. The possibility of Jewish civil emancipation in Europe that followed from the Napoleonic reorganisation of the French legal code brought into sharp focus a series of questions surrounding the so-called 'Jewish Question'. The parameters of this debate were largely shaped by the philosophy of history of Georg Hegel.

In the development of world history, the Jews had retained an exclusive particularity which rendered them inassimilable within civil society:

This religion must necessarily possess the element of exclusiveness, which consists essentially in this — that only the One People which adopts it, recognizes the One God, and is acknowledged by him. The God of the Jewish People is the God only of Abraham and of his seed: National individuality and a special local worship are involved in such a conception of deity. (Hegel, 1956, p. 195)

The solutions to Jewish particularity which emerged in the nineteenth century included: (1) civil assimilation through a political franchise; (2) social assimilation through the revolutionary reorganisation of civil society; and (3) proletarianisation of the Jewish community, combined with a territorial resettlement of the Jewish people. These three solutions broadly correspond to liberalism, Marxism and Zionism. The solutions to the 'Jewish Question' thus generally assume a tabular form.

Solution	Perspective	Theorist
Assimilation	Civic liberalism	Bauer
Revolution	Revolutionary socialism	Marx
Proletarianisation	Zionism	Borochov

All three solutions in some respect involved a diminution or abandonment of religious belief and practice. Alternatively, a movement towards civil assimilation could be combined with a shift away from Orthodox to Reformed Judaism. Paradoxically, the development of national consciousness among the Jewish community was to be achieved by a radical secularisation of their religious particularity — a particularity that had been traditionally their principal defence against Gentiles and assimilation in Gentile society. The solution of the 'Jewish

Question' involved a denial of any specific, public Jewish identity and was thus a major threat to religious consciousness.

Following Hegel's discussion of Jewish particularity, Bruno Bauer, a left Hegelian member of the Berlin Doctors Club, wrote a series of articles on Jewish emancipation in the *Deutsche Jahrbucher* in 1842 (Berlin, 1978; Kolakowski, 1978, vol. 1). Bauer argued that in order to promote the political development of Prussia it was necessary for both Christians and Jews to abandon their religious exclusiveness. Jewish adherence to outmoded Oriental beliefs and practices was a brake on historical development; the impediment of Christian ritualism was an inheritance from its Jewish past. The civil development of both com-munities required a mutual abandonment of religious identities. Religious problems were the product of a political system which denied universal human and civil rights to the population. The solution to the 'Jewish Question' could be secured through political reform and the secularisation of the state.

In response to Bauer, Marx argued in his essay 'On the Jewish Question' that the alienation of Jews was a specific example of the alienation of men as citizens from their roots in society as a whole. Political liberation without social liberation was a superficial solution to the problem of human rights. The pariah status of traditional Jewry and the concentration of Jews in merchant activities had to be resolved by a total transformation of capitalist society. A socialist reorganisation of society would provide the only permanent and total solution to the particularity of traditional Judaism.

Marx and Engels were not sympathetic towards the development of Jewish nationalism in the form of a territorial solution to the 'Jewish Question', as developed by Moses Hess and the early Zionists. In part, this indifference to Jewish nationalism was bound up with Marx and Engels's view that small nations did not provide an adequate basis for capitalist development and hence for urban proletarian radicalism (Davis, 1965). Subsequently, official Marxism came to regard Zionism as merely utopian romanticism. There was, nevertheless, an important connection between the ideas of secular Marxism and radical Zionism.

Much of the theoretical content of proletarian Zionism derived from writers like the Russian Jew, Ber Borochov (1881–1917), who drew a clear distinction between the social structure of Gentile society and the social organisation of the Jewish *shtetl*. Whereas Gentile society had a social structure in the form of a pyramid, with a large base of peasants and workers, surmounted by a narrow peak of professionals, aristocrats and owners of capital, the Jewish *shtetl* of eastern Europe was organ-ised as an inverted pyramid with a narrow band of workers and a broad belt of professionals, intellectuals, merchants and capitalists (Boro-chov, 1937). For Borochov, the solution to Jewish particularity involved a double process of proletarianisation and secularisation. Both processes in the solution of the 'Jewish Question' hinged on a territorial settlement of the Jews, namely, greater Israel. The return of Jews to the Holy Land and the restoration of the promise of the land was thus the principal socialist alternative to bourgeois assimilation. Borochovism offered a radical solution to the particularity of Judaism, which would eventuate in a socialist working-class community, very different from the petty-bourgeois character of the traditional urban *shtetl*. The Jewish settlement of Palestine is thus to be conceived as 'the only intentionally downwardly mobile social movement ever experienced in the history of migration' (Avineri, 1970b, p. 35). Unlike the white colonisation of Africa, Zionism in theory avoided dependence on cheap Arab labour and sought to convert the Jewish middle class into a new working class.

The possibility of civil assimilation of the Jewish population in western Europe in the nineteenth century represented a significant threat to traditional religious values. Religious leaders were anxious that the acceptance of Jews into the political institutions of civil society would entail the loss of a specific Jewish identity and with it a loss of religious belief and practice. The logical conclusion of civil assimilation was Christian baptism and full membership of Jews within the culture of Christian Europe — a conclusion which, for example, Marx's father had accepted by converting to Lutheranism. Large-scale conversion to Christianity was, however, uncommon. In France, middle-class assimilated Jews tended to accept a secular rationalist position rather than theism (Marrus, 1971), or combined Reformed Judaism with French patriotism. The trend towards assimilation in France was, however, decisively blocked by the growing anti-Semitism of the late nineteenth century, which culminated in the Dreyfus Affair, and in Germany the trend was terminated by the growth of National Socialism. With the failure of assimilation, the Jewish community was faced with three possibilities — either a territorial solution along Zionist lines, or a return to the encapsulated traditionalism of Orthodox religion, or migration to the United States.

The relationship between Zionism and religion in the formation of the state of Israel is thus complex and unstable. The earlier settlers from Russia and eastern Europe, who formed the backbone of the kibbutz movement in Palestine, were essentially secular and socialist in their search for an alternative to the religious traditionalism of the Shtetl. There was and is, therefore, a clear-cut division between the secular ideology of Zionism and the theology of Orthodox Judaism. For the Orthodox Jew, the contemporary state of Israel has no ultimate legitimacy without the messianic in-gathering of the Jewish people in the crisis of the Last Day. However, the state of Israel is a Jewish state and it has, in practice, proved difficult to distinguish the Jewish identity from its religious basis — 'as a Jew, how can one reject the God of Abraham, Isaac and Jacob — without rejecting oneself?' (Bell, 1980, p. 315). Since political membership of the state in Israel is based on a Jewish identity, it is difficult to separate political from religious citizenship:

All parties of the Zionist movement — labour Zionism, Religious Zionism and Revisionism — share, above and beyond very real differences of policy and political ideology, a common goal which links them all as members, often conflicting members, of the movement. This goal is the solution of the Jewish problem by way of establishing and consolidating in Palestine a Jewish state *for* Jewish people. (Davis, 1977, p. 7)

Although religious conservatism does not regard contemporary Zionism as the basis of a genuine Jewish state, it does provide a justification for the presence of Jews as a minority within the broader context of the Arab Middle East. A religious identity as the basis of political life tends, therefore, to be reinforced by the precariousness of Israel from a political and military point of view. The growing importance of religious commitment as the basis of political organisation in Israel is, in part, a consequence of the crisis that developed after the Yom Kippur War. The religious promise of the return of the Jews to the land of their forefathers has become increasingly the main political legitimation of Israel against its Arab critics. The religious parties in Israel have thus been able to strengthen their political control over secular Zionism, and the enforcement of religious laws over personal and public life has increased (Ein-Gil, 1981). Rather than Israel experiencing a process of secularisation with the establishment of the state, religion has 'provided the historic *raison d'être* of Israeli existence' (Martin, 1978b, p. 81). The reinforcement of religious values and institutions as the mechanism of national commitment has taken a very different form from the return to religious origins that has been described in the case of Iran. Both forms of 'religious archaism' are, however, closely bound up with the problem of religio-political space as the necessary basis for religious practice.

Summary

In capitalist society, religion withers away at the political and cultural core of the dominant institutions. The state, the family, the school and the factory are shorn of transcendental meaning and significance. The administered society is characterised by a thick network of regulatory institutions which order and contain human activity. The compensation for containment is located in a hedonistic mass, consumerism and privatised leisure. There is also a movement towards esoteric cults among the young and marginal groups, but the hedonism and individualism of these cults often mirror the anomy of other-directed culture in middle-class suburbia. Much of the religious and intellectual deviation of the middle class is thus an attempt to elude rather than challenge contemporary society (Powell, 1962).

On a global scale, however, religion often assumes renewed vitality as the cultural medium of political protest against internal colonialism by subnational cultures or against external colonialism by subordinated nationalism. Religious nationalism often involves a restoration of the past in opposition to the accretions of the present, but this restoration of archaism may also involve a thorough reinterpretation of traditional idioms through the concepts of 'democracy', 'activism' and 'emancipation'. Christian, Islamic and Jewish revivalism in the political arena have a superficial resemblance, but in detail they often correspond to very different social situations. The revival of religious forms often involves a radical secularisation of content.

A number of sociologists (Bellah, 1970a; Bell, 1980), however, have argued that the exhaustion of modernism presages a 'return of the sacred', since the fundamental questions of human existence are no longer satisfied by the tired doctrines of modernism, Marxism and existentialism. The problem of the government of the body — sexuality, procreation and death — is irreducible and pushes men back to a more fundamental response to the question of being.

10 Secular Bodies and the Dance of Death

This study of religion has been an inquiry into openings and closures, of permissions and restrictions on the relations between bodies. In religious cultures or groups, spiritual norms of behaviour are the gateways to bodily experiences, controlling the threat of orgy and permitting legitimate unions. If religion controls the apertures of life through the discipline of female bodies, it also oversees our departures to a space where the contradictions between desire and service are finally resolved. In classical cultures, Pluto the god of fertility was converted or translated by the Romans into Dives, who carried bodies into the flat plain of Asphodel to lead another dreary, unsubstantial life.

These personal comings and goings through the seine of sex and death are collectively part of the reproduction of the species. Our intimate experience of these sexual and mortal processes provides also our most powerful metaphors of spiritual experience. In art, this fusion of sexual and religious metaphors is unavoidable, as in John Donne or Bernini's 'The Ecstatic Vision of St Teresa'; the same is true of evangelical hymnology and the ecstatic writings of Julian of Norwich. In protesting against 'digestive reductionism' even William James was forced to admit that:

It is true that in the vast collection of religious phenomena, some are undisguisedly amatory — e.g., sex-deities and obscene rites in polytheism, and ecstatic feelings of union with the Saviour in a few Christian mystics . . . Religious language clothes itself in such poor symbols as our life affords, and the whole organism gives overtones of comment whenever the mind is strongly stirred to expression. (James, 1929, p. 11)

The union of bodies provides a natural metaphor for the union of souls. A materialist theory of religion will thus have to take seriously the religious significance of the unions of sex and the disunions of death.

Existential problems
It is often held that the pleasures of sex and the fear of death are universal, anthropological experiences which provide the bedrock of all existential problems, and hence the basis of all religious theodicy. Regardless of social differences, our origin in the womb and our closure in the grave are necessary, incontrovertible and universal experiences of men and women. We are born and, sooner rather than later, we go to

our death-beds. Unlike animals, the foreknowledge we have of our own inevitable demise is part of our existential misery that finds conceptual expression in religious theodicy and practical expression in mortuary rituals. Although not denying the universality of the facts of sexual reproduction and death, social differences deeply influence our unique experience of sexuality and finitude, and our location in the social structure closely impinges upon our common religious experiences of the body. Starting with the problem of the fragility of the body and the inevitability of death, it is important to note that death has a social history and that the biology of death is also a socially constructed event.

There is general agreement among sociologists of religion that all religious behaviour is ultimately directed towards the existential problems of humanity and that religious beliefs represent attempts to make sense of the world by reference to a sacred reality. Those sociologists who follow Weber's discussion of theodicy interpret religion as the human response to the problem of meaning and as a cultural shield against the potential chaos of contingent reality. Religion helps us to believe that, despite the existence of injustice, violence and death, life is not without purpose. Religious doctrines:

are concerned with moral problems of human action, and the features of the human situation, and the place of man and society in the cosmos. (Parsons, 1951, p. 368)

Sociologists have often defined religion in terms derived from Paul Tillich as our 'ultimate concern'. Religion is an expression of human anxiety over the depth of existence and the ground of our being:

That depth is what the word *God* means. And if that word has not much meaning for you, translate it, and speak of the depths of your life, of the source of your being, of your ultimate concern, of what you take seriously without any reservation. (Tillich, 1962, pp. 63—4)

On any account, the cycle of individual life — procreation, maturation and death — must be regarded as fundamental to the ground of being, and hence to that which ultimately concerns us without reservation. The oddity is that the majority of textbooks on the sociology of religion over the last two decades have little or nothing to say about the relationship between sex, death and religion in contemporary societies. This observation can be illustrated by taking index citations as a measure of interest in these two issues. Despite this slight treatment of sex and death in relation to religion in contemporary sociology, death in particular has been typically regarded as an event which is central to religion as a set of answers to human dilemmas. It is not uncommon to assume that, since the fear of death is a constant facet of human psychology, religious beliefs in personal immortality are universal features of human society (Argyle, 1964). However, although the

Author	Book	Index citation	
		Death	Sex
Acquaviva, S. S. (1979)	*The Decline of the Sacred in Industrial Society*	10	19
Berger, P. L. (1969)	*The Social Reality of Religion*	19	12
Budd, S. (1973)	*Sociologists and Religion*	5	0
Glock, C. Y. and Stark, R. (1965)	*Religion and Society in Tension*	5	0
Hill, M. (1973)	*A Sociology of Religion*	12	0
Martin, D. (1967)	*A Sociology of English Religion*	0	0
Robertson, R. (1970)	*The Sociological Interpretation of Religion*	0	0
Schneider, L. (1970)	*Sociological Approach to Religion*	0	0
Towler, R. (1974)	*Homo Religiosus*	0	0
Wilson, B. (1982)	*Religion in Sociological Perspective*	3	4
Yinger, J. M. (1961)	*Sociology Looks at Religion*	0	0

finitude of individual existence may be a permanent biological fact, the social nature of death and individual experiences of it are highly variable over time and between social groups. In this respect, recent historical and sociological studies of death are particularly important for the analytical development of the sociology of religion. Of special significance in this field of inquiry is Philippe Ariès's study of western attitudes to death (1974).

Death
There have been very considerable changes in western Christian approaches to the nature of death and dying. The principal transition has been from a social system in which death was frequent, open and communal to one in which the experience of death is closed, private and isolated. In everyday terms, whereas the majority of people traditionally died in their beds surrounded by kinfolk, in contemporary society death is no longer domestic; in the United States approximately 80 per cent of the population die in hospital and in the United Kingdom over 50 per cent experience institutionalised deaths.

There are a number of important contrasts between the experience of death in medieval and modern societies. In pre-modern societies, given the limitations on life expectancy, death was a regular, common and visible experience within the domestic situation; it was an event witnessed by close relatives and friends of all age-groups. Personal deaths were not individualised, being treated as primarily a problem for the surviving group. Burials were typically communal and individual headstones or coffins were unusual. In Ariès's account, each village church in France had a large ditch in which corpses were laid in their shrouds and the bones of the deceased were subsequently collected in the local charnel-house over which the Church exercised communal guardianship. A French fifteenth-century illustration from a Book of Hours shows a grave-digger unearthing bones from previous burials in preparation for a new disposal (Boase, 1972, p. 111). The Church thus acted as the communal guardian of the bones of the dead in anticipation of the day of judgement and resurrection. It was not until the seventeenth century, with the growing influence of Protestantism, that there was a significant emphasis on the individual bodies of the departed and the development of private places of interment.

On the basis of medieval literature, especially the epic poem, Ariès argues contentiously that pre-modern deaths were not deeply problematic, either for the group or the individual. Death was merely another transition, part of a sequence that included conception, maturity and old age. The very regularity and familiarity of domestic deaths made human departures ordinary and matter of fact. The dead were consequently not regarded with loathing and fear.

However, the stability of medieval attitudes towards death was first massively disrupted by the widespread outbreak of pestilence, especially the Black Death, in the fourteenth century. Death ceased to be routine and became fascinating, terrifying amd macabre, since it was now regarded as a punishment and life after death as a trial. Purgatory was extended, elaborated and developed as a place of interrogation and spiritual inquiry. Within the Church, the Council of Florence in 1439 gave orthodox affirmation of this popular interest in purgatory as a place for dividing the wicked from the faithful. On a darker plain, there were popular riots against the Jews, who were accused of spreading the pestilence among Gentile populations (McNeill, 1979). Beginning with the late-thirteenth-century poem, *Le Dit des trois morts et des trois vifs*, carved on the façade of the Church of the Innocents in Paris, the theme of the dance of death became a common, macabre feature of art and literature. Among aristocratic groups, masques were performed by men dressed as skeletons and death was seen to be a force that preyed upon the living. Death personified had become the hunter and rapist of human populations and, by combining themes of putrefaction and sexuality, the dance of death elaborated the parallel of sexual intercourse and the union of life and death. In the artistic fascination with death, putrescence and procreation were mingled in a sinister union.

As the threat of pestilence became less pressing, the gruesome picture of death as naked corruption of the flesh receded and artistic treatment of death became less macabre. Although in England the Protestant Reformation drastically changed the traditional Catholic interpretations of death and purgatory, the English stage was relatively free from religious control by 1600. As a result, Shakespearian tragedy revealed a strikingly secular view of death and dying. The conflict of good and evil, the cosmic role of fortune and the struggle of reason against passion in Shakespeare's art are portrayed without any specifically Christian framework. Although references to hell and heaven abound, they are not informed by any detailed commitment to the Christian viewpoint. Death is merely release from 'life's fitful fever':

> Better be with the dead,
> Whom we, to gain our peace, have sent to peace,
> Than on the torture of the mind to lie
> In restless ecstasy. Duncan is in his grave;
> After life's fitful fever he sleeps well;
> Treason has done his worst: nor steel, nor poison,
> Malice domestic, foreign levy, nothing
> Can touch him further.
>
> (Macbeth, III.ii.19)

Shakespeare's ethical view of life was probably shaped by traditional Christian teaching, and he no doubt assumed the importance of religion for the preservation of social stability, but his treatment of death did not reveal any deep attachment to the hope of resurrection and restoration (Reese, 1953). Death in this perspective is primarily an escape from life.

Perhaps one of the most significant shifts in western attitudes to death took place with the emergence of romanticism in the late eighteenth century as a protest against formalism, containment and the subordination of pleasure. Within the romantic imagination, pleasure and pain were intimately fused, and consequently the marriage of death and beauty became a dominant theme in literature and art (Praz, 1933). The tragic alliance of unrequited young love and premature death emerged as a favoured topic in English poetry and, presumably, among the literate classes. The pattern was established by the verses of Keats, Shelley and Byron; the epitome of this melancholic tradition was found in the death of the young poet Thomas Chatterton (1752—70), described by Wordsworth as 'the marvellous boy, The sleepless soul, that perished in his pride'. The odes of Keats are, in particular, concerned with problems of youthful beauty and the corruption of death. He declared himself in the 'Ode to a Nightingale' to:

> have been half in love with easeful Death,
> Call'd him soft names in many a mused rhyme,
> To take into the air my quiet breath;
> Now more than ever seems it rich to die,
> To cease upon the midnight with no pain

It was the wasting disease of pulmonary tuberculosis that held the literary mind in such horrified fascination and presented the image of youth that 'grows pale, and spectre-thin, and dies'. This narcissistic emphasis on personal, individual death was conceived within a tragic mould without any Christian underpinning.

Although this romantic orientation to death survived a considerable time in literary circles, appearing in Europe, for example, in the work of Gabriele d'Annunzio (1863—1938), the advent of mass warfare and the destruction of civilian populations by mechanised military forces brought about a strongly anti-romantic approach in twentieth-century representations of death. This transition in attitude was especially characteristic of poets of the First World War, and it is interesting to contrast Keats's 'Ode to a Nightingale' (1819) with Wilfred Owen's 'Anthem for Doomed Youth' (1918):

> What passing-bells for these who die as cattle?
> Only the monstrous anger of the guns,
> Only the stuttering rifles' rapid rattle
> Can patter out their hasty orisons.

The solitary death of the consumptive poet was replaced by the mechanised death of masses, and the dominant themes of modern literary expression came to centre on the problem of pointless, ruthless extermination through nuclear warfare and holocaust (Langer, 1978).

Although there is now the permanent threat of nuclear destruction, the nature of death has changed dramatically from the fourteenth to the twentieth centuries. If medieval deaths were typically public, routine and domestic, modern deaths are characteristically private, institutionalised and professionally controlled. The majority of deaths in contemporary industrial society are the consequence of degenerative disease among the geriatric and take place in secluded wards of large hospitals. In England and Wales approximately 87 per cent of all deaths are caused by neoplasms, respiratory and circulatory diseases. It is because death is now commonly associated with old age that, when youthful deaths do take place through misadventure, we regard such 'unwarranted' occurrences as particularly tragic. Stevie Smith's poem 'Not Waving But Drowning' captures this mood well:

Nobody heard him, the dead man,
But still he lay moaning:
I was much further out than you thought
And not waving but drowning.

Poor chap, he always loved larking
And now he's dead
It must have been too cold for him his heart gave way,
They said.

The association of death and old age normally enables us to distance ourselves from our own demise, which is secured in some remote future. In a variety of other respects, death is hidden. It takes place away from the home, typically in a side-ward away from public inspection; it is witnessed not by close relatives, but by neutral experts; the body is suitably treated not by the next of kin, but by professional caretakers; extensive employment of drugs and other treatments even dissociates pain and death; the *disjecta membra* are hygienically treated. Modern death, unlike that monstrous figure that haunted the wild imagination of fourteenth-century engravers of royal sepulchres, is effectively banished from the everyday world of industrial man.

The problem for Ariès and other writers on death (Mitford, 1963; Bowman, 1964; Mack, 1973; Dempsey, 1975) is to explain the American enthusiasm for embalming and the 'memory picture' of the dead at peace with the notion that modern man has banished and denied death. The open coffin and the display of the deceased is an aspect of almost 90 per cent of American funerals. Embalming, which became increasingly popular towards the end of the nineteenth century, traditionally required the presence of a relative of the departed, but now kinfolk are by law excluded from the preparation room. Lay people have thus been replaced by professional experts in the surveillance of the dead (Habenstein, 1962). The arguments for embalming employed by professional funeral directors are presented in terms of aesthetics, therapy and hygiene. In particular, it is suggested that the view of the deceased 'at peace' provides the mourners with a therapeutic memory of their lost ones:

These attitudes toward death frame a view of the proper life that confounds the medieval view of the proper death. The key notion is fulfillment. The life of the individual should rise in an arc through brassy youth to fruitful middle years, and then decline gently toward a death that is acceptable as well as inevitable. The practices of embalming and viewing express these collective representations. The point is to reveal the dead at peace. Because the last hours or days preceding death may have been marred with pain, which is inadmissible, the restored body provides a truer image of death. (Huntington and Metcalf, 1979, p. 205)

The centrality of the embalmed body within the American funeral is paradoxically further evidence of the denial of death within a culture that gives exclusive normative emphasis to youth, fulfilment and achievement. Since death is associated with old age, ageing is socially stigmatised (Johnson and Williamson, 1980).

One crucial aspect of the banishment of death in modern societies is the absence of definite, prescribed rites of mourning. There is no shaving of hair, burning of clothes, periods of seclusion or changes of name. In Britain, the traditional wake has survived in a reduced form among Irish migrants and among the islanders of western Scotland, but in general mourning and the expression of grief have become private and uncertain (Hinton, 1967; Sudnow, 1967). The family of the dying is often isolated within the hospital setting (Kübler-Ross, 1970) and in a wider context:

Increasing disregard of formal mourning has meant that bereaved individuals get little support from society at large and from their families in particular. (Parkes, 1975, p. 24)

The banishment of death is thus joined with the shunning of mourning and mourners.

In a situation of social isolation, the recently bereaved very commonly turn to religion for consolation, although the decline of the theology of heaven and hell has meant that the churches have an uncertain purchase on contemporary patterns of dying and bereavement (Gorer, 1965). Although the bereaved may seek out the services of spiritualist groups, the evidence is that this contact does not lead to permanent membership of a spiritualist group (Parkes, 1975, pp. 71–2). Vieda Skultans (1974) does suggest, however, that spiritualist groups provide general therapeutic services for the elderly and the bereaved by creating intimacy and social contact for these isolated people.

The problem is, however, that in modern society the credibility of personal survival after death has been seriously challenged. Within the churches in America, there is considerable variation between denominations in terms of belief in life after death. For mainstream denominations, less than half the laity are certain that there is life beyond the grave, although Protestant fundamentalists and Roman Catholics are uniformly committed to such a belief (Glock and Stark, 1965, p. 98). Surveys of the general population suggest that some 50 per cent of the population adheres to a belief in personal immortality (ABC Television, 1965). It is difficult to know, however, what weight can be given to these attitudinal responses. Assent to belief in life after death as a philosophical proposition is very different from a living commitment to the full panoply of Christian ritual and practice, within which the believer confidently experiences the supernatural promise of resurrection:

religious belief in general is something different from the acceptance of a set of philosophical ideas. The latter may have no implications for human conduct, but a belief is not *religious*, as Durkheim understood it, unless it is taken seriously, that is, unless something is done about it, either directly or indirectly. (Nottingham, 1954, p. 31)

Belief in life after death, along with the whole mythology of heaven, hell and resurrection, has become an optional extra of modern Christian life.

The problem of death has been solved, not by religious conviction, but by a system of secular practices which neutralise the horror of physical death. Mass death in a nuclear war is a constant anxiety, but not as yet a real experience. In a society dominated by the values of youthfulness and vitality, death has become an embarrassment, rather than an ever-present facet of daily existence. Death has been routinised as the province of experts and professionals so that death 'demands no meaning of a kind which religion has traditionally supplied' (Wilson, 1966, p. 71).

Sex

It is often suggested that, if sex was the forbidden subject of the nineteenth century, death is the taboo topic of the twentieth. In this respect, sex and death have changed roles, since we now speak volubly and compulsively about sex (Foucault, 1979). In this study of religion, it has been argued that religion played a crucial role in subordinating female sexuality in the interests of property transmission and family stability. In this particular respect, this study closely follows the view of Engels, that any treatment of materialism must consider the double process of material and physiological reproduction.

Much contemporary criticism of Engels seems misguided in this respect (Beauvoir, 1972b, pp. 84 ff.), but it is clear that patterns of sexual inequality and the basic forms of the sexual division of labour cannot be explained simply in terms of the dominant mode of economic production and even less in terms of the appearance of private property. The covering of female bodies and the exclusion of women from public roles in antiquity under the impact of Pauline theology represented a major diminution of those freedoms which women had enjoyed in pagan Rome and Greece (Seltman, 1956). The exclusion of women from public roles, particularly from economic activities, may have been intensified by the advent of bourgeois family life in capitalism (Zaretsky, 1976), but it certainly did not have its origin in capitalist private property. In the late nineteenth century, the new emphasis on child care, breast-feeding, intimacy and domestic privacy (Shorter, 1977) reinforced the isolation of women in the nuclear family.

In this analysis of religion, therefore, I have presented the view that there is no rigid or strict association between sexual roles and the mode of production. In feudalism and early capitalism, however, the Christian teaching on female sexuality was functionally important in the preservation and inheritance of property through male hands. Changes in the nature of property and ownership in twentieth-century capitalism broke this functional relationship between sexual morality, religion and property, creating a situation in which the moral control of persons is no longer an essential requirement of economic life. It may be the case, of course, that individual managers of productive units prefer employees to be conventional in their private lives, but these preferences are contingent features of social life. Like Weber, however, my argument is that the new freedom for sexual experimentation develops in a society where individuals are controlled by regulatory practices and by systems of individuation. These societies are not legitimated by a moral code grounded in any sense of religious ultimacy and do not require moral conformity. Political legitimacy and private meaning are now divorced.

In western societies, the Christian religion was historically the principal means for the control of women's bodies, and hence the movement for female emancipation was a struggle against religious conceptualisations of sexuality. In Catholic Europe, the Church is still seen as an important part of that public apparatus by which women are allocated to subordinate social positions. The struggle against female domestication, in Italy for example (Caldwell, 1978), involves a struggle against Catholic teaching on marriage, reproduction and divorce. The movement for female emancipation within the Church involves a considerable redirection of Christianity's masculine theology by, for example, giving special prominence to Maryology (Biezanek, 1964).

The political struggle to change the position of women in society involved essentially an attempt by women to gain control of their own bodies; this required a double confrontation with medicine and with religion. In nineteenth-century America, feminists turned to physiology and hygiene as a better guide to the rational organisation of individual behaviour than traditional religion (Leach, 1981). In a period when women were thought to be subject to a new variety of nervous disorders — insomnia, hysteria, exhaustion and depression — medical reform, diet and contraception offered women a means of medical rationalism which would enable them to enter society on equal terms with men.

This reorganisation of the private life of women was to take place alongside the reorganisation of public health. Salvation and sanitation were to be united in a programme of public reform. Professional employment in nursing, health education and environmental planning began to provide some outlet for the social aspiration of middle-class women (Abel-Smith, 1960; Dingwall and McIntosh, 1978). The hygienic organisation of society at large was the social parallel of rational physiological improvement for the individual woman. These occupational advancements for women were, however, limited and had to be achieved against considerable opposition from professional groups that sought to ensure that health roles for women were largely an extension of their domestic activities into the public sphere. The nursing profession was thus seen as a 'natural' role for women who were physiologically equipped for mothering duties (Gamarnikow, 1978).

One crucial limitation of nineteenth-century feminism was, however, that it frequently reflected the economic individualism of the society in which it was encased. Middle-class women wanted the individual freedoms of men to gain employment in the market-place, where they would hopefully enjoy the same wage levels as male labour. What they sought was the same level of contractual freedom as other labourers within a private capitalist system of production. American feminism thus became isolated from working-class radicalism. When individualism was combined with secularism, the result was that:

> By the 1920s the feminist demand for sexual equality in marriage had degen-
> erated into the equal rights of both sexes to sexual pleasure and orgasmic
> fulfilment, transforming bourgeois women along the way into domestic play-
> mates and little else; later, the radical feminist emphasis on self-ownership
> collapsed into the sober realism of planned parenthood. (Leach, 1981,
> pp. 348—9)

It is in this context that Michel Foucault's view of power as pro-ductive rather than repressive is particularly important. The discourses of medicine and hygiene resulted, not in repressive, but in productive, regulated bodies, slimmed down and manicured for sexuality. The new discourses of the body seek to express and constitute, not suppress and deny sexuality. Whereas the aristocracy depended on practices of blood — primogeniture, lineage and conservation — the bourgeoisie required 'a sound organism and a healthy sexuality' (Foucault, 1981, p. 126). Foucault, however, regards the medicalisation of the population as deeply problematic and less than liberating. The rise of contemporary sexuality is also part of the secularisation of societies; Foucault identi-fies the problem of sexuality with the death of God. The contemporary problems of language, sex and God are located in the person of the Marquis de Sade.

In pre-modern culture, our sexuality found its expression in a language which, at least in principle, connected our bodies with a divine order of supernatural love, fallen creatures and earthly sins. With de Sade's erotic pornography, the ancient connection between our sexuality and the order of the sacred cosmos was broken. Since nothing is absolutely true, everything is permitted, but this cultural permission turns sexuality in on itself without purpose or outlet, apart from pure gratification. Sexual appetite became without limit, now being combined with sadistic cruelty and pure exploitation:

> What characterizes modern sexuality from Sade to Freud is not its having found the language of its logic or of its natural process, but rather, through the violence done by such languages, its having been 'denatured' — cast into an empty zone where it achieves whatever meager form is bestowed upon it by the establishment of its limits. Sexuality points to nothing beyond itself, no prolongation, except in a frenzy which disrupts it. (Foucault, 1977, pp. 29—30)

In the literary imagination of de Sade, the Protestant Ethic of hard work was converted into a sexual ethic that was entirely secular, demanding its own devotion to pleasure as a hard task-master (Beauvoir, 1972a). Our pleasures, suitably commercialised and developed by leisure industries, are now to be explored in a regime of dieting and jogging that seeks no object other than pleasure itself. These pleasures are, of course, significantly modified and channelled along the social divisions of class, sex and age. Like death, sexual pleasure is a physiological fact, but its social nature and distribution are highly unequal.

History and society deeply shape our personal experiences of death and sex. Although the latter is almost regarded as a democratic right, the union of bodies is never without the presence of social class and personal biography:

> But no bed, however unexpected, no matter how apparently gratuitous, is free from the de-universalising facts of real life. We do not go to bed simply in pairs; even if we choose not to refer to them, we still drag there with us the cultural impediments of our social class, our parents' lives, our bank balances, our sexual and emotional expectations, our whole biographies — all the bits and pieces of our unique existences. (Carter, 1979, p. 9)

Although death and sex are universal experiences grounded in our biology, they are nevertheless fragmented by social and cultural divisions. We can only understand these existential dilemmas in terms of a thorough sociological grasp of the social structure in which these private events are publicly located.

Conclusion

Throughout this study of religion, I have attempted to throw doubt on the persistent sociological assumption that in pre-modern societies the lives of people were thoroughly embraced by a common religious culture which gave immediate significance to human existence. More specifically, I have raised questions about the penetration of Christianity into the everyday existence of working-class men and women. There is little convincing evidence that social and political inequality were legitimated by religion for peasants in feudalism or labourers in early capitalism.

In the last analysis, we do not know whether religion made death and sex meaningful for ordinary men, or whether it provided a vague promise of better things to come for the faithful and the righteous. What we do know is that death and sex were highly public events which had major significance for the life of the community. Death typically occurred in the public arena of the home, witnessed by relatives and confessors; its presence and frequency testified to the brevity of human life and, at least in the fourteenth century, death pointed to a real world beyond in purgatory. In a similar fashion, sex was often a public event. Aristocratic couples often had to prove the sexual consummation of their marriage before observing parents (Duby, 1978); children were not excluded from the sexual activities of their parents (Ariès, 1973). In peasant communities, the rural charivari played a major part in the public control of courtship, marriage and fidelity; sexual affection was often remarkably public and overt (Shorter, 1977).

In the modern world, sex and death have become private and secular. Death has receded to the privacy of the side-ward of bureaucratic hospitals; sex has withdrawn to the domestic seclusion of middle-class suburbia. This sexual space is, however, thoroughly invaded by commercialism, television, video 'nasties' and unsolicited pornography. Privatised sex is directly linked to an expanding popular culture of commercialised pleasure. The irony is that, without a common religious tradition, our private sexual deviation has very little public impact on the legitimacy of modern societies; indeed, it would be difficult to know precisely what would constitute sexual deviation between private citizens. A society based on widespread structural unemployment and early retirement may actually require these private pleasures, given the demographic characteristics of western societies.

This is, however, not essentially a 'bread and circus' argument. It is not specifically the case that public organisation by bureaucratic state regulation requires the compensation of personal hedonism. In modern industrial society, private systems of meaning have become uncoupled from public modes of social legitimation. Although a number of radical philosophers (Marcuse, 1972) looked to sexual liberation as an avenue of social transformation, sexual expressivity now appears to have been successfully commercialised and contained.

Personal deviation is largely separated politically and institutionally from the major mechanisms of public regulation. Personal meaning in the form of religious symbolism and practice no longer has significant implications for the distribution of property and power; personal significance and individual religiosity is a frigate without anchorage, radar systems, location or direction. Afloat within the wider system of impersonal regulation of bodies, sexual and religious commitment and deviation are cut off from the social structure and process of the public mainland. Religion as a system of social hooks binding men to the social structure has been reduced to a private range of stylistic options.

The importance of this observation for sociological theory is that personal systems of meaning are not essential for public orders of legitimation. It is perfectly possible, as in modern societies, for personal meanings to be significantly cut adrift from systems of public regulation, control and legitimation. Although conventional sociology of religion was based on the implicit assumption that the social coherence of society depended ultimately on the interpenetration of private and public orders of meaning, in modern societies the social realm of politics is radically disjoined from such interpersonal significance. Private disorders no longer have implications directly for social continuity, which now depends on independent practices of regulation and co-ordination.

We need, therefore, to rephrase the paradox presented by Borges in relation to the parody of bodies. Opting for abstinence or orgy is now an idiosyncratic choice without major social significance; both asceticism and hedonism are highly commercialised, operating outside the zones of political regulation and administration. The parody of fatherhood and mirrors continues but outside the central processes of property production and conservation. God is dead; everything is permitted, at least optionally and provisionally.

The principal explanation of this disjunction is that impersonal property in late capitalism no longer requires the discipline of bodies or the physiological regulation of populations. With the separation of moral bodies and regulated property, religion no longer significantly contributes to the unity of social classes, the discipline of bodies or the reproduction of economic relations. In periods of international crisis, modern societies may occasionally experience high levels of social consensus and moral unity, when religious leaders pray for the nation and the survival of its people, but, in the everyday management of the state and the surveillance of society, religious adherence to central values is in western societies purely marginal.

Liberal democracy has created two largely separate zones of activity between private hedonism and public regulation. Within the private sphere, individuals are relatively free to select a variety of sexual and religious postures that are no longer directly connected with the public operation of politics and economics. The only bridge between the subjective freedom of private citizens and the objective regulation of public activities is not a system of shared religious meanings, but a commercialised popular culture that employs sexual idioms to extend the market for consumer goods. The public realm can thus function in late capitalism without an overarching system of common legitimation grounded in religion, despite the chaos of personal life-styles which is enhanced by the consumer market.

What is Religion?

Within the sociology of religion the problem of defining religion has played a crucial role in the whole development of the discipline (Parsons, 1944). In this particular study of religion, I have chosen to restrict consideration of this analytical issue, because it is often more rewarding to approach these theoretical issues by way of empirical, substantive debates. Furthermore, although the question of the nature of religion has been endlessly discussed by philosophers, sociologists and theologians, the conceptual cows have yet to come home.

Broadly speaking, these debates about the definition of religion have been organised around a number of basic dimensions. There is, for example, a key difference between reductionist and non-reductionist perspectives. The former tend to see religion as an epiphenomenon, a reflection or expression of more basic and permanent features of human behaviour and society. Writers like Pareto, Lenin, Freud and Engels saw religion as the product or mental reflection of economic interests, biological needs or class experiences of deprivation. The implication of reductionism is that religious beliefs are false by reference to certain scientific or positivistic criteria and that the holding of religious beliefs is irrational by reference to criteria of logical thought. The final implication of 'positivist reductionism' is that religion is seen as primarily a cognitive activity of the individual mind which, for various causes, misapprehends the true nature of empirical and social life (Goode, 1951).

A classic nineteenth-century definition of religion was E. B. Tylor's famous 'minimum definition' as 'the belief in Spiritual Beings' (1891, p. 424). Religion arose from the attempts of 'ancient savage philosophers' (p. 428) to make sense of their own mental experiences. This type of definition is thus individualistic, cognitive and rationalist, because it is not specifically concerned with religious practice or symbolism in relation to social organisation, and it accepts the criteria of western science as self-evidently true and the only basis of rationality.

Durkheim and the sacred
The history of the sociology of religion can thus be seen as a theoretical movement away from positive reductionism towards an appreciation of the importance of religious ritual in social organisation and towards an awareness that positivist science is not an appropriate measure of the

rationality of religion. In anthropology, this change in perspective was associated with the demonstration that in 'primitive society' people do make a clear distinction between magic and technology; magic has an important function in structuring situations of uncertainty and danger (Malinowski, 1948).

In sociology, the decisive break with early positivism is often located in Durkheim's distinction between the sacred and the profane, which came to dominate most contemporary approaches to the definitional problems of religion. In *The Elementary Forms of the Religious Life*, published in 1912, religion was defined as:

a unified system of beliefs and practices relative to sacred things, that is to say, things set apart and forbidden — beliefs and practices which unite into one single moral community called a Church, all those who adhere to them. (Durkheim, 1961, p. 62)

The advantage of such a definition is that it recognises the centrality of religious practice to belief, it permits comparative research by avoiding a specifically theistic approach and it pushes the issue of the falsity of individual beliefs into the background. Indeed, for Durkheim, there are no false religions:

All are true in their own fashion; all answer though in different ways, to the given conditions of human existence. (Durkheim, 1961, p. 15)

There was, however, a covert positivism in Durkheim's definition. Religion survived because it fulfilled certain basic social functions, namely, in maintaining common beliefs through ritual practices. The truth of religion was a sociological truth and the referent of religious symbols was not the totemic god, but society itself. The beliefs of the participants were in fact mistaken, since the real object of worship was the social group. Durkheim thus retained a rationalist commitment to the superiority of scientific criteria of truth, since in Durkheim's account religious beliefs must:

be distorted representations of an empirical reality which is capable of correct analysis by an empirical science, this time sociology. (Parsons, 1937, p. 420)

More recent criticisms of Durkheim have questioned the universality and methodological validity of the sacred/profane distinction by arguing that in practice a belief in superhuman beings is basic to any notion of 'religion', including Buddhism (Horton, 1960; Spiro, 1966). The main objection to Durkheim's account is, however, that it fails ultimately to incorporate the actor's own subjective belief and experience of sacred reality. The phenomenology of religion has, therefore, opted for a definition of religion as the experience of the holy (Otto, 1929; Wach, 1971). In the sociology of religion itself, Peter Berger emphasises the importance of the subjective response of the social actor

to the threat of death and chaos to the construction of a religious
world-view, a sacred cosmos (Berger, 1969). Within this perspective,
Weber's treatment of 'the problem of meaning' and especially the
construction of religious theodicies (Weber, 1966) has provided an
alternative to Durkheim's focus on the social functions of the sacred.

Religion and meaningful order

Despite criticism and theoretical development, the Durkheimian perspective remains powerful in most approaches to the issue of defining
religion from a sociological point of view, but this Durkheimian
perspective is typically combined with a Weberian concern for the
question of meaningfulness. For the social actor religion is a response to
the existential dilemmas of human life, especially illness and death, but
this response is itself structured and directed by religious cultures
which have the social effect of binding individuals together in social
collectivities.

A number of prominent definitions of religion in contemporary
sociology combine these two dimensions. Religion is:

(1) a system of symbols which acts to (2) establish powerful, pervasive, and
long-lasting moods and motivations in men by (3) formulating conceptions of a
general order of existence and (4) clothing these conceptions with such an aura
of factuality that (5) the moods and motivations seem uniquely realistic.
(Geertz, 1966, p. 4)

or:

Religion is a set of coherent answers to the core existential questions that
confront every human group, the codification of these answers into a creedal
form that has significance for its adherents, the celebration of rites which
provide an emotional bond for those who participate, and the establishment of
an institutional body to bring into congregation those who share the creed and
celebration, and provide for the continuity of these rites from generation to
generation. (Bell, 1980, pp. 333—4)

or:

Religion is the human enterprise by which a sacred cosmos is established. Put
differently, religion is cosmization in a sacred mode. By sacred is meant here a
quality of mysterious and awesome power, other than man and yet related to
him, which is believed to reside in certain objects of experience . . . The sacred
cosmos is confronted by man as an immensely powerful reality other than
himself. Yet this reality addresses itself to him and locates his life in an
ultimately meaningful order. (Berger, 1969, p. 26)

These definitions are comprehensive, influential and in many respects
persuasive. They avoid ethnocentricity, they do not equate religion
with the Church, they give adequate emphasis to ritual and experience,
and they take religion seriously without uniformly reducing religion to
biology, economic interest or irrational drives.

Cognitive reductionism

Definitions of this sort, however, raise three major problems. First, they often explicitly assume (Luckmann, 1967; Berger, 1969) that all people share a common anthropological need for meaning or transcendence that is ultimately grounded in our biologically 'unfinished' constitution. That is, the problem of meaning is a shared necessity of humanity, irrespective of our sexual, social, ethnic or class identity. The problems of birth, sex and death are universal and uniform. Such definitions fail to take into account the highly variable experiences of 'existential dilemmas' by sex, age or class. They also make assumptions about social uniformity, in that they have to assume the existence of general beliefs and an embracing culture. The sharing of common existential problems presupposes the existence of a shared culture within which these questions have a meaning and significance. The pluralism of modern societies implies, at the very least, the existence of a variety of 'religions' within the 'same' culture. In this situation, religion may not so much bind people together as bind them against each other in a welter of contradictory systems of significance.

Secondly, these approaches fail to ask a basic sociological question: who exactly believes in the importance of existential questions? Throughout this study, I have attempted to suggest that we should not assume the existence of a dominant culture which integrates all social classes within the same moral framework. Existential questions of meaning may influence all sections of a community, but they appear to have a special salience for intellectual strata. For other classes, religion may be tied to mundane ends — success, health, security. These are 'existential issues', but they are formulated at the level of practical actions:

religious or magical behavior or thinking must not be set apart from the range of everyday purposive conduct, particularly since even the ends of the religious and magical actions are predominantly economic. (Weber, 1966, p. 1)

The contemporary concern for the subjective meaning of religion with its emphasis on symbols and on 'coherent answers' may be in danger of 'cognitive reductionism' as the mirror image of previous 'economic reductionism'.

Finally, by concentrating on the individual's response to crises in life, these definitions fail to take seriously the issue, not of definition, but of explanation. The search for a definition of religion should not obscure the sociological inquiry into the effects and consequences of religion for societies divided into social classes.

Religio

This particular study of religion has been conducted from a 'materialist perspective' that is concerned with two issues, namely, 'the production of the means of subsistence' and 'the production of human beings themselves' (Engels, n.d., p. 6). This perspective is concerned, therefore, with the place of religion in respect of the material conditions of economic production and in relation to the physiological reproduction of people.

In many respects, these themes have been approached from a Durkheimian definition of religion. Religion (*religio*) is an obligation or bond; the etymological meaning of religion points to its social functions of discipline and bondage. In particular, in western Christian societies I have argued that historically religion had the function of binding sons to fathers, daughters to mothers and wives to husbands. The discipline of bodies was directed towards the material conservation of economic and political power. This historical approach has grounded the problem of religion in the accumulation of wealth via the organisation of sexuality. It does not follow from this approach that the ultimate meaning of religion can be encapsulated in a simple economic formula.

I have also followed Weber in recognising that religion is a response to certain fundamental questions of meaning, but I have not assumed that the 'problem of meaning' strikes all members of a society in the same way and with equal force. Furthermore, I have not assumed that existential questions can be resolved by a form of cognitive reductionism that regards meaning as a cognitive activity alone. Our existential questions are rooted in the biographical history of bodies — their being in and departure from the world. Weber's problem of meaning can thus be linked with Engels's insistence on the basic problem of the reproduction of human beings. The micro-problem of the meaning of my body is part of the macro-problem of bodies in time and space, so that my experiences are part of those of the species, but mediated by class, sexual identity, age and so forth. The 'coherent answers' of religion are not disembodied responses of mind, but part of my physical experience through my body of the socially structured world. The physicality of the Abrahamic faiths — with their myths of incarnation, resurrection, divine fatherhood, holy men, rituals of purification, sacraments, the symbolism of water and fire, and the body of the chosen people — is ample theological justification for a corporeal sociology of religion. The problem with such an approach, as with all definitions of religion, is its historical specificity.

In so far as this study has accepted the secularisation of religion, the definition of religion in modern society is particularly problematic. Although social-class positions remain important in our experience of modern society, in general we are exposed to the material world of commodities, objects and bodies without the intervening shield of religious meanings. The death of God has left us literally and culturally naked.

Bibliography

ABC Television (1965), *Television and Religion*, London.
Abedin, S. Z. (ed.) (1979), *Journal of the Institute of Muslim Minority Affairs*, vol. 1.
Abel-Smith, B. (1960), *A History of the Nursing Profession*, London.
Abercrombie, N. (1980), *Class Structure and Knowledge. Problems in the Sociology of Knowledge*, Oxford.
Abercrombie, N. and Turner, B. S. (1978), 'The dominant ideology thesis', *British Journal of Sociology*, vol. 29, no. 2, pp. 149—70.
Abercrombie, N., Hill, S. and Turner, B. S. (1980), *The Dominant Ideology Thesis*, London.
Abun-Nasr, J. M. (1965), *The Tijaniyya, a Sufi order in the Modern World*, London.
Acquaviva, S. S. (1979), *The Decline of the Sacred in Industrial Society*, Oxford.
Adams, C. C. (1933), *Islam and Modernism in Egypt*, London.
Algar, H. (1969), *Religion and State in Iran, 1785–1906*, Berkeley, Ca.
Althusser, L. (1969), *For Marx*, Harmondsworth.
Althusser, L. (1977), *Lenin and Philosophy and Other Essays*, London.
Althusser, L. and Balibar, E. (1970), *Reading Capital*, London.
Anderson, L. (1980), 'Freud and Nietzsche', *Salmagundi*, no. 47—8, pp. 3—29.
Anderson, P. (1974a), *Passages from Antiquity to Feudalism*, London.
Anderson, P. (1974b), *Lineages of the Absolutist State*, London.
Andorka, R. (1978), *Determinants of Fertility in Advanced Societies*, London.
Argyle, M. (1958), *Religious Behaviour*, London.
Argyle, M. (1964), 'Seven psychological roots of religion', *Theology*, vol. 67, pp. 1—17.
Arieli, Y. (1964), *Individualism and Nationalism in American Ideology*, Cambridge, Mass.
Ariès, P. (1973), *Centuries of Childhood*, Harmondsworth.
Ariès, P. (1974), *Western Attitudes to Death: from the Middle Ages to the Present*, Baltimore, Ma. and London.
Aron, R. (1968), *Main Currents in Sociological Thought*, Harmondsworth, 2 vols.
Avineri, S. (ed.) (1968), *Karl Marx on Colonialism and Modernization*, New York.
Avineri, S. (1970a), *The Social and Political Thought of Karl Marx*, Cambridge.
Avineri, S. (1970b), 'The Palestinians and Israel', *Commentary*, vol. 49, pp. 31—44.
Bakan, D. (1974), 'Paternity in the Judeo-Christian tradition', in A. Eister (ed.), *Changing Perspectives in the Scientific Study of Religion*, New York, pp. 203—16.
Barnes, R. H. (1974), *Kedang, a Study of the Collective Thoughts of an Eastern Indonesian People*, Oxford.
Baumgarten, E. (1964), *Max Weber, Werk und Person*, Tubingen.
Beattie, J. and Middleton, J. (eds.) (1969), *Spirit Mediumship and Society in Africa*, London.
Beauvoir, S. de (1972a), *The Marquis de Sade*, London.
Beauvoir, S. de (1972b), *The Second Sex*, Harmondsworth.
Becker, L.C. (1977), *Property Rights*, London.
Beetham, D. (1974), *Max Weber and the Theory of Modern Politics*, London.
Bell, D. (1961), *The End of Ideology, on the Exhaustion of Political Ideas in the Fifties*, New York.
Bell, D. (1976), *The Coming of Post-Industrial Society*, Harmondsworth.
Bell, D. (1980), *Sociological Journeys, Essays 1960–1980*, London.
Bellah, R. N. (1964), 'Religious evolution', *American Sociological Review*, vol. 29, pp. 358—74.
Bellah, R. N. (1970a), *Beyond Belief, Essays on Religion in a Post-Traditional World*, New York, Evanston and London.

Bellah, R. N. (1970b), 'Christianity and symbolic realism', *Journal for the Scientific Study of Religion*, vol. 9, pp. 89—96.

Bendix, R. (1966), *Max Weber, an Intellectual Portrait*, London.

Berger, P. L. (1957), 'Motif Messianique et processus social dans le Behaisme', *Archives de Sociologie des Religions*, vol. 4, pp. 93—107.

Berger, P. L. (1969), *The Social Reality of Religion*, London.

Berger, P. L. (1973), 'The obsolescence of the concept of honour', in P. L. Berger, B. Berger and H. Kelman, *The Homeless Mind*, Harmondsworth.

Berger, P. L. and Pullberg, S. (1966), 'Reification and the sociological critique of consciousness', *New Left Review*, no. 35, pp. 56—71.

Berlin, I. (1978), *Karl Marx*, Oxford.

Biezanek, A. (1964), *All Things New*, London.

Birnbaum, N. (1973), 'Beyond Marx in the sociology of religion', in C. Y. Glock and P. E. Hammond (eds.), *Beyond the Classics? Essays in the Study of Religion*, New York, pp. 3—70.

Birnbaum, N. and Lenzer, G. (eds.) (1969), *Sociology and Religion, a Book of Readings*, Englewood Cliffs, NJ.

Black, H. (1902), *Culture and Restraint*, London.

Black, J. S. and Chrystal, G. (1912), *The Life of William Robertson Smith*, Edinburgh.

Blumler, J., Brown, J. R., Ewbank, A. J., and Nossiter, T. (1971), 'Attitudes to the monarchy: their structure and development during a ceremonial occasion', *Political Studies*, vol. 19, no. 2, pp. 149—71.

Boase, T. S. R. (1972), *Death in the Middle Ages, Mortality Judgment and Remembrance*, London.

Bocock, R. (1974), *Ritual in Industrial Society, A Sociological Analysis of Ritualism in Modern England*, London.

Borges, J. L. (1970), *Labyrinths*, Harmondsworth.

Borochov, B. (1937), *Nationalism and the Class Structure, a Marxian Approach to the Jewish Problem*, New York.

Bossy, J. (1975), *The English Catholic Community 1570—1850*, London.

Bottomore, T. (1979), *Political Sociology*, London.

Bourdeaux, M. (1968), *Religious Ferment in Russia*, London.

Bowman, L. (1964), *The American Funeral: A Study in Guilt, Extravagance and Sublimity*, New York.

Boxer, C. (1965), *The Dutch Seaborne Empire 1600–1800*, London.

Boyle, J. A. (ed.) (1968), *The Cambridge History of Iran*, Vol. 5, Cambridge.

Brand, J. (1978), *The National Movement in Scotland*, London.

Braudel, F. (1980), *On History*, Chicago.

Breger, L. (1981), *Freud's Unfinished Journey*, Boston and Henley.

Brøndsted, J. (1965), *The Vikings*, Harmondsworth.

Buber, M. (1956), *Tales of the Hasidim*, London.

Budd, S. (1973), *Sociologists and Religion*, London.

Burckhart, J. (1955), *The Civilization of the Renaissance in Italy*, London.

Caldwell, L. (1978), 'Church, state and family: the women's movement in Italy', in A. Kuhn and A. M. Wolpe (eds.), *Feminism and Materialism, Women and Modes of Production*, London, Boston and Henley, pp. 68—95.

Campbell, C. (1972), 'The cult, the cultic milieu and secularization', in M. Hill (ed.), *A Sociological Yearbook of Religion in Britain*, Vol. 5, pp. 119—36.

Campbell, C. (1977), 'Clarifying the cult', *British Journal of Sociology*, vol. 28, pp. 375—88.

Capaldi, N. (1975), *David Hume, the Newtonian Philosopher*, Boston.

Carlton, E. (1977), *Ideology and Social Order*, London.

Carter, A. (1979), *The Sadeian Woman, an Exercise in Cultural History*, London.

Carter, I. (1974), 'The Highlands of Scotland as an underdeveloped region', in E. de Kadt and G. Williams (eds.), *Sociology and Development*, London, pp. 279—311.

Carver, T. (1981), *Engels*, Oxford.

Cassirer, E. (1954), *The Question of Jean-Jacques Rousseau*, New York.
Castaneda, C. (1968), *The Teachings of Don Juan, a Yaqui Way of Knowledge*, California.
Chaliand, G. (1980), *People without a Country, the Kurds and Kurdistan*, London.
Charnay, J. P. (1971), *Islamic Culture and Socio-economic Change*, Leiden.
Charnay, J. P. (1980), *Les Contre-Orients, ou comment penser l'Autre selon soi*, Paris.
Chaucer, G. (1960), *The Canterbury Tales*, Harmondsworth.
Chenu, M. D. (1969), *L'Eveil de la Conscience dans civilisation medievale*, Paris.
Cheyne, G. (1733), *The English Malady*, London.
Christian, W. A. (1972), *Person and God in a Spanish Valley*, New York and London.
Clark, A. C. (1913), *Handbook for the Attendants of the Insane*, London.
Clarke, B. (1975), *Mental Disorder in Earlier Britain*, Cardiff.
Cohen, W. (1957), *The Pursuit of the Millennium*, London.
Cornaro, L. (1776), *Discourses on a Sober and Temperate Life*, London.
Coward, H. and Kawamura, L. (eds.) (1977), *Religion and Ethnicity*, Waterloo, Ont.
Cragg, G. R. (ed.) (1975), *The Works of John Wesley*, Oxford.
Crapanzano, V. (1973), *The Hamadsha, a Study in Moroccan Ethno-Psychiatry*, Berkeley, Ca.
Cutler, D. R. (ed.) (1968), *The Religious Situation*, Boston.
Dahrendorf, R. (1968), 'Out of Utopia', in R. Dahrendorf, *Essays in the Theory of Society*, London, pp. 107—28
Davis, H. B. (1965), 'Nations, colonies and classes: the position of Marx and Engels', *Science and Society*, vol. 29, pp. 26—43.
Davis, J. C. (1981), *Utopia and the Ideal Society, a Study of English Utopian Writing 1516–1700*, Cambridge.
Davis, K. (1948), *Human Society*, New York.
Davis, U. (1977), *Israel, Utopia Incorporated*, London.
Dawson, R. (1981), *Confucius*, Oxford.
Delumeau, J. (ed.) (1969), *Histoire de la Bretagne*, Toulouse.
Delumeau, J. (1977), *Catholicism between Luther and Voltaire*, London and Philadelphia.
Demerath, N. J. and Hammond, P. E. (1969), *Religion in Social Context: Tradition and Transition*, New York.
Dempsey, D. (1975), *The Way We Die, an Investigation of Death and Dying in America Today*, New York.
Derrida, J. (1976), *On Grammatology*, Baltimore, Md. and London.
Devane, R. S. (1976), *The Failure of Individualism*, London.
Dickson, T. (1978), 'Class and nationalism in Scotland', *Scottish Journal of Sociology*, vol. 2, pp. 143—62.
Dingwall, R. and McIntosh, J. (eds.) (1978), *Readings in the Sociology of Nursing*, Edinburgh.
Douglas, M. (1966), *Purity and Danger*, London.
Duby, G. (1953), *La Sociétié aux XI et XII siècles dans la région mâconnaise*, Paris.
Duby, G. (1978), *Medieval Marriage — two Models from Twelfth-Century France*, Baltimore, Md. and London.
Durkheim, E. (1915), *'Germany above all'. The German Mental Attitude and the War*, Paris.
Durkheim, E. (1938), *The Rules of Sociological Method*, Chicago.
Durkheim, E. (1961), *The Elementary Forms of Religious Life*, New York.
Durkheim, E. (1964), *The Division of Labour in Society*, New York.
Durkheim, E. and Mauss, M. (1963), *Primitive Classification*, London.
Dwyer, D. D. (1978) 'Women, Sufism and decision-making in Moroccan Islam', in L. Beck and N. Keddie (eds.), *Women in the Muslim World*, pp. 585—98.
Edelman, B. (1979), *Ownership of the Image, Elements for a Marxist Theory of Law*, London.
Ein-Gil, E. (1981), 'Religion, Zionism and secularism', *Khamsin*, vol. 8, pp. 105—20.
Eisenstadt, S. N. (1956), *From Generation to Generation: Age Groups and Social Structure*, Glencoe, Ill.

Eister, A. (1967), 'Toward a radical critique of church-sect typologizing' *Journal for the Scientific Study of Religion*, vol. 6, pp. 85—90.

Eliade, M. (1959), *Cosmos and History*, New York.

Elias, N. (1978), *The Civilizing Process*, Oxford.

Engels, F. (n.d.), *The Origin of the Family, Private Property and the State* (1st edn, 1884), Moscow.

Engels, F. (1965), *The Peasant War in Germany*, London.

Engels, F. (1968), *The Condition of the Working Class in England in 1844*, London.

Engels, F. (1975a), *Socialism: Utopian and Scientific*, Peking.

Engels, F. (1975b), *On Marx*, Peking.

Engels, F. (1976), *Ludwig Feuerbach and the End of Classical German Philosophy*, Peking.

Epp, F. H. (1977), *Mennonites in Canada 1786-1920, the History of a Separate People*, Toronto.

Epstein, I. (1959), *Judaism*, Harmondsworth.

Evans-Pritchard, E. E. (1965), *Theories of Primitive Religion*, London.

Fanfani, A. (1933), *Le origini dello spirito capitalistico in Italia*, Milan.

Feuerbach, L. (1953), *The Essence of Christianity*, London (1st edn, 1841).

Firth, S. and Hoorn, J. (1979), 'From Empire Day to Cracker Night', in P. Spearritt and D. Walker (eds.), *Australian Popular Culture*, Sydney, pp. 17—38.

Fischer, M. M. J. (1980), *Iran, from Religious Dispute to Revolution*, Cambridge and London.

Fleischmann, E. (1964), 'De Weber à Nietzsche', *Archives Européennes de Sociologie*, Vol. 5, pp. 190—238.

Foucault, M. (1967), *Madness and Civilization, a History of Insanity in the Age of Reason*, London.

Foucault, M. (1973), *The Birth of the Clinic, an Archaeology of Medical Perception*, London.

Foucault, M. (1977), *Language, Counter-Memory, Practice*, London.

Foucault, M. (1979), *Discipline and Punish: the Birth of the Prison*, Harmondsworth.

Foucault, M. (1980), *Power/Knowledge*, London.

Foucault, M. (1981), *The History of Sexuality, Vol. 1: An Introduction*, Harmondsworth.

Frank, A. G. (1972), *Sociology of Underdevelopment and the Underdevelopment of Sociology*, London.

Freud, S. and Breuer, J. (1978), *Studies in Hysteria*, Harmondsworth.

Freund, J. (1968), *The Sociology of Max Weber*, London.

Freund, J. (1979), 'German sociology in the time of Max Weber' in T. Bottomore and R. Nisbet (eds.), *A History of Sociological Analysis*, London, pp. 149—86.

Frith, S. (1978), *The Sociology of Rock*, London.

Galloway, A. D. (1974), 'The Meaning of Feuerbach', *British Journal of Sociology*, vol. 25, pp. 135—49.

Gamarnikow, E. (1978), 'Sexual division of labour: the case of nursing', in A. Kuhn and A. M. Wolpe (eds.), *Feminism and Materialism, Women and Modes of Production*, London, pp. 96—123.

Gaskin, J. C. A. (1976), 'Hume's critique of religion', *Journal for the History of Philosophy*, vol. 14, pp. 301—11.

Geertz, C. (1966), 'Religion as a cultural system', in M. Banton (ed.), *Anthropological Approaches to the Study of Religion*, London, pp. 1—46.

Geertz, C. (1968), *Islam Observed, Religious Development in Morocco and Indonesia*, New Haven, Conn., and London.

Gellner, E. (1964), *Thought and Change*, London.

Gellner, E. (1969a), 'A pendulum swing theory of Islam', in R. Robertson (ed.), *Sociology of Religion*, pp. 115—38.

Gellner, E. (1969b), *Saints of the Atlas*, London.

Gellner, E. (1970), 'Concepts and society', in D. Emmett and A. MacIntyre (eds.), *Sociological Theory and Philosophical Analysis*, London, pp. 115—49.

Gellner, E. (1980), 'In defence of Orientalism', *Sociology*, vol. 14, pp. 295—300.

Geoghegan, V. (1981), *Reason and Eros: the Social Theory of Herbert Marcuse*, London.
George, K. and George, C. H. (1953—5), 'Roman Catholic sainthood and social status', *Journal of Religion*, vol. 5, pp. 33—5.
Giddens, A. (1972), *Politics and Sociology in the Thought of Max Weber*, London.
Giddens, A. (1978), *Durkheim*, London.
Giddens, A. (1979), *Central Problems in Social Theory*, London.
Gilsenan, M. (1973), *Saint and Sufi in Modern Egypt, an Essay in the Sociology of Religion*, Oxford.
Glock, C. Y. (ed.) (1973), *Religion in Sociological Perspective*, Belmont, Ca.
Glock, C. Y. (1976), 'Consciousness among contemporary youth, an interpretation', in C. Y. Glock and R. N. Bellah (eds.) *The New Religious Consciousness*, Berkeley, Ca., pp. 353—66.
Glock, C. Y. and Bellah, R. N. (eds.) (1976), *The New Religious Consciousness*, Berkeley, Ca.
Glock, C. Y. and Stark, R. (1965), *Religion and Society in Tension*, Chicago.
Goffman, E. (1969), *The Presentation of Self in Everyday Life*, London.
Goldmann, L. (1973), *The Philosophy of the Enlightenment, the Christian Burgess and the Enlightenment*, London.
Goldthorpe, J. H. (1978), 'The current inflation: towards a sociological account', in F. Hirsch and J. Goldthorpe (eds.), *The Political Economy of Inflation*, London, pp. 186—214.
Goode, W. J. (1951), *Religion Among the Primitives*, Glencoe, Ill.
Goodridge, R. M. (1975), 'The ages of faith — romance or reality?' *Sociological Review*, vol. 23, pp. 381—96.
Goody, J. (1962), *Death, Property and the Ancestors*, Stanford, Ca.
Goody, J. (1977), 'Against "ritual" — loosely structured thoughts on a loosely defined topic', in S. F. Moore and B. G. Myerhoff (eds.), *Secular Ritual*, Assen, pp. 25—35.
Goody, J., Thirsk, J. and Thompson, E. P. (eds.) (1978), *Family and Inheritance, Rural Society in Western Europe, 1700–1800*, Cambridge.
Gorer, G. (1965), *Death, Grief and Mourning*, London.
Gouldner, A. W. (1967), *Enter Plato: Classical Greece and the Origins of Social Theory*, London.
Gramsci, A. (1971), *Selections from the Prison Notebooks*, London.
Grans, F. (1967), 'Social utopias in the Middle Ages', *Past and Present*, no. 38, pp. 3—19.
Gregorovius, F. (1948), *The Ghetto and the Jews of Rome*, New York.
Grierson, H. J. C. (1956), *Milton and Wordsworth, Poets and Prophets*, London.
Habakkuk, H. J. (1950), 'Marriage settlements in the eighteenth century', *Transactions of the Royal Historical Society*, vol. 32. pp. 15–30.
Habenstein, R. W. (1962), 'Sociology of occupations: the case of the American funeral director,' in A. M. Rose (ed.) *Human Behavior and Social Processes, an Interactionist Approach*, London, pp. 225—46.
Habermas, J. (1976), *Legitimation Crisis*, London.
Halliday, F. (1979), *Iran: Dictatorship and Development*, Harmondsworth.
Hanham, H. J. (1969), *Scottish Nationalism*, London.
Hartung, F. (1957), *Enlightened Despotism*, London.
Hechter, M. (1975), *Internal Colonialism, the Celtic Fringe in British National Development 1536–1966*, London.
Hegel, G. W. F. (1956), *The Philosophy of History*, New York.
Held, D. (1980), *Introduction to Critical Theory, Horkheimer to Habermas*, London.
Henderson, W. (1976), *The Life of Friedrich Engels*, 2 vols., London.
Henderson, W. and Chaloner, O. (1959), *Engels as Military Critic*, London.
Henson, M. A. (1975), *Giles of Rome and the Medieval Theory of Conception*, London.
Hepworth, M. and Turner, B. S. (1982), *Confession: Studies in Deviance and Religion*, London.
Herberg, W. (1960), *Protestant, Catholic, Jew*, New York.
Hibbin, S. (1978), *Politics, Ideology and the State*, London.

Hill, M. (1971), 'Typologies sociologique de l'ordre religieux, *Social Compass*, vol. 18, pp. 45—64.

Hill, M. (1973), *A Sociology of Religion*, London.

Hill, M. and Turner, B. S. (1971), 'John Wesley and the origins of ascetic devotion', in M. Hill (ed.), *A Sociological Yearbook of Religion in Britain*, Vol. 4, pp. 102—20.

Hill, M. and Turner, B. S. (1975), 'Methodism and the pietist definition of politics: historical development and contemporary evidence', in M. Hill (ed.), *A Sociological Yearbook of Religion in Britain*, Vol. 8, pp. 159—80.

Hill, S. (1981), *Competition and Control at Work, the New Industrial Sociology*, London.

Hindess, B. and Hirst, P. Q. (1975) *Pre-Capitalist Modes of Production*, London and Boston.

Hinton, J. (1967), *Dying*, Harmondsworth.

Hirst, P. Q. (1976), *Social Evolution and Sociological Categories*, London.

Hirst, P. Q. (1979), *On Law and Ideology*, London.

Hirst, P. Q. and Woolley, P. (1982), *Social Relations and Human Attributes*, London and New York.

Hobsbawm, E. J. (1963), *Primitive Rebels*, Manchester.

Hodgson, M. G. S. (1960), 'A comparison of Islam and Christianity as framework for religious life', *Diogenes*, no. 32, pp. 49—74.

Hodgson, M. G. S. (1964), 'Islam and image', *History of Religions*, vol. 3, pp. 220—60.

Hodgson, M. G. S. (1974), *The Venture of Islam*, 3 vols., Chicago and London.

Hollingdale, R. J. (1973), *Nietzsche*, London and Boston.

Holloway, J. and Picciotto, S. (1978), *State and Capital, a Marxist Debate*, London.

Horton, R. (1960), 'A definition of religion and its uses', *Journal of the Royal Anthropological Institute*, vol. 90, pp. 201—26.

Hourani, A. H. (1946), *Syria and Lebanon, a Political Essay*, London.

Hourani, A. H. (1962), *Arabic Thought in the Liberal Age*, London.

Hubert, H. and Mauss, M. (1964), *Sacrifice: its Nature and Function*, London.

Hume, D. (1963), *On Religion*, London.

Hunt, E. K. (1981), *Property and Prophets, the Evolution of Economic Institutions and Ideologies*, New York.

Hunter, J. (1976), *The Making of the Crofting Community*, Edinburgh.

Huntington, R. and Metcalf, P. (1979), *Celebrations of Death, the Anthropology of Mortuary Ritual*, Cambridge.

Hyppolite, J. (1969), *Studies on Marx and Hegel*, London.

Jafar, M. and Tabari, A. (1981), 'Iran: Islam and the struggle for socialism', *Khamsin*, vol. 8, pp. 83—104.

James, W. (1929), *The Varieties of Religious Experience*, London.

Jansen, G. H. (1979), *Militant Islam*, London.

Jay, M. (1973), *The Dialectical Imagination: a History of the Frankfurt School and the Institute of Social Research 1923–1950*, London.

Johnson, E. S. and Williamson, J. B. (1980), *The Social Problems of Aging*, New York.

Kantorowicz, E. H. (1957), *The King's Two Bodies, a Study in Mediaeval Political Theology*, Princeton, NJ.

Karim, A. K. N. (1956), *Changing Society in India, Pakistan and Bangladesh*, Dacca.

Kaufmann, W. (1974), *Nietzsche, Philosopher, Psychologist, Anti-Christ*, New Jersey.

Kautsky, K. (1925), *The Foundations of Christianity*, London (1st edn, 1908).

Keddie, N. R. (1966), *Religion and Rebellion in Iran: the Tobacco Protest of 1891–1892*, London.

Keddie, N. R. (1968), *An Islamic Response to Imperialism*, Berkeley and Los Angeles, Ca.

Khaldun, Ibn (1958), *The Muqaddimah, an Introduction to History*, 3 vols., London.

Kiernan, V. G. (1972), *The Lords of Human Kind*, Harmondsworth.

Kiernan, V. G. (1982), *European Empires from Conquest to Collapse 1815–1960*, London.

Koebner, R. (1951), 'Despot and despotism, vicissitudes of a political term', *Journal of the Warburg and Courtauld Institutes*, vol. XIV, pp. 275—302.

Kolakowski, L. (1978), *Main Currents of Marxism, its Origin, Growth and Dissolution*, 3 vols., Oxford.

Kolakowski, L. (1982), *Religion*, London.

Korsch, K. (1970), *Marxism and Philosophy*, London.

Krell, D. F. (1981), 'Analysis', in M. Heidegger, *Nietzsche, Vol. 1, The Will to Power as Art*, London and Henley, pp. 230—57.

Kritzeck, J. (1973), 'Dervish tales', in L. F. Rushbrook Williams (ed.), *Sufi Studies, East and West*, New York, pp. 153—7.

Krygier, M. (1979), 'Weber, Lenin and the reality of socialism', in E. Kamenka and M. Krygier (eds.), *Bureaucracy, the Career of a Concept*, London, pp. 61—87.

Kübler-Ross, E. (1970), *On Death and Dying*, London.

Ladurie, E. Le Roy (1974), *The Peasants of Languedoc*, Urbana, Ill.

Ladurie, E. Le Roy (1980), *Montaillou*, Harmondsworth.

Ladurie, E. Le Roy (1981), *Carnival in Romans, a People's Uprising at Romans, 1579–1580*, Harmondsworth.

Langer, L. L. (1978), *The Age of Atrocity, Death in Modern Literature*, Boston.

Larrain, J. (1982), 'On the character of ideology, Marx and the present debate in Britain', *Theory, Culture and Society*, vol. 1, pp. 5—22.

Lasch, C. (1980), *The Culture of Narcissism*, London.

Lea, H. C. (1896), *A History of Auricular Confession and Indulgences in the Latin Church*, 2 vols., London.

Leach, W. (1981), *True Love and Perfect Union, the Feminist Reform of Sex and Society*, London and Henley.

Le Bon, G. (1895), *Psychologie des foules*, Paris.

Lenin, V. I. (1965), *On Religion*, Moscow.

Lévi-Strauss, C. (1969), *Totemism*, Harmondsworth.

Lévi-Strauss, C. (1976), *Tristes Tropiques*, Harmondsworth.

Lewis, B. (1961), *The Emergence of Modern Turkey*, London.

Lewis, B. (1967), *The Assassins, a Radical Sect in Islam*, London.

Lewis, C. S. (1936), *The Allegory of Love*, London.

Leyser, K. J. (1979), *Rule and Conflict in an Early Medieval Society Ottonian Saxony*, London.

Lilge, H. (1960), *Heinrich Heine, Biographie und Auswahl*, Bielefeld.

Ling, T. (1966), *Buddha, Marx and God*, London.

Ling, T. (1968), *A History of Religion East and West*, London.

Ling, T. (1980), *Karl Marx and Religion, in Europe and India*, London.

Loewith, K. (1970), 'Max Weber and Karl Marx', in D. Wrong (ed.), *Max Weber, Maker of Modern Sociology*, Englewood Cliffs, NJ, pp. 101—21.

Luckmann, T. (1967), *The Invisible Religion, the Problem of Religion in Modern Society*, New York and London.

Lukács, G. (1971), *History and Class Consciousness*, London.

Lukes, S. (1973a), *Individualism*, Oxford.

Lukes, S. (1973b), *Emile Durkheim, His Life and Work*, London.

Lukes, S. (1975), 'Political ritual and social integration', *Sociology*, vol. 9, no. 2, pp. 289—308.

McDonough, R. (1978), 'Ideology as false consciousness: Lukacs', in Centre for Contemporary Cultural Studies Working Paper in Cultural Studies, no. 10, *On Ideology*, London, pp. 33—44.

Macfarlane, A. (1978), *The Origins of English Individualism*, Oxford.

MacIntyre, A. (1967a), *A Short History of Ethics*, London.

MacIntyre, A. (1967b), *Secularization and Moral Change*, London.

MacIntyre, A. (1967c), 'The idea of a social science', *Aristotelian Society Supplementary Proceedings*, pp. 95—114.

MacIntyre, A. (1969a), *Marxism and Christianity*, London.

MacIntyre, A. (1969b), 'The debate about God', in A. MacIntyre and P. Ricoeur (eds.), *The Religious Significance of Atheism*, New York and London, pp. 3—29.

MacIntyre, A. and Ricoeur, P. (1969), *The Religious Significance of Atheism*, New York and London.

MacIver, R. M. (1917), *Community, a Sociological Study*, London.

Mack, A. (1973), *Death in American Experience*, New York.
MacLaren, A. A. (1974), *Religion and Social Class: The Disruption Years in Aberdeen*, London and Boston.
Maclean, I. (1980), *The Renaissance Notion of Women*, Cambridge.
McLellan, D. (1970), *Marx before Marxism*, London.
McLellan, D. (1973), *Karl Marx, his Life and Thought*, London.
McNeill, W. H. (1979), *Plagues and People*, Harmondsworth.
Macpherson, C. B. (1962), *The Political Theory of Possessive Individualism*, London.
Malinowski, B. (1948), *Magic, Science and Religion*, New York.
Mandel, E. (1969), *The Marxist Theory of the State*, New York.
Mann, M. (1973), *Consciousness and Action among the Western Working Class*, London.
Mannheim, K. (1960), *Ideology and Utopia*, London.
Marcuse, H. (1972), *Eros and Civilization*, London.
Marrus, M. R. (1971), *The Politics of Assimilation, the French Jewish Community at the Time of the Dreyfus Affair*, Oxford.
Marshall, G. (1980), *Presbyteries and Profits, Calvinism and the Development of Capitalism in Scotland 1560–1707*, Oxford.
Marshall, T. H. (1950), *Citizenship and Social Class*, Cambridge.
Martin, B. (1981), *A Sociology of Contemporary Cultural Change*, Oxford.
Martin, D. (1962), 'The denomination', *British Journal of Sociology*, vol. 28, pp. 1—14.
Martin, D. (1967), *A Sociology of English Religion*, London.
Martin, D. (1969), *The Religious and the Secular*, London.
Martin, D. (1972), 'Great Britain — England', in H. Mol (ed.), *Western Religion, a Country by Country Sociological Inquiry*, The Hague.
Martin, D. (1978a), *A General Theory of Secularization*, Oxford.
Martin, D. (1978b), *The Dilemmas of Contemporary Religion*, Oxford.
Marx, J. and Ellison, D. (1975), 'Sensitivity training and communes, contemporary quests for community', *Pacific Sociological Review*, vol. 18, pp. 442—60.
Marx, K. (1847), *Misère de la Philosophie, résponse à la philosophie de la misère par M. Proudhon*, Paris.
Marx, K. (1971), *A Contribution to the Critique of Political Economy*, London.
Marx, K. (1972), 'The future results of the British rule in India', in K. Marx and F. Engels, *On Colonialism*, New York.
Marx, K. (1973), *Grundrisse*, Harmondsworth.
Marx, K. (1974), *Capital*, 3 vols., London.
Marx, K. and Engels, F. (1955a), *On Religion*, Moscow.
Marx, K. and Engels, F. (1955b), *Selected Correspondence*, Moscow.
Marx, K. and Engels, F. (1956), *Werke*, Berlin.
Marx, K. and Engels, F. (1963), *Letters to Americans 1848–95*, London.
Marx, K. and Engels, F. (1965), *The German Ideology*, London.
Marx, K. and Engels, F. (1968), *Selected Works*, London.
Marx, K. and Engels, F. (1972), *On Colonialism*, New York.
Marx, K. and Engels, F. (1974), *The German Ideology*, London.
Mauss, M. (1920), *The Gift, Forms and Functions of Exchange in Archaic Society*, London.
Mauss, M. (1979), *Sociology and Psychology*, London, Boston and Henley.
Mead, G. H. (1934), *Mind, Self and Society*, Chicago.
Merquior, J. G. (1980), *Rousseau and Weber, two Studies in the Theory of Legitimacy*, London, Boston and Henley.
Merton, R. K. (1957), *Social Theory and Social Structure*, New York.
Migdal, J. S. (1980), *Palestinian Society and Politics*, Princeton, NJ.
Miranda, J. P. (1980), *Marx against the Marxists, the Christian Humanism of Karl Marx*, London.
Mitford, J. (1963), *The American Way of Death*, New York.
Mitnick, B. M. (1980), *The Political Economy of Regulation*, New York.
Mol, H. (ed.) (1972), *Western Religion, A Country by Country Sociological Inquiry*, The Hague.

Moore, S. F. and Meyerhoff, B. G. (eds.) (1977), *Secular Ritual*, Assen.
Moseley, K. P. and Wallerstein, I. (1978), 'Precapitalist social structures', *Annual Review of Sociology*, vol. 4, pp. 259—90.
Nairn, T. (1975), 'Old Nationalism and New Nationalism', in G. Brown (ed.), *The Red Paper on Scotland*, Edinburgh, pp. 22—57.
Nairn, T. (1977), *The Break-Up of Britain, Crisis and Neo-nationalism*, London.
Nasr, S. H. (1966), *Ideals and Realities of Islam*, London.
Needham, R. (1963), 'Introduction', *Primitive Classification*, in E. Durkheim and M. Mauss, London, pp. vii—xlviii.
Needleman, J. and Baker, G. (1978), *Understanding the New Religions*, New York.
Nelson, B. (1968), 'Scholastic *rationales* of "conscience", early modern crises of credibility and the scientific technocultural revolutions of the 17th and 20th centuries', *Journal for the Scientific Study of Religion*, vol. 7, pp. 155—77.
Nelson, B. (1969a), 'Conscience and the making of early modern cultures: the Protestant ethic beyond Weber', *Social Research*, vol. 36, pp. 4—21.
Nelson, B. (1969b), *The Idea of Usury, from Tribal Brotherhood to Universal Otherhood*, Chicago.
Nelson, J. T. (1977), 'Inauguration rituals', in P. H. Sawyer and N. Wood (eds.), *Early Medieval Kingship*, Leeds, pp. 50—71.
Newcomb, H. (1862), *Christian Character: a Book for Young Ladies*, Edinburgh and New York.
Niebuhr, H. R. (1929), *The Social Sources of Denominationalism*, New York.
Niebuhr, H. R. (1949), *The Kingdom of God in America*, New York.
Nietzsche, F. (1910), *The Genealogy of Morals, a Polemic*, Edinburgh.
Nietzsche, F. (1933), *Thus Spake Zarathustra*, London.
Nietzsche, F. (1967a), *The Will to Power*, New York.
Nietzsche, F. (1967b), *The Birth of Tragedy*, New York.
Nietzsche, F. (1968), *Twilight of the Idols and the Anti-Christ*, Harmondsworth.
Nietzsche, F. (1973), *Beyond Good and Evil*, Harmondsworth.
Nietzsche, F. (1974), *The Gay Science*, New York.
Nietzsche, F. (1979), *Ecce Homo*, Harmondsworth.
Nieuwenhuijze, C. A. O. van (1958), *Aspects of Islam in Post-colonial Indonesia: Five Essays*, The Hague.
Nisbet, R. (1967), *The Sociological Tradition*, London.
Nottingham, E. K. (1954), *Religion and Society*, New York.
Oakley, F. (1973), 'Celestial hierarchies revisited: Walter Ullmann's vision of medieval politics', *Past and Present*, no. 60, pp. 3—48.
Obeyesekere, G. (1968), 'Theodicy, sin and salvation in a sociology of Buddhism', in E. Leach (ed.), *Dialectic in Practical Religion*, Cambridge, pp. 7—40.
O'Leary, de Lacy (1969), *How Greek Science Passed to the Arabs*, London.
Ollman, B. (1971), *Alienation: Marx's Critique of Man in Capitalist Society*, Cambridge.
Olssen, E. A. (1968), 'Marx and the Resurrection', *Journal of the History of Ideas*, vol. 44, pp. 131—40.
Otto, R. (1929), *The Idea of the Holy*, London.
Owen, E. R. J. (1969), *Cotton in the Egyptian Economy 1820–1914*, London.
Packe, M. (1954), *John Stuart Mill*, London.
Parkes, C. M. (1975), *Bereavement, Studies of Grief in Adult Life*, Harmondsworth.
Parkin, F. (1972), *Class Inequality and Political Order*, London.
Parkin, F. (1982), *Max Weber*, London and New York.
Parsons, H. L. (1964), 'The prophetic mission of Karl Marx', *Journal of Religion*, vol. 44, pp. 52—72.
Parsons, T. (1937), *The Structure of Social Action*, Glencoe, Ill.
Parsons, T. (1944), 'The theoretical development of the sociology of religion', *Journal of the History of Ideas*, vol. 5, pp. 176—90.
Parsons, T. (1951), *The Social System*, New York.
Parsons, T. (1963), 'Christianity and modern industrial society', in E. A. Tiryakian (ed.),

Sociological Theory, Values and Social Cultural Change, Essays in Honour of Pitrim Sorokin, New York, pp. 33—70.

Parsons, T. (1973), 'Durkheim on religion revisited: another look at the elementary forms of the religious life', in C. Y. Glock and P. E. Hammond (eds.), *Beyond the Classics: Essays in the Scientific Study of Religion,* New York, pp. 156—80.

Pashukanis, E. B. (1978), *Law and Marxism, a General Theory,* London.

Peel, J. D. Y. (1971), *Herbert Spencer,* London.

Peters, E. (1970), *The Shadow King, Rex Inutilis in Medieval Law and Literature,* New Haven, Conn., and London.

Pettazzoni, R. (1954), 'Confessions of sins: an interpretation', in *Studies in the History of Religions,* Leiden, pp. 48—62.

Pickering, W. S. F. (1975), *Durkheim on Religion,* London and Boston.

Plant, R. (1973), *Hegel,* London.

Plekhanov, G. V. (1940), *The Role of the Individual in History,* London.

Poggi, G. (1978), *The Development of the Modern State, a Sociological Introduction,* London.

Poll, S. (1969), *The Hasidic Community of Williamsburg, a Study in the Sociology of Religion,* New York.

Pope, L. (1942), *Millhands and Preachers,* New Haven, Conn.

Popper, K. R. (1945), *The Open Society and its Enemies,* London.

Postan, M. M. (1972), *The Medieval Economy and Society,* London.

Poulantzas, N. (1973), *Political Power and Social Classes,* London.

Poulantzas, N. (1975), *Classes in Contemporary Capitalism,* London.

Poulantzas, N. (1978), *State, Power, Socialism,* London.

Powell, E. H. (1962), 'Beyond utopia, the "Beat Generation" as a challenge for the sociology of knowledge', in A. M. Rose (ed.), *Human Behavior and Social Processes, an Interactionist Approach,* London, pp. 360—77.

Praz, M. (1933), *The Romantic Agony,* Oxford.

Prestwich, M. (1980), *The Three Edwards, War and State in England 1272–1377,* London.

Rasmussen, K. (1931), *The Netsilik Eskimos, Social Life and Spiritual Culture,* Copenhagen.

Redfield, R. (1955), *The Little Community: Viewpoints for a Study of the Human Whole,* Uppsala.

Redfield, R. (1965), *Peasant Society and Culture,* Chicago.

Reese, M. M. (1953), *Shakespeare, his World and his Work,* London.

Reisman, D. (1961), *The Lonely Crowd,* New Haven, Conn., and London.

Renan, E. (1863), *Vie de Jesus,* Paris.

Renan, E. (1896), *The Poetry of the Celtic Races and Other Studies,* London.

Richardson, J. (1977), *Conversion Careers, in and out of New Religious Groups,* Beverly Hills, Ca.

Richey, R. E. (ed.) (1974), *American Civil Religion,* New York.

Ridley, J. (1977), *The Roundheads,* London.

Rigby, A. and Turner, B. S. (1972), 'Findhorn Community, centre of light: a sociological study of new forms of religion, in M. Hill (ed.), *A Sociological Yearbook of Religion in Britain,* vol. 5, pp. 72—86.

Rigby A. and Turner, B. S. (1973), 'Communes, hippies et religions secularisées: quelques aspects sociologiques de formes actuelles de religiosite', *Social Compass,* vol. 20, pp. 5—18.

Robbins, T. (1969), 'Eastern mysticism and the resocialization of drug users: the Meher Baba cult', *Journal for the Scientific Study of Religion,* vol. 8, pp. 308—17.

Robertson, D. W. (1980), *Essays in Medieval Culture,* Princeton, NJ.

Robertson, R. (ed.) (1969), *Sociology of Religion,* Harmondsworth.

Robertson, R. (1970), *The Sociological Interpretation of Religion,* Oxford.

Robertson, R. (1978), *Meaning and Change, Explorations in the Cultural Sociology of Modern Societies,* Oxford.

Robertson, R. and Holzner, B. (eds.) (1980), *Identity and Authority, Exploration in Theory and Society,* Oxford.

Rodinson, M. (1961), *Mahomet*, Paris.
Roover, R. de (1967), *San Bernardino of Siena and Sant'Antonino of Florence, the Two Great Economic Thinkers of the Middle Ages*, Boston.
Rosenwein, B. H. and Little, L. K. (1974), 'Social meaning in the monastic and mendicant spiritualities', *Past and Present*, no. 63, pp. 4—32.
Roth, G. and Schluchter, W. (1979), *Max Weber's Vision of History, Ethics and Methods*, Berkeley, Ca.
Rousseau, J.J. (1960), *Politics and the Arts, Letter to M. d'Alembert on the Theatre*, Glencoe, Ill.
Rousseau, J. J. (1973), *The Social Contract and Other Discourses*, London.
Royster, J. E. (1972), 'The study of Muhammad: a survey of approaches from the perspective of the history and phenomenology of religion', *Muslim World*, vol. 62, pp. 49—70.
Runciman, W. G. (1969), 'The sociological explanation of "religious" beliefs', *Archives européennes de sociologie*, vol. 10, pp. 149—91.
Russell, B. (1945), *History of Western Philosophy*, London.
Said, E. W. (1978), *Orientalism*, London.
Schmidt, A. (1971), *The Concept of Nature in Marx*, London.
Schneider, L. (ed.) (1964), *Religion, Culture and Society, a Reader in the Sociology of Religion*, New York, London and Sydney.
Schneider, L. (1970), *Sociological Approach to Religion*, New York.
Schneider, L. and Dornbusch, S. M. (1958), *Popular Religion, Inspirational Books in America*, Chicago.
Schutz, A. (1972), *The Phenomenology of the Social World*, London.
Schwarzfuchs, S. (1979), *Napoleon, the Jews and the Sanhedrin*, Boston and Henley.
Scott, J. (1979), *Corporations, Classes and Capitalism*, London.
Seger, I. (1957), *Durkheim and his Critics on the Sociology of Religion*, Columbia.
Seltman, C. (1956), *Women in Antiquity*, London.
Semmel, S. (1974), *The Methodist Revolution*, London.
Sennett, R. (1974), *The Fall of Public Man*, Cambridge.
Seve, L. (1975), *Marxism and the Theory of Human Personality*, London.
Shahak, I. (1981), 'The Jewish religion and its attitude to non-Jews', *Khamsin*, vol. 8, pp. 27—61 and vol. 9, pp. 3—49.
Shariati, A. (1979), *On the Sociology of Islam*, Berkeley, Ca.
Shariati, A. (1980), *Marxism and other Western Fallacies: an Islamic Critique*, Berkeley, Ca.
Shils, E. (1981), *Tradition*, London and Boston.
Shils, E. and Young, M. (1953), 'The meaning of the coronation', *Sociological Review*, vol. 1, pp. 63—82.
Shiner, L. (1966), *The Secularization of History*, Nashville, Tenn.
Shmueli, E. (1969), 'The appeal of Hasidism for American Jewry today', *Jewish Journal of Sociology*, vol. 11, pp. 5—30.
Shorter, E. (1977), *The Making of the Modern Family*, London.
Siebert, R.J. (1976/7), 'Horkheimer's *Sociology of Religion*', *Telos*, no. 30, Winter, pp. 127—44.
Siebert, R.J. (1977/8), 'Fromm's theory of religion', *Telos*, no. 34, Winter, pp. 111—20.
Silverman, D. (1975), *Reading Castaneda*, London.
Simmel, G. (1968), *The Conflict in Modern Culture and other Essays*, New York.
Singer, P. (1980), *Marx*, Oxford.
Sklair, L. (1970), *The Sociology of Progress*, London.
Skultans, V. (1974), *Intimacy and Ritual, a Study of Spiritualism, Mediums and Groups*, London.
Smith, A. D. (1971), *Theories of Nationalism*, London.
Smith, G. L. (1973), *Religion and Trade in New Netherland*, Ithaca, NY and London.
Smith, W. C. (1957), *Islam in Modern History*, New York.
Smith, W. R. (1889), *Lectures on the Religion of the Semites*, Edinburgh.
Smout, T. C. (1972), *A History of the Scottish People, 1560-1830*, London.

Snelling, C. and Whiteley, O. (1974), 'Problem-solving behavior in religious and para-religious groups', in A. Eister (ed.), *Changing Perspectives in the Scientific Study of Religion*, pp. 315—34.

Sohn-Rethel, A. (1978), *Intellectual and Manual Labour — a Critique of Epistemology*, London.

Sombart, W. (1962), *The Jews and Modern Capitalism*, New York.

Sperry, W. L. (1946), *Religion in America*, New York.

Spiro, M. (1966), 'Religion: problems of definition and explanation', in M. Banton (ed.), *Anthropological Approaches to the Study of Religion*, London, pp. 85—126.

Stark, W. (1967), 'Max Weber and the heterogony of purposes', *Social Research*, vol. 34, pp. 249—64.

Stark, R. and Glock, C. Y. (1965), 'The "New Denominationalism" ', *Review of Religious Research*, vol. 7, no. 1, pp. 8—17.

Stark, R. and Glock, C. Y. (1968), *American Piety, the Nature of Religious Commitment*, Berkeley and Los Angeles, Ca.

Stedman-Jones, G. (1971), 'The Marxism of the early Lukács', *New Left Review*, no. 70, pp. 11—60.

Steiner, F. (1956), *Taboo*, London.

Stelling-Michaud, S. (1960), 'Le mythe du despotisme oriental', *Schweizer Beitrage zur Allgemeinen Geschichte*, vol. XVIII, pp. 328—46.

Stern, J. P. (1979), *A Study of Nietzsche*, Cambridge.

Stone, D. (1978), 'Human potential movement', *Society*, vol. 15, pp. 66—8.

Stone, L. (1973), *Family and Fortune, Studies in Aristocratic Finance in the Sixteenth and Seventeenth Centuries*, Oxford.

Strauss, D. F. (1835), *Das Leben Jesu*, Berlin.

Strawson, P. F. (1959), *Individuals, an Essay in Descriptive Metaphysics*, London.

Strong, T. B. (1975), *Friederick Nietzsche and the Politics of Transfiguration*, Berkeley, Ca.

Sudnow, D. (1967), *Passing On, the Social Organization of Dying*, Englewood Cliffs, NJ.

Tambiah, S. J. (1976), *World Conqueror and World Renouncer, a Study of Buddhism and Polity in Thailand against a Historical Background*, Cambridge.

Tarde, G. (1901), *L'Opinion et la foule*, Paris.

Taylor, G. R. (1953), *Sex in History*, London.

Taylor, K. (1975), *Henri Saint-Simon 1760–1825. Selected Writings on Science, Industry and Social Organisation*, London.

Telford, J. (ed.) (1931), *The Letters of John Wesley*, London.

Tentler, T. N. (1974), 'The summa for confessors as an instrument of social control', in C. Trinkaus and H. A. Oberman (eds.), *The Pursuit of Holiness in late Medieval and Renaissance Religion*, Leiden, pp. 103—26.

Thomas, K. (1971), *Religion and the Decline of Magic*, London.

Thompson, E. P. (1963), *The Making of the English Working Class*, London.

Thulstrup, N. (1980), *Kierkegaard's Relation to Hegel*, Princeton, NJ.

Tillich, P. (1962), *The Shaking of the Foundations*, Harmondsworth.

Tiryakian, E. A. (1981), 'The sociological import of a metaphor: tracking the source of Max Weber's "Iron cage" ', *Sociological Inquiry*, vol. 51, pp. 27—33.

Tocqueville, A. de (1946), *Democracy in America*, London.

Touraine, A. (1974), *The Post-Industrial Society*, London.

Towler, R. (1974), *Homo Religiosus: Sociological Problems in the Study of Religion*, London.

Trevor-Roper, H. (1967), *Religion, the Reformation and Social Change*, London.

Troeltsch, E. (1931), *The Social Teaching of the Christian Churches*, London.

Turner, B. S. (1970), *The Decline of Methodism, a Study of Religious Organisation and Commitment*, unpublished Ph.D. thesis, University of Leeds.

Turner, B. S. (1971), 'The re-appraisal of Tylor's concept of religion: the ineractionist analogy' *International Yearbook for the Sociology of Religion*, vol. 7, pp. 139—49.

Turner, B S. (1971/2), 'Belief, ritual and experience: the case of Methodism', *Social Compass*, vol. 8, pp. 187—201.

Turner, B. S. (1972a), 'Rationality, symbol and action: the social basis of the sociology of religion', *Sociological Analysis*, vol. 2, no. 2, pp. 37—47.

Turner, B. S. (1972b), 'The sociological explanation of ecumenicalism', in C. L. Mitton (ed.), *The Social Sciences and the Churches*, Edinburgh, pp. 233—45.

Turner, B. S. (1974a), *Weber and Islam, a Critical Study*, London.

Turner, B. S. (1974b), 'The concept of social "stationariness": utilitarianism and Marxism', *Science and Society*, vol. 38, pp. 3—18.

Turner, B. S. (1976), 'Origins and traditions in Islam and Christianity', *Religion: a Journal of Religion and Religions*, vol. 6, pp. 13—30.

Turner, B. S. (1977a), 'Class solidarity and system integration', *Sociological Analysis*, vol. 38, pp. 345—58.

Turner, B. S. (1977b), 'Confession and social structure', *Annual Review of the Social Sciences of Religion*, vol. 1, pp. 2—58.

Turner, B. S. (1978a), 'Orientalism, Islam and capitalism', *Social Compass*, vol. XXV, pp. 371—94.

Turner, B. S. (1978b), *Marx and the End of Orientalism*, London.

Turner, B. S. (1980), 'Capitalism and feudalism in Iran, 1502—1979', in Georg Stauth (ed.), *Iran: Precapitalism, Capitalism and Revolution*, Saarbrucken, pp. 53—114.

Turner, B. S. (1981a), *For Weber, Essays on the Sociology of Fate*, Boston, London and Henley.

Turner, B. S. (1981b), 'Marginal politics, cultural identities and the clergy in Scotland', *International Journal of Sociology and Social Policy*, vol. 1, no. 1, pp. 89—113.

Turner, V. (1969), *The Ritual Process, Structure and Anti-structure*, London.

Tylor, E. B. (1891), *Primitive Culture: Researches into the Development of Mythology, Philosophy, Religion, Language Act and Customs*, 2 vols., London.

Ullmann, W. (1969), *The Carolingian Renaissance and the Idea of Kingship*, London.

Ullmann, W. (1975), *Medieval Political Thought*, Harmondsworth.

Urry, J. (1981), *The Anatomy of Capitalist Societies*, London.

Valentini, N. and Meglio, di C. (1974), *Sex and the Confessional*, London.

Veith, I. (1965), *Hysteria, the History of a Disease*, Chicago and London.

Vermes, G. (1973), *Jesus the Jew*, Harmondsworth.

Waardenburg, J. (1978), 'Official and popular religion in Islam', *Social Compass*, vol. 25, pp. 315—41.

Wach, J. (1971), *Sociology of Religion*, Chicago and London.

Waldock, A. (1961), *Paradise Lost and its Critics*, Cambridge.

Ward, H. (1888), *Robert Elsemere*, London.

Watt, M. M. (1969), *Islamic Revelation in the Modern World*, Edinburgh.

Webb, K. (1978), *The Growth of Nationalism in Scotland*, Harmondsworth.

Weber, M. (1949), *The Methodology of the Social Sciences*, edited by E. Shils and H. Finch, Chicago.

Weber, M. (1951), *The Religion of China*, New York.

Weber, M. (1952), *Ancient Judaism*, New York.

Weber, M. (1958), *The City*, New York.

Weber, M. (1961), *From Weber, Essays in Sociology*, edited by H. Gerth and C. Wright Mills, London.

Weber, M. (1965), *The Protestant Ethic and the Spirit of Capitalism*, London.

Weber, M. (1966), *The Sociology of Religion*, London.

Weber, M. (1968), *Economy and Society*, 2 vols., Berkeley, Los Angeles, Ca., and London.

Weber, M. (1977), *Critique of Stammler*, New York.

Weintraub, K. J. (1978), *The Value of the Individual, Self and Criticism in Autobiography*, Chicago and London.

Wertheim, W. F. (1961), 'Religious reform movements in South and Southeast Asia', *Archives de Sociologie des Religions*, vol. 12, pp. 52—62.

Westergaard, J. and Resler, H. (1975), *Class in a Capitalist Society*, London.

Westermarck, E. A. (1968), *Ritual and Belief in Morocco*, 2 vols., New York.

Whyte, W. H. (1956), *The Organization Man*, New York.

Wieruszowski, H. (1963), 'Roger II of Sicily, rex-tyrannus in medieval political thought', *Speculum*, vol. 38, pp. 46—78.

Williams, B. A. O. (1963), 'Hume on religion', in D. F. Pears (ed.), *Hume: a Symposium*, London, pp. 77—88.

Williams, G. (ed.) (1978), *Social and Cultural Change in Contemporary Wales*, London.

Williams, R. (1976), *Key Words*, London.

Williams, R. M. (1965), *American Society, a Sociological Interpretation*, New York.

Wilson, B. (1959), 'An analysis of sect development' *American Sociological Review*, vol. 24, pp. 3—15.

Wilson, B. (1966), *Religion in Secular Society, a Sociological Comment*, London.

Wilson, B. (1970a), *Religious Sects, a Sociological Study*, London.

Wilson, B. (ed.) (1970b), *Rationality*, Oxford.

Wilson, B. (1976), *Contemporary Transformation of Religion*, London, Oxford and New York.

Wilson, B. (1982), *Religion in Sociological Perspective*, Oxford and New York.

Winch, P. (1958), *The Idea of a Social Science*, London.

Wittfogel, K. (1957), *Oriental Despotism, a Comparative Study of Total Power*, New Haven, Conn., and London.

Wolf, E. R. (1971), *Peasant Wars in the Twentieth Century*, London.

Wolin, S. S. (1961), *Politics and Vision*, London.

Worsley, P. (1970), *The Trumpet Shall Sound*, London.

Worsley, P. (1972), 'Franz Fanon and the "lumpenproletariat" ', *Socialist Register*, pp. 193—230.

Yinger, J. M. (1961), *Sociology Looks at Religion*, New York.

Yuval-David, N. (1980), 'The bearers of the collective: women and religious legislation in Israel', *Feminist Review*, vol. 4, pp. 15—27.

Zaretsky, E. (1976), *Capitalism, the Family and Personal Life*, London.

Zaretsky, I. and Leone, M. (eds.) (1974), *Religious Movements in Contemporary America*, Princeton, NJ.

Zborowski, M. and Herzog, E. (1962), *Life is with People, the Culture of the Shtetl*, New York.

Zeldin, T. (1970), *Conflicts in French Society*, London.

Index